PARIS WAS A WOMAN

PARIS WAS A WOMAN

PORTRAITS FROM THE LEFT BANK

ANDREA WEISS

HarperSanFrancisco

A Imprint of HarperCollinsPublishers

FIRST EDITION

Library of Congress Cataloguing-in-Publication Data
Available Upon Request

ISBN 0–06–251313–3 (pbk.)

95 96 97 98 99   10 9 8 7 6 5 4 3 2 1

CONTENTS

To my nieces
Jennifer Levy-Lunt,
une femme de la rive gauche
and Isabella Jane Schiller,
une femme de l'avenir

DRAMATIS PERSONAE

Berenice Abbott – American photographer, she began her career by taking portraits of her friends in Man Ray's studio during her lunch hour.

Margaret Anderson – Founder and editor of *The Little Review*, one of the most important avant-garde literary magazines between the wars.

Djuna Barnes – Novelist, journalist, satirist and visual artist, her best known work is the 'underground classic', *Nightwood*.

Natalie Clifford Barney – Immensely wealthy, and notoriously lesbian, American writer and salon hostess who lived in Paris for 70 years.

Sylvia Beach – A Presbyterian minister's daughter, she established the bookshop, Shakespeare and Company, and was the first publisher of James Joyce's *Ulysses*.

Germaine Beaumont – The protégée and intimate friend of Colette, she was a French journalist and novelist who was awarded the prestigious Prix Theophraste Renaudot for literature.

Romaine Brooks – American painter of intense portraits in muted colours, she was the lifelong friend of Natalie Barney.

Bryher (Winifred Ellerman) – English heiress, publisher, writer, patron of the arts, and anti-fascist resistance worker, she was the lifelong friend of poet H.D.

Lily de Clermont-Tonnerre – A close friend of Natalie Barney's and Gertrude Stein's, she was a controversial writer of extreme political views, first on the left and in later years on the right.

Colette – One of France's most highly regarded authors, Colette wrote hundreds of short stories, novels and essays.

Nancy Cunard – English scion of the Cunard steamship family, she dismissed her parents' upper-class values to become a poet, wide-eyed radical, and founder of the avant-garde Hours Press.

H.D. (Hilda Doolittle) – Poet and novelist based primarily in London, with forays into Paris, she was muse to Ezra Pound, analysand of Sigmund Freud, and a proponent of 'Imagism'.

Janet Flanner – American journalist who commented in *The New Yorker* on life in Paris for 40 years.

Gisèle Freund – German-Jewish refugee photographer who photographed all the famous and soon-to-be famous writers in France.

Eileen Gray – Irish designer and architect who evolved her own sparse, elegant Modernist style, and who lived on the Left Bank of Paris for 75 years.

Radclyffe Hall – English author of the controversial novel *The Well of Loneliness* (1928) which pleaded sympathy for lesbians and was banned in Britain until 1948.

Jane Heap – Co-editor, with Margaret Anderson, of *The Little Review*, and unofficial literary agent for Gertrude Stein.

Marie Laurencin – French painter who frequented the salons of Natalie Barney and Gertrude Stein.

Georgette LeBlanc – French opera singer who lived for twenty years with editor Margaret Anderson.

Mina Loy – English-born Modernist poet and designer, her work was published in many of the small literary magazines.

Adrienne Monnier – French writer and editor, she ran the leading book-shop for French avant-garde literature, La Maison des Amis des Livres.

Noel Murphy – American singer whose home in Orgeval, outside Paris, was a weekend gathering-place for many of the expatriate women.

Solita Solano – Editor, novelist, poet and journalist, she compromised her own writing career to provide emotional and practical support to Janet Flanner for 50 years.

Gertrude Stein – The best known and most prolific of the female Modernist writers in Paris, she was also an art collector and ran a weekly salon.

Alice B. Toklas – Lifelong companion, secretary, publisher, and muse to Gertrude Stein.

Renée Vivien – A gifted poet, neighbour of Colette and lover of Natalie Barney, she died in Paris at the age of 31.

Dolly Wilde – An English writer who strongly resembled and admired her uncle Oscar; she abused drugs and alcohol to the point of self-destruction.

Thelma Wood – Silverpoint artist and sculptor, she had a tortured romance with Djuna Barnes in Paris in the twenties.

PREFACE

Often films start out as books, but in my case this book grew out of a film project. My partner Greta Schiller and I felt that time was overdue for a comprehensive documentary film on the women of the Left Bank. We began the enormous research and fundraising work, never dreaming that four years would pass before we saw its completion.

I have had many wonderful experiences in the process. Visiting the Fonds Littéraire Jacques Doucet in Paris, for instance, Greta and I were taken in to a small closet off the main reading room. We wondered what on earth would be revealed by the head archivist, François Chapon; he had already shown us Natalie Barney's furniture, paintings, and chest of private love letters. We were completely surprised by what came next – François Chapon, who had known Natalie Barney when he was a young man, opened a beautiful inlay box to reveal a plait of her hair.

From Paris Greta and I hired a car and drove down to Bilignin, the village in the Rhône region where Gertrude and Alice had their country home. Using *The Alice B. Toklas Cookbook* as our travel guide, we stopped in some of the best hidden-away country restaurants in all of France. We laughed about how fortunate we were that this trip ostensibly was our 'work'. We loved coming upon, at long last, the signs indicating Bilignin, placed on each end of a little country lane. Between the two village signs were fewer than a dozen farmhouses, many cows, a beautiful double row of old, sturdy oak trees and a big gate – behind which stood Gertrude and Alice's big grey house. We could have been in the 1930s when Gertrude and Alice lived there; we almost could have been in the 1830s as well, for how little the village has changed.

I want to thank the many people who made possible my research for both the film and book: at the Library of Congress, Beverly Brannon in the prints and photographs division and Fred Bauman in the manuscripts division. At the Fonds Littéraire Jacques Doucet, Nicole Prevot and François Chapon. At the Sylvia Beach collection at Princeton University, Margaret Sherry. For assistance with the letters, manuscripts and photographs of Djuna Barnes, Ruth M. Alvarez at the McKeldin Library, University of Maryland at College Park, and L. Rebecca Johnson Melvin at the University of Delaware Library. At Yale University, Beinecke Rare Book and Manuscript Library, Patricia Willis and Daniele McClellan.

Most of my research took place in these archives, where I sifted through letters, photographs, and other worn, fragile materials, feeling inspired and transported by them into the past. Nonetheless, I also read numerous contemporary books on the subject and I am deeply indebted to the scholars and biographers who paved the way for me and brought attention to these women's lives and work, including Shari Benstock, Noel Riley Fitch, Catharine R. Stimpson, Meryl Secrest, Brenda Wineapple, and in particular, Karla Jay, who supported this project all along the way.

Frances Berrigan, executive producer, and Greta Schiller, director, of the documentary film have been the best possible colleagues on this project, and I look forward to many more collaborations with them both. My agent, Faith Evans, immediately saw exciting possibilities in what was, back then, just a vague idea – which it may well have stayed had it not been for her enthusiasm and consistent encouragement. My editor Sara Dunn firmly believed in the project throughout (even though she kept trying to restrain my growing selection of photographs) and gave me invaluable guidance. I want to thank as well all the others at Pandora who skilfully transformed the manuscript into a book, including Belinda Budge, Miranda Wilson, Michele Turney, designers Jo Ridgeway and Jerry Goldie and my copy editor Ruth Petrie. Elizabeth Wilson kindly read the book in manuscript form; her comments, always so intelligent, are greatly appreciated. Thanks also to Marina Ganzerli, Miles McKane, Kirsten Lenk, and Florence Fradelizi for their assistance with the research in crucial moments. For help in tracking down obscure references and images and juggling all sorts of details, my endless thanks to Melissa Cahill Tonelli.

The photographer Gisèle Freund, who agreed to be interviewed for the film, subsequently spent many enlightening hours with us on various trips to Paris. For her inspired conversation, carried on in a baffling mixture of French, German, and English (she speaks four languages, but, according to her, none of them well) she has my total admiration. Many thanks to Berthe Cleyrergue and the late Sam Steward for also agreeing to be interviewed and offering their precious first-hand memories.

Mark Finch was always an interested, sympathetic listener to my ideas and frustrations throughout the writing of both this and my previous book. I wish it were possible to thank him for his unflagging confidence in me, and for his countless acts of genuine friendship over the past decade.

OVERLEAF **Adrienne Monnier entering her bookshop, the birthplace of several Modernist literary movements.**

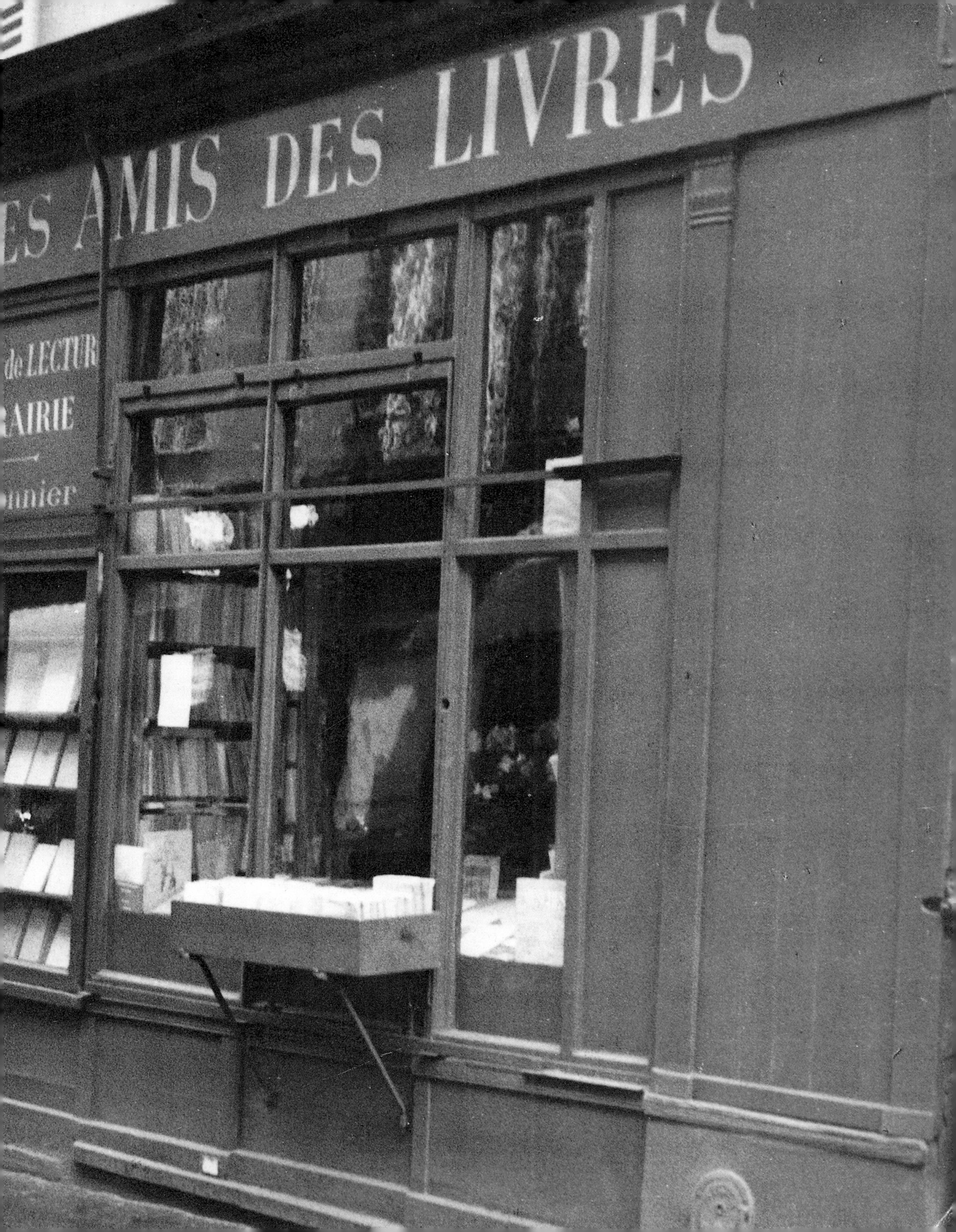
ES AMIS DES LIVRES
de LECTUR
AIRIE
nnier

INTRODUCTION:

PARIS WAS A WOMAN

Renée Vivien dreamt of Paris, 'that loved and longed-for city '; for Colette it was the 'City of Love'. Janet Flanner believed that the Seine gave Paris a special anatomy which made her 'one of the loveliest cities left on earth'. It was the Left Bank of the Seine which first called out to Adrienne Monnier, and years later continued 'to call me and to keep me'. Sylvia Beach stated, with typical modesty and understatement, that she was 'extremely fond of Paris, I must confess'. Djuna Barnes would cry out, more passionately, 'there's a longing in me to be in Paris'.

Women with creative energy and varying degrees of talent, women with a passion for art and literature, women without the obligations that come with husbands and children, were especially drawn to the Left Bank, and

LEFT **'Paris, 1929': The Left Bank as seen through the eye of German photographer Marianne Breslauer.**

never with more urgency and excitement than in the first quarter of this century. It was not simply its beauty but that rare promise of freedom which drew these women to it. They came from as near as Savoy and Burgundy and from as far as London, Berlin, and New York, Chicago, Indiana and California – before the days of the aeroplane. They came for their own individual, private reasons, some of which they themselves perhaps never fully fathomed. But they also came because Paris offered them, as women, a unique and extraordinary world.

Individual biographies of many of these women have been published in the past decade, and Shari Benstock's impeccable resource, *Women of the Left Bank*, serves as both thoughtful literary analysis and detailed group biography of the female Modernists. Conferences have been held on the writings of Djuna Barnes, and newly edited and restored manuscripts of Gertrude Stein have been published. Women artists, writers, scholars, publishers and many others continue to be inspired and fascinated by the women of the Left Bank, and the stories of their lives and works are no longer restricted to academic circles.

This growing body of work on the Paris of the 1920s and 30s calls into question the myths and clichés which have become enshrined in the popular imagination, fuelled by the many accounts of American male expatriates such as Robert McAlmon's *Being Geniuses Together** and Samuel Putnam's *Paris Was Our Mistress*, which emphasize the bars and brothels inhabited by the macho, hard-drinking artists. Their nameless, ever-patient wives barely got a look-in. More recently, Humphrey Carpenter embellishes these myths in his *Geniuses Together*, a boastful chronicle of boozing, gambling and sexual exploits. We learn that Hemingway was recklessly gambling away his wife Hadley's money at the Paris racetracks while James Joyce and Robert McAlmon were slogging their way through an entire menu of French drinks. Malcolm Cowley, who later wrote *Exile's Return: A Literary Odyssey of the 1920s*, got into a violent bar brawl with the proprietor of the Rotonde and so earned himself admission into the inner sanctum of the male expatriate community.

The twin emphases on drinking and sexual exploits dominate the image we now have of Paris in the twenties. Yet the women's experiences of both of these 'freedoms' was very different. Sylvia Beach was a teetotaller, and although it was she who introduced the legendary writers James Joyce and Valery Larbaud to each other, she did not join them when they met, regularly, 'in that American bar in the Latin Quarter, whither his friend James Joyce calls him whenever he wants to read a new work to [Larbaud]'.[1] Natalie Barney claimed that 'being born intoxicated, I drink only water', although she was occasionally seen taking a few sips of an excellent French wine. Gertrude Stein and Alice Toklas, it is well known, had no tolerance for drunks; they were not invited a second time. The English writer and publisher, Winifred Ellerman, who called herself Bryher, preferred water to wine and soon after arriving in Paris decided to refuse all alcohol since 'drinks and *la poésie pure* did not mix'. She looked at the drunken faces of a group of male Modernists and, 'Suddenly I realised to my horror that it was a vicarage garden party in reverse. These rebels were no more free from the conventions that they fastened upon themselves than a group of old ladies gossiping over their knitting.'[2]

Janet Flanner, who loved nothing more than a good gossip, washed down with an aperitif of cinzano and fruit juice at the Café des Deux Magots, would probably not have agreed, and neither would Nancy Cunard or Djuna Barnes, who often joined her there. Yet all three were hard-working writers drawn to Paris for the freedom it offered women – the freedom to work. When we look at the cumulative accomplishment of these authors, poets, painters, book publishers, photographers, 'little magazine' editors and booksellers, it becomes clear that the continually fostered myth of lazy afternoons in cafés and wild nights in Montparnasse bars simply does not fit.

'Sexual freedom' was also a part of the mythology – and also, something most of the Modernist women could do without. According to Djuna Barnes' biographer, Andrew Field, women did want this freedom, but simply weren't able to handle it: ' . . . sexual freedom came too suddenly, and [they were] ill-prepared to cope with the freedom of Paris. The stage set was magnificent, but most could not master their parts.'[3]

He assumes that so-called sexual freedom was indeed a goal for women, or that it meant the same thing to women as to men. But did the model of sexual freedom for men – sex without commitment, or with many partners instead of one – comprise freedom for women? For whom was the stage set magnificent; for whom was it designed?

When Robert McAlmon tried to kiss Adrienne Monnier in a taxi he received not a polite rebuke but a heavy bite on his lip. Ezra Pound tried a similar move on Bryher, with equally unsuccessful results. These were but two of many women on the Left Bank for whom sexual freedom did not mean being readily available to men, but rather freedom from the heterosexual imperative. It meant freedom to love as they chose – in their case, other women.

There were, inevitably, unpleasant literary consequences for women who rejected individual men or men in general. Ezra Pound felt Djuna Barnes's literary reputation was overrated and 'in need of deflating'. Men labelled Nancy Cunard a nymphomaniac and therefore fair game, so when Richard Aldington walked in and, in her words, 'pounced', she paid a high price for refusing his 'favours'. Aldington viciously attacked her as being a predatory, ruthless destroyer of men in his short story 'Now Lies She There'. William Carlos Williams, a man who had been shocked by the presence of lesbians at Natalie Barney's salon, wrote publicly about Adrienne and Bryher in such unwarranted terms of disgust that Bryher was driven to seek legal recourse.

When we pay attention to these women's stories, we find a different image of Paris emerging, which is not that of one long party lasting the entire decade of the twenties. Even the unrelenting cultural fascination with 'the twenties' ignores the reality that many of the expatriate women arrived in Paris much earlier (Natalie Barney and Eileen Gray, for instance, came in 1902; Gertrude Stein in 1903), and stayed much later. Most made Paris their permanent home, surviving one or even two world wars.

How did this city appear to them upon their arrival? They became enchanted by the busy outdoor market at Les Halles on the Right Bank, the romantic bookstalls and fishermen along the Seine, the outdoor café by the lake in the Bois de Boulogne where ladies of leisure met for lunch. They walked by children playing with wooden sailboats in the fountain in the Luxembourg Gardens. The sounds they heard most often were of church bells and of horses' hooves on cobblestone passageways. They settled on the Left Bank, close to the river, and began to work. There they created three milieux which were to change the cultural landscape of Paris: Sylvia

Beach's and Adrienne Monnier's bookshops in the rue de l'Odéon, and Natalie Barney's and Gertrude Stein's salons in the rue Jacob and rue de Fleurus, respectively.

It was not that Paris was culturally more 'liberated' than England or America in its attitudes towards women, but simply that it left its foreigners alone. Asked why she liked to live among the French, Gertrude Stein wrote, 'Well the reason is very simple their life belongs to them so your life can belong to you . . . '[4]

If the goal was to have their lives belonging to themselves, it was no coincidence that virtually all the women writers and artists in Paris had neither husbands nor children. (Some of the women who found themselves pregnant, such as Janet Flanner and Djuna Barnes, had miscarriages or abortions or, in the case of Romaine Brooks, gave the child up for adoption. The few with children – H.D. and Colette each had a daughter – were not regularly based in Paris and also had other people to care for the children.) Of those who had married at some point, all were divorced or widowed. Katherine Anne Porter, an American expatriate writer in France who *was* married, betrayed feelings of jealousy towards Gertrude Stein for being able to have her own life. After Gertrude's death, she wrote about her in *Harper's Magazine*, situating her in

> the company of Amazons which nineteenth-century America
> produced among its many prodigies: not-men, not-women,
> answerable to no function in either sex, whose careers were
> carried on, and how successfully, in whatever field they chose
> . . . who lived in public and by the public and played out their
> self-assumed, self-created roles in such masterly freedom as
> only a few early medieval queens had equaled. Freedom to
> them meant precisely freedom from men and their stuffy rules
> for women. They usurped with a high hand the traditional
> masculine privileges of movement, choice, and the use of
> direct, personal power . . . [5]

This 'company of Amazons' was a self-consciously created community whose lives intertwined in multiple, often surprising ways. Yet they were not a monolithic group; divisions and conflicts existed along lines of

ABOVE **Gertrude Stein with the young sculptor and silverpoint artist Thelma Wood: their contrasting appearances reveal some of the disparity in age, sexuality, and economic class among the women in Paris.**

nationality, economic class, talent, artistic priorities, political perspective, and sexuality. Gertrude Stein's and H.D.'s writing had nothing in common, yet friendship and respect for each other's work overrode literary differences.

Their financial situations were as varied as their artistic goals. Some were heiresses, as Natalie Barney, Romaine Brooks and Bryher were, while some like Djuna Barnes lived on the *largesse* of others. Others, such as Alice B. Toklas, lived on small family allowances. Janet Flanner was the only one with a regular pay check; Berenice Abbott recalled that Janet always could afford to dress elegantly as a result.

Many of the women were lesbian or bisexual; all felt a primary emotional, if not sexual, attachment to other women. Yet there were many ways of defining (or not defining) their romantic attachments: Gertrude Stein wrote about her 'wife', Janet Flanner talked of her 'emotional friendships', and Sylvia Beach was silent on the subject. Their intimate relationships also arranged themselves in a variety of constellations which, in forging new territory, followed no set pattern or predetermined rules.

Although the women were of different nationalities and religions, they were all white, despite there being many influential Black American women living in Paris at that time – who were attracted to Paris precisely because they found no 'colour bar' there. Author and editor Jesse Redmon Fausset had found that in Paris 'nobody cares – not even Americans, it seems – whether an artist is white, black or yellow or, as Forster says in *A Passage to India*, "pink-gray"'.[6] She met more writers and artists in four months in Paris than she had in four years in New York. But in general the encounters between black and white women did not lead to enduring friendships.

Among the outstanding black women entertainers who made Paris their home were Josephine Baker, Bricktop, Adelaide Hall, Florence Mills and Mabel Mercer, while Elizabeth Welch was a frequent visitor from England. Florence Mills and Adelaide Hall were stars of The Blackbirds, an all-black show of over 100 performers which played at the Moulin Rouge. Originally brought over for the tourists and expatriates, the troupe found its best audience among the enthusiastic French. Of all the Black Americans performing on the Parisian stage, Josephine Baker was indisputably the most celebrated. She arrived in 1925 at the age of 18, as part of a chorus line with the first Black American stage company ever to tour Europe. Just off the ship and on the train to Paris, she fell immediately in love with France – but that was nothing compared with the way France would soon fall in love with her.

ABOVE **The singer and nightclub owner Ada Smith, nicknamed
'Bricktop' because of her red hair.**

Bricktop was born Ada Smith in Chicago, and ran a popular club
across town in Montmartre, where she sang Cole Porter songs like an angel
and knew all her customers by name. Although English painter Nina
Hamnett, American writer Kay Boyle and the famous Montparnasse model
Kiki were all seen on occasion in Bricktop's, she was better friends with her
'regulars' – among them Robert McAlmon (whom she called 'the big
spendin' man') and Man Ray who could always be found at the bar.

There were few social connections between the black entertainers
and the white literary women. Janet Flanner and Adrienne Monnier both
wrote enthusiastically about Josephine Baker's performance, but neither
mentions meeting her, despite Colette being their mutual friend. During the
twenties, Colette was one of Josephine Baker's closest friends, their
intimacy based in part on a shared love of animals.

While black entertainers were dazzling Paris with their Afro-
American rhythms and styles, other, mostly European, women were
flocking to Paris and shaking up its cultural life on other fronts.

Architecture, photography, painting, ballet, theatre and costume design and filmmaking were just some of the visual and performing arts of the 1920s in which women pioneered and flourished. From Russia, the avant-garde painters and theatre designers Alexandra Exter and Natalya Goncharova came to Paris where Cubist, Futurist, and Constructivist influences were discernible in their colourful, rhythmically active compositions. From England, Modernist designer and architect Eileen Gray came to Paris to discover Cubism and art deco and to enjoy the companionship of other female visual artists, including Romaine Brooks and Berenice Abbott. From Germany, photographers Marianne Breslauer and Germaine Krull arrived and used the city itself as their model for Modernist compositions in black and white. From France, Germaine Dulac was an innovator of avant-garde filmmaking, often with a focus on women's themes. Most of these visual artists crossed paths with the literary women and the confluence of such creativity had cultural implications for them all. The cast of characters was not limited to either women or foreigners, but the *mise-en-scène* of pre-war Paris was both international and female.

Paris has often been imagined as a mysterious, seductive woman, both mistress and muse to generations of male poets. Women drawn to the allure of Paris were also responding to the female qualities of a city which allowed them to express themselves in less conventional, more substantive ways than simply as romanticized mistress or muse. Whatever perspectives, needs, or backgrounds the women of the Left Bank seem to have in common, it was the intangible but irresistible promise of Paris that united them. Gertrude Stein wrote in 1939 that, 'The only personality I would like to write about . . . is Paris, France, that is where we all were, and it was natural for us to be there.'[7] As they searched to find and create the conditions by which they could love and work and live, they transformed the character of the city itself. For them, Paris was neither a fantasized young *cocotte*, clichéd old mistress, nor the idealized muse of the male poet's imagination. For nearly half a century, she became a fascinating, creative, intelligent woman.

*Robert McAlmon wrote *Being Geniuses Together: 1920–1930* in 1938. It was revised, with additional material by Kay Boyle, in 1968.

ADRIENNE ▪ ▪ MONNIER

CHAPTER 1

ODÉONIA: THE COUNTRY OF BOOKS

Twenty-three year old Adrienne Monnier realized a childhood dream in November 1915 when she opened a small bookshop on the rue de l'Odéon in the sixth arrondissement. Its location in the heart of the artistic and intellectual centre of Paris was no accident:

> The Left Bank called me and even now it does not cease to call me and to keep me. I cannot imagine that I could ever leave it, any more than an organ can leave the place that is assigned to it in the body.[1]

She loved books passionately and read each one before bringing it into her shop. What we perceive as an 'ordinary' and practical business (although at

LEFT A portrait of Adrienne Monnier in her favourite setting – surrounded by books. Painted by her brother-in-law, Paul Emile Bécat.

the time, hardly ordinary for women) she managed to turn into an intellectual and artistic profession. Her bookshop soon became the hub of French avant-garde literature, the birthplace for more than one Modernist movement, and a spontaneous literary salon for many famous and soon-to-be famous writers, including André Breton, Paul Valéry, Colette, Guillaume

Apollinaire, Jules Romains, Jean Cocteau, Léon-Paul Fargue and André Gide.

Almost four years after Adrienne had opened her bookshop, the young American Sylvia Beach established her own English language bookshop, Shakespeare and Company. Alice B. Toklas later recalled that within just a few months, Sylvia had become a 'literary personality'. Janet Flanner describes the two booksellers:

The immediate compatibility of these two extraordinary women – Mlle Monnier, buxom as an abbess, placidly picturesque in the costume she had permanently adopted, consisting of a long, full gray skirt, a bright velveteen waistcoat, and a white blouse, and slim, jacketed Sylvia, with her schoolgirl white collar and big colored bowknot, in the style of Colette's *Claudine à l'école* – eventually had an

LEFT Sylvia worked as a volunteer farm hand in Touraine, as all the men had left for the front. She then volunteered for the Red Cross in Serbia at the war's end.

important canalizing influence on French-American literary relations as they flowed, almost like a new major cultural traffic, up and down the Rue de l'Odéon.[2]

An American minister's daughter from Princeton, New Jersey, Sylvia Beach had come to Paris at the age of 29 because of a professed love for France and for contemporary French literature. It was 1917, four years into the worst war in history, and before long she left Paris to enlist in the war effort. It would be two years before she returned, bringing an engraved cigarette lighter as a gift for Adrienne Monnier, whom she had met shortly after her arrival in France. Sylvia Beach's biographer, Noel Riley Fitch, describes that initial meeting:

> The story began in Paris on a cold, gusty March afternoon in
> 1917. A shy young woman named Sylvia Beach hesitated at the
> door of a Left Bank bookshop and lending library, La Maison
> des Amis des Livres. The owner, a self-assured young French
> writer and publisher named Adrienne Monnier, got up quickly
> from her desk and drew her visitor into the shop, greeting her
> warmly. The two talked the afternoon away, each declaring
> love for the language and literature of the other.[3]

The developing relationship between Sylvia and Adrienne was crucial to the flowering of English and American literature in France. It was the example and inspiration of Adrienne Monnier which guided Sylvia towards her life's calling in the service of literature. From the practical perspective, Adrienne was the one who took on the logistical problems of setting up Shakespeare and Company, obtaining the necessary business permit and negotiating with the concierge of the former laundry. Sylvia recalled that when they first went to view the premises, Adrienne

> point[ed] to the words 'gros' and 'fin' on either side of the door,
> meaning they did both sheets and fine linen. Adrienne, who
> was rather plump, placed herself under the 'gros' and told me
> to stand under the 'fin'. 'That's you and me,' she said.[4]

This sense of humour was key to their relationship, perhaps even more

The two young women who found themselves at the centre of French-American literary relations.

important than their shared love of French literature. Adrienne wrote:

This young American displayed an original and most attaching personality. She spoke French fluently with . . . an energetic and incisive way of pronouncing words . . . In her conversation there were neither hesitations nor pauses; words never failed her; on occasion she deliberately invented them, she proceeded then by an adaption of English, by a mixture or extension of French vocables, all that with the exquisite sense of our language. Her finds were generally so happy, so charmingly funny, that they at once came into usage – our usage – as if they had always existed; one could not keep from repeating them, and one tried to imitate them. To sum it up, this young American had a great deal of humor, let us say more: she was humour itself.[5]

Their devotion to each other lasted until Adrienne's death in 1955, when Katherine Anne Porter wrote to Sylvia: 'Adrienne – you and Adrienne, for I thought of you together, even though you were both so distinct as individuals and friends in my mind . . . ' [6]

Ostensibly in the same profession, Adrienne's focus was books and words while Sylvia's was readers and writers. Perhaps it was these different emphases which softened any potential competition between the two establishments, so much so that Sylvia 'always consulted [Adrienne] before taking an important step. She was such a wise counselor, and she was, besides, a sort of partner in the firm.'[7]

Educated in Latin and French, philosophy, mathematics and history, Adrienne had a love of words and books not limited to those written by others; she published a volume of poetry in 1923, called *La Figure*, and a collection of prose in 1932. In addition to her bookshop work she managed to contribute articles to numerous journals including *Commerce* and *Mesures* (for both of which she was the administrator for a short while), *Nouvelle Revue Française*, *Figaro Littéraire*, and *Les Lettres Nouvelles*. Widely accepted as a leading authority on French avant-garde literature, she received letters from around the world. The great Russian film director, Sergei Eisenstein, requested that she 'writ[e] me a line or two about what is the great "*épatage*" of to-day in French literature!'[8]

Sylvia, by contrast, had no formal education and did not write anything but her highly guarded memoirs late in life, and a translation of *Barbarian in Asia* by Henri Michaux. To Bryher she confessed that ' . . . I only wish I had exercised with the pen a little all these years, and now knew how to write, as Gertrude would call it, but I didn't and don't.'[9] In a letter to the editor of her memoirs, she turned her inhibitions about writing into a joke:

> About my education, the less said the better. I ain't had none: never went to school and wouldn't have learned anything if I had went. You will have to copy what goes for T.S. Eliot: say I have degrees from all those places, same as him.[10]

Janet Flanner, with that acerbic tongue she was known for in her political journalism, claimed that

> Sylvia herself did not have a literary mind or much literary taste though in time a certain sense of literature rubbed off into her from the people around her. What she instinctively recognized and was attracted to was merely literary genius or flashes and fractions of it, or of tremendous great talent . . . [11]

This talent preferably came in the form of a writer. Even more than books, it was the writers that she loved most and made her life's work, evidenced by the shop's interior in which more wall space was devoted to portraits of writers than to books. Man Ray and Berenice Abbott were 'the official portraitists of "the Crowd"', as Sylvia Beach dubbed them, until Gisèle Freund came through Paris in the mid-thirties and made a career of photographing all the great writers and thinkers on the Left Bank.

In 1919, Sylvia was in the process of choosing a path for her own career which would not seem 'useless' in comparison to her war efforts. She responded to her mother's futile pleas to return to Princeton by sending a telegram: 'Opening bookshop in Paris. Please send money.' Not wealthy herself, her mother obliged with $3,000. Sylvia was able to open the shop.

ABOVE According to Janet Flanner, this cheque represented Sylvia's mother's life savings, which she sent so that Sylvia could open her bookshop.

ABOVE **Adrienne and Sylvia during a Sunday outing to Rocfoin, where Adrienne's family lived. Occasionally James Joyce (seated, left) would join them.**

Like Sylvia, Adrienne had no brothers and therefore was the recipient of some family money. Her father, a postal clerk who worked on the trains, received compensation for near fatal injuries in a railroad accident, the only money her family ever had. Adrienne, a staunch pacifist, believed herself 'blessed by the Goddess of War': in addition to the compensation money, the recruitment of men into the First World War created unprecedented professional opportunities for women such as herself. Adrienne always found these two factors which enabled her to open her shop – world war and family tragedy – ironic and bittersweet.

After the initial start-up funds, Sylvia continued to receive occasional financial assistance from her mother, who often sold her jewellery for this purpose. Adrienne's family sent both Adrienne and Sylvia fresh vegetables from their home in Rocfoin, a small town southwest of Paris, where for many years the two women spent their Sundays. These contributions supplemented the meagre earnings of the two bookshops.

Sylvia described her first meeting with the people who would become two of her most regular book-borrowers in the shop's early days:

Not long after I had opened my bookshop, two women came . . . One of them, with a very fine face, was stout, wore a long robe, and, on her head, a most becoming top of a basket. She was accompanied by a slim, dark whimsical woman: she reminded me of a gypsy.[12]

They were, of course, Gertrude Stein and Alice B. Toklas. Gertrude set out to help the shop by circulating an advertisement for it:

LEFT **Shakespeare pulled out his hair whenever books were overdue in the lending library.**

RIGHT **Adrienne formally invited Gertrude and Alice to her house, soon after they had joined Sylvia's lending library.**

LA MAISON DES AMIS DES LIVRES

7, RUE DE L'ODÉON - PARIS - VIe

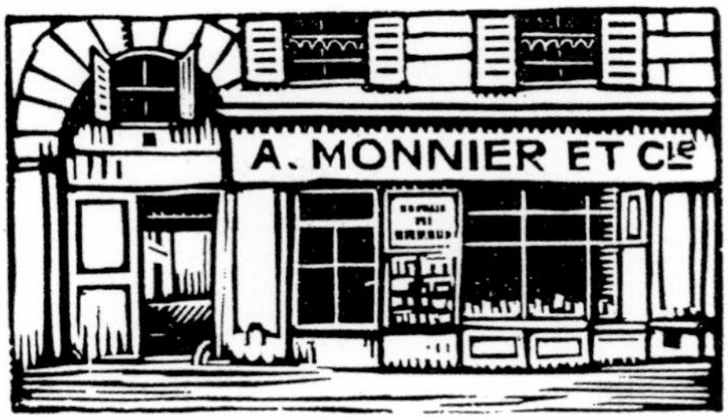

3 avril 1920

Chère Mademoiselle,

Je vous rappelle que c'est mercredi 7 que nous goûtons chez moi : 18 rue de l'Odéon (5 h.)

En attendant le grand plaisir de vous voir, je vous envoie, ainsi qu'à votre amie, l'assurance de ma vive sympathie

Adrienne Monnier

Not a country not a door send them away to sit on the floor.
Cakes. This is not the world. Can you remember.

Alice and Janet Flanner both claimed this succeeded in drawing in new customers.

From the start, Sylvia and Adrienne were much more than booksellers. Adrienne, in particular, was determined to alter people's, and especially women's, reading habits and relation to books. In her essay 'Les Amies des Livres', she offered a feminist analysis of women's relationship to books, and catered to that relationship in the way she ran her bookshop: she sold inexpensive volumes for curious readers rather than first editions for scholars and collectors, and allowed customers to take books home for a time before deciding whether to buy them. Her free lending library was the first ever in France. Sylvia and Adrienne saw themselves as not only sellers and lenders but also readers and lovers of books, charged with the mission of imparting this love to their customers. Bryher wrote that Sylvia was known for 'finding by some intuitive process that she and Adrienne Monnier alone seemed to me to possess, the exact book that an enquirer needed for his development at that particular moment'.[13]

In 1921 Shakespeare and Company moved around the corner so that it was almost directly opposite Adrienne's bookshop, and Sylvia moved into Adrienne's apartment a few doors away. After that, Bryher felt that

there was only one street in Paris for me, the rue de l'Odéon. It
is association, I suppose, but I have always considered it one of
the most beautiful streets in the world. It meant naturally Sylvia
and Adrienne and the happy hours that I spent in their
libraries.[14]

Bryher and Sylvia became friends soon after the shop opened, and they remained close for the rest of their lives. After more than thirty years of friendship, Sylvia wrote,

RIGHT **The English writer and publisher Bryher, who used her family
wealth to support Shakespeare and Company during its many
financial crises.**

36

It was in one of the earliest days of 'Shakespeare and Company'
that you came into my bookshop and my life, dear Bryher, and
that we became a Protectorate of yours. We might have had the
words: 'By Special Appointment to Bryher' painted above the
door.[15]

The sister bookshops on the rue de l'Odéon soon became a cultural centre
of Europe, serving as a gathering place where writers from all over the
world met, collected their post and read the latest in the proliferation of
literary magazines. The French poet Jules Romains introduced poetry
readings at La Maison des Amis des Livres shortly after he met Adrienne in
1917. She had lured him into the bookshop by writing, 'At 7 rue de
l'Odéon there is a bookseller who loves your work.' Soon after, he came by
and inquired after Monsieur Monnier. She was thrilled that he hadn't
guessed her gender, perhaps suspecting that he would not have taken her
seriously enough to come at all. She need not have worried:

I saw in front of me a girl with a round, rosy face, with blue
eyes, with blond hair, who, it appeared almost at once, had just
entered the service of literature as others decide to enter the
service of religion . . . Already her voice was authoritative and
charming; very watched over, very limpid, at once full of music
and assurance.[16]

Although poetry readings predominated, occasionally other, non-literary
events were held as well, such as a tea in honour of Paul Robeson at
Shakespeare and Company, at which he sang Negro Spirituals, thus
performing the opening concert of his European tour. The first exhibition of
photographs by Gisèle Freund was held in La Maison des Amis des Livres.

In the mid-thirties, Gisèle Freund left Germany at a day's notice with
a suitcase containing her unfinished doctoral dissertation, a change of
clothing, and a few Deutschmarks. She had been alerted that the police
were looking for members of her student group, involved in resistance
activities in Frankfurt. Grateful to be safe from the Nazis, she arrived in
Paris, not knowing she was the only one of her group to survive. She
resumed her studies at the Sorbonne and one day, while browsing through

the outdoor stalls on the rue de l'Odéon, selected a book by Jules Romains to buy for two francs. As she opened the shop door of La Maison des Amis des Livres, she met the woman, twenty years her senior, who would become the most influential person in her life. The two women became fast friends, and on busy days Gisèle would help Adrienne in her shop.

Meanwhile Gisèle began taking photographs, using free stock from the front and tail ends of moving picture film. She asked filmmaker friends Bunuel, Dali and Cocteau to give her these otherwise unusable 'short ends', thus enabling her to get started in 35mm still photography. One day she suggested to Adrienne:

> I have an idea, I have a new film in colour, I would love to
> photograph all your friends in colour. And she said 'that's a
> wonderful idea,' she was always open for new ideas you see,
> and therefore in less than a year I made all these photographs
> which now are worldwide known. Not everybody knows who
> did them, but the photographs are known.[17]

Adrienne decided to hold an exhibition of the photographs in her shop. She rented fifty chairs, hung a white sheet on the wall, and invited the leading authors of Paris to watch their own images projected on the wall. She even reviewed the exhibition in her bookshop magazine:

> I have come back from a voyage to the country of faces. A long
> voyage undertaken in the company of Gisèle Freund. It was she
> who was the pilot, she who held the rudder, she who operated
> the machine for exploring faces. This machine was an ordinary
> camera loaded with film sensitive to colors . . . Yes, my voyage
> with Gisèle Freund has been a great adventure. All the more so
> because she is a bold photographer and conceals nothing, not
> she . . . Thanks to her, we are rich in excellent pictures of most
> of our best writers. It should be said that her way of projecting
> the photos on a screen gives very surprising results. Here light
> plays the role of a sculptor . . . [18]

**OVERLEAF From the balcony of Gisèle Freund's hotel room Adrienne
Monnier looks out over her beloved Left Bank.**

And Simone de Beauvoir recalled:

> The place was crowded with famous writers. I don't remember
> who was there; what has stayed eternally in my mind, however,
> is the sight of the chairs lined up in rows, the screen glowing in
> the darkness, and the familiar faces bathed in beautiful color
> . . . All the consecrated authors as well as the new talents with
> a still-uncertain future drifted across the screen before our
> eyes.[19]

Sylvia and Adrienne were cultural diplomats and ambassadors, introducing
writers and artists to each other and delicately balancing artistic
temperaments. In the early 1920s, Sylvia Beach introduced Gertrude Stein
to French writers such as Valéry Larbaud, the bookshop's official
'godfather', whom Gertrude subsequently invited to her salon. In the mid-
thirties Sylvia and Adrienne held a large reception in honour of the editors
and contributors to *Life and Letters Today*, which Sylvia insisted be a cross-
cultural affair. She wrote to Bryher, 'I think it is very important for you all to
be present, on account of the friendly relations with French writers. And
you know it won't be at all formal, never is in our house, and people don't
dress up here . . . '[20] Sylvia also played the role of 'tour guide' for young
American writers hoping to meet Gertrude Stein:

> Gertrude Stein's admirers, until they had met her and discov-
> ered how affable she was, were often 'skeered' to approach her
> without proper protection. So the poor things would come to
> me, exactly as if I were a guide from one of the tourist agencies,
> and beg me to take them to see Gertrude Stein.
>
> My tours, arranged with Gertrude and Alice beforehand,
> took place in the evenings. They were cheerfully endured by
> the ladies in the pavillon, who were always cordial and hos-
> pitable.[21]

Bryher, in her memoirs, wrote that Sylvia 'was the perfect Ambassador and
I doubt if a citizen has ever done more to spread knowledge of America

RIGHT **The cultural ambassador in front of her embassy.**

abroad . . . Great and humble she mixed us all together . . . , the bond between us being that we were artists and discoverers.'[22]

One young American that she took under her wing was an unknown journalist and 'wannabe' writer named Ernest Hemingway. He spent hours in the shop, reading and occasionally buying the many experimental 'little magazines' on sale while Sylvia and her assistants babysat his son Bumby. Sylvia found that Hemingway had 'the true writer's temperament' which she admired from the start. Adrienne quietly predicted that of all the unknown expatriates adrift in Paris trying to write, Hemingway would be the one to succeed. But Sylvia placed her bet on someone else.

In 1920 Sylvia met James Joyce at a dinner party at the home of French poet André Spire, to which she had been brought by Adrienne and he by Ezra Pound. She recognized him as the author of *A Portrait of the Artist as a Young Man*, although how she came upon this book she couldn't recall: 'I don't know. You can never tell how a bookworm gets hold of a book. They simply make for this diet of theirs.'[23] She approached him, trembling, and asked, 'Is this the great James Joyce?' to which he quietly replied, 'James Joyce,' and she shook what she described as his 'limp, boneless' hand.

Her passionate belief in Joyce's genius led Sylvia into a tremendously risky and courageous undertaking: the publication of *Ulysses*, in 1922,

BELOW Ernest Hemingway claimed he could write letters but not mail them. As he was in the shop virtually every morning, he probably hand-delivered this letter to Sylvia.

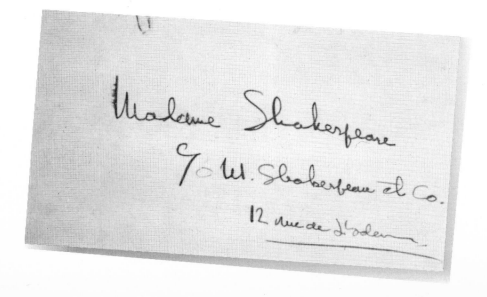

ABOVE **Sylvia, Adrienne and *Ulysses*, disguised as *Shakespeare's Works in One Volume.***

when no established publisher would touch it. Sylvia attempted it because she was, in the words of Janet Flanner, 'the intrepid, unselfish, totally inexperienced, and little-moneyed young-lady publisher'. [24] Three similarly intrepid, unselfish and inexperienced women had tried unsuccessfully before her. When Harriet Weaver started the Egoist Press in London specifically for this purpose, the British printers refused to set the type. Margaret Anderson and Jane Heap began publishing *Ulysses* piecemeal in their *Little Review*, then still based in New York, only to have three issues seized by the United States Post Office and a fourth land them in court on an obscenity charge. It managed to become a book only because the French printers in Dijon did not understand English. Even by its eighth edition Sylvia's shop was selling it, at purchasers' request, in false dust covers because of the lingering controversy surrounding it; one cover gave

it the title 'Shakespeare's Works in One Volume', another 'Merry Tales for Little Folks'.

Beach served as the 'midwife' to Joyce's career, devoting herself to publishing and promoting his work and ensuring that Joyce and his family of four had adequate funds. This twelve-year involvement was not only an immense emotional and financial drain on her, it lead to the threat of imprisonment and to eventual bankruptcy. Thus the facts of Sylvia's life seem to portray a woman who, although living an unconventional lifestyle and taking extraordinary risks, still behaved in a traditionally female way: as the tireless, unpaid housekeeper to male genius, the modest, self-effacing minister's daughter, and ultimate acquiescing victim of male greed.

Such a portrait only shows one side of Sylvia Beach. We know that she was an entertaining storyteller with a sharp, ironic wit and a knack for pantomime, and who, with no formal education, spoke four languages. Before settling in Paris, she had travelled throughout Europe, supporting the suffrage movement in Italy, writing articles such as 'Spanish Feminism in 1916', and attracting much attention in her trousers and short hair in Touraine during the war.

After her death, Sylvia's friends wrote about her as a woman of intense loyalties and passions, who was strong-willed, intelligent and endlessly energetic: 'Has anyone imagined that Sylvia's devotion to her chosen writers was selfless? She was a barbed-wire fence of self.'[25]

Selfless or not, it seems that Sylvia leaned on Adrienne to set limits which she herself did not set on the demands of customers and friends. It was Adrienne who, in 1931, finally put a stop to Joyce's endless financial loans and emotional demands. At a time when Joyce had reached god-like stature, Adrienne wrote him a scathing letter exposing him as a manipulative fame-and-fortune-seeker, a letter Sylvia never would have written. In her memoirs, Sylvia Beach described the insanity of Joyce's demands during the publication of *Ulysses*, but it is impossible to know whether her lack of bitterness in the telling veiled, as Joyce himself assumed it did, unspoken hostility.

. . . James Joyce and *Ulysses* had practically taken over the

LEFT 'I worshiped James Joyce,' Sylvia confessed.

bookshop in the rue de l'Odéon. We attended to Joyce's correspondence, were his bankers, his agents, his errand boys . . .
The printers, like everyone else connected with this great work,
found out that it was invading their lives . . . They followed my
orders to supply Joyce with all the proofs he wanted, and he
was insatiable. Every proof was covered with additional text
. . . Joyce told me he had written a third of *Ulysses* on the
proofs.[26]

Janet Flanner celebrated the publication of *Ulysses* in her *New Yorker*
column and described the excitement in Paris when the first copy appeared
in Shakespeare and Company's shop window, but bemoaned Joyce's unfair
treatment of Sylvia:

[Sylvia was like a] beast of burden struggling beneath the crush-
ing load of a singular author's genius and egotisms, heavy as
stones or marble in the case of the Dubliner Joyce . . . All of
Joyce's gratitude, largely unexpressed, should have been
addressed to her as a woman. For the patience she gave him
was female . . . She always gave more than she received.
Publishing *Ulysses* was her greatest act of generosity.[27]

The expression of Joyce's gratitude seems to have been limited to a short
poem he wrote for Sylvia upon receiving the first copy of *Ulysses* on his
fortieth birthday ('Who is Sylvia'), and a comment he made privately to a
third party, 'All she ever did was to make me a present of the ten best years
of her life.'[28] For her part, Sylvia did not see publishing the novel as a
present or an act of generosity. The greatness of Joyce's work demanded
sacrifices from everyone, herself especially, and she had little resentment
about its emotional and financial cost to her personally:

Up to the last minute, the long-suffering printers in Dijon were
getting back these proofs, with new things to be inserted somehow, whole paragraphs even, dislocating pages. [They] suggested that I call Joyce's attention to the danger of going beyond my
depth; perhaps his appetite for proofs might be curbed. But no,
I wouldn't hear of such a thing. *Ulysses* was to be as Joyce

wished, in every respect.

I wouldn't advise 'real' publishers to follow my example, nor authors to follow Joyce's. It would be the death of publishing. My case was different. It seemed natural to me that the efforts and sacrifices on my part should be proportionate to the greatness of the work I was publishing.[29]

Among Sylvia's sacrifices for *Ulysses* were two of her best customers. Gertrude Stein called at the shop one day to withdraw her support and announce that thereafter she would patronize the American Library on the Right Bank instead.

Sam Steward, a young American in Paris in the thirties who was close to Gertrude Stein, recalls that she 'felt a little frozen out, or at least a little wounded by the fact that Sylvia Beach had paid so much attention to the publication of Joyce's *Ulysses* and had not really done much about Gertrude's writing.'[30]

But before long it was Sylvia who was frozen out. When Joyce became rich and famous, he thanked Sylvia by breaking their publishing contract and selling rights that belonged to her. According to Gisèle Freund,

Hemingway was unknown. All these people [who later became the most famous writers of our century] were unknown. And they became known through Adrienne and Sylvia. To publish *Ulysses*, this was incredible! This Sylvia Beach did, and she went bankrupt, thanks to Joyce. She had not a penny left, nothing. And then he made a very big arrangement with an American publisher and forgot about the arrangement he had made with Sylvia Beach.[31]

Very late in the procedure (only six months before Adrienne's angry letter attempting to sever ties with him) Joyce produced a contract between himself and Sylvia, described by Janet Flanner as 'a strange, Jesuitical document' which granted Sylvia world rights in *Ulysses*. Contract in hand, she tried to sell the book to an American publisher, Curtis Brown, who withdrew his offer when Sylvia requested what she thought 'a modest estimate of the value that *Ulysses* represents to me'. Sylvia confided to her sister, 'It must be because of my sex that they think I wouldn't charge them anything.'[32] Joyce himself was to violate the contract soon after; the next deal for an American edition he signed behind her back with Random House, and pocketed a 45, 000 dollar advance. Sylvia called Joyce in anger and released him from all of her claims to *Ulysses*.

Gertrude Stein was also angry about James Joyce, and it was more than a matter of simple jealousy. She felt her book, *The Making of Americans*, written almost two decades before *Ulysses* but not published until 1925, suffered unfairly from the ordeal that the printers in Dijon had already undergone with *Ulysses*. Robert McAlmon, who was publishing it through his Contact Editions, wrote to her,

> Neither Mr. Joyce or Miss Beach estimated rightly on the no. of
> words in *Ulysses* . . . The work [Making of Americans] has
> stayed too long unpublished but the error made by my believ-
> ing Joyce knew how many words were in his book will of
> course mean a great difference in the quotation I can expect
> from the printer. It will be almost double.[33]

The 'long-suffering' printers in Dijon survived the two Modernist epics of the decade, *Ulysses* and *The Making of Americans*, only to have *Ulysses* return for publication in a French edition at the end of the decade. Adrienne Monnier was the novel's first French-language publisher, again no small task. The French novelist Valery Larbaud, who thought *Ulysses* to be 'as great as Rabelais', became its official translator. During the long, arduous publication process, Adrienne held a bilingual public reading by Larbaud and Joyce in her bookshop.

Although the business of the shop took most of her energy, Adrienne somehow managed to launch her own magazine, the short-lived *Navire d'Argent* (she later published the *Gazette des Amis des Livres* as well). In it she introduced in translation the work of English, American and German writers to France. T. S. Eliot was speaking for many when he wrote that 'to

RIGHT **Gisèle Freund's portrait of James Joyce with his publishers,
taken when relations between them were already strained.**

Adrienne Monnier, with *Navire d'Argent*, I owe the introduction of my verse to French readers',[34] although Adrienne and Sylvia together had translated his 'Love Song of J. Alfred Prufrock'. Adrienne found the translation relatively easy, unlike '*The Wasteland*', which she and Sylvia 'would never have dared to attack'. Adrienne also compiled and published the first bibliography of English literature available in French.

In the first issue of Adrienne's *Navire d'Argent* was a short monologue, 'Homme buvant du vin', by J.-M. Sollier. The surname was Adrienne's mother's, and the pseudonym was her own. This was just one in a collection of Adrienne's prose pieces she later collected in a book and published herself. In *Navire*'s final issue, devoted to poetry in May 1926, she included two poems of her own. According to Gisèle Freund, the pseudonym was a function of her femaleness:

> When she wrote a book under the name of her grandfather [her mother's maiden name], under the name of Sollier, everybody thought it was a marvelous book. It was a wonderful book until they heard it was Adrienne. The only writer who knew about it was Léon-Paul Fargue, and when he told the others this is Adrienne Monnier, all those who had thought it was wonderful became quiet. Nobody wanted to speak about it anymore because she was much more useful to the writers, to help them, to publish them, and as a seller of their books, than to write herself, which is what she always wanted. She did everything for other people. And this made her embittered. Today a woman would just do it but in those times, you see, she just couldn't do it . . . [35]

If the need to hide her own authorship was particularly female, so was her literary style. Referring not to her poetry but to her 'gazettes', the critic Jean Amrouche has written:

> Her art of telling is in close correspondence with her art of liv-

RIGHT Déjeuner Ulysses: A luncheon given in honour of the appearance of a French edition of *Ulysses*, published by Adrienne Monnier in 1929.

MORALITÉS
PAUL VALÉRY
LE NAVIRE D'ARGENT
A LA MAISON DES AMIS DES LIVRES
CHEZ ADRIENNE MONNIER
INTRODUCTION

ing. Her writings name, point out, evoke, paint, or describe real objects with which she had dealing and which life bore forth to her whose welcome always preceded the offering . . . That took place, I saw it the way I am telling it, with the joy that I took in it, that is what clearly underlies most of the gazettes.[36]

Adrienne's literary style is almost too vibrant and sensual to fit under the category 'criticism'. In her essay 'Lunch with Colette' the menu is virtually transformed from words on a page to tastes in one's mouth, both pleasant and not:

Today there are snails. 'Ah, no!' says Colette, 'it's the only thing I've never been able to eat. I've tried to enjoy them, but nothing goes down except the juice.' In my corner I exult, for I have a horror of snails, and I have never even wanted to put one of them in my mouth.

The dialogue Adrienne re-created from her lunch with Colette has that spontaneity and disorder of real life: one moment fortune-tellers, the next Colette's occasional 'urge to kill' someone. Adrienne's words convey her *joie de vivre* – despite her living through poverty, world wars and health torments which would eventually end her life in suicide.

Looking back on her life, Sylvia wrote that her three great loves had been Adrienne Monnier, James Joyce and Shakespeare and Company. The

LEFT *Le Navire d'Argent*: Adrienne's self-published journal, which included her own writings under a pseudonym.

RIGHT The publication of Adrienne's *Gazettes*, a volume of philosophical and critical essays about literature and politics, which she published under her own name.

LA MAISON DES AMIS DES LIVRES
7, RUE DE L'ODÉON, PARIS VIᵉ

Nouvelle Direction : Jacques LAMY

Lundi 14 Décembre, de 16 à 19 heures
Adrienne Monnier signera son livre

Les Gazettes d'Adrienne Monnier

(Cette signature sera la seule faite par l'auteur)

Les personnes qui désirent des exemplaires sur bon papier *(voir prospectus ci-joint)* sont priés de les souscrire dès maintenant. Il sera réservé des exemplaires du premier tirage de l'édition courante sur demande faite à l'avance. Ecrire ou téléphoner : DAN. 07-41

first heartache accompanying these loves was the severing of her ties with Joyce, but within ten years Sylvia would also move out from Adrienne and lose Shakespeare and Company as well.

For the first time in twenty-two years, Sylvia went back to the United States in 1937 on the occasion of her father's eighty-fourth birthday. Her return was delayed by several months when she learned she needed a hysterectomy and then several weeks of rest. Upon her eventual return home, she discovered that Gisèle Freund had moved into her apartment and become more intimate with Adrienne. The refugee photographer had been taken in by them the previous winter and Adrienne had arranged a 'marriage of convenience' for residency purposes; but now, as Shari Benstock put it, she 'represented a threat to Sylvia's relationship with Adrienne'.[37] Sylvia promptly moved across the street to live above her shop, but continued to eat her meals with Adrienne and Gisèle as her new apartment had no proper kitchen.

There were other reasons to continue meals with Adrienne. Bryher recalled that they were 'a unique experience, first to eat the dinner

ABOVE **A quiet afternoon at home, when Sylvia still lived with Adrienne at 18, rue de l'Odéon, down the street from the two bookshops.**

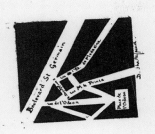

On " SHAKESPEARE AND COMPANY'S " bookshelves will be found not only the Classics, but the works of english and american authors of to-day, from Hardy, Shaw, Chesterton, Alice Meynell, Henry James, Edith Wharton... to the younger georgian and american authors.

Hitherto, french readers have encountered a certain difficulty in keeping in touch with recents movements across the Channel and on the other side of the Atlantic; but with the arrival upon the scene of " SHAKESPEARE AND COMPANY " that difficulty no longer exists.

— Henceforth, the french public will have an opportunity to follow closely in the newest reviews, anthologies, etc., the modern poetry and prose of England, Ireland and America.

SHAKESPEARE AND COMPANY
—— Sylvia Beach ——
8, Rue Dupuytren - Paris (VI)

ABOVE This bookmark, predating the move to rue de l'Odéon, is addressed to French readers interested in finding English-language books, although the majority of the customers in the twenties were English and American.

because she cooked better than anyone whom I have ever known, and then to listen to the conversation of some of the finest minds in France . . . Sylvia, of course, had been adopted by them all.'[38]

Sylvia turned her energies to salvaging the financially drained Shakespeare and Company, an effort to which her many friends, especially Bryher, rallied. According to Gisèle Freund, there were times when Sylvia would have died of hunger had it not been for Bryher. A cheque for 4,000 French francs arrived just at the point when Sylvia 'was feeling like giving up the whole "racket"!'. She called Bryher her 'wonderful fairy godmother'.

As if the financial disaster of *Ulysses* were not enough, international events conspired to destroy her bookshop. Soon after the stock market crash of 1929, Sylvia began feeling the effects of the Depression: not only could customers afford fewer books, but there were far fewer customers. Although her clientele had always been international, the mainstay of her business was American expatriates, most of whom repatriated as soon as the dollar fell against the franc. She admitted to Bryher that her business was 'practically at a standstill'. Finally, in great sadness, she resorted to selling some of her treasured first editions and private manuscripts.

When Sylvia confided to André Gide that she might have to close down, it was the French writers from Adrienne's shop across the street who came to her rescue. They formed a committee of some of the most important writers of the day, and issued a successful subscription appeal. Expatriate stragglers also pitched in and Janet Flanner recalled that poetry readings helped to gain new subscribers:

> Valéry recited some of his most beautiful poems – including 'Le Serpent,' at Joyce's special request, although no mention is made of Joyce's reading anything. . . T. S. Eliot came over from London to give a reading, and even Hemingway consented to read aloud from his works when Stephen Spender agreed to make it a double bill. And so Shakespeare and Company was saved . . . [39]

But it was only a short reprieve. Sylvia lost her third great love in 1941 when a German officer in occupied Paris insisted on buying her personal copy of *Finnegans Wake*. Several times previously she had thought the time had come when she would have to close the shop, but she had survived each crisis and ignored her father's pleas to return to America. When France entered the war, it was her government who pleaded. Sylvia somehow 'had resisted all efforts of my embassy to persuade me to return to the United States . . . Instead, I had settled down to share life in Nazi-occupied Paris with my friends.'[40] But when Sylvia refused to sell her private copy, the officer threatened to return and confiscate all her books. That afternoon, Sylvia, with the help of Adrienne and her concierge, emptied out thousands of books, letters, pictures, as well as the tables and chairs, carrying them up four flights to a vacant apartment and safety. Sylvia painted over the bookshop sign on the building, and within two hours Shakespeare and Company had disappeared.

The Nazis did come back another time to arrest Sylvia and place her in an internment camp with other expatriate Americans who dared to stay in their adopted homeland. But the remains of what had been Shakespeare and Company were never found; they survived as a hidden treasure until the liberation of Paris.

RIGHT **The contents of what had been Shakespeare and Company, including the sign above the premises, removed to a vacant apartment for safe-keeping during the Occupation.**

CHAPTER 2

THE WRITER AND HER MUSE

In September 1907, Gertrude and Alice first met in Paris where they would remain, together, for the next four decades. In *The Autobiography of Alice B. Toklas*, Gertrude described their meeting, presumably as she wanted Alice to have experienced it:

> I was impressed by the coral brooch she wore and by her voice.
> I may say that only three times in my life have I met a genius
> and each time a bell within me rang and I was not mistaken
> . . . The three geniuses of whom I wish to speak are Gertrude
> Stein, Pablo Picasso and Alfred Whitehead.

Alice herself described her first impressions of Gertrude with even more adulation:

> She was large and heavy with delicate small hands and a beau-
> tifully modeled and unique head . . . She had a certain physi-
> cal beauty and enormous power . . . I was impressed with her
> presence and her wonderful eyes and beautiful voice – an
> incredibly beautiful voice . . . Her voice had the beauty of a
> singer's voice when she spoke.[1]

One Sunday evening in the winter of 1908, Gertrude Stein was writing at

LEFT The writer and her muse.

ABOVE **'We were so wifely.'**

the large wooden table in her studio. The walls around her were crammed
with peculiar, nonsensical paintings. Wearing her usual writing garb of a
monk-like brown robe, she suddenly stood up, gathered up her papers and
rushed out of the room. She hurried into the kitchen, pausing only to catch
a savoury whiff of her dinner cooking on the stove. Gertrude loved good
food, and especially Alice's American cooking, but even more she loved
her own writing – which Katherine Anne Porter has called 'no doubt the
dearest of Miss Stein's possessions'.[2] Full of excitement, Gertrude told
Alice, 'You'll have to take whatever you're cooking off the stove so it won't
burn or stop cooking it entirely for you must read this.'[3]

It was neither poem, novel, nor play she had just finished but rather
'Ada' – a word-portrait, the first of dozens she would write throughout her
lifetime. She invented this literary form out of the deep affinity she felt with
the Cubist portraits of her artist friends, particularly Picasso. Her friendships

served as a wellspring of her writing; her word portraits, written between 1908 and 1946, were tributes to great friendships with 'ordinary' mortals as well as with such luminaries as Raoul Dufy, Marcel Duchamp, Francis Picabia, Isadora Duncan, Sherwood Anderson, Hemingway, Cézanne, Max Jacob, Juan Gris, Francis Rose, Picasso, Matisse, Man Ray, Edith Sitwell and Madame de Clermont-Tonnerre.

Many of these individuals weren't yet famous when Gertrude wrote about them, and many of the portraits weren't of famous people at all. The question of fame was something Gertrude considered of no importance, either in her friendships or her word-portraits. What mattered in the word-portraits even more than the personality of the subject was the vitality and essence of her writing. Gertrude saved and cherished a comment published in the *Sunday Observer* in 1939 which claimed that Joyce's style in *Finnegans Wake* had 'its precedents in Lewis Carroll and Gertrude Stein, who was the first, so far as I know, in her "Portrait of Mabel Dodge", to strive for a new effect from the contortions of grammar and syntax'.

The story of Alice putting dinner on hold to listen to Gertrude's first 'word portrait' gives us an insight into Alice's importance, already secure a year after they had met, as Gertrude's confidante, intended reader, muse, editor, memory prod for incidents and events, and even virtual 'collaborator' (Alice's creative deciphering of Gertrude's illegible scrawl, and her correction of Gertrude's mistakes or introduction of new textual errors raises interesting questions of authorship).

Had Alice performed her literary services for a great man, it is likely she'd only now be recognized as a subject fit for rescue from obscurity by a literary biographer. But unlike a conventional wife, Alice was allowed to occupy a central role in Gertrude's writing and public life so that she lives on in our collective cultural memory while the wives of Gertrude's male contemporaries, such as Picasso, Hemingway, or Ezra Pound, remain largely unknown to us.

Like the rest of the world, Gertrude Stein believed genius to be male. In her early, unpublished notebooks, Gertrude wrote of the artist Elie Nadelman:

Nadelman, like Pablo and Matisse have a maleness that belongs to genius . . . Pure passion concentrated to the point of vision.

If maleness belongs to genius, where did that leave Gertrude Stein? After such confident pronouncements about Picasso and Matisse she wrote more tentatively, 'moi aussi perhaps'. She interpreted maleness as a social role rather than biological essence, thus not excluding herself from the province of genius. In her relationship with Alice, she assumed the more conventionally male role, or, as Catherine R. Stimpson describes it, 'As they violated the rules of sex, they obeyed those of gender.'[4]

Yet Gertrude's writing was not so obedient, and took on a playful fluidity of gender. In 'Didn't Nelly and Lilly Love You' (1922), the story of Gertrude's and Alice's birthplaces and their meeting in Paris starts out with the polarized 'he' and 'she' and ends up with the more ambiguous 'we' and 'I':

> . . . It was a coincidence that he moved there and that she
> stayed there and that they were and that he became to be there
> and she came not to be fair, she was darker than another, how
> can a sky be pale and how can a lily be so common that it
> makes a hedge. I do know that she never met him there . . .
> We never met . . . Now actually what happened was this. She
> was born in California and he was born in Allegheny,
> Pennsylvania.
> . . . I love her with an a because I say that she is not afraid.
> How can I tell you of the meeting.
> . . . She came late I state that she came late and I said what
> was it that I said I said I am not accustomed to wait.
> We were so wifely.

The resulting ambiguity could be maddening to some, as it was to Natalie Barney, who nonetheless realized that Gertrude's 'obscurity' functioned as 'the better part of discretion'. Gertrude's seemingly opaque style made possible her 'improper' and audacious subject matter, so carefully disguised at times that the lesbian centre of her writing was never

RIGHT 'Slowly and in a way it was not astonishing but slowly
I was knowing that I was a genius . . . It is funny this thing of
being a genius, there is no reason for it, there is no reason that it
should be you . . . ' – *Everybody's Autobiography*

fathomed. Having read steadily through 'Didn't Nelly and Lilly Love You', Natalie Barney claimed she couldn't 'make out whether they did or didn't – the chances being two against one they didn't'.[5]

Behind the ever-shifting pronouns lurk Gertrude's fears and doubts about identity, her own and everyone else's. Her own family identity she considered a nuisance, while recognition by her little dog was reason enough to know 'I am I'. Later she even doubted this: 'I became worried about identity . . . I was not sure but that that only proved the dog was he and not that I was I.' When she told Alice that it is impossible for anyone to know oneself for sure, Alice, not plagued by such worries, answered, 'That depends on who you are.'[6]

Gertrude wrestled with what she called 'the subject of identity' to the end of her life. In her last work, *The Mother of Us All*, she wrote of her heroine, Susan B., 'I have had to be what I have had to be. I could never be one of two I could never be two in one as married couples do and can, I am but one all one, one and all one . . . '

This was only partially true of Susan B. Anthony (who spent much of her life with the married Elizabeth Cady Stanton), but it was particularly untrue of Gertrude. Gertrude may have had to be what she had to be, but she was always one of two, or even more so two in one. Her writing and Alice's 'wifely' role as nurturer and caretaker were inseparable, interdependent entities, much as Gertrude and Alice were. In one of Gertrude's notebooks, she intermingled their names, coming up with 'Gertrice/Altrude'. Another notebook has a draft of an essay in her own hand on one page, with a shopping list in French in Alice's hand on the next. Alice's list also includes, in English, some crucial household tasks, such as taking their poodle Basket to the 'farmacy'. The daily tasks outlined in Alice's unselfconscious writing, and undertaken solely by her, made possible Gertrude's selfconscious writing on the next page, which, appropriately enough, Gertrude titled 'how to write'.

Even more than as caretaker, Alice served as muse and inspiration for Gertrude. Catherine R. Stimpson writes, 'Stein wrote both out of and about her immediate world. Toklas supplied that world with raw material: events, tales, domestic details, tension, sexuality, and flair. Stein returned those materials to her as comparatively finished texts.'[7] Gertrude's notebooks are filled with doodlings and private expressions in the margins around her manuscripts, revealing her subconscious and liminal preoccupations. In the notebook which holds the manuscript to *An American in France*, she made a line drawing of two figures resembling herself and Alice; opposite it she wrote:

> Prime de Merit
> I love she
> She is adorably we.
> When it is she
> She is me.
> She embroiders
> beautifully.

On the last page of this notebook, it was more than Alice's embroidery to which Gertrude paid tribute:

> Tongue like a whip.
> Dear little tongue.
> Red little tongue.
> Long little tongue.
> Let little be mine.
> [in very small, faint letters:]
> yes yes yes

These private musings came to Gertrude in the middle of other literary endeavours – virtually all of which were *also* tributes to Alice – indicating that Alice as lover and muse was never far removed from Gertrude's creative process. Occasionally these marginal scrawls were sufficiently distracting from the manuscript at hand for them to move to central prominence. In her notebook for 'Why I Do Not Live in America' written in July-August 1928 for publication in *transition* magazine, Gertrude drew in pencil a primitive rosebud vase, underneath which she wrote: 'A vase of flowers for my rosebud'. The rosebud theme stayed in her mind, for a few papers later she interrupted her treatise on America to write in big letters across two pages a poem which was to become famous – without, however, its revealing last line:

A
ROSE IS A
ROSE IS A
ROSE IS A
ROSE
She is my rose.

Judy Grahn, in *Really Reading Gertrude Stein*, tells us that these lines are usually misunderstood:

> Large numbers of the reading public . . . believe she meant that
> roses are tedious, tiresomely all alike, when she meant the
> opposite, that every time you see a rose it is a different experi-
> ence because it is located at a different place in the 'sentence'
> of your life; and moreover that a rose 'is,' has existence beyond
> our clichés about it.[8]

Gertrude created new relations between words, even between the same words. She did not call this repetition, but rather insistence, since through the repeating, meanings change.

She used words, not to describe the world around her, but to reproduce that world in language and sound. Consequently, her writing seemed more and more abstract, to the point where many could not follow her. Among them was her friend Natalie Barney although she was willing to give Gertrude the benefit of the doubt. Years later she wrote, referring to Gertrude, 'we must be patient with geniuses, as they are most patient with themselves, and follow themselves even where we cannot follow them.'[9] Bryher was more sure of the benefits of Gertrude's experimentation with language: 'Her attack on language was necessary and helped us all, even if we did not follow her.'[10]

One afternoon Gertrude Stein and Alice Toklas strolled down the rue de Rennes, which was lined with junk shops and antique dealers as it still is today. Gertrude was struck by group of Spanish porcelain figures in a shop window, centring around what she thought was St Ignatius. Despite her love of modern art, Gertrude's tastes ran towards the kitsch. Alice contradicted her about St Ignatius, and claimed it may not even be Spanish, but suggested they buy it nonetheless. Suddenly Gertrude didn't want it any more, especially if it wasn't as she first saw it. 'I've got it inside me now and it would only interfere,' she answered.

Who makes it be what they had as porcelain.

Saint Ignatius and left and right laterally be lined.

All Saints.

To Saints.

Four Saints

And Saints.

Five Saints.

To Saints.

Last Act.

Which is a fact.

The porcelain figures found their way into the opera *Four Saints in Three Acts* which Gertrude Stein wrote in collaboration with composer Virgil Thomson and designer/painter Florine Stettheimer. It premiered, with an all-black cast, to rave reviews in New York in 1934. One way or another, Gertrude used and transformed virtually everything she experienced.

Bryher was in the United States for the premiere of Four Saints in Three Acts. She later wrote, 'The evening remains for me one of the most triumphant nights that I ever spent watching a stage . . . Gertrude's text soared out magnificently and with it her, and our, rebellion against outworn art.'

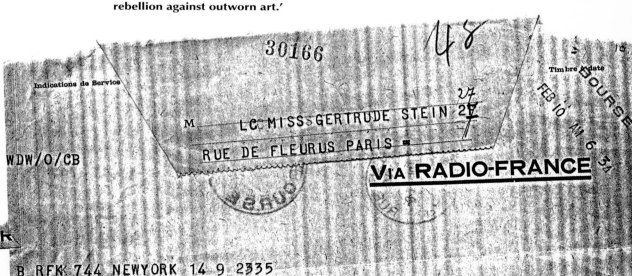

Some of Gertrude's contemporaries found her transformations easier than others; not surprisingly, they were most often writers themselves. What *is* surprising is that the American writer William Carlos Williams, who seems to have generally despised the women in the Left Bank Modernist community, was one of her most vocal supporters. He wrote a 'Manifesto' in defence of Gertrude's work, which he believed to be 'in many ways of all American literary works the most modern'. He appreciated her 'revolutionary' approach to words themselves, detached from their associations in the world:

LEFT Gertrude collaborated with composer Virgil Thomson on *Four Saints*. He claimed that that 'her discovery of the opera as a poetic form' was a result of her friendship with him.

BELOW Virgil Thomson's tribute to Gertrude Stein. He also wrote a composition for Alice B. Tolkas.

Dear Gertrude

It still resembles you

love

Virgil

The feeling is of words themselves, a curious immediate quality quite apart from their meaning . . . It is simply the skeleton, the 'formal' parts of writing, those that make form, that she has to do with, apart from the 'burden' which they carry . . . It is a revolution of some proportions that is contemplated the exact nature of which may be no more than sketched here but whose basis is humanity in a relationship with literature hitherto little contemplated . . . [11]

Ernest Hemingway, a young reporter for the *Toronto Star* in the early 1920s, was another devotee of Gertrude's. He would trade on his association with her ('Gertrude Stein and me are just like brothers') to enhance his own literary reputation. His letters to her in the early days of their friendship reveal a mentor/pupil relationship:

November 9, 1923

I am going to chuck journalism I think. You ruined me as a journalist last winter. Have been no good since . . . I've thought a lot about the things you said about working and am starting that way at the beginning. If you think of anything else I wish you'd write it to me. Am working hard about creating and keep my mind going about it all the time.

Within a year he had given up journalism altogether and was writing fiction. He wrote to Gertrude in August 1924, 'I have finished two long short stories, one of them not much good, and the other very good . . . but isn't writing a hard job though? It used to be easy before I met you . . . '

Kenneth Macpherson, who edited the little magazine *Close-Up* with Bryher, was also among the small circle of those who had an appreciation of Gertrude's work. When writing to solicit some of her work for his magazine, he acknowledged that, 'I consider that you have done more toward the advancement of thought in art than almost any other writer. Apart from which, one derives a real and stimulating pleasure from your writing.' Shortly afterwards, he wrote again: 'I must say that your writing

Works: Ferrestone Press, West Norwood

Telephone: 6111 Central.
Telegrams: "Franalmer, Fleet, London."

Frank Palmer,
Publisher.

**/K.W.

NEW YORK
AND MELBOURNE

14, Red Lion Court,
Fleet Street,
London, E.C.

27th January, 1913.

Dear Madam,

    I have read through a portion of the MS which
you gave me on Friday, but I regret that I cannot make
you any proposition concerning the same. I say I have
only read a portion of it, because I found it perfectly
useless to read further, as I did not understand any of it.
I have to confess to being as stupid and as ignorant as
all the other readers to whom the book has been submitted.

    I herewith return the MS.

      Yours faithfully,

      for Frank Palmer.
      K.W.

Miss Gertrude Stein,
      Knightsbridge Hotel,
         Knightsbridge, S.W.

and your feeling for words always seemed to me brilliant and inspired. I so hope you will send more, and very soon, and also frequently . . . '

Such a request for more work, even by the 1920s, is unique among Gertrude's vast correspondence with editors and publishers who, over the years, came up with increasingly creative epistles in trying to reject, yet again, the manuscripts she relentlessly submitted. In two of the earliest of such letters, the editors are simply stumped:

Duffield and Co., Publishers, August 14, 1906

Dear Miss Stein:

. . . we hardly see our way clear to making you any offer of publication of 'Three Histories'. The book is too unconvention-al, for one thing, and if I may say so, too literary . . . This, at any rate, would be our unfavorable prognosis.

Sidgwick and Jackson, Ltd., London. January 29, 1913

Dear Madam,

We are returning herewith your MS. entitled 'MANY MANY WOMEN', as we are unable to offer to publish it for you.

Under ordinary circumstances we should like to recommend another publisher to whom the work might appeal; but we regret to say that we do not think it probable that you will find any publisher for work of this kind . . .

The rejection letters continued throughout the 1910s and '20s, but without further confessions to being stupid or 'at sea'. By the mid–1920s, it was the ignorant readers rather than publishers who were to blame. In London, Jonathan Cape doubted 'sufficient sales', while in New York, Alfred Knopf 'frankly [didn't] believe that we have progressed enough, even though you think we have, in modern literature to make [publication] possible . . . '

And so the publishing world rejected Gertrude Stein, but only after she herself had dismissed the values of the entire literary establishment. During the rebellious spirit of the twenties, the rejections may have actually enhanced her reputation; Bryher recalled that, 'If a manuscript was sold to an established publisher, its author was regarded as a black sheep and for his own safety moved to the Right Bank.'[12] Although Gertrude did not write for fame or recognition, the decades without it did take their toll. Many years after her death, her friend, the Russian painter Pavel Tchelitchew, reflected on what this isolation must have meant to Gertrude:

> If you realized that she worked insistently, every day, to be
> published the first time by a real publisher, publishing house,
> after she was sixty. But I wonder who will do that, who will
> have the insistence, you understand, the obsession, the surety,
> the purity of insistence to do that. No concessions. She used to
> tell me, 'Don't you ever dare to make concessions. Then one
> walks down, down, down, down.'[13]

Even after she received her long awaited recognition in her sixties, she continued to give young novelists the same advice she gave Tchelitchew as a young man: 'Let nothing else get in but that clear vision which you are alone with. If you have an audience it's not art. If anyone hears you it's no longer pure.'[14]

But it is one matter to have an audience in your head while writing and quite another to have an audience reading your work when finished. Out of unwavering confidence and belief in Gertrude, not to mention sheer frustration, Alice started publishing the works herself in 1930. She established a press, Plain Edition, and extended her job as Gertrude's personal typist and editor into being her publisher as well. They financed the press with their reluctant sale of a Picasso:

> When Gertrude could not find a publisher she sold the beautiful
> Picasso painting of the girl with the fan held in the air, which
> quite broke my heart. And when she told Picasso, it made me
> cry. But it made it possible to publish the Plain Edition.[15]

Had Gertrude Stein not collected Picasso's paintings in the early twentieth century, she would not have been able to finance her own work twenty years later. And were it not for Gertrude Stein, it is possible that Picasso's paintings might still have been unsaleable in 1930, much as her writings were.

When no one would publish Gertrude's *G.M.P*, Alice printed 500 copies herself, with the initials of the title spelled out and rearranged.

MATISSE PICASSO
AND GERTRUDE STEIN

with two shorter stories
by
GERTRUDE STEIN

PLAIN EDITION
27 - *rue de Fleurus* - 27
PARIS

Directors
HERBERT JONATHAN CAPE
G. WREN HOWARD
Telephone
MUSEUM 9011, two lines

JONATHAN CAPE LIMITED
Publishers
THIRTY BEDFORD SQUARE
LONDON W.C.1

Telegrams
CAPAJON, WESTCENT
LONDON
Marconigrams
CAPAJON, LONDON

Nov.2oth.25.

Miss G.Stein,
27 rue de Fleurus,
Paris.

Dear Madam:-

We are sorry to return your MS "G.M.P."
without being able to make you an offer for its
publication. We fear, however, that we could not
make sufficient sales for it to satisfy you or
ourselves.   Tnanking you,

We are,

Yours very truly,
Jonathan Cape Ltd

Twenty five years earlier, Janet Flanner reminds us,

> Gertrude Stein, rich in enthusiasm but modest in means, and
> then about as unknown as a writer as Picasso was as a painter,
> began her famous and eclectic Picasso collection and her
> friendship with him, which over the years have been two of the
> most important personal elements in the Picasso legend. For her
> first Picasso, she and her brother Leo paid Sagot the art mer-
> chant 150 francs and all three quarreled about the picture's
> merits.
>
> It was the early, exquisite, conventional nude, 'A Little Girl
> with Basket of Flowers.' Miss Stein, who was already ripe to
> prefer stranger sights in art, thought the girl looked classically
> flat-footed . . . After Miss Stein became close friends with
> Picasso, she bought directly from him. She says that from 1906
> to 1909 the Stein family controlled the Picasso output, since no
> one else wanted it.[16]

It wasn't difficult to maintain this control: neither had much money and
often Picasso would trade a painting for some eggs or would barter with her
for other essentials. When Gertrude fell in love with Cézanne's portrait of
Mme Cézanne wearing an extraordinary green dress, she bought it outright,
much to the annoyance of her family who thought she must be mad. As
Gertrude came into a bit more money, she began to collect paintings by
Juan Gris and Picabia, also not yet in demand.

Even today, art historians have a hard time crediting Gertrude Stein
for her visionary role in modern art, although the paintings she selected
were eventually to be scooped up by the Museum of Modern Art in New
York. Most like to claim it was Leo Stein rather than his younger sister
Gertrude who first recognized Picasso's genius. Biographers with an
inexplicable anti-Gertrude Stein bias often suggest that her admiration for
Picasso was not reciprocated, despite evidence of their friendship. Picasso
named Gertrude and Alice the godparents of his child (as did Hemingway)
and by 1919 had begun to give Gertrude paintings as ironically, such was
his success that she could no longer afford to buy them. In the mid-
twenties, Picasso surprised Gertrude by making etchings for a forthcoming

limited edition of her 'Birthday-Book' which she had written for his son.

Granted, Gertrude Stein was not alone in 'discovering' Picasso: the poets Max Jacob and Guillaume Apollinaire also championed his work. But Gertrude and Leo, and then Gertrude and Alice, collected his paintings while others only laughed at them. According to Pavel Tchelitchew, Gertrude 'was the one who discovered great French painters. She and her brothers paid their attention to Matisse in old good days when Matisse was unknown . . . Then Gertrude Stein discovered Picasso . . . She was the one who had believed in him. She was the one whom he painted. She was really his great friend and protector.'[17]

Their important and volatile friendship continued for over four decades, from 1905 to Gertrude's death. Fame cost Picasso most of his other early friendships but it never came between the two. Although neither spoke nor read the other's mother tongue, they seemed to understand each other implicitly. Gertrude always felt that there was a 'particularly strong sympathy between Picasso and myself as to modern direction'.[18] During one of the eighty or ninety sittings for Picasso's portrait of her, she mentioned that she heard with her eyes and saw with her ears. Picasso immediately agreed to this method.[19]

Whether it was his ears or his eyes which were responsible, none of their friends thought the portrait resembled Gertrude. 'Never mind,' Picasso replied, 'in the end she will manage to look just like it.' He was upset when she cut her hair – 'and my portrait!' was his response.

Picasso and Gertrude became especially close during these sittings for the now famous portrait. Every Saturday, he and his lover Fernande would walk Gertrude home across Paris and stay for dinner. These weekly meals coincided with the beginning of the informal salons. Gertrude wrote,

> Little by little people began to come to the rue de Fleurus to see
> the Matisses and the Cézannes, Matisse brought people, every-
> body brought somebody, and they came at any time and it
> began to be a nuisance, and it was in this way that Saturday
> evenings began.

Soon, meeting Gertrude Stein would be considered a rite of passage into the Modernist movement. Janet Flanner, who was frequently there, recalled,

Her studio was the most fascinating of any place in Paris,
because everyone did go there, about once a week she'd have
a tea party . . . And she always led the conversation, well
Gertrude led everything . . . When she laughed everyone in the
room laughed. It was more than a signal, it was a contagion of
good spirits. . . . While Gertrude orated and made the pattern
of the conversation, Miss Alice B Toklas was sitting behind a
tea tray. It was as if Gertrude was giving the address and Alice
was supplying all the corrective footnotes.[20]

It has become legendary that the wives were restricted to hearing the
corrective footnotes. Although Janet 'always thought behind the tea tray
was the best place to be', the segregated arrangement particularly annoyed
Sylvia Beach, even though she was not a wife herself: 'I knew the rules and
regulations about wives at Gertrude's. They couldn't be kept from coming,
but Alice had strict orders to keep them out of the way while Gertrude
conversed with the husbands . . . I couldn't see the necessity for the
cruelty.'[21] But then Sylvia was very defensive about wives. In a letter to
Bryher, who had asked if any women would be attending a 'famous
reception' she and Adrienne had organized for French writers, she
answered,

I was amused and interested to see in your letter to Adrienne
that you would have liked to see what women were being invited, if any. All have wives and will be accompanied by same,
and very fine wives they are, mostly. But aside from the two
brilliant exceptions of Colette and Adrienne Monnier, I can't
mention a single woman writer in France to-day [i.e. French]
who is any good. That's the plain truth. . . . There is nothing to
compare with the English and American women writers.
Strange, isn't it.

If Sylvia and Adrienne surrounded themselves with writers, Gertrude
'attracted and influenced not only writers but painters, musicians, and least
but not last, disciples', according to Natalie Barney. 'She, instead of offering
helpless sympathy, often helped them out, by changing an *idée fixe* or

obsession into a fresh start in a new direction.'[22] In this way Gertrude advised and supported many young artists and writers who went on to become famous.

Some, but not all, would be grateful to Gertrude for this help and encouragement for the rest of their lives. Pavel Tchelitchew was one:

I am very pleased to come to talk to you about Gertrude Stein. She was my great friend, in fact I owe her everything that happened to me since the time I met her. Because from a very obscure person I suddenly became a young artist on whom there was put a spot of light . . . I liked Gertrude Stein because there was something in her extremely friendly, extremely good, extremely maternal, and something like somebody one has always known . . . [23]

Gertrude Stein is so often likened to a man among men at these salons, while Alice is the wife surrounded by other wives, that Pavel Tchelitchew's choice of the word 'maternal' leaps out as incongruous and even suspect. But most of the men surrounding Gertrude at her salon were homosexual, and much younger than she. According to Sam Steward, a young homosexual who befriended her in the 1930s,

. . . the ladies generally were entertained by Alice and talked to her about recipes and 'female' things. Whereas Gertrude liked to talk with the men who were present, the husbands, and the young homosexual writers and artists that flocked to Gertrude and were her most devoted fans and admirers.[24]

Pavel Tchelitchew and his partner Allen Tanner were two of the many young men who admired Gertrude. Others included the English painter Francis Rose, American photographer George Platt Lynes, the French writer René Crevel, German photographer Horst P. Horst, composer and writer Paul Bowles, and the choreographer Frederick Ashton (who choreographed Gertrude Stein's 'The Wedding Bouquet' and performed it at Sadlers Wells in London in 1937).

Gertrude did pay attention to women at the salon, but only if they weren't also wives. Samuel Putnam recalled that, contrary to legend, 'it is

ABOVE 'Group of Artists' by Marie Laurencin, 1908. 'In the early
days Marie Laurencin painted a strange picture, portraits of
Guillaume [Apollinaire], Picasso, Fernande and herself. Fernande
told Gertrude Stein about it. Gertrude Stein bought it and Marie
Laurencin was so pleased. It was the first picture of hers any one
had ever bought.' – from *The Autobiography of Alice B. Toklas*

RIGHT Painter Marie Laurencin was a regular at Gertrude and
Alice's salon.

also my impression that there were more women than men among Stein's devotees. What moral there is to this, I am sure I do not know; but if one is to judge from the reports brought back, she appeared to get on better with the women . . . '[25] Edith Sitwell was always flattered that Gertrude was respectful toward her at the salons as she had heard that women were treated as Alice's visitors. Marie Laurencin, although the 'mistress' of poet Guillaume Apollinaire before the First World War, was respected by Gertrude as an extraordinary artist in her own right. She attended the salon regularly, Gertrude bought some of her paintings, and, despite an interlude of coolness following the publication of Gertrude's *Autobiography of Alice B. Toklas*, the two women remained friends until Gertrude's death.

Like Janet Flanner, Bryher preferred Alice's company at the salons, and would slip away from Gertrude to join Alice's conversation. Although on occasion Gertrude requested of Bryher that they talk over certain literary ideas, Bryher felt she could not offer Gertrude sufficient intellectual stimulus. And, furthermore, she only admired Gertrude whereas she loved Alice.

Picasso relished in the international flavour and sexual ambiguity of the gatherings. According to his biographer John Richardson, Picasso 'was used to seeing Gertrude in the company of other emancipated women'.[26] The salon conversations were scintillating, in part because Gertrude was always at the centre of them, and in part because the guests did not get progressively drunk and mentally impaired. One of the salon regulars recalled that this was in marked 'difference with my other American friends who used to go in cafés, drinking cocktails and discussing and discussing till they didn't know what they were talking about [while Gertrude] was having teas . . . '[27] Gertrude herself did not find this café life interesting. She wrote, 'Drinkers think each other are amusing but that is only because they are both drunk. It is funny the two things most men are proudest of is the thing that any man can do and doing does in the same way, that is being drunk and being the father of their son.'

Four years after Gertrude sat for Picasso's famous portrait, she began writing her own portrait of Picasso. After unsuccessfully submitting it to several journals, together with her portrait of Matisse, Gertrude Stein found a publisher in the New York photographer and art collector Alfred Stieglitz.

Stieglitz accepted the portraits for his magazine *Camera Work* in 1913, and printed them alongside reproductions of paintings by Picasso and Matisse.

The following year, the *New York Times*, to Gertrude's delight, dubbed her a 'Cubist of Letters'. But the publisher Alfred A. Knopf, then at Doubleday, responded thus to the *Camera Work* experiment:

Dear Mr Stieglitz —

Thank you for the Stein issue. I can see many possible causes
for the lady's spasms but none for their publication . . . — tho I
know nothing of Matisse and Picasso but the pictures in
Camera Work: perhaps they could only be explained thru such
spasms as G.S had gone thru. I don't object to her doing what
she did but I do object to having to see it in print! at any rate
when unadorned by any apologies or explanations on her part.

Knopf must have come to regret this letter, even if he never came to see any value whatsoever in 'This one always had something coming out of this one. This one was working. This one always had been working. This one was always having something that was coming out of this one.'

Gertrude did not respond to Knopf; indeed, she rarely answered her detractors, however strange their criticisms seemed to her. She believed, 'Being intelligible is not what it seems. Everybody has their own English . . . You will see, they will understand it. If you enjoyed it, then you understand it.'[28]

Stieglitz, who ran a gallery in New York, was along with critic Henry McBride among the first in the United States to acknowledge the Modernist movement in art. Henry McBride, considered the 'dean of American art critics', came to appreciate the work of Picasso, Matisse, Braque, and Léger through his association with Gertrude Stein, whom he often went to visit in Paris.

The letters between Gertrude Stein and Henry McBride constitute an informal history of modern art and artists. Early on, Gertrude promised to 'let you know if anything new creeps up in Paris in the art way . . . ' During the First World War Gertrude gave McBride an informal report on the activities of all the artists they admired. After chastising him for his briefly pro-German stance, she asked, 'Perhaps you would like to know about the painters.' She listed their itineraries:

> Braque is at the front in the trenches. Derain is an Incidist but
> so far has been laid up with a leg. Apollinaire is in training to
> be a conductor of cannon and is incidentally learning to ride
> and getting fat . . . Picabia is driving an automobile. Delaunay
> is so to speak not a patriot. All the Americans are red cross and
> are working hard at it in a most engaging uniform. I guess that's
> all . . .

Gertrude herself was among those in an engaging Red Cross uniform, as was Alice, Sylvia Beach and many other American women. Gertrude and Alice drove around the countryside in their Ford truck, which they named Auntie, dispensing supplies to French war hospitals and later doubling as an ambulance service. Alice recalled that

> There were no official agencies . . . You were Americans help-
> ing the French, so you appealed to Americans. Well, I appealed
> to my father. He was very good. His Club sent an ambulance
> when we wanted it and sent an x-ray performance . . . Our
> supplies all came from private people . . . comforts and ban-
> dages, and surgical instruments and things of that kind.[29]

Gertrude and Alice distributed these supplies and the only arguments ever witnessed between them were sparked by Gertrude's efforts to park the truck.

In a letter of November 1915, Gertrude wrote, 'There is no use talking about the war it is not fit to talk about.' But she did talk – and write – about the war, during it and for years afterwards. Among her pieces were 'Accents in Alsace' and 'The Deserter', both rejected by *Harper's*, *Everybody's Magazine*, and other publications. Nonetheless, meeting all sorts of people through her war work made her more convinced that there were readers for her work, if only she could reach them. 'Accents in Alsace' is a political satire, but like everything else Gertrude wrote, it is really about Alice: 'In me meeney miney mo. You are my love and I tell you so.'

ABOVE **After World War One, Alice found that Paris 'like us was sadder than when we left it', although Gertrude was proud to receive this certificate.**

Gertrude was never savvy about politics and often made stupid, even reactionary comments for which she is ridiculed to this day. But she lived through and wrote intimately about the horrors of war; indeed, it became one of her strongest themes. When the German army entered Paris during World War II, Gertrude and Alice escaped to their summer home in the South, and it is said that their entire village conspired to keep the presence of the two American Jews there a secret.

Wars I Have Seen documents her observations through the two world wars. In it she addresses large political questions, such as why statesmen declare war, not as a political theorist would but with the simplicity and directness of a child:

> they are still believing what they are supposed to believe
> nobody else believes it, not even all their families believe it but
> believe it or not, they still do believe it . . . And so naturally
> they believing what they are supposed to believe make it possi-
> ble for the country to think they can win a war . . .

When she drops her childlike observations in favour of political analysis — for example she 'always thought [Pétain] was right to make the armistice [with Germany]' — she clearly overreaches her grasp. But she is in full command when she moves from broad, rambling storytelling to sudden, unnerving personal detail:

> And now in June 1943, it is trying, there are so many sad things
> happening, so many in prison, so many going away, our den-
> tist's son and he was only eighteen and he should have been
> taking his entrance university examinations and he with others
> in a camion took shoes and clothes and weapons to give to the
> young men who had taken themselves to the mountains, to
> avoid being sent away, and what has happened to him and to
> them.

Novelist Richard Wright defended Gertrude's writing ever since his 'ears

LEFT During the Occupation, Gertrude and Alice grew most of their food in their garden. Villagers conspired to keep their presence in the French countryside a secret from the Germans.

were opened' by *Three Lives* 'for the first time to the magic of the spoken word. I began to hear the speech of my grandmother, who spoke a deep, pure Negro dialect . . . ' Richard Wright remained a loyal reader of what he called 'Steinian prose' and reviewed *Wars I Have Seen*: 'I know of no current war book that conveys a more awful sense of the power of war to kill the soul, of the fear, the rumor, the panic, and the uncertainty of war.'[30]

At the war's end, Gertrude Stein turned her home into a beckoning harbour for American soldiers adrift in a sea of fear, panic and uncertainty. If she was too old to provide the material support she had given to French soldiers during the First World War, her emotional support for American soldiers during the Second may have been equally significant. Learning of her death the following year, one soldier wrote to Alice,

Dear Miss Toklas:

You may remember me as the sergeant named Billy who used to come to your house last summer to talk . . .

It seems that everyone in this country has had their say about Miss Stein; and it must be gratifying . . . – to see how much she meant emotionally as well as intellectually to her country, and to see how quickly she has become a genuine American legend.

I have no special articulateness or perception and . . . merely wanted to tell you how much you both did for so many of us who were just emerging from bitter experiences. We thought of your home as an outpost of all we could take pride in; you both made us feel a special excitement and obligation in just being Americans; and you both gave us something to hold us against the flood of disillusion that follows any victory . . . Sincerely William C. Haygood [Chicago]

Gertrude had become particularly patriotic during the Second World War, although she had always identified strongly with being an American,

RIGHT **An American in France.**

America is my country and Paris
is my home town and it is as it has
come to be.

despite almost half a century in France. She connected her role as literary innovator and cultural pioneer to being a Californian with an intrinsic affinity for the new. She has been called 'the voice of American common sense, American pragmatism, America living in the present'.[31]

Despite her sweeping and often offensive generalizations about various national and racial characteristics, her writings on America and Americans are usually poignant and apt. Being an American in France was the experience which both made it possible for her to write and was what she often wrote about.

Gertrude Stein and Alice B. Toklas were fiercely American, but in thirty years, they returned to their native shores just once, in 1934, for the lecture tour Gertrude made following the overnight success of *The Autobiography of Alice B. Toklas*. The publication of the immensely readable, entertaining 'autobiography' was the turning point in Gertrude's life: at 58 she received her first book contract and the recognition as a writer for which she had worked for so long. The book was reprinted for the Book-of-the-Month Club, and many predicted a Pulitzer prize.

America treated Gertrude Stein's tour as the return of its prodigal daughter. Her ship was met by newsreel cameramen and journalists of every hue. *The Saturday Review of Literature* ran a banner headline: 'Exile's Return'; the *New York Post* reported, rather unpleasantly: 'That grand old expatriate . . . returned to these shores today after thirty-one cloistered years in Paris. She brought with her Alice B. Toklas, her queer, birdlike shadow . . . . her girl Friday talked about Miss Stein, when she talked at all.'

The media are fascinated by, but just can't figure out, the relationship between Gertrude and Alice.

Alice Toklas Hides in Shadows of Stein

Mouselike Companion Does Not Show Exotic Air Author Claims for Her.

By EVELYN SEELEY.

EVERYBODY knows Gertrude Stein and her brilliant wit and esoteric writings. Everyone has argued over her these many years. But almost nobody knows Alice B. Tok her indispensable and willing shadow, and some eve

SomeoneCalled Stein Sails With Alice B. Toklas

Bon Voyage Party Presents New Slant on Question of Who's No. 1 of That Pair

Secretary Rules Roost

Employer Has a Hard

'Coming back to the United States after 31 years everything seizes
my interest and seizes it hard. The buildings in the air and the people in the street, they're all exciting.' – Gertrude Stein, interviewed
at Columbia University on NBC radio, 12 November 1934.

Other newspapers debated whether Alice Toklas actually existed, or
whether it was she who really called the shots in their relationship.

Of course, the press made plenty of jokes about Gertrude's writing,
and most journalists could not resist a few paragraphs in parody of her
repetitive style. *The Detroit News* announced that 'A New York literary
analyst professes to understand the poems of Gertrude Stein. It complicates
the matter considerably, as we must now try to understand the analyst.'
Less humorously, the *Journal of the American Medical Association* ran an
article by B.F. Skinner, which analyzed Gertrude's writing for indications of
mental disorder.

OVERLEAF 'Quite unexpectedly suddenly my name has become very
well known in America and publishers over there are eager . . . '

Despite such insults, Gertrude thoroughly enjoyed her trip around America, most of which she had never seen before. She sent a card to Janet Flanner, postmarked February 1935, 'My dear Janet, Yes we are having a good time a really good time and it is very exciting and very natural and we like it a lot, and do not pine [?] at all for Paris, certainly I liked having your letter lots of love Gtde.'

Gertrude also loved the sudden fame and fortune. She bought a new car and a Hermes coat for her dog Basket.

And suddenly she was receiving unsolicited letters from publishers; this one came from Scribner's: 'Dear Miss Stein . . . I am interested to hear that you are working on a novel; you must naturally realize that we should always be interested in anything you do.'

Ironically, it was not her painstakingly developed literary innovations which brought Gertrude before the reading public. The book which catapulted her to fame was not even written in her own enigmatic repetitive style, but rather adopted the ordinary, direct speaking voice of Alice B. Toklas. Alice, of course, denied that she played any role other than typist: 'Oh no. What could I contribute?'[32] Yet Virgil Thomson, who knew them both well, claims that:

> This book is in every way except actual authorship Alice
> Toklas's book; it reflects her mind, her language, her private
> view of Gertrude, also her unique narrative powers. Every story
> in it is told as Alice herself had always told it.[33]

If this is true, then privately Gertrude's success must have been bittersweet. Gertrude, obsessed with the question of her own identity, became famous for writing in someone else's voice. As Katherine Anne Porter put it: 'She had never learned who she was, and yet suddenly she had become somebody else.'[34]

She was also somebody else because fame changed her. It had to. As she wrote in *Everybody's Autobiography*,

RIGHT **Janet Flanner seems to have been as overwhelmed by Gertrude and Alice's American tour as they themselves were.**

December Tenth

dear Gertrude, I'm glad I refused to do a Profile of you for
The NewYorker —my reason was excellent; I said since I couldn't
write about you better than you'd written about yourself in
Autobiography, I felt it was improper to write at all – for
if I'd written it and it had been added to everything else
they've written and pictured about and around you, the name
of the magazine would have to be changed from/NewYorker
to/Gertruder. Or maybe/Gertrudest. Are you and Miss Toklas
have a good or a bad time, or a mixture, or nothing of either
enough to be sure until later? Why don't you both run for
President while you're out there, you could get the job easy.
Friends in New York sent me the boat interviews, one of which
seemed to me excellent, intelligent. You seem to me to make
such sense in what you say I can't see how anybody find it
cryptic or anger-making; maybe I'm 42 and know that,
though; maybe when I was 32 I didn't know what you meant
either. This is to thank you for sending me the Autobiography
in French and to wish you and Miss T a Merry Christmas and
to tell you I think you're both superb. an ordeal by
soda-pop which burns and is licquid but is neither fire nor
water; you've both come through immortally.

              Love and greetings,

                              Janet F

... suddenly it was all different, what I did had a value that made people ready to pay, up to that time everything had a value because nobody was ready to pay. It is funny about money. And it is funny about identity. You are you because your little dog knows you, but when your public knows you and does not want to pay for you and when your public knows you and does want to pay for you, you are not the same you.

It was not whether she wrote as Gertrude or as Alice, or even how she wrote at all; it was the fascinating friendships she wrote about which placed the book at the top of the bestseller lists. *The Autobiography of Alice B. Toklas* chronicles these famous friendships – and was to be responsible for ending many of them.

While Gertrude and Alice were touring their homeland, trouble was brewing in their home town. *The Autobiography* produced a storm of protest, mostly by those depicted in its pages. The anger was so great that *transition magazine*, edited by Eugene Jolas, published a supplementary issue titled 'Testimony against Gertrude Stein' solely to allow the 'injured parties' to 'correct what was said about them'.

Lurking behind some of these 'corrections' seem to be deeper, private angers, and perhaps resentment over her new-found fame. For example, Matisse wrote, 'With regard to the purchase of the Cézanne [which Gertrude had incorrectly described]: there was no tent in the picture, it was a Cézanne with three women bathers and several trees . . . ' He charged Gertrude with deliberately writing this falsehood about the painting.

Braque has a more legitimate claim. He was understandably upset because Gertrude wrote that Picasso had invented Cubism, whereas Braque felt he and Picasso were engaged in a joint 'search for the anonymous personality . . . ' Clearly Gertrude's version made Braque's personality too anonymous for his liking.

RIGHT **After the publication of *The Autobiography of Alice B. Toklas*, some of Gertrude Stein's former friends set out to establish that she was not 'in any way concerned with the shaping of the epoch she attempts to describe' and that 'she had no understanding of what really was happening around her'.**

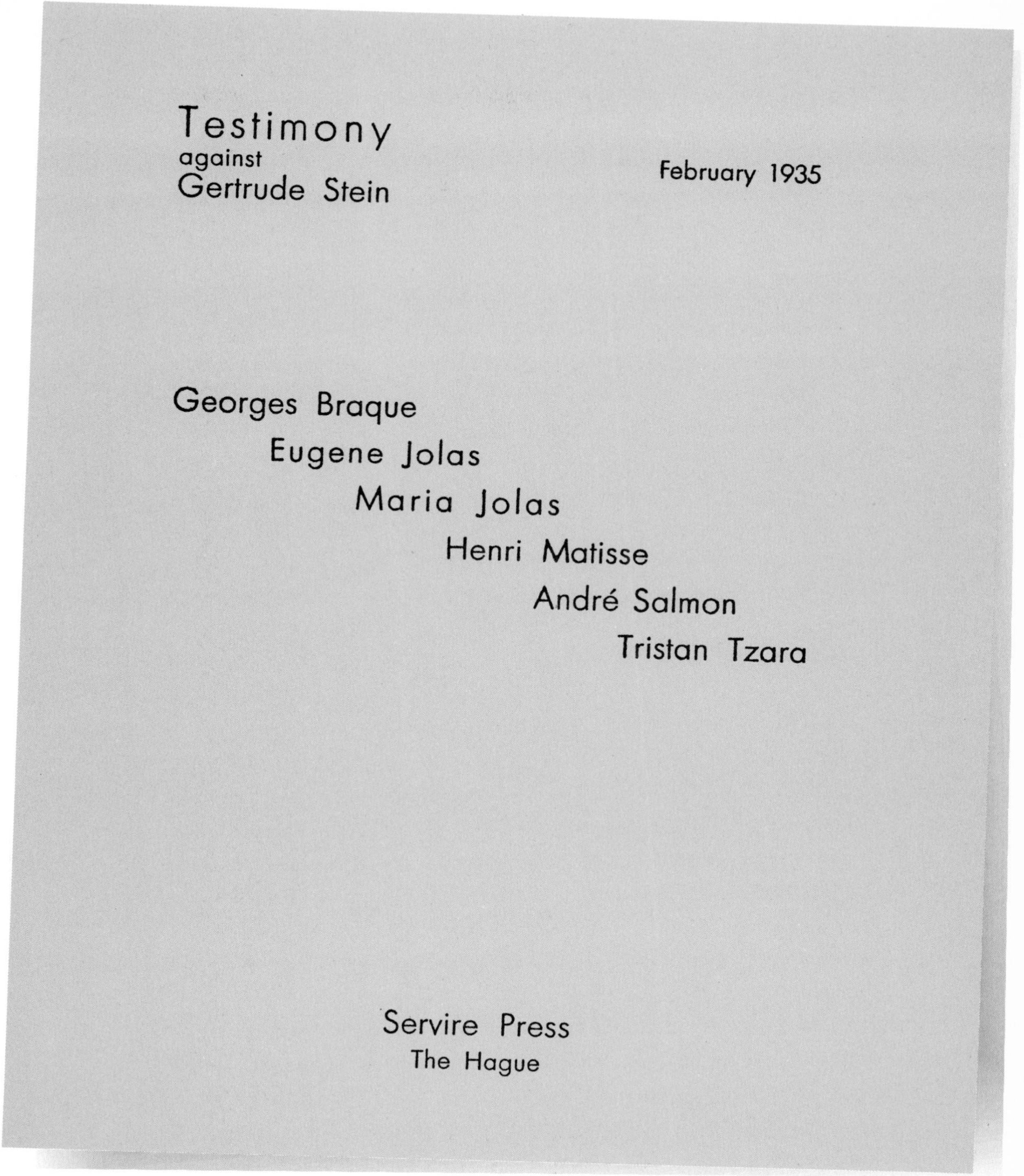

Testimony
against
Gertrude Stein

February 1935

Georges Braque

Eugene Jolas

Maria Jolas

Henri Matisse

André Salmon

Tristan Tzara

Servire Press

The Hague

The famous falling out between Hemingway and Gertrude Stein also involved a bruised male ego. In *The Autobiography*, Gertrude claimed that Hemingway was a great pupil of hers: 'He copied the manuscript of *The Making of Americans* and corrected the proof . . . In correcting these proofs Hemingway learned a great deal and he admired all that he learned.'

Hemingway, after Gertrude's death, tried to set the record straight in his 'Letter of Exceptional Literary Importance'. He couldn't totally refute that she had been his mentor, but suggested that theirs was a more reciprocal relationship:

> I always loved her very much . . . She had, or Alice had, a sort
> of necessity to break off friendships and she only gave real loy-
> alty to people who were inferior to her. She had to attack me
> because she learned to write dialogue from me just as I learned
> the wonderful rhythms in prose from her . . .

Janet Flanner never found traces of Hemingway's style in Gertrude Stein's dialogue, but noticed that 'her rhythms emerged in the style of Ernest Hemingway . . . He and Sherwood Anderson were the two people who were most affected, most influenced by, the quietude of her speech and felt that in the rhythm of the repetitions in her writing they arrived at their own styles.'[35]

Writing is a solitary venture. Hemingway, Sherwood Anderson, Scott Fitzgerald and many others learned from Gertrude Stein but, as Hemingway rightly points out, 'Then you have to do it alone and by yourself and keep on learning; only you are alone . . . ' Nonetheless, it is not difficult to imagine how Gertrude must have felt as she watched her 'proteges' go on to greater critical and popular acclaim while she remained ridiculed and unpublished for so long. They must have loved her constant dismissals of their success: ' . . . if the outside [world] puts a value on you then all your inside gets to be outside. I used to tell all the men who were being successful young how bad this was for them . . . '[36]

Publicly Gertrude always denied harbouring hard feelings. When a publisher told her, 'We want the comprehensible thing, the thing the public can understand,' she answered with, 'My work would have been no use to anyone if the public had understood me early and first.'[37] She put up a tough front:

> I found the money to publish [*Three Lives*, her first book]
> myself. No publisher would look at it. But that did not discour-
> age me; I was not the first author who paid his own admission.
> . . . Lack of popular success . . . is the last of my worries. I am
> working for what will endure, not for a public. Once you have
> a public you are never free. . . . The early setbacks aid the
> eventual greatness. Quick success is killing.[38]

But it was the lack of success, year after year, which was killing. Throughout her many unpublished decades the negative responses did bother Gertrude enormously. Privately she wrote in 1913, 'it's getting anything at all printed thats my worry'. Three years later she wrote, 'Get kind of sad and restless every now and then because I can't be published. Would love to be published.' Often when sending her manuscripts to editors, she'd anticipate the rejection and ask them to read the submissions several times before deciding. She confided to a friend, 'I do so love to be printed. Even the war has not made me less fond of that.'

Over thirty years later, on her death bed, Gertrude made her last request: that all her many unpublished manuscripts see their way into print. Alice was to outlive her by over twenty years, until that enormous task was accomplished and she could join Gertrude in Père Lachaise cemetery in Paris.

In those lonely decades, Alice wrote several books of her own, including her memoirs, *What is Remembered*. It might well have been titled *What is Forgotten* for, according to Alice, 'I could have begun with the beginning and given you everything connected with every day along the line. Until Gertrude died. I lost my memory then, because I think I was upset and my head, when it came back, just wasn't clear.'[39] If Gertrude is best known for what she wrote with Alice's 'unique narrative powers' and in Alice's persona, Alice ends her own life story with Gertrude's death and in Gertrude's famous last words: 'What is the answer? I was silent. In that case, she said, what is the question?'

CHAPTER 3

AMAZONES ET SIRÈNES

'As an Amazon, Miss Barney was not belligerent.
On the contrary, she was charming, and all dressed in
white with her blond coloring, most attractive.
Many of her sex found her fatally so . . . '
—**Sylvia Beach, *Shakespeare and Company***

By 1972, the year she died in Paris at the age of 95, Natalie Clifford Barney had long been a legendary figure in France. She had written countless poems and 13 books, been immortalized by other writers in at least half-a-dozen works of fiction and in numerous memoirs, and had hosted an international salon for many of the leading writers, artists, and intellectuals of this century. But none of this was the reason for her legendary status.

Rather, she was what her biographer George Wickes has aptly called 'unquestionably the leading lesbian of her time'.[1] She devoted her life to praising the joys of, and indeed promoting an ethos of, lesbianism.

Natalie surrounded herself with a coterie of beautiful women, virtually all of whom were former, present or future lovers. While in her twenties, she and the poet Renée Vivien travelled to Lesbos to set up a lesbian school for poetry and love (the scheme was curtailed when Renée's other lover, a wealthy Dutch baroness, hauled her back to France). The qualities of

ABOVE **'Our understanding natures coincided, completing one
another' – Natalie Barney left, on her relationship with
Romaine Brooks.**

Sappho that Natalie admired – a love of beauty and sensuality, the freedom
to love without jealousy or moral judgment – were signposts by which she
set out to live her own life. Although her plans for Lesbos were stymied,
Natalie gathered a similar community of women around her in Paris, and
held pagan rituals in her garden.

Usually these theatrical events were attended only by women, but
one afternoon when Colette performed, André Germain was on hand to
record it for posterity. In his book about Proust, Germain devoted a chapter
to the literary women of the era which he titled 'Amazones et Sirènes' (In
Remembrance of Things Past, Proust had titled *his* chapter on these women

'Sodom and Gomorrah'). Germain recalled:

> Several years later I was to see Colette again, naked this time
> and imitating a faun. It was in a garden which belonged to a
> friend whose every wish I then obeyed, Nathalie [sic] Clifford
> Barney . . . Nathalie had summoned me for a ceremony in
> honor of a poetess whom I had not known but pursued beyond
> the grave, Renée Vivien. The poems murmured and at the end
> sobbed by that unfortunate young woman [Renée] struck me
> and charmed me, despite their pagan audacity . . . [2]

In a recent study of the work of both Renée Vivien and Natalie
Barney, Karla Jay has attempted to restore Natalie Barney's reputation as a
poet which has been eclipsed by the notoriety she has achieved as a
seductress of women. Alas, Jay found in the end that her literary
achievements amounted to many but not
much. Her calling as a poet could never
match her calling as a lover, despite her
pursuit of a lesbian aesthetic in which poetry
and love were inseparable. There are
moments of brilliance in her writings, yet
her far greater literary contribution rested in
identifying and promoting the creative
genius of others. Her wide capacity for love
nourished and supported a century of
female creativity, not only her own but
that of her innumerable lovers and
intimate friends. Her art was that of love,
and she was a prolific artist, much to the
chagrin of her jealous lifelong partner,
the painter Romaine Brooks.

Natalie and Romaine were both
enormously wealthy American
expatriates in Paris, but here their
similarities ended. Romaine wrote to
Natalie after half a century together:

ABOVE **Natalie held pagan rituals and 'theatricals' for women in her garden. Participants included Colette, Sarah Bernhardt and Eva Palmer.**

LEFT **Poet Renée Vivien with Natalie – they fantasized reviving the golden age of Sappho.**

> [I'm] thinking about our long friendship
> which on my part is as great as ever; of
> our natures that differ fundamentally:
> you needing people as fuel for producing
> the sparks that animate your rare gift of
> rapid words and I needing solitude for
> creating . . . my world of art . . .

But Natalie believed that their fundamentally different natures complemented each other and enabled their relationship to endure where others burnt themselves out. From Renée Vivien to Djuna Barnes to Dolly Wilde (Natalie's lover of ten years), Natalie Barney was repeatedly drawn to extraordinarily gifted women who were bent on self-destruction. Of Djuna Barnes, Natalie wrote: 'A rough diamond sort of genius who cut everything to pieces and then blamed the cuts.' In her memoirs, she reflected on why her relationship with Romaine broke from this pattern, and how the relationship kept Romaine from joining the ranks of the 'self-destroyers':

> They were a wild, bacchanalian lot . . . and although I sympa-
> thized with them, I could not suffer their fate. Had I not ridden
> wild horses myself and been carried away, but they had not
> thrown me nor had I risen to such heights, perhaps because I
> had neither their gifts nor their guts. But Romaine who had
> both, had hewn her way through equally adverse circumstances
> and soberly braved hardships surpassing theirs and come out
> on top with her all-dominating art . . . putting her soul into
> everything she believed in or loved or undertook. The intensity
> with which . . . would make such a pursuit unbearable had not
> our understanding natures coincided, completing one another.

ABOVE **Romaine painted Natalie as 'L'Amazone' in 1920.**

LEFT **Romaine's calm, powerful self-portrait, painted in 1923
when she was 49.**

THE ALLURE OF PARIS

Natalie and Romaine were the first among the community of American expatriate women to arrive in Paris; both came intermittently in the 1890s and Natalie returned to settle in Paris in 1902. 'This wild girl from Cincinnati' as Natalie was dubbed, was not only a very rich heiress, but also incredibly appealing. On a visit to France with her family in 1899, she had, at 22, seduced one of the most sensuous and famous Parisian courtesans of *la belle époque*, Liane de Pougy. In *Idylle saphique*, a novel which rocked the social world of upper-class Paris on its publication in

BELOW 'This wild girl from Cincinnati' took Paris by storm.

1901, Liane de Pougy had written an explicit, thinly-veiled account of this affair – the first of many works of fiction inspired by Natalie (two years later she made an appearance in one of Colette's *Claudine* books). Natalie's father hauled her back to Washington where her family was then living and, futilely, selected an eligible fiancé from her many male suitors.

Natalie, too, celebrated the notorious love affair in *Lettres à une connue*, which her publisher decided was too scandalous to print, and in *Quelques Portraits – Sonnets de Femmes*, 34 love poems to women. Illustrated by her mother – who had not known exactly how the illustrations would be used – the slender volume created a scandal in Washington. Newspaper headlines read 'Sappho in Washington' – but it was her being 'in Washington' and not being a 'Sappho' which disturbed Natalie. She was already beyond needing society's approval:

> I considered myself without shame: albinos aren't reproached
> for having pink eyes and whitish hair, why should they hold it
> against me for being a lesbian? It's a question of nature: my
> queerness isn't a vice, isn't 'deliberate', and harms no one.
> What do I care, afterall, if they vilify or judge me according to
> their prejudices?

Fortunately her mother was sympathetic to Natalie's frustrations. A painter who had studied with Whistler in Paris, Alice Pike Barney took her daughter away from the dull, stifling, upper-class Washington society that Natalie so disliked and returned to the Paris they both loved. To Natalie, 'Paris has always seemed . . . the only city where you can live and express yourself as you please.'[3]

Of all the American expatriate women in Paris, Natalie seems to have brought the lightest cultural baggage, and certainly none of the American Protestant morality, with her to France. She was equally at home in English and French, both of which she spoke in an antiquated nineteenth-century style. She privately published her volumes of lesbian love poems in classic French romantic style, but moved rather carelessly between one literary form and another in her poetry, epigrams, novels, plays, memoirs and autobiographical texts. She prioritized living over writing, saying that, 'My life is my work, my writings are but the result.'[4]

NATALIE CLIFFORD BARNEY

PENSÉES
D'UNE
AMAZONE

Les sexes adverses, la guerre et le féminisme.
Choses de l'Amour.
Pages prises au roman que je n'écrirai pas.
Autres éparpillements.

PARIS
ÉMILE-PAUL FRÈRES, ÉDITEURS
190, RUE DU FAUBOURG-SAINT-HONORÉ, 100
PLACE BEAUVAU
—
1921

Natalie Barney's epigrams, or pensées, as she called them, can be seen as capsules of feminist logic, turning around masculine assumptions with feminine wit in much the way Oscar Wilde turned around heterosexual assumptions with homosexual wit. In her *Pensées d'une amazone* she wrote about the masculinity of war and its futility; the ridiculousness of men and the oppression of women:

If love existed among men, they would have already found the means of proving it.

Man, that incompletely weaned creature . . .

If maternity worked backwards, beginning with the pains of childbirth, there would still be mothers, but they would be willing heroines, not victims of a mistake or wretched martyrs of one of nature's tricks.

The Frenchman is, in fact, absentminded; he has submitted to the war; he has equally submitted to victory, and will not even condescend to profit from it.

ROMAINE BROOKS: WORKING OUT LIFE THROUGH ART

For Romaine Brooks, in direct contrast to Natalie Barney, her work was her life. In her work she exorcised the demons of her childhood – an insane brother and a cruel, unloving mother – a time so awful that those who read her unpublished memoirs refused to believe them. Romaine arrived in Paris by way of Rome, Capri, London and St Ives, after a brief marriage to a

RIGHT 'Mother Nature' by Romaine Brooks, 1930. When Natalie convinced Romaine to exhibit her drawings in Paris in 1931, a reviewer wrote that 'One must think them dictated to the author by who knows what demon. . . . '

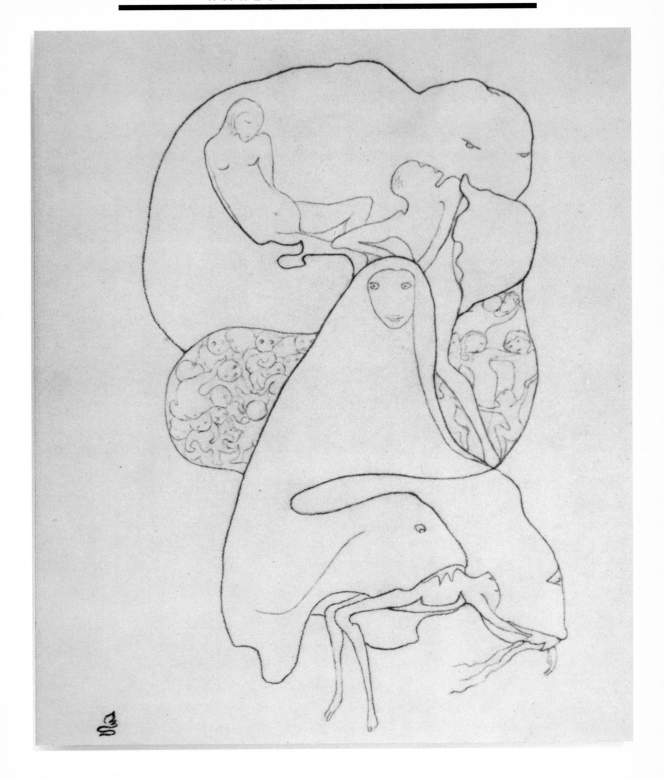

homosexual man, an unwanted child given up for adoption, a serious bout of pneumonia, and several unsatisfactory love affairs. After this long and difficult journey, Romaine was homeless and restless. She found serenity only in her work. For fifteen years she painted in obscurity, isolation, and poverty (her great wealth came suddenly, upon her mother's death). As the first and only woman student in the Art Academy in Rome, she had suffered humiliating harassment and ridicule as well as near-starvation.

Not at all gregarious by nature, Romaine's acquaintances were mainly people she met through Natalie, and most of these she didn't like. But she befriended one shy artist who was to become a close friend: the Irish-born designer and architect, Eileen Gray. Eileen had moved to Paris in 1902, to be in the company of independent, creative women. Her participation in the 1913 *Salon des Artistes Décorateurs* brought her sparse, Modernist designs to the attention of art collector Jacques Doucet, her first patron, and earned her critical acclaim.

Similarly, Romaine's first exhibition, in Galeries Durand-Ruel in 1910, was a big success – but, sadly, it could also be seen as the peak of her career. Although influenced to some extent by the Symbolists, Romaine's work pays no notice of the far more significant art movement of the nineteenth century, Impressionism. Unlike Eileen Gray, who was influenced by the geometry of Cubism and of the Dutch De Stijl group, Romaine did not care for artistic trends and painted as though the twentieth century and its many artistic shake-ups were not occurring around her. As time went on, she was increasingly discredited for being outmoded and out of touch – as though she were a journalist who didn't bother to read the newspaper, rather than a painter guided by her own mind's eye.

THE SALON, OUT OF TIME

Natalie Barney also seemed to exist outside of time. She is now viewed as embodying the contradictions of the *belle époque*, a period caught in the tension of looking forward to the new century while clinging reluctantly to the old. But her contemporary Marguerite Yourcenar disagreed, saying to her when Natalie was already in her nineties: 'Really, the eighteenth century is your time, much more than la Belle Époque. How young you are, Natalie, for a contemporary of Madame du Deffand and Rivarol.'[5] Although snubbed by the more staid members of upper-class French society because of her sexual notoriety, in fashion, politics and resistance to anything new, Natalie was as old-fashioned and conservative as they.

She flouted social convention in certain circles, but she craved social acceptance in others. When her young lover Renée Vivien died of anorexia, alcoholism and a broken heart, Natalie sent her poems about Renée to the leading man of letters in France. Remy de Gaurmont was at once the editor of the influential *Mercure de France*, a prolific poet, essayist and novelist, literary critic of the Symbolist movement and mentor to, among others, T. S. Eliot and Ezra Pound. Despite a disfiguring disease which kept him in seclusion, he befriended Natalie and published elegant essays in *Mercure de France* addressed to a mysterious Amazon. The consequence of his unrequited love for Natalie Barney in his dying years was that she achieved an artistic and social prominence she could never have gained otherwise, and which she desperately needed to fulfil her social ambitions. In 1909, she established a salon in her Left Bank house that would continue for 60 years and encompass many French, American and English artists, writers and celebrities including André Gide, Jean Cocteau, Paul Valéry, Colette, Ezra Pound, Gertrude Stein, Edith Sitwell, Ford Maddox Ford, Sherwood Anderson, Marie Laurencin, Thornton Wilder, Janet Flanner, Gabriele D'Annunzio, Edna St Vincent Millay, Isadora Duncan, Rainer Maria Rilke and Djuna Barnes.

According to Solita Solano, journalist and friend of Janet Flanner, 'Natalie did not collect modern art; she collected people, and you could be sure of being dazzled any Friday (her day) you dropped in for tea.'[6] On one particularly dazzling Friday Greta Garbo showed up, brought by her lover Mercedes D'Acosta. Garbo created quite a stir, according to Truman Capote, as Natalie and her friends 'thought of Garbo as the *ne plus ultra* of what they were all about.'[7]

For 45 of those 60 years, Natalie Barney was dutifully served by her housekeeper Berthe Cleyrergue. Janet Flanner has called Berthe 'so loyal, she practically took on Natalie's taste', whereas Natalie called her 'my librarian, manager, receptionist, nurse, handyman, cook, chambermaid,

and confidence man, companion of my winters and of all the troubles that she helps me to iron out . . . '[8] Berthe knew most of the salon guests and the gossip surrounding them (exchanging it with a select few at the door before they came in), if not the literature for which they were renowned. She describes the salon:

> It was the literary salon itself. There were literary – poetry conversations, about which book had just come out. It was young people coming with their manuscripts. So there was Madame Radelais, Janet Flanner, Germaine Beaumont, who would take the manuscripts and eight or ten days later, or a fortnight later, bring them back to tell this young man or woman, if it was any good. And then, they would be recommended to a publisher. Gertrude Stein used to come; there were a lot of people. Colette was a great friend. In 1928, together with Miss Romaine Brooks, Colette was a friend to Miss Barney, the very best of her friends all her life, for 62 years. Miss Barney would always say this to me, so, if she said it, I can repeat it.[9]

ABOVE One of the salon regulars was Germaine Beaumont, short-term lover and long-term friend of Natalie Barney's, whom after forty years she still called 'My Natalie'. As Solita Solano indicated on this photograph, she was the protégée of Colette, but also was a highly regarded writer in her own right.

LEFT Natalie Barney, as Remy de Gaurmont's L'Amazone.

COLETTE IN LITERATURE AND LOVE

Janet Flanner has confirmed that Colette, regardless of her three husbands and several female lovers, was, after Romaine Brooks and Lily de Clermont-Tonnerre, one of the great loves of Natalie's life:

> [Natalie] was intimate with Colette . . . Colette must have been
> more satisfactory than almost anyone else in her life. Then
> there were the younger women, whom it would not be fair to
> name, since they were people with whom Natalie merely fell
> in love . . . [10]

One of France's most celebrated and esteemed authors, Colette immortalized the lesbian society of Paris in her *The Pure and the Impure*, which Colette considered to be her best book. The shocked and offended readers of a Paris weekly, *Gringoire*, in which it was serialized in 1930, disagreed: after its fourth instalment the editor, bowing to his readership, discontinued the serialization so abruptly that, according to Janet Flanner, 'the word FIN, The End, appears in the middle of a sentence that is never completed'.[11]

In her introduction to an English translation of *The Pure and the Impure*, Janet Flanner wrote that she could 'think of no other female writer endowed with this double [male and female] comprehension whereby she understood and accepted the naturalness of sex wherever found or however fragmented and reapportioned'.[12] Perhaps Colette's ability to live in male and female, heterosexual and homosexual, worlds all at once gave her this double comprehension. Natalie Barney, however, had another view of Colette's serial marriages: she wrote in her 1929 book, *Adventures of the Mind*, that Colette loved, among other things, 'having one man at a time in order to keep her in slavery'.

Colette was on her third (and last) husband by the time she wrote *The Pure and the Impure*; she had come a long way from being a bawdy music hall performer to earning France's highest award, the Legion of Honour.

RIGHT **'Colette seemed to have a hermaphroditic duality in her understanding and twofold loyalties,' according to Janet Flanner.**

She could now afford to be the cool, detached observer of the sexual escapades of her youth, whereas in her early autobiographical novels, she had written from the midst of her tumultuous and disreputable life, motivated by passion and revenge.

When Colette first married the theatre editor, Parisian wit and general man-about-town known as Willy, she was just a country girl of nineteen and he considerably older and already established. By then he had an entire literary factory on the go, hiring ghostwriters by the dozens. He added Colette to their numbers, and locked her in a room to write her schoolgirl memoirs to which, like everything else, he put his own name. But, she wondered, what choice did she have? 'It was marry Willy or become an old maid or a teacher.'[13]

What Willy didn't expect was the overnight sensation *Claudine à l'école* created. This led to a demand for Claudine sequels and plays that only Colette herself could fulfil. Decades later, when her name had been restored to the title page, she still credited Willy, not as author, nor even literary collaborator, as he liked to imagine himself, but for getting her work published in the first place:

> When I had finished, I handed over to my husband a closely-written manuscript . . . He skimmed through it and said: 'I made a mistake, this can't be of the slightest use . . . ' Released, I went back to the sofa, to the cat, to books . . . The exercise books remained for two years at the bottom of a drawer. One day Willy decided to tidy up the contents of his desk.
>
> 'Fancy,' said Monsieur Willy. 'I thought I had put them in the waste-paper basket.' He opened one exercise book and turned over the pages . . . He swept up the exercise-books haphazard, pounced on his flat-brimmed hat and rushed off to a publisher . . . And that was how I became a writer.
>
> But that was also how I very nearly missed becoming a writer. I lacked the literary vocation and it is probable that I should never have produced another line if, after the success of *Claudine à l'école*, other imposed tasks had not, little by little, gotten me into the habit of writing.[14]

Although one of France's greatest writers, Colette always doubted her literary skills and her right to claim a 'literary vocation'. She felt it was only strenuous self-discipline, rather than talent, that enabled her to write: 'If I were to relax the merciless control I inflict on my prose, I know well that I would soon cease to be the anxious and diligent prose writer that I am and become nothing more than bad poet.'[15]

After their messy divorce, in which Willy tried to claim all future revenue from Colette's writings published under his name, Willy wrote that the marriage had been the only respectable solution to Colette's scandalous behaviour. In one of his later novels he portrays her 'as an intelligent and sly country girl, poor as a churchmouse, who cannot marry in her own village because of a fugue with a music teacher'. Although Willy's was a piece of fiction, Colette disputed the facts: the piano teacher was a woman, in Paris, and she and Willy were already married.

In her own early fictions Colette stuck so closely to the facts that she barely paused to alter the names of her schoolmates in the *Claudine* series, causing them tremendous embarrassment and lifelong hostility towards her. Janet Flanner, in her introduction to *The Pure and the Impure* described what she called Colette's 'favourite writing formula' as 'autobiographic novelizing' and went on to easily decode the characters. Of the character 'La Chevalière' whose 'real title was too weighty to be mentioned' Janet Flanner wrote:

> Stripped of all the fictitious trappings with which Colette loyally
> sought to disguise her, she was easily recognizable to Parisians
> as the ex-Marquise de Belboeuf, with whom Colette had lived
> for six years after the end of her first marriage . . . She looked
> like a distinguished, refined, no-longer-young man, for she
> always wore men's clothes, indeed wore quite a lot of them,
> which made her look plump [to] hide what might have seemed
> her effeminate figure . . . She was addressed as Monsieur le
> Marquis.[16]

The infamous couple created a scandal virtually everywhere they went. They performed together in music hall pantomimes throughout France, with the ex-Marquise, known as 'Missy', playing the male role. Reviewing

Colette's performance in a pantomime in 1906, a critic called on Lesbos to imply that Colette was playing to the women rather than the men in the audience: 'She struck some ceremonial poses, during which her skirt rose still higher, and the Mytilène élite became delirious.' At the Moulin Rouge, the sold-out, black-tie opening crowd was so scandalized by the near-nudity, female cross-dressing, and, above all, by the kiss between Colette and Missy that it turned into a screaming, fighting mob; the show was shut down by the police.

On the domestic front, however, Missy and Colette settled into peaceful bliss. Colette's mother, who closely followed in the press the unconventional behaviour of her daughter, was relieved that after the disastrous marriage to Willy, 'you have with you someone who loves you truly'. Janet Flanner recalled that this domesticity centred around good food: 'Her household always included an excellent devoted cook for Colette was a gourmet and a good cook herself . . . '[17] But it was precisely her cooking for which Colette apologized:

ABOVE **When Missy and Colette performed a music hall pantomime at the Moulin Rouge, the police shut down the show.**

[Undated] Dearest Janet

How kind of you. This poor lunch I gave you, which gave me
the pleasure of your company only deserved that you would
say: My girl you are not much of a hausfrau. And I'll remember
your quiche lorraine as a remarkable peace [sic] of cement . . .
When do I take you to a decent dinner?[18]

The arrangement between Missy and Colette, seemingly modelled on
heterosexual marriage, and Missy's notorious cross-dressing, are matters
Colette has her characters take up in *The Pure and the Impure*:

' . . . a couple of women can live together a long time and be
happy. But if one of the two women lets herself behave in the
slightest like what I call a pseudo-man, then . . . '

'Then the couple become unhappy?'

' . . . You see, when a woman remains a woman, she is a
complete human being. She lacks nothing, even as far as her
amie is concerned. But if she ever gets it into her head to try to
be a man, then she's grotesque. What is more ridiculous, what
is sadder, than a woman pretending to be a man? On that subject, you'll never get me to change my mind. La Luciènne, from
the time she adopted men's clothes, well! . . . Do you imagine
her life wasn't poisoned from then on?'

'Poisoned by what?'

Many of the 'female figures in this transvestite society of the "Pure and the
Impure"', as Janet Flanner called them, were modelled on women who
attended Natalie's weekly salon.

Truman Capote commented that the salon was fascinating for its
literary connections as well as its sexual intrigue:

Miss Barney's circle was not limited to lesbians . . . She had
tout Paris. Many of them were friends of Proust who had been
characters in *Remembrance of Things Past* – like the Duchesse
de Clermont-Tonnerre. Miss Barney would say to me very
specifically that she wanted me to meet somebody because that
person was so-and-so in Proust.[19]

THE ADVERSE SEXES: WAR AND FEMINISM

The Duchesse de Clermont-Tonnerre, whose aristocratic family went as far back as Henry IV, was by no means as stuffy as her name. Financially ruined by divorce and then by war, she earned her own way as a writer, volunteered in a military hospital during the First World War, and, in numerous radical newspaper editorials and public lectures, advocated communism, for which she earned the nickname, 'The Red Duchess'. Natalie had to bail her out financially on occasion. Although politically at odds with each other, Lily de Clermont-Tonnerre was Natalie's Great Love during the Great War, and the reason Natalie could not tear herself away from France, even after she had packed and shipped her belongings back to the United States. In her memoirs she recalled Lily's plea:

> On the first of August [1914] in Paris, my French friend [Lily] asked: 'You are not going back to America, are you?'
>
> 'My family is awaiting me there, my trunks and my papers have already left for Le Havre.'
>
> 'But you, you were with us in peace, you won't leave us now there is to be war?'

Lily prevailed; ironically, had she not, Natalie would never have met Romaine during those years, although later neither could remember which year it was. From the start Romaine had to share Natalie with Lily de Clermont-Tonnerre, as she would have to do with all of Natalie's other lovers for the next half a century. But she admired and respected Lily, unlike most of Natalie's subsequent liaisons. It was Lily who introduced Romaine to Eileen Gray; Eileen had worked as an ambulance driver under Lily's supervision during the First World War.

Romaine had great respect for women war workers generally, and painted her powerful 'La France Croisée' whose face, recalling that of the dancer Ida Rubenstein, Romaine's previous lover, shows the strength and calm with which women met the horrors of war. The painting inspired four poems by Gabriele D'Annunzio, with whom Romaine also had had a

ABOVE 'Elisabeth de Gramont' by Romaine Brooks, 1924.
Despite their romantic triangle, Romaine admired Lily de Clermont-
Tonnerre, who used the pen-name Elisabeth de Gramont.

tortured love affair. The poems, together with a reproduction of her painting, were published as a booklet to raise money for the Red Cross.

The poet Lucie Delarue Mardrus, a close friend of Colette's, also volunteered as a nurse during the war.

She was married to Dr Joseph-Charles Mardrus (whom Natalie always called Dr Jesus-Christ Mardrus), famous for his translation of *The Arabian Nights* into French. Nicknamed 'Archangel Amazon', Lucie Delarue Mardrus was another lover of Natalie Barney's and wrote about their love in overtly erotic poetry (posthumously published by Natalie as *Nos secrètes amours*) and a play, *Sapho désesperée*. Her husband had endured the affair for two years, but now that he was completing the sixteenth and final volume of *The Arabian Nights*, he turned his attentions back to his wife and promptly carried her off to Africa.

Lucie later portrayed Natalie in an unflattering – indeed, devastating – light in her 1930 novel, *L'Ange et les Pervers*, where her character heartlessly plays with her lovers' emotions.

For you are terribly American, for all your cosmopolitan airs.
You make twenty-five rendezvous all over Paris for the same
hour . . . You have the restless disease which comes from
being dragged around ocean liners, trains, and hotels while too
young, like all little Yankees who are too rich . . .

You invent little situations, you play childish games with
love. At bottom you are a bunch of schoolgirls – dangerous
schoolgirls at that – for in the midst of all this there is a man
who loved his wife and who has lost her, a woman who was
leading a peaceful life and who is now launched on adventures
that lead her astray.

Harsh words, but after their tumultuous affair, Lucie and Natalie settled into a lifelong friendship, and Lucie divorced 'Jesus-Christ'.

Despite the decision of her many friends, including fellow Americans Sylvia Beach, Gertrude Stein and Alice B. Toklas, to enlist in the war effort,

LEFT **'La France Croisée' by Romaine Brooks, 1914. Romaine's portrait of a Red Cross nurse as a symbol for France at war.**

Natalie wanted no part of the 'ambulance aids' brigade, as she sarcastically referred to them. Natalie felt that war was a logical extension of ordinary male aggression, of which women were the innocent victims. Her *Pensées d'une amazone* opens with a section which gives pithy expression to these theories, entitled 'The Adverse Sexes: War and Feminism'. While her friends were facing the daily horrors of military hospitals, Natalie was organizing a congress of female pacifists. The meetings were held in Natalie's Temple of Friendship, a small, four-columned Doric temple built

A drawing of the temple in Natalie's garden. As if expecting Natalie Barney to live at this address some day, the temple had been inscribed with the words 'à l'amitié' – 'to friendship'.

in a corner of the wild, spacious garden hidden away in the courtyard at 20 rue Jacob. Some women claimed these pacifist meetings were the only place where it was safe to express any fear or hatred of war, which did nothing to bring peace but somehow made them feel better.

Although her political views were conservative, bordering on the fascist, anti-semitic and outright bizarre as she got older, Natalie Barney was in some ways her own brand of devout feminist, espousing a feminism which did not extend to all womankind, despite her claim that 'we endeavored to include women of all classes, professions and all countries' in the pacifist meetings held in her temple. Nor was she much concerned with women's entry into politics and other male dominated fields, although she would have been pleased if women took over the business of running society altogether. In her memoirs she wrote:

With or without [women's] rights everything seems to be going on much as before their voting and never was their influence

more needed – and lacking . . . If the voices of women are
hushed up like children's – they the courageous mothers of
men – if they have no worthy representatives of their cause, if
they cannot rule equally with men over the lives together created, should not the stronger in the instinct of race preservations
prevail; and the Matriarchal again dominate the Patriarchal?

The most practical application of her feminist ideals could be found in her
devotion to encouraging, advocating, and even financing women's literary
and artistic endeavours. Although not known for her generosity, she used
some of her seemingly infinite funds to publish privately women writers, to
award a 'Renée Vivien Prize' and to support those, such as Djuna Barnes,
who fell on hard times. Natalie's Académie des Femmes was her answer to
the Académie Française, that venerable but blinkered institution which
excluded women. Colette had been promoted to the highest position
permitted a woman within the Legion of Honour, but still could not be
elected to the Académie Française on account of her gender; she was of
course a founding member of Natalie's Académie. Although many men,
from Rainer Maria Rilke to Ezra Pound (with whom she would play tennis
in the 1920s) attended Natalie's salon, the special Académie des Femmes
gatherings would always be dedicated to honouring a woman writer and
would at times be open to women only.

Among the women honoured by the Académie were Djuna Barnes,
Edna St Vincent Millay and Gertrude Stein and it was here that Colette
performed a selection from her play *La Vagabonde* in 1922.

A CLASH OF CENTURIES: NATALIE BARNEY AND GERTRUDE STEIN

In her own, informal way, Natalie probably did more than anyone, aside
from Sylvia Beach and Adrienne Monnier, to bridge French and expatriate
literary communities in Paris. In 1926 she wrote to Gertrude Stein,

The other night 'au Caméléon' I realized how little the French
'femmes de lettres' know of the English and Americans and vice

versa . . . I wish I might bring about a better 'entente,' and hope therefore to organize here this winter, and this spring, readings and presentations that will enable our mind-allies to appreciate each other . . . Colette has promised to act a scene from her 'Vagabonde' which is to appear later in a theatre in Paris – I should like to add at least one anglo-saxon to this first group, and thought that you, presented by yourself would make a good representation – and balance the French trio. Will you! Shall we? . . . Hoping my 'petit projet' may meet with your approval and receive your participation. With affectionate greetings to you and your friend, in which Romaine Brooks joins me -

It is hard to imagine that Natalie Barney, with her nineteenth- (or even eighteenth-) century style and her flamboyant lesbian sexuality, and Gertrude Stein, with her avant-garde literary style and her traditional 'companionship' with Alice B. Toklas, had much in common. Most commentary about Gertrude Stein denies altogether the importance of women in her life aside from Alice, and characterizes her as 'male identified'. But actually she had many close female friends, and Natalie Barney was certainly one of them, as the many letters between them indicate. Berthe recalls,

Gertrude Stein and Miss Toklas were not only invited for the receptions, but for the lunches. We always invited Gertrude Stein for lunches because she was an astonishing personage – physically and every way. At first I was frightened of her . . . I took her for a man. When I learned she was a woman, I said: 'That's not true.' But really they were very intimate friends, very, very intimate.[20]

Natalie pursued friends as ardently as she pursued lovers, and was known to be as constant in friendship as she was inconstant in love. Her relationship with Gertrude was one that she cultivated, slowly and persistently. It came to fruition only in the mid–1920s after they had known of each other for 23 years. Years after the initial invitation to Gertrude to read at her salon – for which Natalie had translated into French some of the pages from Gertrude's *The Making of Americans* – Natalie was still intent on building Franco-American relations between literary women. On 9 January 1931, when Natalie was expecting Gertrude and Alice for tea, she invited along Colette and Lucy Mardrus 'and a few others I know are sympathetic to you'.

Natalie herself was not completely sympathetic to Gertrude's writing, which had little in common with her own. She wrote, 'Being a writer of pensées, I like to find a thought as in a nut- or seashell, but while I make for a point Gertrude seems to proceed by avoiding it . . . I cannot see where so simple a dissociation of words from their subject leads us.'[21]

Although in no way literary peers – it is probable that Gertrude found Natalie 'simple-minded' when it came to literature – the two women would gossip and talk for hours about gastronomy while indulging in cakes at Rumplemayer's on the rue de Rivoli. They regularly went for neighbourhood walks together, accompanied by Gertrude's white poodle, Basket. After Gertrude's death, Natalie recalled these walks in a foreword she wrote for the publication of Gertrude's *As Fine as Melanctha*:

> Often in the evening we would walk together; I, greeted at the door . . . by Gertrude's staunch presence, pleasant touch of hand, well-rounded voice always ready to chuckle. Our talks and walks led us far from war paths. For generally having no axe to grind nor anyone to execute with it, we felt detached and free to wander in our quiet old quarter where, while exercising her poodle, 'Basket', we naturally fell into thought and step. Basket, unleashed, ran ahead, a white blur, the ghost of a dog in the moonlit streets:
>
> Where ghosts and shadows mingle -
> As lovers, lost when single.
>
> The night's enchantment made our conversation as light, iridescent and bouncing as soap bubbles, but as easily exploded when touched upon – so I'll touch on none of them for you, that a bubble may remain a bubble! And perhaps we never said *'d'impérissables choses'*.[22]

Natalie introduced Lily de Clermont-Tonnerre to Gertrude, and the two women became great friends. According to Gertrude Stein's *Autobiography of Alice B. Toklas,*

> She and Gertrude Stein pleased one another. They were entirely
> different in life education and interests but they delighted in
> each other's understanding. . . . One day [Lily announced,] the
> time has now come when you must be made known to a larger
> public. I myself believe in a larger public. Gertrude Stein too
> believes in a larger public but the way has always been barred.
> No, said Madame de Clermont-Tonnerre, the way can be
> opened. Let us think.
>
> She said it must come from the translation of a big book,
> an important book. Gertrude Stein suggested the Making of
> Americans . . . That will do exactly, she said. And went away.
> Finally and not after much delay, Monsieur Bouteleau of Stock
> saw Gertrude Stein and he decided to publish the book.

Gertrude Stein was not so successful when she similarly solicited a publisher on behalf of Natalie Barney. In 1935, a year after Gertrude's first great 'literary success', she used her new, formidable reputation to recommend that Harcourt Brace and Co. publish Natalie's *Aventures de l'esprit.* (Djuna Barnes had tried to find Natalie a publisher in New York in 1930, also without success.) Harcourt Brace wrote back on June 3, 1935 that 'it would suffer from comparison with *The Autobiography of Alice B. Toklas* which covers a number of the same people and to a considerable extent the same period, and yet Miss Barney's book is really far less clever and interesting.'

When she received the rejection letter from Harcourt, Natalie wrote Gertrude that

> I am lazy enough to be relieved at not having to go over those
> old 'Aventures de l'esprit' – though it would have done Dolly
> [Wilde] good to go on translating them. I've other fish to fry –
> small fish that may please the American taste better? I remain
> very grateful to you for opening Harcourts eyes to my existence.
> Lots of love N.

The story of Natalie and Gertrude's short-lived falling out has been told many times. Alice's quip as to where Natalie found her many women – in the lavatory of the Louvre department store – was countered by Natalie's retaliation: she announced that the relationship between Gertrude and Alice was 'entirely innocent'. But when asked if there was any rivalry between Natalie and Gertrude, the composer Virgil Thomson, who knew both women well, denied it:

> I can't conceive that there was any because they weren't doing
> the same thing [with their respective salons] . . . She'd come to
> Gertrude's house, and Gertrude would come to hers, and
> they'd write little *pneumatiques* all the time. Besides which,
> they were exchanging literary people. If the Sitwells came over
> and were around Gertrude's, she'd probably take them to
> Natalie's or have Natalie in or furnish them to Natalie for some
> soiree. If you've got Edith Sitwell on your hands, you don't
> want to see her every day.[23]

Edith Sitwell could be tedious. She wrote in 1927 to Gertrude that 'We arrive in Paris a week today. Please may a horde of us invade you on Friday afternoon (the 27th) at about 3:30 . . . ' Natalie and Gertrude found themselves commiserating one evening in Shakespeare and Company, when Edith Sitwell neglected to mention Gertrude's name even once, in a lecture purportedly about Gertrude's writings.

But Edith Sitwell could be helpful as well. She wrote a long article on Gertrude's work for *Vogue* in 1925, 'The Works of Gertrude Stein: A Modern Writer Who Brings Literature Nearer to the Apparently Irrational World of Music', and a favourable review of *The Making of Americans* for T.S. Eliot's *The New Criterion*. In 1925 she tried to place Gertrude's *Portraits and Prayers* with several publishers in London, but after meeting with no success, she offered instead to 'kill somebody soon, – a reviewer, or possibly a publisher . . . I should like to do something drastic to the idiot who sent your book back.'

According to Natalie's neighbour, Elizabeth Eyre de Lanux, who attended the salon religiously throughout the 1920s and 30s, Gertrude Stein was a regular: 'Gertrude Stein was always there – the permanent occupant of right wall center, knees wide-spread, dressed in stout tweeds and mountain climbing boots; she seemed a game warden scrutinizing the birds.'[24]

Gertrude's poodle Basket would also attend Natalie's Friday salons, 'so perfectly groomed that he seemed to be enameled' according to another salon guest.[25]

A 'RENDEZVOUS AMONG LADIES'

Janet Flanner was also 'one of the pillars' of Natalie's salon, as she called it – she was also regularly in attendance at Gertrude's – but denied knowing Natalie very well 'because if you weren't in love with her – which I certainly was not, since I brought up the topic – you didn't know as much about her . . . I never felt that I knew her at all well, really.'[26] Perhaps not, but Janet was close to many of the same women in Natalie's circle, including Natalie's lover, Dolly Wilde. Publicly Janet wrote with typical humour and detachment in her *New Yorker* 'Letter from Paris' about Oscar Wilde's niece, who showed up at a Parisian party 'looking both important and earnest'. Privately, however, Dolly sent Janet the following undated letter, which suggests a certain intimacy between the two:

> Dear grey & white Janet Your hair is your fortune and there is a nuance about you that makes you rare and exceptional. Be content and comforted. I want to thank you for the bouquet. The pleasure is undescribable – like all enchantment and there is something sad about being unable to tell the secret of pleasure. Be clever enough to enter the core of secret magic and leave me the tedium of explanation . . . If this letter is incoherent – it is nervousness and hopeless darling.[27]

As a journalist covering life in Paris, Janet relied on Natalie's intimate friendships and far-reaching connections in French society for the inside

RIGHT **Dolly Wilde, whom Janet Flanner found to be more a literary character than a writer of literature.**

story which occasionally worked its way into her fortnightly 'Letter from Paris' in the *New Yorker*. Natalie supplied the crucial information to Janet of what Mata Hari wore the day she faced the firing squad: contrary to the legend that she wore a mink coat with nothing underneath, she actually 'died wearing a neat Amazonian tailored suit, specially made for the occasion, and a pair of new white gloves'.

How did Natalie know? Mata Hari was a salon regular. One time she wanted to ride in to the salon on an elephant, but Natalie said, 'No, there are cookies and tea, and we can't have an elephant in my garden.' So she rode in, nearly naked, on a circus horse instead.

A professional commentator on virtually everything and everyone, Janet Flanner was reticent on the subject of Natalie Barney, claiming that she didn't know much, that she was 'a very spotty recollector', and that Natalie 'is a perfect example of an enchanting person not to write about'. Yet as an old woman she did recall with charming detail both Natalie and her damp, *démodé* house, from the paintings of nymphs hanging from the ceiling, to the luxurious pale blue silk sheets Natalie used. Janet Flanner's recollections of the salon focus on the social and sexual rather than literary aspects of the proceedings:

> . . . Introductions, conversation, tea, excellent cucumber sand-
> wiches [in tribute to those served in Oscar Wilde's *The
> Importance of Being Earnest*], divine little cakes Berthe baked,
> and then the result: a new rendezvous among ladies who had
> taken a fancy to each other or wished to see each other again.[28]

Because of Natalie's overt lesbianism, many women, from Janet Flanner to Djuna Barnes to Gisèle Freund, later played down their association with her, although letters and other evidence survive to contradict their denials of friendship. Gisèle Freund claims she was warned by Adrienne Monnier not to attend Natalie's salon, even though Adrienne and Sylvia were often in attendance themselves:

> [Natalie] received every Friday her friends. It was not consid-

**LEFT Journalist Janet Flanner relied on Natalie's personal connec-
tions for her *New Yorker* column.**

ered decent to go there. And so Adrienne said, 'You better not go there.' She never said why, but . . . I didn't go. I never met these people.[29]

The reason may well have been to protect Gisèle, not from indecency but from Natalie herself. Sylvia and Adrienne privately thought of Natalie as 'the breaker of so many hearts – a real killer, Miss B.'[30]

THE WELL OF LONELINESS

Sylvia Beach makes a point of establishing in her memoirs that she was *not* at Natalie Barney's salon on one particularly risqué evening:

> At Miss Barney's one met the ladies with high collars and
> monocles, though Miss Barney herself was so feminine.
> Unfortunately, I missed the chance to make the acquaintance at
> her salon of the authoress of *The Well of Loneliness*, in which
> she concluded that if inverted couples could be united at the
> altar, all their problems would be solved.[31]

It is likely that Gertrude and Alice *were* at Natalie's on this occasion, for, improbable though it may seem, they became friendly with Radclyffe Hall and Una Troubridge around this time, or at least friendly enough to receive postcards from the two English women who were staying at the Grand Hotel Bristol in Merano, Italy shortly after passing through Paris.

Although Radclyffe Hall ('John') and her lover Una, Lady Troubridge seem to have been close friends with Natalie and Romaine for a time, they were more frequently spotted, with their monocles and long cigarette holders, at the Café des Deux Magots than at Natalie's salon.

Radclyffe Hall reputedly hated the idea of promiscuity, for which Natalie was famous. Indeed, she portrayed Natalie as Valerie in her

RIGHT 'Una, Lady Troubridge' by Romaine Brooks, 1924. Romaine found the male posturing of Radclyffe Hall and Una Troubridge ridiculous, and painted Una as a virtual caricature – after which the friendship was permanently strained.

famous, controversial lesbian novel, *The Well of Loneliness*, first published in 1928:

> Most of her sketches were written in French, for among other
> things Valerie was bilingual; she was also quite rich, an
> American uncle had had the foresight to leave her his fortune;
> she was also quite young, being just over thirty, and . . .
> good-looking. She lived her life in great calmness of spirit, for
> nothing worried and few things distressed her. She was firmly
> convinced that in this ugly age one should strive to the top of
> one's bent after beauty . . . she was *libre penseuse* when it
> came to the heart; her love affairs would fill quite three
> volumes, even after they had been expurgated. Great men had
> loved her, great writers had written about her, one had died, it
> was said, because she refused him, but Valerie was not
> attracted to men . . .

The Well of Loneliness goes on to describe the first impressions of a literary salon, clearly modelled on Natalie's:

> So pleasant was it to be made to feel welcome by all these
> clever and interesting people – and clever they were there was
> no denying; in Valerie's salon the percentage of brains was gen-
> erally well above average. For together with those who them-
> selves being normal, had long put intellects above bodies, were
> writers, painters, musicians and scholars, men and women
> who, set apart from their birth, had determined to hack out a
> niche in existence.

Romaine figured in an earlier novel of Radclyffe Hall's, *The Forge*, and as a minor character in *The Well of Loneliness*; she also appeared in a book by Bryher. Yet her largest and most unflattering literary role was in another novel published in 1928, Compton MacKenzie's *Extraordinary Women*. Focussing on a group of lesbians in Capri, *Extraordinary Women* is as explicit a novel as *The Well of Loneliness*. Unlike *The Well*, however, which was burned in the cellars of Scotland Yard, *Extraordinary Women* met with no trouble at all from the censors, no doubt because it ridiculed lesbianism more than it promoted tolerance or understanding – which presumably is what a good novel about lesbians should do.

The censors did not seem to care that the lesbian love in *The Well of Loneliness* was portrayed negatively, as distressing or even harrowing – but Radclyffe Hall's friends and contemporaries certainly did. Colette wrote to Una Troubridge (who had adapted Colette's *Chéri* for the stage) that the characters' emotions in *The Well of Loneliness* were wrong: 'an abnormal man or woman should never feel abnormal, quite the contrary'.[32] Janet Flanner thought the book's premise was misguided: 'her whole analysis was false and based upon the fact that the heroine's mother, when expecting her, had hoped for a boy baby, which as a daughter, Miss Hall interpreted literally'.[33]

Janet, at the time, held her usually scathing tongue when it came to reviewing the book in print. She avoided any mention of its literary merits, and joked instead about its value as contraband: 'Its biggest daily sale [in Paris] takes place from the news vendor's cart serving the de luxe trains for London, La Flèche d'or, at the Gare du Nord.' When a theatrical version of the novel was staged in Paris, the kindest thing Janet could find to write in her review is that the character of Stephen Gordon 'made up in costume what she lacked in psychology'.

Romaine did not object to her appearance in Bryher's novel, and wrote, 'What a pleasure again to see fragment in your book! Was a bit shy at first – so much about myself, but now am so glad. When will you be in Paris?' Yet she was less than pleased with *The Well of Loneliness*, and not only because of her own depiction. To Natalie she revealed her honest response: 'a ridiculous book, trite, superficial, as was to be expected. A digger-up of worms with the pretension of a distinguished archaeologist . . . She has watched me with the eye of a sparrow who sees no further than the window-pane.' No further than the window-pane – the ultimate insult from an artist whose gaze seemed to bore right through the body and into one's soul, so much so that Romaine has been dubbed 'The Thief of Souls'.

THE PORTRAIT NOT PAINTED

Throughout the 1920s and 30s, Romaine had designs on Gertrude's soul. She begged Gertrude to sit for her portrait, pleading that

> Since my last portrait painted several years ago no one has occupied so important a place in my mind as yourself. I have always wanted to paint you as you know; but tendencies some-how stronger than all else forced me to work at quite other things: subconscious drawings and even 'memoires' for which I have no particular talent. Now your portrait comes again forcibly to the foreground . . .

There was always one excuse or another, and in the end it never came about. Once when the two couples were spending an afternoon together in Bilignin at Gertrude's and Alice's country house, Romaine was suddenly inspired to paint the whole group, but Natalie had other plans:

> Another meeting with this inseparable couple took place in their *jardin de cure* at Bilignin, on another summer afternoon . . . The four of us – for Romaine Brooks had come along with me – and Basket, all curves and capers, lent a circus effect to the scene . . .
>
> Meanwhile Romaine, contemplating our group and finding it 'paintable,' wished to start a picture of it then and there, before the light or her inspiration should fade. But I the disturb-ing element of the party, because of a clock in my mind and in duty bound to pleasures, insisted that Romaine and I were due elsewhere. So this picture of us all was left unpainted: *mea culpa!*[34]

During the Second World War, Romaine again wrote to Gertrude: 'Often think of portrait not yet painted. Is your new poodle like Basket?'

Shortly after Gertrude's death in 1946, as Natalie was trying to place a painting of Romaine's in the Tate Gallery in London, she suddenly recalled Romaine's desire to paint Gertrude's portrait. To Alice she wrote, 'What a pity that [Romaine] never did Gertrude's portrait, but then the Picasso is and should perhaps remain unique.' Gertrude probably preferred it this way anyway, as she felt Picasso's portrait 'is the only reproduction of me, which is always I'.[35]

Natalie's friendship with Gertrude and Alice during the war years indicates a deep gulf between her genuine sympathy and concern for those she knew personally and her complete insensitivity, prejudice and brutishness when it came to the rest of humanity. Her acceptance of the popular trend of anti-semitism was not mitigated by her close friendship with two American Jews in hiding in the French countryside. Under the influence of her fascist and equally politically confused friend, Ezra Pound, who was living in Mussolini's Italy, Natalie decided the Axis had 'superior leadership and cause' and in 1939 she moved with Romaine to Italy, 'that Latin sister, until ours comes to her senses, finds herself again and puts her house in order'.

ABOVE Not one to allow the sweep of fascism across Europe to interfere with her personal pleasures, Natalie kept up her membership in the Paris racing club in 1939.

There is no question that Natalie's political views were indefensible. She was always muddled and misguided when it came to politics, but clear as a bell when it came to friendships and personal loyalties. Her anti-semitic views were abstractions, incongruous with her feelings about people she knew (including her beloved mother, who was half-Jewish). From Italy she sent poems and letters to Gertrude and Alice, signing them 'with love to you both, from both [her and Romaine], your not unhappy exile (as the verses enclosed prove!)'.

Many decades later, when Alice died, she was buried in the same grave Gertrude occupied in Père Lachaise cemetery in Paris. Romaine and Natalie found this so romantic that they devised a similar joint-burial plan – but it never came to pass since Natalie, whose art was love, had one more masterpiece in mind. She fell in love with Janice Lahovary, wife of a diplomat, who left her husband and two sons in order to care for Natalie in her old age. The novelist and journalist Germaine Beaumont found it 'marvellous, not to find love at 88, but to find a co-respondent'.[36] Romaine, who had put up with Natalie's infidelity for over fifty years, was less enthusiastic. Initially she tolerated the arrangement, and even visited Natalie at Janice Lahovary's home (where a lift was installed for Natalie who could no long climb stairs). But one day she finally had had enough.

Romaine told Berthe, who was still Natalie's housekeeper and confidante: 'It was all over from the minute that creature managed to slip between us. I thought I was going to end my days with Miss Barney. Now it's impossible. Let her leave me in peace!' Both women were in their nineties when Romaine broke off the relationship, refused Natalie's desperate apologies and love letters, and died alone in the south of France.

Natalie's tireless heart, which had long ruled her body, mind, and soul, was finally broken. She might otherwise have lived forever, but died soon after her beloved Romaine.

LEFT **Natalie Barney in middle age, still the Amazon.**

CHAPTER 4

CITY OF DARK NIGHTS

Perhaps the greatest enigma of Paris literary life between the wars was, and remains, Djuna Barnes. Men and women of all persuasions found her irresistible, falling for her considerable beauty, glamour, intelligence and sharp wit. Today, darker and more disturbing qualities than these continue to attract readers and scholars to her life and work. But, then as now, it is virtually impossible to extricate a 'real' identity from the myth that has become Djuna Barnes – partly because she herself believed in the myth and left little behind to contradict it, and partly because her life offers up the kind of Hollywood or tabloid legend our culture loves so well. Like Tennessee Williams, Rainer Werner Fassbinder or Jane Bowles, Djuna Barnes brings together the familiar but endlessly fascinating scenarios of tortured creativity, tragic homosexuality, and the genius drowning in booze. While her life alternately substantiates and invalidates these scenarios, the 'facts' of her life surpass anything that Hollywood could have dreamt up.

Born in New York State in 1892, Djuna Barnes grew up in a 'bohemian' household which included not only her grandmother, parents

LEFT **Djuna Barnes 'A beautiful woman, very tall, very "majestic" she was a real character. Really.'**
– Berthe Cleyrergue, housekeeper to Natalie Barney.

and their three children, but one of her father's several mistresses and *her* various children. This family has been called sexually unconventional but is perhaps more aptly described as exploitative and sexually abusive. Her closest 'parent' was her grandmother, Zadel Barnes Budington, herself an early feminist and prolific writer, yet it is likely that this closeness bordered on incest – certainly the many letters Zadel wrote to Djuna are pornographic, and make reference to sexual activity between them. Her father attempted to rape the teenaged Djuna, an event she recounted years later to her friend Emily Coleman. When she reached seventeen, her father, with her mother's collusion, gave her as a sexual sacrifice to the brother of his live-in mistress (who later became his second wife) – a parental betrayal that has been variously described as a marriage to, or a rape by, her much older uncle, although no legal documents verifying a marriage have been found. Not surprisingly, the traumas of her childhood haunted her for the rest of her life, resurfacing, through various literary forms and strategies, in her early drama *The Dove* as well as in her major works: *Ryder* (1928), *Nightwood* (1936), and *The Antiphon* (1958).

In 1910, at the age of 18, Djuna started publishing poetry. Two years later she moved to Greenwich Village, began art studies at the Pratt Institute, and found a reporting job with the *Brooklyn Eagle*, thus embarking on a journalistic career that would continue intermittently for 25 years.

Although Djuna did not consider her journalism as serious writing and wrote out of financial necessity, even in this she engaged in the extraordinary and the spectacular. She crawled around a female gorilla's cage in an attempt to commune with her; she underwent forced feeding for a sympathetic article on English suffragettes. Under the pseudonym Lydia Steptoe, she wrote several feminist satires on women's conventional roles. But always she

Haunted by the traumas of her childhood, Djuna drew this double portrait of herself as simultaneously woman and child.

ABOVE **Djuna Barnes pioneered a kind of participatory journalism: here she is being rescued by a fireman's rope from atop a skyscraper.**

distinguished these pieces from her private, creative and non-commercial writing: poetry (most of which from this period has been lost), short stories, and one-act plays, which were produced by the avant-garde Provincetown Players in Greenwich Village.

The details of her life between the years 1912 and 1920 are scant and conflicting – something she would have enjoyed. Obsessed with privacy, she concealed and contradicted biographical facts, even while the deeper truths of her life invariably surfaced through her writing. We do know that in these years she was in love with women and men, apparently having had a brief marriage to writer Courtenay Lemon after the 'arranged' marriage to her uncle ended, although no legal record for this second marriage exists

145

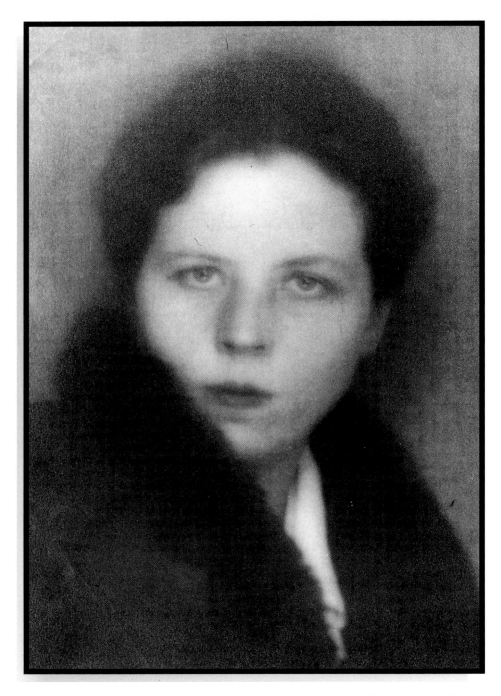

ABOVE **Djuna Barnes: 'Certainly she was one of the most talented and, I think, one of the most fascinating literary figures in the Paris of the twenties.'** — Sylvia Beach

either. Her lovers from this time included, possibly, the homosexual painter Marsden Hartley (although *his* biographer disputes it), the poet Mary Pyre (Djuna nursed Mary until she died in 1919 of tuberculosis), and, briefly, Jane Heap, co-editor with Margaret Anderson of *The Little Review*. *The Little Review* had moved from Chicago to New York and then on to Paris, and had published Djuna widely in these years. It is rumoured that Djuna hated Margaret Anderson for taking Jane Heap away from her; Djuna's dislike did not wane when the three all found themselves settled in Paris.

It was her writings in *The Little Review* as well as a chapbook of eight poems and five drawings, *The Book of Repulsive Women* (a satire on the way men look at women's bodies), which brought Djuna's reputation, as both writer and visual artist, to Paris before her actual arrival in 1919. She settled into the Hotel Angleterre on the rue Jacob, adorned in Peggy Guggenheim's elegant black cape and other cast-off clothing, and each morning she wrote in bed.

Djuna had a brief affair with Natalie Barney, a rite of passage not

**Djuna drew these caricatures of three personalities in Paris:
the poet Mina Loy who became her close friend, the homosexual artist
Marsden Hartley with whom it is rumoured she had a brief affair, and
'spiritual mother of all the Modernists' as she was called here, Gertrude
Stein. Djuna never forgave Gertrude for admiring her legs – a sure
indication to Djuna that Gertrude did not also admire her writing.**

uncommon among attractive female arrivals in Paris at that time. Djuna became a regular 'fixture' at Natalie's lesbian soirées and drew on this circle of women to write *Ladies Almanack*. Although Djuna's sexual practice was not fixed, her writing was: from the outset, it utilized lesbian-coded language and lesbian themes, culminating in the particularly explicit *Ladies Almanack*, privately printed in Paris in 1928, and published under the pseudonym, 'A Lady of Fashion'. Natalie Barney had written in January of that year to Richard Aldington, ex-husband of the poet H. D., about publishing it, arguing on the basis of potential sales:

> All ladies fit to figure in such an almanack should of course be eager to have a copy, and all gentlemen disapproving of them. Then the public might, with a little judicious treatment, include those lingering on the border of such islands and those eager to be ferried across.[1]

But, in the end, it was printed by Contact Editions, Robert McAlmon's press (Djuna felt its name to be a misnomer as it didn't have much contact to or with anything). Robert McAlmon had been married to Bryher for a time, a financial arrangement designed to free Bryher from the clutches of her enormously wealthy family. The divorce settlement of £14,000 which he received from her shipping magnate father earned him the nickname Robert McAlimony and enabled him to establish Contact Editions. So it is ironic that *Ladies Almanack*, a far more radical lesbian book than Radclyffe Hall's *The Well of Loneliness*, published in the same year, was unwittingly financed by Bryher's family.

Djuna Barnes dismissed *Ladies' Almanack* as a 'slight satiric wigging' and 'jollity', and claimed it was written 'in an idle hour' for a 'very special audience'. The most immediate special audience for it was her lover Thelma Wood, an American silverpoint artist and sculptor whom Djuna had met in 1920 or 1921; Djuna apparently wrote it to amuse Thelma during a stay in hospital. But Djuna's efforts on behalf of the book belie her attempts, later in her life, to trivialize it. She not only hand-coloured 50 of the 1050 copies, but hawked it herself on the streets of Paris when its distributor fell through. Sylvia Beach also helped by carrying it in Shakespeare and Company.

'Djuna was a very haughty lady, quick on uptake, and with a wise-
cracking tongue that I was far too discreet to try and rival . . . '
– Robert McAlmon

Despite the lack of distributor, *Ladies Almanack* quickly became the talk of the town, with much speculation as to who was who.

While the book is riddled with private references, innuendoes and allusions which make for amusing, if baffling, reading, we are fortunate that Natalie Barney and Janet Flanner both annotated their copies.

Natalie Barney: Dame Evangeline Musset

born lesbian and on a mission to recruit others, who says to her father

> Am I not took after your very Desire, and is it not the more commendable, seeing that I do it without the Tools for the Trade, and yet nothing complain?

Mina Loy: Patience Scalpel

the one staunch heterosexual, she

> belongs to this Almanack for one Reason only, that from Beginning to End, Top to Bottom, inside and out, she could not understand Women and their Ways as they were about her, above her and before her.

(Nonetheless, by August even Patience Scalpel starts to make a move towards women.)

Dolly Wilde: Doll Furious

> . . . Amid the rugs Dame Musset brought Doll Furious to a certainty. ". . . Ah!" [Dame Musset] sighed, "there were many such when I was a Girl, and in particular I recall one dear old Countess who was not to be convinced until I, fervid with Truth, had finally so floored her in every capacious Room of that dear ancestral Home, that I knew to a Button, how every Ticking was made! And what a lack of Art there is in the Upholstery Trade, for that they do not finish off the under Parts of Sofas and Chairs . . . There should . . . be Trade for Contacts, guarding that on which the Lesbian Eye must, in its March through Life, rest itself."

Three of Djuna Barnes' drawings for *Ladies Almanack*.

Romaine Brooks: Cynic Sal

"The Night-Light of Love," said Saint Musset, "burns I think me in the slightly muted Crevices of all Women . . . There is one . . . on whom I have had a Weather Eye these many years. . . . Her Name is writ from here to Sicily, as Cynic Sal. She dressed like a Coachman . . . , but she drives an empty Hack. And that is one Woman," she said, "who shall yet find me as Fare, and if at the Journey's end, she still cracks as sharp a Whip, and has never once descended the Driver's Seat to put her Head within to see what rumpled meaning there sits, why she may sing for her Pains, I shall get off at London and find me another who has somewhat of a budding Care for a Passenger."

Two British women,

Radclyffe Hall: Tilly Tweed-in-Blood

sported a Stetson and believed in Marriage (between women; she wanted to put the question to the House of Lords), and

Una Troubridge: Lady Buck-and-Balk

sported a Monocle and believed in Spirits:

They came to the Temple of the Good Dame Musset, and they sat to Tea, and this is what they said: "Just because woman falls, in this Age, to Woman, does that mean that we are not to recognize Morals? What has England done to legalize these Passions? Nothing! Should she not be brought to Task, that never once through her gloomy Weather have two dear Doves been seen approaching their bridal Laces, to pace, in stately Splendor up the Altar Aisle, there to be United in Similarity, under mutual Vows of Loving, Honouring, and Obeying, while the One and the Other fumble in that nice Temerity, for the equal gold Bands that shall make of one a Wife, and the other a Bride?"

Janet Flanner and Solita Solano: The messengers Nip & Tuck

They alert Dame Musset to women she might recruit.

> "We come . . . to let you know there is a Flall loose in the Town who is crying from Corner to Niche, in that lamenting Herculean Voice that sounds to us like a Sister lost, for certainly it is not the Whine of Motherhood, but a more mystic, sodden Sighing. So it seems to us, as Members of the Sect, we should deliver to you this piece of Information, that you may repair what has never been damaged."
>
> "It shall be done, and done most wily well," said the Dame . . . "Where was she last seen, and which way going? . . . To scent, we will chase her into a very Tangle of Temptation!"

Duchesse de Clermont-Tonnerre: Duchess Clitoressa of Natescourt.

> Already, when Evangeline appeared to Tea to the Duchess Clitoressa of Natescourt, women on the way . . . would snatch their Skirts from Contamination . . .

Ladies Almanack has been called a lesbian creation myth, beginning with the birth of 'the first Woman born with a Difference'. Ridiculing the sexology of its day, it turns Havelock Ellis's image of the dangerous lesbian seducer into, as claimed in the foreword to the most recent edition, '"one Grand Red Cross" for women's sexual relief'! *Ladies Almanack* also eschews the 'lesbianism as cruel trick of nature' stance of *The Well of Loneliness*, offering it instead as a welcome departure from heterosexual aggression. Rather than pleading for sympathy or tolerance, *Ladies Almanack* relies on lesbian innuendo and codes to speak to lesbians directly, leaving others to make of it what they will. 'Showing their Signs and their tides; their Moons and their Changes; the Seasons as well as a full Record of diurnal and nocturnal Distempers', *Ladies Almanack* celebrates the lesbian body.

There is nothing in *Ladies Almanack* and, indeed, little in the bits and pieces we know of her life during the early and mid–1920s to fit the images of tragic homosexual or tortured writer we've come to associate with Djuna Barnes. The first few years with Thelma Wood were genuinely joyful ones. From 1922, the two women lived together on the Left Bank, first at 173 Blvd St Germain and later at 9 rue St Romain. Djuna's letters to Natalie Barney describe their life together as peaceful and productive: 'We are very quiet: Thelma is painting, I trying a novel, a short story, and a play, all at once!' The following year, Bryher visited them and reported to H.D. that the two women were happy together. They conceived of their relationship as an idyllic family, with Djuna as 'Momma' or 'Junie' and Thelma as 'Papa' or 'Simon'; their cat Dilly was a surrogate child. They wrote each other loving letters:

> 'I love you my very own –
> forever -
> Simon
> I also kiss you a great many
> kisses.'

ABOVE **Thelma Wood, 'Berlin 1921', which is where and when she first met Djuna.**

LEFT **This exhibition of Thelma's drawings in 1926 'caused much excitement' according to the *New York Telegram,* which found her work to 'have a delicate exotic beauty all their own'.**

RIGHT **Thelma in the early idyllic days of her relationship with Djuna.**

154

And Djuna's most autobiographical novel, *Ryder* (1928), which chronicles her unusual family history, was dedicated to T. W.

Before the city of light became a city of dark nights for Djuna Barnes, she was an integral part of the vibrant female artistic community which congregated not only at Natalie Barney's Friday salon but also informally at each other's homes. Janet Flanner regularly retreated to the home of Noel Murphy in the village of Orgeval in order to escape the pressures of Paris, and was highly selective about whom she and Noel would invite there, but Djuna was among the inner circle. A frequent guest, she could often be found in their garden, sunbathing in the nude. Writer Kathryn Hulme described first seeing Djuna with Janet Flanner and Solita Solano at the Café Flore, where the three women, drinking martinis in tailored suits and white gloves, looked like three Fates.[2]

One of Djuna's closest friends was Mina Loy. Born in London, Mina was a woman graced with, or perhaps burdened by, multiple talents: she was by turns a poet, painter, playwright, actress, and designer. To the extent that she was known in her day, it was mostly as a Modernist poet, but it was Modernism with a twist. Her poems, published in *The Little Review*, combined her literary experimentation with an interest in feminist themes, while her novels also explored aspects of her Jewish identity. Ezra Pound, the self-appointed authority on Modernist poetry, announced that he had read quite a bit of 'rubbish' by her but called one of her works 'the utterance of clever people in despair, or hovering upon the brink of that precipice . . . '-faint praise. Perhaps because she actually lived on that brink, Mina Loy saw only two volumes published during her lifetime: *Lunar Baedecker*, which, like Djuna's *Ladies Almanack*, was published by Robert McAlmon's Contact Editions (1923), and, much later, *Lunar Baedecker and Timetables* (1958).

Eugene Jolas, editor of *transition*, wrote about Mina Loy's work, admiring the fact that it took years for her to produce anything: 'In this age of mechanical over-production and standardized esthetics, it is a real delight to meet a writer who works with almost Stoic slowness . . . "One must have lived ten years to write a poem," she said.'[3]

It is ironic that Mina Loy would so admire the prolific Gertrude Stein, who wrote daily at breakneck speed, virtually without revision (although according to Virgil Thomson she first 'waited always for the moment when she would be full of readiness to write').[4] Privately Mina Loy wrote Gertrude intimate letters: 'Dearest and only Gertrude . . . I long to see you. Most love to you both.' Publicly she honoured her in a poem published in *Transatlantic Review*:

> Curie
> of the laboratory
> of vocabulary
> she crushed
> the tonnage
> of consciousness
> congealed to phrases
> to extract
> a radium of the word.

Mina Loy was a regular at both Natalie Barney's and Gertrude's Stein's salons, where she was occasionally accompanied by Djuna Barnes. In 1927, she gave a talk at Natalie's about Gertrude Stein and on a different afternoon read from her own work, thus earning herself a place in Djuna Barnes' *Ladies Almanack* as the sole heterosexual woman, Patience Scalpel.

Mina had married a fellow art student in 1904, but they became estranged, both took other lovers, and eventually divorced, leaving her with two children (a third had died in infancy). Moving between Paris, Florence and New York, she met the poet/boxer/draft dodger Arthur Cravan in 1917, who became the great love of her life. Arthur Cravan was a hero to the Surrealists and Dadaists in Paris; this gave Mina Loy a certain, dubious stature among them when she returned to Paris in the twenties. Her romance with the wild Arthur resulted in another child and enormous heartache. When she married him in Mexico City in 1918, it marked the end, rather than the beginning, of their relationship. He disappeared shortly after in the desert; his body was never found.

When *The Little Review* sent out a questionnaire to all previous contributors for their last issue, Mina answered the question 'What was the happiest moment in your life?' by saying, 'Every moment I spent with

ABOVE AND RIGHT The close friendship between Djuna Barnes and Mina Loy was rooted in their shared artistic and emotional temperaments.

Arthur Cravan'. For the next question, 'and the unhappiest?' she wrote 'the rest of the time' – for her that would be another forty years.

Unlike the other Modernist women on the Left Bank, Mina Loy ended up back in Paris as a single mother, now with two children to support (her first husband had taken one of the three). This she did by opening a lampshade design business with the financial backing of Peggy Guggenheim. She had ingenious designs for inventions as well, including children's games, window washers, and other practical items, none of which she ever patented. In her Modernist literary efforts, her stunning beauty, her numerous gifts as a visual artist, and her prolonged agony in matters of the heart, one can readily see the basis of Mina Loy's close friendship with Djuna Barnes.

Although her closest friends were women, Djuna Barnes was also admired by many of the male writers and artists who congregated in Paris in the twenties. She was respected as a writer rather than because she was in a position to publish, introduce, distribute, publicize or otherwise assist the men. This respect for her writing didn't necessarily correspond with comprehension, but then clarity was not high on the list of Modernist literary requirements, as Janet Flanner tells us:

> Djuna had written a play that she showed to T. S. Eliot; he told her that it contained the most splendid archaic language he had ever had the pleasure of reading but that, frankly, he couldn't make head or tail of its drama. She gave it to me to read, and I told her, with equal candor, that it was the most sonorous vocabulary I had ever read but that I did not understand jot or title of what it was saying. With withering scorn, she said, 'I never expected to find that you were as stupid as Tom Eliot.' I thanked her for the only compliment she had ever given me.[5]

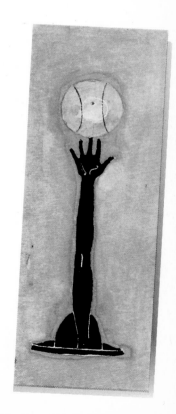

RIGHT **Mina Loy's design for one of her many lamps. She had a good eye for design but a bad head for business.**

The intrepid Djuna Barnes not only was on first-name basis with T. S. Eliot but, according to Janet Flanner, was the only person allowed to call James Joyce 'Jim' – something even Hemingway didn't dare. The ever proper Mr Joyce, however, continued to call her Miss Barnes, just as he called Sylvia (as she was known to everyone else), Miss Beach. Joyce, 'with the strange formality of a polyglot genius in exile, remained Mr Joyce' to everyone besides Djuna Barnes.[6]

Soon after her arrival in Paris, Djuna wrote an essay for *Vanity Fair* about her first encounters with James Joyce, whom she clearly admired from the start:

ABOVE **A sketch of James Joyce by Djuna Barnes, n.d.**

And then, one day, I came to Paris. Sitting in the café of the Deux Magots, which faces the little church of St. Germain des Prés, I saw approaching out of the fog and damp, a tall man, with head slightly lifted and slightly turned, giving to the wind an orderly distemper of red and black hair, which descended sharply into a scant wedge on an out-thrust chin . . .

It has been my pleasure to talk to him many times during my four months in Paris. We have talked of rivers and of religion, of the instinctive genius of the church which chose, for the singing of its hymns, the voice without 'overtones' – the voice of the eunuch. We have talked of women; about women he seems a bit disinterested. Were I vain, I should say he is afraid of them, but I am certain he is only a little skeptical of their existence. We have talked of Ibsen, of Strindberg, Shakespeare . . . We have talked of death, of rats, of horses, the sea; languages, climates and offerings. Of artists and of Ireland. . .

He has, if we admit Joyce to be Stephen [Daedelus], done as he said he would do. 'I will not serve that which I no longer believe, whether it call itself my home, my fatherland, or my church; and I will try to express myself in my art as freely as I can, using for my defense the only arms I allow myself to use: silence, exile and cunning.'

This is somehow Joyce, and one wonders if, at last, Ireland has created her man.

When James Joyce's *Ulysses* was published in 1922, it was considered *the* Modernist masterpiece. Reading it piecemeal in *The Little Review*, Djuna despaired of her future as a writer: 'I shall never write another line. Who has the nerve after this?'[7] Critics later berated her for imitating (and poorly at that) Joyce's style, even though Sylvia Beach, who knew Joyce's style better than anyone, claimed emphatically that Djuna's work 'did not resemble that of any other writer of the time'.[8] Although he must be considered an influence on Djuna's work, her writing influenced his as well, particularly *Finnegans Wake*, published three years after *Nightwood*. Joyce himself didn't feel that Djuna's writing was derivative of his – he gave

ABOVE 'Red cheeks. Auburn hair. Grey eyes, ever sparkling with delight
and mischief . . . : that's the real Djuna as she walks down Fifth Avenue,
or sips her black coffee, a cigarette in hand, in the Café Lafayette.'
– Guido Bruno

her the original annotated manuscript of *Ulysses* and considered her among
the select few with whom he would discuss his work. Apparently sharing
her low opinion of journalism, he wrote to her with the following 'literary
advice': 'A writer must never write about the extraordinary. That is for the
journalist.'

Djuna Barnes did not take his advice. In her life and her writing, she
was consistently drawn to the extraordinary. In the writing of *Nightwood*,
her greatest work, she began closest to home, with her relationship with
Thelma – which by now was not ordinary by any standards – and over the
years kept re-writing and transforming her novel towards the extraordinary,
the fantastic, and the bizarre.

Although *Nightwood* is larger, more complex, and finally far more interesting as a novel than the 'facts' of Djuna and Thelma, one can readily see its autobiographical origins, especially in its tracing of the painful, destructive path upon which she and Thelma had embarked. The initial relationship between Nora and Robin in *Nightwood* clearly recalls the early, idyllic days between Djuna and Thelma.

> She stayed with Nora until mid-winter. Two spirits were work-
> ing in her, love and anonymity. Yet they were so "haunted" of
> each other that separation was impossible. Nora bought an
> apartment in the rue du Cherche-Midi. Robin had chosen it. In
> the passage of their lives together, every object in the garden,
> every item in the house, every word they spoke, attested to their
> mutual love, the combining of their humors.

By 1924 or early 1925, the romance between Djuna and Thelma began to turn increasingly volatile, strained by their excessive drinking and Thelma's promiscuity. After one particularly heavy night, Thelma proposed marriage to Peggy Guggenheim.

More disturbing to Djuna was Thelma's affair with the poet and playwright Edna St Vincent Millay, an old acquaintance of Djuna's from the Provincetown Players days, who came temporarily to Paris to escape her supposedly 'sexually liberated' lifestyle in Greenwich Village. There was no love lost between Djuna and 'Vincent' (as Millay was often called) even before the affair with Thelma Wood. Djuna's biographer, Andrew Field, claims that this was because 'Barnes was jealous of the successs of Millay'.[9] When Edna St Vincent Millay wrote her most overtly lesbian play, 'The Lamp and the Bell', based on her intense college relationship with Charlotte ('Charlie') Babcock, she wrote to her sister Norma Millay: 'But don't let any of the Provincetown Players get hold of it to read. I mean this most seriously. They would hate it, & make fun of it, & and old Djuna Barnes would rag you about it, hoping it would get to me.'[10] With her stunning red hair, her lovers of both genders and all persuasions, her writing which she divided into 'serious' plays and poetry, or income-generating journalism and feminist satire (also under a pseudonym), and her own 'tragic streak' of alcoholism and, later, extreme isolation, Edna St Vincent Millay's life oddly paralleled Djuna Barnes's.

According to Berthe Cleyrergue:

> Thelma Wood was living with Djuna in Natalie Barney's house
> when I met her in 1925. It was a complete disaster. For a month,
> they left everything everywhere. It was the beginning of the end
> for the two of them, and when Thelma was the first to leave,
> Djuna went to the Hotel Angleterre, rue Jacob, and that is
> where she began to drink and drink and drink. They phoned me
> from the Hotel Angleterre to come and get her. I brought her
> back to the rue Jacob and there I nursed her for a month . . . [11]

In June 1927, the first break in the relationship occurred when Thelma left
for America; she wrote this heart-wrenching letter from the ship:

> Dearest one – You said something just as I was leaving that
> makes things seem a little less terrible – maybe you didn't mean
> it – you said it so softly – that we could meet in New York and
> maybe Simon would be different. But you see how Silly Simon
> must clutch on anything to make him stronger – you see I can't

think of anything ahead that doesn't mean you -

I keep saying, 'Simon you've got to be a man and take your medicine' – but then always in my head goes 'there is no Simon and no Junie' and I can't bear it and go crazy . . . I feel so shy at saying anything for fear it sounds like excusing which God knows I don't – but I've thought over it all and I think if I didn't drink maybe things wouldn't have suffered [?] – as that is usually when I get involved [with someone else]. Now Simon will not touch one drop till you come to America and I'll have my exhibition done – and I'll try and be financially independent – and then maybe if you still care – and look him over – and he again looks sweet to you Perhaps we could try it a new way – and if you will I will never again as long as you love me take one small drop of anything stronger than tea.

Although nothing – not the drinking, the affairs, nor the financial dependency – changed in their relationship, the letter was apparently

BELOW Waiting impatiently for some word from Djuna . . .

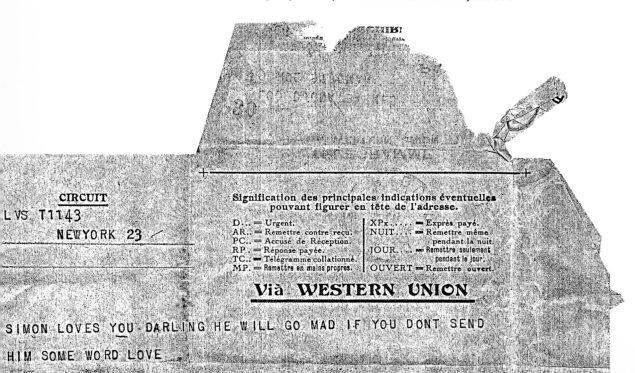

persuasive, for they were reunited in Paris later that year. They made a home together at 9 rue St Romain (which Djuna was able to buy from the proceeds of *Ryder*). But Thelma's penchant for other women drove them to a torturous break-up. This time Thelma wrote Djuna:

> Djuna beautiful – . . . I knew I had lost you – I realized every misdeed committed in eight years would come back – that every one in Paris would be against me . . . The knowing you saw us, I had said such terrible things I hated myself . . . I did not want such a thing to be known between us – something I did not care about – It seemed a shame for foolishness to spoil us – I wanted no *acknowledged* disloyalty and after you came back from N.Y. I loved you so terribly – and my one idea was to wipe out the fact I'd been stupid . . . As for the rest of our eight years you seemed to have had a pretty rotten time – with my brutishness and I'm sorry – sorry.

Thelma stayed with the 'other woman', Henrietta Metcalfe, in the United States, and Djuna stayed on alone in Paris, worn out by years of intense passion, drinking and heartache. The desperate pleas from Thelma continued to arrive via letter but Djuna had had enough.

> I dream of you every night – and sometimes Djuna I dream we are lovers and I wake up the next day and nearly die of shame. Taking advantage in my sleep of something I know so intimately – and something you do not wish me to have. It's like stealing from you and I feel the next day like cabling 'forgive me' and sitting up all night . . . I'd do anything in the world to please you a little – but what is it I can do? I don't know which foot forward I'm so certain both are wrong.

A desire for revenge, an attempt to exorcise her personal demons, and those magical, inexplicable motives for which writers write, even in their darkest hours, were forces which combined to propel Djuna Barnes into the voracious writing project she engaged in for over eight years, from 1927 to 1935, which eventually became *Nightwood*.

It has been suggested that in the writing of *Nightwood*, and specifically in the creation of Robin, Djuna Barnes conflated her relationship to Thelma with the sexual abuse of her childhood.[12] Djuna wrote to Emily Holmes Coleman, a friend she had met through Peggy Guggenheim, 'I am up to my neck here in my lost life – Thelma & Thelma only – & my youth – way back in the beginning when she had no part in it & yet she is the cause of my remembrance of it.' Djuna admitted that the character of Robin Vote was modelled on Thelma – which she knew would anger her – but claimed, unconvincingly, that Nora Flood was based on Thelma's lover Henrietta Metcalf rather than on herself. It was, undeniably, Djuna who followed Thelma in anguish just as Robin followed Nora in *Nightwood*:

> Suffering is the decay of the heart. In the beginning, after Robin went away to America, I searched for her in the ports. I sought Robin in Marseille, in Tangier, in Naples, to understand her, to do away with my terror. I said to myself, I will do what she has done, I will love what she has loved, then I will find her again. At first it seemed that all I should have to do would be to become 'debauched', to find the girls that she had loved; but I found that they were only girls that she had forgotten. I haunted the cafés where Robin had lived her nightlife; I drank with the men, I danced with the women, but all I knew was that others had slept with my lover.

Ultimately *Nightwood* is much more than a road map to the disintegration of a tortured love affair. It has been considered a visionary allegorical tale of the rising tide of fascism across Europe, in which Jews, homosexuals and other marginalized outsiders constitute Hitler's degenerate *Untermenschen*. Some have read it as a feminist reworking of Dante's *Divine Comedy*, in which the price paid for personal and sexual freedom is judgement and damnation; others have claimed it is a lesbian rage against the clergy and a 'feminist-anarchist call for freedom'. The novel is open to such a range of

**RIGHT 'Djuna was tall, quite handsome, bold-voiced, and a remarkable talker, full of reminiscences of her Washington Square New York life and her eccentric childhood somewhere up the Hudson.'
– Janet Flanner**

interpretations precisely because its author was not interested in the 'realistic'. She claimed to work with her intuition and over the years of rewriting, she transformed her 'remembrance of time and pain' into something quite beyond her personal history.

Emily Holmes Coleman served as 'midwife' to the novel, nurturing and encouraging Djuna's writing to such an extent that Djuna's mother found such behaviour to be not 'normal'. As the publishers' rejections continued to arrive, Emily, determined to find a publisher at any cost, argued that Djuna should eliminate the story of Felix (the Jew Nora later marries), reduce the story of the Doctor Matthew O'Connor (a transsexual with dubious medical credentials), and stick closely to her central narrative: the tragic relationship between Robin and Nora. Djuna refused, insisting that

> Robin's marriage to Felix *is* necessary to the book for this reason (which you can not know, not having lived with a woman having loved her and yet circulated in public with the public aware of it) that people *always* say, 'Well of course those two women would never have been in love with each other if they had been *normal,* if any man had slept with them, if they had been well f— and had born a child.' Which is ignorance and utterly false, I married Robin to prove this point, she had married, had had a child yet was still 'incurable'.

As for the transsexual doctor, he plays an indispensable role as well. Andrew Field argues that Dr O'Connor is the key to the narrative:

> [The story of *Nightwood*] is the profound and impossible love of a woman who contemplates and understands for a woman who rages and destroys . . . There is, too, the very great problem of perspective because Dr. O'Connor is both of and not of the main story. Dr. O'Connor is an entire Greek chorus put into a single character, and that character, moreover, stands very near to the reader so that his apparent dimensions are much enlarged. Once that is seen, once the painterly trick of perspective is grasped, whereby the main story is moved upstage where it must appear somewhat reduced, then *Nightwood* has a plot.[13]

In late 1931, Djuna was recovering from an appendicitis operation and the American writer Charles Henri Ford moved in with her, which led to a brief, unstable affair (before he moved on to a relationship with the painter Pavel Tchelitchew). But Djuna was restless, sick of Paris and unsure where else to go. To friends she complained that 'Montparnasse has ceased to exist. There is nothing left but a big crowd . . . Montparnasse is all over. And Greenwich Village is all over. It's all all over.'[14] Keeping Paris as her base, Djuna moved aimlessly to New York, to Tangier, to Peggy Guggenheim's English country house, where she continued working on *Nightwood*, to London, and back to Paris.

T.S. Eliot, then senior editor at Faber and Faber, is usually credited with rescuing the manuscript of *Nightwood* from its endless, discouraging rounds of publishers' rejections. Sylvia Beach wrote that: 'Fortunately, T. S. Eliot, with his usual discernment, sought her out and ushered her to the place she deserves to occupy.'[15] But Emily Coleman virtually forced Eliot to take Djuna's manuscript, which he did, despite reservations, while cutting it down by two-thirds its length.

When it was finally published in 1936, *Nightwood* was largely ignored by critics, although it has since achieved a kind of cult status. It received a few terrible reviews, but even the favourable ones did not know what to make of it – calling it 'Strange and Brilliant', 'Queer, Morbid, and Interesting', 'The Twilight of the Abnormal'.

Djuna
Barnes
Nightwood
Intro. by T. S. Eliot

"*One of the three great prose books ever written by a woman.*"
—Dylan Thomas

Paperbook, $1.35

NEW DIRECTIONS

It seems odd that Djuna Barnes's lesbian themes were so overtly presented while Gertrude Stein's were so carefully disguised. Yet Gertrude Stein was ridiculed and despised for being a lesbian, whereas Djuna Barnes was respected and accepted within the heterosexual Modernist community. Shari Benstock suggests a reason for this paradox: it was inconceivable 'that a woman as beautiful as Barnes might be lesbian' and therefore her lesbian themes were read as 'confirmation of the degradation and innate depravity of homosexuality, turning these texts against themselves'.[16]

During the mid- to late-1930s, Djuna Barnes was in and out of hospital. Solita Solano recalled that 'when in trouble' Djuna would stay with her and Janet Flanner, and on occasion they would have to take her to the American Hospital. She became increasingly quarrelsome and violent, and was considered insane by the staff in the nursing home where she was recuperating from her, at least, second nervous breakdown. For a time her friends didn't know to where she had disappeared. Just as war was breaking out across Europe, Emily Coleman found her and Peggy Guggenheim provided her boat fare back to New York, even though she doubted that Djuna, frail and penniless, would survive the journey.

Djuna Barnes's self-portrait around the time her illnesses began.

In 1939, Djuna Barnes settled in New York. Natalie Barney regretted not getting a chance to say farewell and wrote, 'for farewell you must! and not let little love affairs lead to such extremes! Why not go back . . . to pull yourself together for the sake of your great gift?'

But Djuna Barnes had no more love affairs, little or large, and not much materialized from her great gift in the following forty-odd years. Having told Robert McAlmon in Paris that ' . . . I might as well go back to Greenwich Village and rot there', that is essentially what she did. Although she still attempted to write, 'very slowly, tear everything up, more or less, and start all over again'[17] – she spent the rest of her life bitter and reclusive, addicted to drugs and alcohol, and financially supported by Natalie Barney, Peggy Guggenheim and, occasionally, Janet Flanner.

In 1943, Peggy Guggenheim's Manhatten gallery ran an exhibition of Djuna Barnes's drawings and paintings, the only public acknowledgement she received for her parallel career as a visual artist. Her years of frustrated writing did produce a last novel, *The Antiphon*, published in 1959. But these public events did not lure her out of private seclusion. She never even managed to see her old friend Mina Loy, also back in New York and living an equally reclusive life on the Bowery. Although for decades Djuna Barnes refused interviews and scorned the publication of various memoirs and biographies which romanticized the Paris of old, in her seventies she wrote to Natalie Barney, 'of course I think of the past and of Paris, what else is there to remember?'

During the Occupation of Paris, Djuna wrote this article, a lament for the Paris that was no more.

KILHAM

Lament for the Left Bank
by DJUNA BARNES

Personally I would give all I have, except what I got from it, to be back in Paris again as it was, sitting at a bistro table with its iron legs in the sawdust from the escargot baskets, the cheap, badly-pressed cotton napkin coming off all over my best cloak—that napkin with its hems always half turned and heavy with the blood-red of yesterday's burgundy—a carafe of vin ordinaire before me, an oval dish of salade de tomate, a bowl of cress soup, a blanquette de veau, green almonds—anything—only to hear again the sad, angry popping of the taxi horns, the gracious flowing language chattered by clerks off for two hours of food and argument. To see the patchwork theatrical placards on the kiosks, the pink-paper lampoons on the plaster wall of the house across the

ing traffi
horse tail
blue-blou
screamin
to that is
door parl
    And th
fallen co
walls ma
only a m
If you m
leave; if y
At a café
be as bitt
house can
street doe

Few An
    ground,
toward th
Anthony
Barbusse's
chalked u
*Quiet on
The Enor
A Farewe
    Well?
    Those v
family alw
to much a
ing to not
would hav
clair Lewi
Sherwood
Puerto Ric
the wester
might hav
Taine and

CHAPTER 5

LETTERS FROM PARIS

JANET TO GENÊT

Janet Flanner's will, written in Paris in 1923, requested that any papers found after her death be destroyed by fire without first being opened or perused, as 'one writes down many thoughts and hopes during one's life that seem trivial and unsightly if one is not alive to defend them.'

Janet amended her will in later years, and Solita Solano saved most things that Janet was inclined to throw away. When the two women were in their late seventies, Solita donated the lot (minus any reference to their sexual lives) to the Library of Congress, despite a previous letter from Janet to the library which claimed she had nothing of value. It's fortunate for us, because during the many years she was living and working in Paris, Janet Flanner was possibly the single most influential writer on the Left Bank.

Such a pronouncement would greatly surprise Janet Flanner herself,

LEFT Janet Flanner, in front of a portrait of her lifelong friend, Solita Solano.

despite her having received the Legion of Honour from the French government in 1947, an honorary doctorate from Smith College in 1958, and many other public honours. In 1964, when she was compiling an anthology of her writings from the twenties and thirties, she still found many of her thoughts trivial and unsightly, and was embarrassed that they had made their way into print even the first time around. Ever self-doubting, she considered herself 'merely' a journalist, not quite a writer.

As the personality behind the pen name 'Genêt', Janet Flanner for half a century wrote a fortnightly 'Letter from Paris' for publication in the *New Yorker* magazine. In this letter she commented cleverly and often wisely on everything from *haute couture* to the ballet, new music, modern art, and even the rise of fascism. She wrote not as an outside observer but as a participant who experienced firsthand the cultural world around her. Her popular column, read by Americans thirsty for knowledge about Parisian life, became an institution in its own right in which virtually all the artists and writers of the Left Bank are immortalized. Her position as a journalist for a new but increasingly important cultural magazine gave her an entrée to everyone and everything, and resulted in a privileged overview of life in Paris across the social spectrum.

ABOVE **Solita Solano, shortly after she met Janet Flanner.**

Janet was strategically placed at the centre of the Modernist movement in Paris, yet she was traditional to the point of romanticism: 'I wanted beauty, with a capital B. I came to find the art and culture I couldn't find in America.'[1] In her *New Yorker* letter she would repeat this barb through her cultural contrasts: 'We recall that while America was making candles, Paris was making Voltaire.' She might be excused such an insult for she came from the American heartland herself. Born in 1892, she was of solid, middle-class, midwestern Protestant stock, but despised what she saw

ABOVE **Janet and Solita in Crete in 1921, where Solita wrote
travelogues for *National Geographic*.**

as the puritanism, materialism, hypocrisy and standardization of America.
She described, with typical Flanner humour, how her background came in
useful for life in France: 'My mother's people came from a Quaker
settlement in Indiana. I was brought up as a semi-Quaker. That's probably
why I get along so well in France – I attach an importance to religion,
especially if I don't have to practise it . . . '[2]

A trip to Europe at the age of seventeen introduced her to 'the
beauties of Europe, the long accretions of architecture and poetry and
civilization and education . . . '[3] But it would be some time before she
returned to the continent. At 26, she came a step closer: she moved from
her home of Indiana to New York City with her new husband, Lane Rehm.
Shortly after their arrival, she fell in love with Solita Solano, four years her

senior. Janet was struck by Solita's 'large swimming eyes of an intense blue'.[4]

When the two first met at the end of the First World War, Solita had run away from her husband and was now working as drama critic for the *New York Tribune*. The opportunity to travel together came when Solita was offered an assignment in Constantinople and Crete for *National Geographic*; the two women set off for southern Europe and the Levant in 1921, hardly a conventional act for 'unescorted' middle-class, married American women at that time.

In 1922, Janet and Solita settled in Paris and took two rooms in the extremely narrow Hotel Napoléon Bonaparte, a fourth-floor walk-up in the rue Bonaparte. Solita described its appeal:

> Having given up our jobs, we romantically had little money . . .
> The Hotel Napoléon Bonaparte was perfect for our purposes;
> it cost a dollar a day and was near the Seine, the Louvre, and
> the auto buses. Its charms were certainly not in its amenities;
> those we built in ourselves much later . . . The top floor was
> important to us all, for next to room 20 was the hotel's unique
> bathroom, barely containing a tub and chair . . . Our ideal, all-
> purpose hotel – no domesticity, privacy for work and study, all
> delights free and within walking distance . . . [5]

ABOVE **Janet's watercolour painting of her room in the Hotel Napoléon Bonaparte in Paris.**

Here they lived together for almost two decades, until France entered the Second World War. The two women remained intimate for the rest of their lives, despite the complications – and there were many – of other partners. Janet chose Paris not only for its art and culture but also to get away from her husband, to whom she felt she had behaved criminally (she felt guilty most of her life for having married him primarily to get out of Indiana). Paris offered her the freedom to live as she wished with Solita.

The pair often appeared in costume at Natalie Barney's afternoon tea parties in the garden, or would be seen sipping cocktails with Djuna Barnes at the Café Flore or lunching with the English heiress Nancy Cunard at their favourite restaurant, La Quatrième République in the rue Jacob. Solita imagined how they must have appeared to others while offering a vivid recollection of what Janet was like at that time:

ABOVE Janet wrote on the back of this: 'Watercolour sketch I did for a wall panel as an illustration of reality, and to be painted by Gene McCowan in a projected flat in Montparnasse which I never took with Solita Solano. This idea was to be a corrective to painters who paint useless portraits of people instead of descriptions of the lives they lead.'

The combined looks of the trio must have been striking: Nancy's Egyptian head with Nefertiti's proud eyes and fine taut mouth painted scarlet . . . ; Janet, two years before she was *The New Yorker*'s Genêt and still not quite recovered from Henry James and Walter Pater, was magnetically hand-some in a way which she claimed could be seen, under the surface of her large intelligent features, that 'I'm going to look like Voltaire one day.' She was voluble from birth. Painters begged her to stop talking and sit for them . . . Janet's hands should be spoken of; they were two small rarities which served but two conscious purposes – two-fingered typing (and at what staccato speeds!) and the maintaining in awkward, practical position the ever-breathing cigarette. [6]

When Janet was not at Natalie Barney's, Café Flore or La Quatrième République, she was at the Café des Deux Magots. And it was precisely this debauched café life, and the envy it provoked in others, which landed her the job at the *New Yorker*.

Back home in New York, her friend Jane Grant loved the witty, newsy, personal letters she received from Janet, and asked Janet to write a bi-weekly letter for the magazine she and her husband Harold Ross were starting up: '"You need to get to work," I wrote, for she had declared she was going to loaf at the Deux Magots the rest of her life – maybe write a book when the spirit moved her.'[7]

The spirit had already moved her to write one book, *The Cubicle City*, a novel about New York which G.P. Putnam's Sons published in 1925. Solita was even more productive. By the time Janet had begun her *New Yorker* job in 1925, Solita had written two novels, *The Uncertain Feast* (1924) and *The Happy Failure* (1925), and was at work on a third, *This Way Up* (1926). The positive reviews which greeted her first novel give some insight into the double bind in which women writers, trying to be simply 'writers', were often trapped, even in the 'liberated' twenties. The *Paris Tribune* found that

Although written by a woman, [*The Uncertain Feast*] has not the usual feminine garrulity that makes women writers produce enormous volumes without feeling or insight. Her story is told in sharply chiseled sentences and stark evocations of moods. She has 'measure' and analysis. She stands over the corpses of emotions and dissects them without shuddering. To be sure, in the portraiture of women and their enigmatic banalities she is less successful than in the pathological

introspection of men's minds and souls. Her women always
seem slightly unreal, but when she begins to paint men, she
gives us unforgettable impressions of keen understanding. [8]

Despite such backhanded compliments, Solita's novels didn't sell well and
she was forced to resume journalism. She also attempted poetry, some of
which was published in small magazines or included in her 1934 volume,
Statue in a field, privately printed in Paris.

Janet's letter for the *New Yorker* not only replaced her own attempts
at fiction but soon overshadowed Solita's literary efforts as well. With the
creation of 'Genêt', Solita's work was henceforth divided between her own
writing and her new function as personal editor, sounding board and
literary assistant to Janet, or, as she modestly described herself fifty years
later, 'Genêt's friend, amateur sec'try and guardian of the thesaurus'.[9] Solita
later extended her unpaid editorial services to Nancy Cunard, Ernest
Hemingway and Margaret Anderson, and translated into English the poetry
of other close friends, such as Colette's protégée, Germaine Beaumont.

Janet had higher regard for fiction, yet her *oeuvre* was really
journalism, about which she seemed to be forever apologizing. In her old
age, as special guest speaker before the American Institute of Arts and
Letters annual meeting in New York, she described herself self-
denigratingly:

I must be the single mere journeyman writer who is a member
of this august national institute . . . I represent the lower class
in writing. I am only a reporter. You other writing members
are poets, novelists, historians, playwrights, literary critics,
commentators on state affairs. In any case, the gentry of writing who write books. I only write columns . . . [10]

She took to those columns 'like a duck takes to water – tentatively at first
and then with a wild abandon'.[11] She wrote a unique kind of journalism that
she hammered out and defined. She would move from the Stavisky fraud
scandal to regulations on the price of wheat, from the funeral procession of
a French historian specializing in Napoleon to a street scrimmage between
teenage Royalists and France's next Prime Minister, Leon Blum, often

within the same sentence. Not only did this give her readers a fascinating insight into how her mind worked, it made them feel present at the moment of writing. And although her style had the ease of a clever conversation, she said of it:

> It hasn't always been easy. I'm a nitpicker. Writing, contrary to what a lot of readers think, isn't just a question of knocking out words. The thoughts count just as much. So does the information and the rhythm . . . If something doesn't work, I start again from scratch – using the same thought but new words.[12]

She was a keen observer, but not at all an objective or detached one; objectivity and detachment weren't even professional aspirations. Her personality was in everything she wrote, and became more, not less, pronounced as she gained confidence as a writer. She later wrote,

> This was a new type of journalistic foreign correspondence, which I had to integrate and develop, since there was no antecedent for it. The *New Yorker*, at its beginnings, was also like an oversized minnow learning to swim. It had not yet found its style, and it was to take me some time before I began to find my own, which instinctively leaned toward comments with a critical edge, indeed a double edge, if possible. Criticism, to be valid, in my opinion, demanded a certain personal aspect or slant of the writer's mind.[13]

Her fascinating and at times highly unconventional connections between the arts, fashion, daily life and the economy ensured for her a respected and continued place in the magazine. Jane Grant remembered that, 'Her criticism of art, music, public figures, her coverage of expositions and important events were so expertly handled that her feature was soon influential in the magazine. She had established a new standard, constructed a new mold.'[14] At a time when the *New Yorker* featured a regular column, 'On and Off the Avenue: Feminine Fashions', and ran large ads for Paris hats ('straight from the Paris openings') at Macy's and

LEFT **A portrait of 'Genêt of the *New Yorker*'.**

Bamberger's department stores, Flanner would slip into her piece on Parisian fashion an unexpected aside on the exploitation of French women workers by the fashion industry. When she wrote about the expatriate experience in France, she was careful to consider the French perspective on Americans in their city, who seemed rich in a country and among a people still struggling under the financial burden of World War I.

The striking contrast between American wealth and French poverty after the war may have moved her to remind her readers of this discrepancy, or perhaps she was only thinking of her editor's admonition. Her sole guideline from the *New Yorker* was to try and get at what the French people thought, rather than focus solely on the opinions of expatriates. Janet frankly did not usually know what the French thought, even if she knew what the French press, which she perused constantly, said. She often wrote about France in her column and elsewhere with sweeping generalizations bordering on stereotype, but as she loved French culture, these generalizations are invariably harmless and usually charming:

> The French are perhaps too civilized as a rule to have much
> taste for [nature]. They largely think all trees are elms if in
> parks or willows if by water because Corot painted them like
> that and made his fortune when his far better art, his early por-
> traits, failed to sell . . . And certainly the French are not real
> bird lovers except when the bird is a quail or a pheasant, lying
> hot on its toasted canape with a watercress salad.[15]

Sometimes she gave up searching for such far-flung explanations and simply admitted to not understanding why the French were so unrelentingly French. She wrote,

> Every country eats well in some ways, in its own opinion and
> at its own table. But everyone eats better in Paris. And there is
> no explanation for this . . . There is no valid explanation why
> the French, more than anyone else for the past four hundred
> years . . . have been uninterruptedly and greatly talented in
> painting; or why for the same length of time they wrote great
> literature, or when they did not, at least wrote great French

writing, which is, of course, a different thing. These cases of protracted talent in nations are mysteries of the population and parenthood.[16]

As a participant in the French and, especially, expatriate artistic community on the Left Bank, Janet wrote regularly about its activities, and here she was on much more solid ground. As a feminist, she was particularly interested in the accomplishments of women. In 1927, when leading French filmmaker Germaine Dulac began *Schemas*, a new magazine on film and photography, Janet Flanner found it worthy of mention for her American audience. In 1929 she reported on Nancy Cunard's opening of her Hours Press; in 1933 she announced the forthcoming publication of Gertrude Stein's *Autobiography of Alice B. Toklas*; in 1935 she publicized a sale of manuscripts at Shakespeare and Company, which had fallen on hard times. Similarly she commented on the appearance of new illustrated editions of work by painter Marie Laurencin, the publication in *transition* magazine of sections from Djuna Barnes' forthcoming novel *Ryder*, and the exhibition of Marie Monnier's embroidered tapestries 'to rebuke the impatient eye' at her sister Adrienne's bookshop, La Maison des Amis des Livres.

PARIS IN BLACK AND WHITE

In April 1927, Janet Flanner reviewed an exhibition of photographs by fellow American expatriate Berenice Abbott, at the Sacre du Printemps. The exhibit included portraits of leading Modernists, including André Gide, Sylvia Beach, James Joyce, Djuna Barnes, and Jean Cocteau, which Janet Flanner cryptically called 'poetic and brief. The poet himself has been eliminated.'

Berenice Abbott had been an independent photographer for two years, having worked for Man Ray as assistant and occasional model. She brought to her photography a background in design, painting, and sculpture, as well as her apprenticeship experience. She had been especially invaluable to Man Ray in the darkroom because she had 'this knack for printing. I could feel the space in the print . . . I had an uncanny sense about developing prints.'[17] But soon she began to take photographs herself on her lunch break; mostly they were portraits of her friends – Thelma Wood, Marie Laurencin, Eileen Gray and Edna St Vincent Millay. She was averse to imposing an image on her subject and instead brought out, without romanticizing or analysing, the image created by her subjects themselves. Janet Flanner was impressed with her Modernist approach: 'The frippery of lights, false and stimulating, is not Miss Abbot's [sic] genre. Stolidly, as if almost accidentally, she arrives at a posturing of her subject so that mind and matter are clothed and balanced against a sensitive plate.'

The *Paris Tribune* ran a review of her photographs, further emphasizing their Modernist qualities:

> She is a skillful worker in black and white, using these two
> extremes with careful precision. She molds and shadows with
> the experience of an artist and the effects derived are what
> might be called 'camera-drawn studies'. In her work is
> manifested an extreme opposition to all traditional ideas and
> methods . . . she finds it necessary to represent her sensitive
> impression of the person apart from any analysis or study of
> character. Her portraits are characterized by their broad
> simplicity and their lack of attention to detail.[18]

For the use of Man Ray's studio during the lunch hour, Berenice Abbott would pay him half of any fees she collected. But her salary was so low that soon she was paying him more than he was paying her, at which point she went into business herself. She was not the only woman to apprentice with Man Ray; the American Lee Miller and the German-born Marianne Breslauer both came to Paris in 1929 and found themselves working in his studio. Marianne Breslauer photographed the city extensively, and made many portraits of artists, including Picasso and Vollard.

When Berenice Abbott and Man Ray parted ways, Bryher gave Berenice her first camera as a gift. Bryher would later write to Sylvia Beach

RIGHT Man Ray took this photograph of Berenice Abbott, which she developed.

that she 'tried always to do what [I] could for the real artists, and especially the woman artist'. Berenice Abbott was supported by Bryher in another, more indirect way, which was through Bryher's financial backing of Sylvia Beach's Shakespeare and Company. Not only were Berenice's photographs on permanent exhibition in the bookshop but, as both photographer and poet, she was represented in the little magazines sold in the shop as well. As Shakespeare and Company was the primary outlet for them, as well as the meeting point for their contributors, Sylvia rightly considered herself the 'mother' of these journals, which was no small task. For it was, in the words of Bryher, 'the moment of glory for the little reviews'.[19]

THE LITTLE REVIEW

Margaret Anderson began *The Little Review* 'because I wanted an intelligent life'. What she meant by intelligent was holding creative opinions; what she meant by art was actually ideas about art. Margaret Anderson could not find creative opinions in Indiana in 1912, just as Janet Flanner failed to a few years later. Trained as a pianist, Margaret Anderson was, in the words of Janet Flanner, 'the born enemy of convention and discipline – a feminist romantic rebel with an appetite for Chopin and for indiscriminate reading.'[20]

Margaret went first to Chicago where she landed a job as a bookshop clerk, earning eight dollars a week. On impulse and a shoestring she started *The Little Review*. Not being one to settle for second best, she was determined it would become the most important magazine in the western world. She knew nothing about publishing, not even 'that you had to read proofs when they came from the printer,' she later recalled.[21]

The first issue appeared in March 1914, and featured, among other items, a critique of 'The Cubist Literature of Gertrude Stein': ' . . . she has eliminated verbs and sentence structure entirely, flinging a succession of image-nouns at the reader. One can surely not accuse her of "prettiness".'

RIGHT **Bernice Abbott's well-known portrait of her friend Janet Flanner, wearing the top hat of Nancy Cunard's father.**

This was mild stuff compared to the third issue, published in May 1914, which scandalized Chicago by praising the ethics of the anarchist Emma Goldman, who had arrived in town for a lecture.

Margaret thrived on controversy, and launched a subscription campaign to raise funds for the next issue. She had barely enough to eat, and not enough for rent, so she moved, with her sister and her sister's two young sons, and even the volunteer office assistant, to the shores of Lake Michigan. There they staked a tent and began work on the next issue which featured the first in a series on Nietzsche. Margaret later wrote, 'Since we were a revolutionary magazine, Nietzsche was naturally our prophet.'[22] A group of 'revolutionary Nietzschean beachcombers' made good copy for the *Chicago Tribune* and the resulting publicity brought in enough subscriptions to rescue them from tent-living just before the freezing Chicago winter set in.

Margaret Anderson was impressionable and restless, intellectually as well as physically; she was by turns as interested in anarchism, feminism, or psychoanalysis as she was in art. The journal was given a more defined character once Margaret brought on Jane Heap to be the assistant editor. They promptly brought out an issue of 64 blank pages, with the pronouncement that none of the contributions was up to their standards. They were not willing to compromise with the public, having subtitled the journal 'A Magazine of the Arts, Making no Compromise with the Public Taste', and likewise would not compromise with mediocre contributors.

Jane Heap was a brilliant woman with a fascinating past. Her father headed a mental asylum in the midwest, and Jane had grown up among the patients, drawn to the interesting and instructive ways their minds worked.

In the twenties in Paris, the male Modernists, including Ezra Pound and Robert McAlmon, found Jane's overt lesbianism and male cross-dressing threatening. Margaret and Jane must have made a striking pair of contrasts, for Janet Flanner has described Margaret Anderson as 'so pretty and feminine a creature'. They also perceived their personalities as complementary – in Jane Heap's metaphor, Margaret was the buzz and Jane the sting.

Margaret and Jane and the magazine were, after a brief move to California, now settled in New York. Ezra Pound was appointed as the

European editor, a mixed blessing, it seems. He brought with him a small subsidy and a large number of manuscripts by Yeats, T. S. Eliot, Wyndham Lewis, James Joyce and himself. But at the same time he had 'designs' on the vulnerable magazine: 'I want an "official organ" (vile phrase). I mean I want a place where I and T. S. Eliot can appear once a month . . . and where Joyce can appear when he likes . . . *Definitely* a place for our regular appearance . . . '[23]

The *Paris Tribune* reported that editors Margaret Anderson and Jane Heap had been misguided,

ABOVE **Margaret Anderson;**
LEFT **Jane Heap. The buzz and the sting.**

confused and lacking in aesthetic judgment until Ezra Pound 'stepped in as European editor and his influence seems to have given *The Little Review* a sort of direction for the time being . . . '[24] It was pronouncements such as these that enabled history to distort and minimize the contributions of women to the Modernist movement. Indeed the *New York Times Literary Supplement*, reviewing a reissue of *The Little Review* in 1968, could get away with claiming that 'Pound was the only participant in *The Little Review* who knew what he was doing and had the executive force to do it.'

It was not the first magazine run by women that Ezra Pound had attempted to 'influence': he was foreign correspondent for Harriet Monroe's *Poetry Magazine*, where he published his dogma on Imagism and 'introduced' the poet H.D. He subsequently took over the English journal, the *New Freewoman*, which lost its feminist focus and changed its name to *The Egoist* within six months of Pound becoming its literary editor.

Although Pound's 'power base' at *The Little Review* enabled it to attract interesting writers, at times his affiliation also worked against them. The poet Amy Lowell felt that 'Margaret Anderson has gone over body and soul to Ezra', a charge Margaret forever denied. H.D. found Pound's behaviour at *The Little Review* reason enough to stay away, 'to keep out of the purlieus'. She had been asked by Margaret Anderson to contribute regularly but decided against it on account of Pound's involvement: 'Me thinks, for the present, we will keep entirely out.'[25]

James Joyce, however, wanted entirely in, and his epic *Ulysses* came out in 23 monthly instalments between 1918 and 1920 in *The Little Review*. The U.S. Post Office put the torch to three issues it deemed obscene, which Margaret felt was

> like a burning at the stake, as far as I was concerned. The care
> we had taken to preserve Joyce's text intact; the worry over
> the bills that accumulated when we had no advance funds;
> the technique I used on printer, bookbinder, paper houses –
> tears, prayers, hysterics, or rages – to make them push ahead
> without a guarantee of money; the addressing, wrapping,
> stamping, mailing; the excitement of anticipating the world's
> response to the literary masterpiece of our generation . . . and
> then a notice from the Post Office: BURNED.[26]

That, however, was not the end of the saga. The Committee for the Suppression of Vice, headed by a Mr Sumner, issued an injunction against the magazine on the grounds of obscenity and the women were dragged into court. Their lawyer and short-term benefactor, John Quinn, represented them in the lost cause. Or more accurately, he represented James Joyce and his literary merits, neither of which was on trial, because he felt the two women were 'damned fools' without 'an ounce of sense' for even attempting the publication of *Ulysses* in the first place. Janet Flanner later recalled that not a single newspaper printed a defence of either James Joyce or his senseless editors, for fear of being associated with the scandal. The *Paris Tribune* questioned whether Margaret Anderson and Jane Heap 'ever really understood' *Ulysses*, despite the ordeal its publication put them through. A high point in the proceedings must have been when one of the three elderly male judges assumed a chivalrous, protective attitude toward Margaret and wouldn't allow the offending passages of the novel to be read aloud in her presence – as if she had never read them herself.

Jane Heap and Margaret Anderson were fingerprinted and the magazine was fined $100. It is possible they would have fared better had Jane represented them herself, for she certainly had a persuasive way with words. On the matter of obscenity and its headmaster, Mr Sumner, she wrote: 'It was the poet, the artist, who discovered love, created the lover, made sex everything that it is beyond a function. It is the Mr Sumners who have made it an obscenity.'

Undefeated, the persistent team moved on to the less puritanical city of Paris in 1923 and carried on publishing. Francis Picabia had become their French editor the year before, but that caused no conflict since, according to Margaret, 'We had never had anything from him except a Picabia number.'[27] Margaret and Jane had found and printed leading French avant-garde writers without Picabia's help, and would continue to do so.

Ezra Pound no longer served as foreign editor; most accounts simply reported that a base in Paris alleviated the need for a European editor. But perhaps the editors, finally encountering him in person, also hastened his departure. After their first meeting, when he was 38 years old, Margaret commented that 'it will be more interesting to know him when he has grown up.'[28]

ABOVE Margaret Anderson and Jane Heap (centre, standing) met
their foreign editor Ezra Pound (far right, standing) for the first
time when they arrived in Paris. They also met Man Ray (with
camera), his model Kiki (standing behind him), Modernist poet
Mina Loy (kneeling) and filmmaker/poet Jean Cocteau (with cane),
among many others.

Margaret Anderson soon left *The Little Review* as well, but without removing her own name from the masthead. It was not the court case, the financial penalty, the negative publicity, the obscene hate letters she received, or even her impoverished existence which made her finally give it up. It was simply that she had found something new which commanded all her attention: an actress and singer named Georgette LeBlanc, who for twenty years had been the on- and off-stage leading lady for the Belgian poet and playwright, Maurice Maeterlinck.

Janet Flanner recalled, 'From the first, [the two women] formed an attachment with all the signs of permanence.'[29] The signs weren't wrong: they turned out to be inseparable until Georgette's slow, painful death from cancer twenty years later. Her *Herald Tribune* obituary in 1941 suggests Georgette had a hand in Maeterlinck's perceived genius:

> Her influence on the life and work of the Belgian poet was
> concededly profound. In recent years, since Maeterlinck's pen
> has been inactive, there has been conjecture as to whether it
> was the break with Mme LeBlanc that was responsible for the
> dimming of a talent that for thirty years had burned so brightly.

Apparently Georgette LeBlanc's own talents did not dim with the break from Maeterlinck. She continued to give concerts and poetry recitals in New York and Paris which, according to Janet Flanner, 'literally moved her listeners to tears'. For Janet, who despised Georgette's music, they might have been tears of misery, but she ignored her personal dislike and duly clarified the weepy response of Georgette's devoted audience: 'tears of pleasure, tears of tenderness'. Relying on her early professional music training, Margaret accompanied Georgette on the piano.

Whether or not Georgette LeBlanc and her piano accompanist were paid for these recitals Janet does not report, but somehow the two were no better off financially than when Margaret carried the burden of *The Little Review*. More astonishingly, their poverty did not seem to cramp their lifestyle. When Margaret wrote her memoirs, an entire volume of which she devoted to chronicling her intimate friendship with Georgette LeBlanc, she recalled, 'At this time we had less money than anyone in the world (including those who have none at all), but we spent twenty years in five of the more celestial French chateaux.'

The first of these chateaux was owned by Georgette LeBlanc's sister and her husband, and the stories Margaret Anderson told about her life there with Georgette as unpaying and unwanted family boarders would make any sane person get a job and move into humbler quarters within an hour. Instead, Georgette wrote poetry and they both became devotees – and eventually proselytizers – of the Russo-Greek mystic Georges Gurdjieff whom they had met in the early twenties. Margaret and Georgette lived intermittently for several years at Gurdjieff's chateau retreat, which counted for another of their French celestial homes. Among their successful converts to his doctrine were Jane Heap and Solita Solano. The ever-cynical Janet Flanner was never susceptible.

ABOVE **Djuna Barnes's sketch of singer Georgette LeBlanc.**

Meanwhile, Jane Heap continued on until 1929 as the sole working editor of *The Little Review*. No longer an 'official organ' for Pound, its scope broadened. It successfully avoided aligning itself with the various warring factions in the art world while giving space to many of them. Margaret Anderson felt relieved that the magazine was in Jane Heap's capable hands. For her, Jane was 'the most interesting thing that had happened to *The Little Review*. To me the expression, the formulation, of her thoughts amounted to genius.'[30]

Jane Heap used her position to help writers she believed in, and to introduce their work to editors and publishers. In particular, she was virtually the self-appointed literary agent for Gertrude Stein. In 1924, she brought Gertrude's writings to the attention of T. S. Eliot, then at *The Criterion*, an English quarterly. Having read nothing of Gertrude's writings despite her enormous output during the previous fifteen years, he was

ABOVE **Jane Heap, a formidable personality who took over the running of** *The Little Review.*

grateful to Jane for landing a manuscript on his desk. Within a year T. S. Eliot had agreed to publication and wrote to Gertrude, 'I am immensely interested in everything you write.'[31]

Many letters passed between Jane Heap and Gertrude Stein between 1923 and 1928 in which personal expressions of friendship were intermingled with business and professional concerns. In 1925, Jane Heap was deeply involved in selling Gertrude's epic, *The Making of Americans*, to an American publisher. She first tried to retrieve the original material and rights from publisher Bob McAlmon for $1000 – which she didn't have and he surely didn't need. Jane wrote to Gertrude, 'I'll get 3 Lives reprinted as well . . . God – how I have planned and worked for this – I hope it will go through.'

But it proved impossible, chiefly because of McAlmon's increasing paranoia. Jane reported a year later on why it hadn't moved forward: 'I have seen Bob several times, always drunk. When I talked to him about the book he cursed and said he knows nothing about it – . . . I had a short talk with Sylvia – Bob has told her that you are cheating him or trying to cheat him.'

For her pains, Jane was rewarded with 'J.H. Jane Heap' which Gertrude wrote in 1928:

> Jane was her name and Jane her station and Jane her nation
> and Jane her situation. Thank you for thinking of how do you
> do how do you like your two percent. Thank you for thinking
> how do you do thank you Jane thank you too thank you for
> thinking thank you for thank you. Thank you how do you.
> Thank you Jane thank you how do you do. An appreciation of
> Jane.

Gertrude wanted to write a further tribute to Jane Heap for the final issue of *The Little Review* in 1929, but Jane and Margaret (back as co-editor for the grand finale) wanted her instead to answer the questionnaire they had put to all their former contributors. The magazine folded in 1929 in part because it felt it had achieved what it set out to do: to be a voice for the renaissance in the arts which began before the First World War.

But rather than celebrate their success, the editors ended on a

ABOVE **Jane Heap and Margaret Anderson became disillusioned
with art, but here they are (last two on right) in the studio of the
sculptor Brancusi (far left) with Dadaist Tristan Tsara, an unidentified woman, and poet Mina Loy.**

disappointed note. Interested not so much in art as in ideas about art, Margaret Anderson felt that 'even the artist doesn't know what he is talking about. And I can no longer go on publishing a magazine in which no one really knows what he is talking about. It doesn't interest me.' Jane Heap was more damning of the art than the artists, who were not to blame. Rather it was the times in which they lived: 'No doubt all so-called thinking people hoped for a new order after the war. This hope was linked with the fallacy that men learn from experience. Facts prove that we learn no more from experience than from our dreams.' Her grim comments on human nature complement an equally grim assessment of the review's history: 'We have given space in *The Little Review* to 23 new systems of art (all nearly dead), representing 19 countries. In all of this we have not brought forward anything approaching a masterpiece . . . '

More than of the times they lived in or of the artists themselves, Jane and Margaret were unjustly critical of the work they themselves had done.

They had survived fifteen years of financial, legal, and artistic obstacles to publish the work of unknown writers and artists, many of whom became world-renowned. In Janet Flanner's *New Yorker* column which, after all, was read by a much larger and more mainstream public, Janet regularly reminded her readers that the work of Max Ernst and many others who were now 'newsworthy' was first seen in New York in the pages of *The Little Review*.

Jane Heap didn't care, however, about which work subsequently became famous; she cared only about whether it was a masterpiece, and that question she answered invariably in the negative. Even *Ulysses*, for which the magazine is remembered (if remembered at all), she found 'too personal, too tortured, too special a document to be a masterpiece in the true sense of the word'.

Personal and tortured perhaps, but *Ulysses* eventually became a classic. In the beginning it met with indifference, if not hostility, from *The Little Review* readers. According to Janet Flanner, it was years later, after Sylvia Beach had published *Ulysses* in book form, that Americans began smuggling a contraband copy along with their contraband liquor when they returned from Paris. 'At first, it must be admitted, the only motive was the titillation of owning something rare and illegal,' Janet recalled, and it was only later that 'there was an increasing awareness of the importance of *Ulysses* as literature'.[32]

The large body of work by women that appeared in the pages of *The Little Review* and other small magazines did not have the notoriety of *Ulysses* and therefore did not survive in print long enough to stand a chance of being discovered 'as literature'. Solita Solano, Mina Loy, Bryher, Djuna Barnes and many other women who were regularly published in the little magazines and small presses have been largely forgotten today, as Joyce's *Ulysses* might easily have been had it not attracted notice for other reasons. Solita Solano's fiction, now long forgotten, was favourably reviewed in its time, although even then a comparison with James Joyce was inevitable: 'Miss Solano is the poet of emotional crises. Over her book hovers the phenomenon of *Ulysses*. But she has forged her own style . . . kinetic . . . tremendously evocative of New York . . . the rush of the subway is in every ideation of her heroes and heroines.'[33]

Thirty years after the demise of *The Little Review*, Bryher looked through a stack of journals with faded covers and plenty of misprints, and found that they still 'blazed with vitality'. She reflected that 'there were the now famous names beside those of whom nothing more was heard' without stating the obvious: with the sole exception of Gertrude Stein it was the male names which had become famous.[34] Mina Loy, for example, was an important Modernist poet who has been totally forgotten. Perhaps because she wrote a feminist manifesto calling for women to 'leave off looking to men to find out what you are not — seek within yourselves to find out what you are', she rarely receives a single mention in memoirs and chronicles of the period, unless it is for her great beauty, or even the beauty of her daughters. Yet e.e cummings, who emulated her innovative use of spacing and broken lines, while applying them to ridiculing petty, superficial ladies or detailing his encounters with prostitutes, is read today by students everywhere. Although history has, for the most part, passed these women's writings by, they were as important in their day as the works of Ernest Hemingway, James Joyce, Ezra Pound and e.e. cummings — all of them known only by a small group of dedicated Modernists and read only within the pages of innovative, avant-garde little magazines.

CLOSE-UP AND FARTHER AWAY

Not all the little magazines were based in Paris, and not all were published by women, but both as contributors and publishers women figured significantly in the little magazine and small press movement. After Pound was dismissed from *The Little Review*, he, together with Ford Madox Ford and Ernest Hemingway, attempted to publish the short-lived *Transatlantic Review*, but it collapsed within a year. Eugene Jolas and Elliot Paul, and later Jolas and his wife Maria, ran the far more successful *transition*, which published the work of many women writers. The Black Sun Press was established in 1924 by the upper-class Bostonian Harry Crosby and his wife, Polly Jacob, who called herself Caresse. In 1929 Harry shot himself in what was apparently a suicide pact with another woman. Caresse carried on the small press work alone, printing beautiful editions of Hemingway,

William Faulkner, Kay Boyle, Max Ernst, Carl Jung, George Grosz and Dorothy Parker.

Bryher and H.D. were each involved in editing a little magazine at one time from outside Paris; H.D. 'sub-edited' *The Egoist* from London in 1916 and, a decade later, Bryher began *Close-Up* from her home in Switzerland, but the two must be counted among the Left Bank literary community because of their elaborate ties to Paris.

Bryher's position as co-editor, with Kenneth Macpherson, of *Close-Up: An International Magazine Devoted to Film Art*, was the starting point for many of her closest friendships in Paris. The magazine's subtitle was loosely interpreted, and there was always room for poetry by H.D. or stories by Gertrude Stein. Her first letters to Gertrude began rather formally:

> I have always, from the time I read 'Three Lives' and met you, valued your opinion very highly. And I look forward to seeing you again, in the autumn.

> Your manuscript arrived this morning and excited us both. It is one of the finest things you have done, I feel. There is a great feeling of depth and continuity about it, like a short but perfect novel.

BELOW Gertrude was always annoyed at Margaret Anderson for not paying *The Little Review's* writers, but Bryher made sure Gertrude was paid for her contributions to *Close-Up*.

Gertrude was impressed with the first two issues of *Close-Up* and was glad to be associated with it. Over the following years she and Alice invited H.D. and Bryher many times to their country house in Bilignin or to come and see them 'at any hour' in Paris. Although Gertrude and H.D. were embarked on very different literary endeavours, they exchanged books and, in letters to Bryher, Gertrude wrote favourably about H.D.'s writings. Bryher's closest friend in Paris was Sylvia Beach, who was of course the main, perhaps only, salesperson for *Close-Up* in Paris. But even if she hadn't been, Bryher never passed through Paris without spending time with Sylvia and Adrienne. It is in her private letters to Sylvia that the reasons for her and H.D.'s frequent distance from Paris become clear, from Bryher's perspective at least.

H.D. and Bryher each had histories with men who were extremely well-known and relatively influential among expatriates on the Left Bank and this was reason enough for H.D. and Bryher to stay away. Ezra Pound had known H.D. since 1901 when she was 16; they had been engaged to be married and subsequently involved in a tortured romantic triangle while in the United States. Pound considered H.D. his protégée, whose poetry he 'corrected' in the tearoom of the British Museum before naming her 'H.D. Imagiste' by scrawling it at the bottom of her page. The long, complicated relationship with Pound ended when H.D. married Richard Aldington in 1913, but they remained in close contact until H.D.'s death. It is not clear whether she told Pound about her true feelings for Bryher, whom Pound never liked, for H.D. shrugged off a romantic attachment. In one letter to him, she hinted that her relationship with Bryher was merely repayment for childcare services: 'Br. looked after Perdita [H.D.'s daughter] and as that seemed to be the only thing I was hanging on for . . . I looked after Br. Of course, this is all very bald . . . but I am tired of mincing matters and "pretending".'[35] It is possible that H.D. similarly downplayed her feelings for Pound to Bryher.

Bryher was attempting to divorce Robert McAlmon, who was well-known if not well-liked among writers and bartenders in Paris. Despite his own failure as a writer, he derived status by being the sole publisher on the Left Bank who didn't have to worry about financial risk, and also by being the only person James Joyce could always rely on to pay his bar tab. Both

H.D. and Bryher were disturbed by the amount of drinking that went on around Bob McAlmon and 'the Bunch', as their friends in Paris were called; for this reason they tended to avoid the city altogether. In retaliation, McAlmon would call Bryher 'a frightened rabbit' who wasn't tough enough 'to "take" Paris', which Bryher claimed was untrue. H.D. also felt that she was out of place in fashionable Parisian gatherings. She wrote to Bryher, explaining her reluctance to join her in Paris:

> (April 28, 1924) Now my dear child, don't worry. You know I love you and if I said I wanted you to go alone with the French crowd, it was only that you are young and sweet and I feel I am not elegant and enough up-to-date! But I will try not to be sly and silly. It is only that I feel démodé with elegant people.

When H.D. was in Paris a few years later without Bryher, she enjoyed being at the centre of the literary scene, to which she was introduced by Sylvia Beach and Ezra Pound. She wrote to Bryher in Switzerland, 'I do, do miss you but had no idea, I could so enjoy Paris.' She especially 'clicked' on this trip with poet and publisher Nancy Cunard, whom she had never much liked before. She described a typical day in Paris to Bryher, whom she addressed as 'Darlingest Fido':

Bryher (LEFT) was completely devoted to H.D. (ABOVE), both the woman and the poet.

I went out . . . and got a really charming lunch at a new place
I have found very much in the open opposite the Luxembourg
Gardens Medici fountain. That is nice . . . I mean finding
these places where really one would know Fido would be
content with the food and everything. I had the half of a half a
bottle of very delicious wine, I will give Dog too when he
comes . . . wrote about 20 cards, coffee and smoked while
Sorbonne students and art students trailed past and a boy
played the violin . . . It appears that the Paris better-sort group
is pro Hilda Aldington now [H.D.], I suppose the sheer under-
world is pro Arabella [Richard Aldington's new wife], anyhow
it is funny to be 'in' it again . . .

The husbands made things particularly uncomfortable for H.D. and Bryher
at times, and given the biases of English law they were difficult to divorce.
Bryher explained to Sylvia Beach,

H.D. would have long ago divorced Aldington had the proceedings been in any way decent or possible . . . I could get
the marriage [to Robert McAlmon] annulled on the grounds of
technical virginity. I don't want to bring up a lot of medical
details but shall be forced to, if R. to whom I have been consistently decent, does not do his share of getting the papers
through.

When the divorce finally did go through, on the grounds of desertion, it
meant Bryher could not be seen in Paris very often. She wrote to Sylvia on
27 March 1927, 'As I am "deserting" R. it is judged better for me not to be
around too much . . . ' That same year, she confided in Sylvia the financial
payoff he was to receive:

My father is buying back the securities settled on him, which
should give him a capital of about fifteen thousand dollars and
he will get his allowance up to the end of this year . . . This is

**RIGHT Bryher was tough enough to 'take Paris', but preferred the
shores of Cornwall, where she first met H.D., and the isles of
Scilly, from which she took her name.**

of course in confidence. I have not heard of or from him late-
ly, except for a short business letter.

Bryher had married McAlmon in order to be left alone by her enormously
wealthy family and to be free to travel with H.D. When the divorce went
through, she made a far more sensible, although initially equally
complicated, choice for her second marriage: her good friend and H.D.'s
lover, the Scottish editor and filmmaker, Kenneth Macpherson. In addition
to appeasing Bryher's family, the marriage shielded H.D. and Macpherson's
affair from H.D.'s husband Richard Aldington. Through Bryher and H.D.,
Macpherson met the writer Norman Douglas, with whom he would live for
many years in Capri.

Bryher and Kenneth Macpherson began *Close-Up* from the village of
Territet in Switzerland, where she had moved for tax purposes. There, in
1930, they built a Bauhaus villa on the shores of Lake Geneva where
Bryher lived, occasionally with Macpherson and intermittently with H.D.
throughout the next decade.

The magazine was the first ever devoted to the *art* of film, which
Macpherson emphasized was indeed an art form: 'People are still apt to
sneer when you talk of films being art . . . It has been a film industry, film
industry . . . . But we are going to talk film art at them until the right balance
is established.' Apparently people were ready to listen, because the initial
printing of 500 copies an issue sold out and had to be expanded to 5000 at
a time when other little magazines didn't reach outside their small but loyal
following.

Through Macpherson, Bryher and H.D. became interested in film
aesthetics and in filmmaking as well. Together they produced several short
films and one 'underground' style feature called *Borderline* which starred
H.D., Bryher, and Paul Robeson. But Bryher came to feel that the visual
power of film competed with her own creative powers as a writer. She
eventually lost interest, especially with the increased use of sound in the
1930s, which to her mind destroyed the cinema's development and turned
it into 'the art that died', as she called it. They ceased publishing *Close-Up*
in 1933, due largely to the introduction of sound film.

Bryher used her inherited wealth to endow other marginal artistic and

ABOVE **The aristocratic Englishwoman Nancy Cunard,
granddaughter of the founder of the famous Cunard steamship company.**

literary projects as well. She generously supported Shakespeare and
Company until its closure, at which point she sent personal cheques
directly to Sylvia. Although she wrote a number of books herself, primarily
historical novels and works about education, Bryher's foremost literary
priority throughout her life was the support and promotion of H.D.'s
creative genius. As Alice did for Gertrude, and Solita did for Janet, so
Bryher did for H.D. – she spared no expense or personal sacrifice to ensure
that H.D. was always free to write.

ABOVE **Nancy at work at her Hours Press.**

Another British woman who used her family's great wealth to underwrite literary endeavours was Nancy Cunard. Knowing nothing whatsoever about printing, she established The Hours Press at her country house in Normandy in the spring of 1928, an event which Janet Flanner publicized in the *New Yorker* as 'an item of exceptional interest to New York bibliophiles'. The *Paris Tribune* also found Nancy's activities noteworthy, and ran a long article with a comparably long title: 'Nancy, the Last of the Famous Cunarders, Steers Her Hand Press into the Stormy Literary Seas of the Montparnasse Surrealists'.

The initial publication list included *Canto* by Ezra Pound, *A Plaquette of Poems* by Iris Tree, *The Eaten Heart* by Richard Aldington, and a French translation by Louis Aragon of Lewis Carroll's *The Hunting of the Snark*, all in limited, signed editions. Nancy used a Belgian hand press with eighteenth-century type, and loved the smell of printer's ink, the feel of different paper stock, and the physical and aesthetic work of making beautiful books. According to the *Paris Tribune* announcement,

> Miss Cunard had decided that certain writings by moderns
> looked better in books than in manuscripts. So she bought a
> printing press and went to work . . . She had ideas about
> printing, in regard to type, size and form which no one seems
> to know where she learned. No doubt, they just came to her,
> as she herself did to the print shop.[36]

Nancy was one of the few heterosexual women in her tight-knit group of female friends in Paris. Bryher recalled that she was so stunning that all heads turned when she walked into a room, and even the *Paris Tribune* reported that, 'The pulse of the Inner Circle of Montparnasse is beating much faster now', since Nancy Cunard returned to the Left Bank from her country house in Normandy.

Through her relationships with men she was drawn into various campaigns and causes; her romance with French poet Louis Aragon involved her, briefly and uneasily, in the otherwise largely male Surrealist literary movement. Her subsequent, seven-year off-and-on relationship with Henry Crowder, a Black-American jazz musician in Paris, not only scandalized her upper-crust English family but introduced her to the

ABOVE Solita, Janet and Nancy were considered a 'fixed triangle', which
Nancy alluded to when she signed this photo to Janet and Solita.

'Afro-American cause', as she called it, which changed her life and started her on a path of occasionally misguided but always passionate and dedicated political activism.

Nancy's greatest literary achievement was the compiling, editing, and designing of the unprecedented anthology *Negro*, published in 1934, which consisted of 855 pages, 550 illustrations, some 150 contributors, two-thirds of whom were black, from three continents. Her greatest lost cause was the Spanish Civil War, to which she gave herself body and soul. Indeed, she never fully accepted that war *had* been lost, no doubt either a contributing symptom or a manifestation of her later loss of sanity.

Janet's 'Paris Letter' profile of Nancy was written long before her descent into alcoholism and madness, when Janet could still simply describe her as

> one of England's best, if most infrequent, poets . . . Miss
> Cunard has long been an intransigent hub of modern literary
> interests, has a small and severe collection of great modern
> paintings and an enormous collection of African art, is still
> beautiful, a tireless traveler and a remarkable letter-writer.

FRIENDSHIPS AND HOSTILITIES

Among the American, British, German and French women in the Modernist community in Paris, there were bound to be close friendships – and equally passionate animosities. Nancy Cunard, Solita Solano, and Janet Flanner formed an exceptionally close-knit family which functioned for each of them as a surrogate blood-tie for the rest of their lives. Solita described them as 'a fixed triangle' which 'survived all the spring quarrels and the sea changes of forty-two years of modern female fidelity . . . '[37] On the other hand, Margaret Anderson and Gertrude Stein quarrelled from mutual disdain; in fact, they despised each other. In *The Autobiography of Alice B. Toklas*, Gertrude admitted that 'Gertrude Stein then and always liked Jane Heap immensely, Margaret Anderson interested her much less.' Djuna Barnes also wasn't particularly keen on Margaret Anderson, whom she didn't respect, or on Gertrude Stein either, for that matter, who 'had to be the centre of everything. A monstrous ego.'[38] In virtually any group, whatever the constellation, Janet Flanner seemed to be on good terms with everyone, and it was her wide network of friends which served to link small clusters of women together into a 'community'. Even Djuna Barnes, who could be particularly acerbic, wrote affectionately to her 'dearest Jannie'.

Margaret Anderson tried to hide her immense dislike of Gertrude Stein from Janet, knowing how close the two were. She wrote the following letter, perhaps to get her annoyance about Gertrude out of her system, but refrained from mailing it to Janet:

> Gertrude and I never changed our minds about one another
> . . . I knew we could never be friends. There was something
> so *hearty* in her, and so much authority involved in the hearti-
> ness. She and Jane [Heap] 'got on' marvelously, but then Jane
> could be hearty when necessary. I can't, and I can think of no
> one whose heartiness, combined with such serious self-love
> and intensity, could repel me as much as Gertrude's . . . My
> reactions to her were like my reactions to certain music –
> 'Please don't play it in my hearing, I can't bear it.'

An interesting metaphor for Margaret to chose, for her beloved Georgette's singing had the same effect on Janet: it made her 'want to jump into the Seine'.[39]

But hiding the letter hardly meant hiding its contents, particularly from such a perceptive woman as Janet Flanner. Janet had her own misgivings about both Margaret (her 'mysticism' and lack of common sense) and Gertrude (her writings, which she often claimed not to understand), but she managed to keep such differences from overshadowing her genuine devotion to each. After their deaths, she even wrote about the animosity between Margaret and Gertrude in her *New Yorker* column, although she kept herself well out of it.

> Probably it was inevitable that Gertrude and Margaret would
> not get along, since both were outstanding egotists. Quite
> often, they would meet in a country house in Orgeval, outside
> Paris, invited by a mutual friend for Sunday lunch. In such

meetings, it was Gertrude's psychology that dominated. Gertrude talked only when she had something to say of definite interest – to herself, and thus, by extension, to her listeners, because she was intelligent and a splendid talker. Her nature was so solid that it reduced Margaret to the two opposite elements always the uppermost in her own personality – violent agreement and violent disagreement . . . The Orgeval lunches invariably developed, by the second cups of coffee which ended them, into small verbal wars. These were Margaret's particular delight, and if she was able to say, as she drew on her topcoat to go home, that she'd never had better conversation, it was her way of acknowledging that she had been involved in battles with almost everyone at the table and felt that she had triumphed in most of them.

The Orgeval gatherings were held at the home of Noel Murphy, another American woman who had been drawn to France. Noel was a singer with whom Janet fell passionately in love, an event which did not demand much change in her undomesticated domestic arrangements with Solita. Janet still shared the hotel rooms with Solita in Paris, and she and Solita retreated separately to the countryside of Orgeval – Janet to

RIGHT **Solita Solano was one of the many American women who stayed in Paris long after the stock market crashed and the 'tourists' had gone home.**

Noel Murphy, and Solita to someone else she had met, Libby Jenks Clark. Their relationship, committed as ever, opened up to accommodate new loves.

Janet started spending as much time in Orgeval as in Paris (Solita joked in 1932 that Janet 'lives with me when she remembers it'[40]) to be with Noel but also to answer her growing need for a retreat from the pressures and demands of work. In the idyllic setting of Orgeval she could think and have time to write. Janet's job remained the same in form only as the twenties gave way to the thirties.

Unlike the vast majority of male expatriates who packed up and repatriated from whence they came as rapidly as the pound or dollar fell against the franc, Gertrude Stein, Janet Flanner, Margaret Anderson, Nancy Cunard, Eileen Gray, Sylvia Beach, Djuna Barnes, Natalie Barney and most of the other expatriate women remained in France. They had no desire to leave and no place other than Paris that they could call home. The photographer Berenice Abbott was one of the few who left; returning to New York, she documented its decline during the worst years of the Great Depression.

But for those who stayed on in France, their leisurely arguments over Sunday lunch in the garden in Orgeval would soon become an impossible luxury: before the decade was out they would gather instead to huddle around the radio for news bulletins, wondering what might happen, what to do, and where to go.

While Gertrude and Janet and other friends were still lunching in the garden, Bryher had already begun using her base in Switzerland and her vast family funds to help Jewish and anti-fascist refugees escape from Germany. The first few refugees showed up in 1933, but by 1934 the exodus had grown drastically. Bryher had been in Berlin in 1932 and was horrified by the tense atmosphere and violence of the Nazis' coming to power. She believed the first-hand stories of the many refugees who came across the border, accounts far bleaker than those in the newspapers. She tried to alert journalists and politicians in other European countries, but met with insult or ridicule.

RIGHT **The beautiful American singer, Noel Murphy, with whom Janet was smitten.**

ABOVE In the 1930s, Janet retreated to Noel's house in Orgeval to
write and relax.

Nancy Cunard also became involved in the fight against fascism although on France's western rather than eastern border. She wrote continuously from Spain for numerous publications, the most respected of which was the *Manchester Guardian*, condemning the British and French governments for their lack of support for the Spanish republic. She reported passionately on the plight of Spanish refugees, started fundraising drives in England, and donated her own money to help refugees escape into France.

Janet also shifted her priorities from literature and art to politics in the thirties. She was not a correspondent from the front line; her strengths lay more in commentary than reportage. She did eventually go to the Spanish border as refugees were teaming across it, and to Nazi-controlled Austria – for a vacation, oddly enough – but found 'history looks queer when you're standing close to it.' Her more comfortable approach was to read, cull, synthesize and analyse European news for the American public, although she was frustrated that with events occurring so quickly her news was often history by the time it reached her readers.

Janet commented with typical sarcasm on the news of the 1929 stock market crash reaching Paris – 'at the Ritz bar the pretty ladies are having to pay for their cocktails themselves.' But with the departure of the American tourists who had always been good for target practice, coupled with the alarming European political events of the early thirties, Janet's style became less flippant and casual, more serious and urgent. Jane Grant at the *New Yorker* recalled, 'In 1930 she casually carried a paragraph about politics. No comment or criticism from Ross [the editor]. She became bolder.' She began to analyse the complex French political scene prior to World War II, with observations both sharp and authoritative.'[41]

In 'All Gaul is Divided', a brilliant essay written in September 1939 at Noel's house in Orgeval, Janet explained why she had shifted her interests from art to politics; why she felt it inappropriate to write about the arts when the world was in such crisis:

> The arts are peace products. Paris was at peace [in the twen-
> ties] and its arts flourished . . . Certainly when men are fright-
> ened of having their bodies dismembered in a war is no
> moment to inquire, as they start running for cannons, 'Are you

still fond of Picasso's blue period' or 'Do you think Proust's works so bourgeois that they cannot survive?'

Janet was not by nature a radical, nor did she, initially, hold strong political views beyond a passion for justice. Yet she pushed herself to become an authority on European politics as dangerous economic and political forces battled their way through the thirties, and she was radicalized in the process. Although she despaired of her own ignorance, the breadth of her knowledge, from which she culled her references, and the sharpness of her mind which produced clever, often brilliant, associations, made Janet Flanner more than a 'mere' journalist. Rather, she was the confident, intelligent voice of her generation.

Like the rest of that generation, however, she was slow to realize the extent to which the Nazis were becoming a genuine threat to western civilization. Her profile of Hitler in 1936 comments on his penchants for music and picnic lunches, his unphotogenic appearance and the physical acrobatics required by the 'Heil Hitler' salute. Her tone was politically noncommittal, portraying him as pathetic and foolish rather than dangerous.

When Berlin put on its best face for the 1936 Olympic Games, Janet went with Noel Murphy to cover it for the *New Yorker*. The massive propaganda strategy behind the Olympics was successful, and Janet, like many other foreign visitors, was impressed with the dazzling pageantry and German organizational skills. She reported on forthcoming changes anticipated in Germany, among them an undertaking she didn't find unreasonable: 'a redistribution of real estate, now valuable for the first time since the inflation, and, in Berlin especially, still owned by non-Aryans.' Finding the Nazi regime now into its 'adult stride', she seemed to miss the ominous meaning behind her own words: 'Only a determined deaf-and-blind visitor to any corner of this land could fail to see and hear the sight, the sound, of Germany's forward march.'

But the vast majority of the world did fail to see and hear. Bryher herself took evidence to the government and the press in England which, with the one exception of the *Manchester Guardian*, would invariably dismiss it on the grounds of it being too controversial or against the

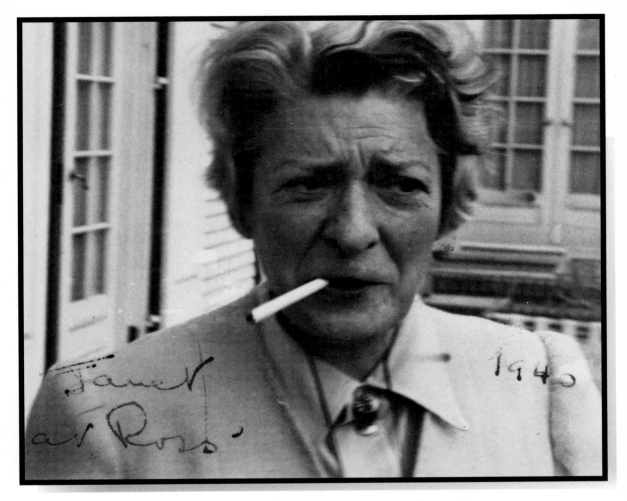

Janet as Ross

1940

ABOVE **Over the years, Janet slowly developed into the confident, intelligent voice of her generation.**

government's policy with Germany at the time. In fact, she would often use copies of *The Times* to hide documents she was smuggling into Germany for refugee visas, so pro-Nazi was the newspaper that the German officials rarely bothered anyone carrying it into the country. Bryher felt sure that the Nazi regime would have collapsed in its infancy had Europe responded swiftly and strongly to its persecution of its own people. Because it hadn't, she remained ashamed of her country for the rest of her life.

As if to justify her own lack of foresight, Janet Flanner later looked back from the brink of war in France to discern how the grim situation had come about under everyone's eyes:

> The scene did not really grow grave until the middle of the
> 1930's. The acts of transition that led to the change were vari-
> ous, slow, insensible, incredible, and in no special instance,
> except by a morbid fortune teller, could their eventually rapid
> melodramatic outcome have been foretold. Indeed much of
> what has happened to Europe in the past five years looks as if
> it had been seen darkly through a glass and by a complicated
> Cassandra.

If Janet was not a morbid fortune teller, she did at least see the present moment as clearly as just about anyone, and for the most part her interpretation was right on target. She may have been slow in waking up to the Nazi threat, but when she did, she was fully alert. According to Shari Benstock,

> That her perceptions of the moment still agree with history's
> assessment of this era suggests a *déjà vu* effect, as though her
> commentaries derived their impetus from a later perspective.
> History has rarely proven her wrong in the analysis of artistic
> movements or political developments.[42]

The political developments she lived through and wrote so passionately and intelligently about began to take such bizarre turns as the decade progressed that she felt as though she had come full circle in her writing to where she had begun: with fiction. In her old age, she wrote about this irony:

> I had in my early twenties meant to be a very superior young
> novelist. I actually wrote a novel, before I started writing for
> Ross. Virgil Thomson – who then lived in Paris finally asked
> me to let him read it . . . [he said] I did not seem to have as
> much talent for fiction as for wishing to write . . . In any case,
> European and French politics had started developing their
> appalling capacity for sounding like fiction, for sounding like
> horrifying thrillers . . . For someone like me who had failed to

write novels, because I lacked the creative parthenogenetical gift of being able to image fiction, as a form of self-fertilization within my own mind, I was well supplied as a journalistic reporter by what happened to millions who could not help themselves against such history . . . There have been many times, in my reporting for the 'Letter from Paris' for the *New Yorker* during these last seven or eight years, when it felt as if I were indeed writing fiction. This is my great recompense.[43]

ABOVE **As a war correspondent, Janet Flanner sometimes felt as though she were writing fiction.**

EPILOGUE

The occupation of Paris by the German army in June 1940 put an end to the French and expatriate community of women on the Left Bank. Those who had developed full, independent lives in Paris were reluctant to leave, yet they were forced to scatter and retreat. No longer a woman, Paris barely had any human qualities left at all. The city's soul, according to Janet Flanner, had been put up 'for sale for German cash'.

Perhaps it was just as well that many of the expatriates did not see their beloved city in this sad condition. Janet Flanner felt that 'anybody who loved Paris and grieves at its plight is fortunate not to see it now because Paris would seem hateful.'[1] Some fled to parts of the country not yet occupied; others swiftly escaped from France altogether. Late one afternoon in June 1940, Gisèle Freund was warned by friends to leave Paris immediately, and by morning she had become a refugee for the second time. Taking only her bicycle, she boarded a train for the south of France, where she expected to stay only a few months. She later departed for Argentina, and wasn't to return to France until after the liberation. Adrienne noted the timetable in her 'Occupation Journal', hiding her emotions behind stony silence: 'Morning at 7:40 departure Gisèle Gare d'Austerlitz. Rose at 5:00, alert at 5:10. Came back from station on foot, passing in front of Saint-Geneviève.'[2]

Of the French women, most stayed and managed to eke out an existence. Colette wrote 'To Those Who Stay in Paris' for *Paris-Soir*, and explained that 'every time there is a war, I spend it in Paris. First you have to stock up on coal, and don't forget the potatoes . . . You need a lot of

ABOVE AND PREVIOUS PAGE 'Anybody who loved Paris . . . is fortunate not to see it now.' When Sylvia and Adrienne looked out at their beloved *arrondissement* under the Occupation, they could hardly believe their eyes.

wool sweaters to wear in the cellar during alerts.'[3] Her friend Adrienne Monnier, having no other source of income, kept her shop open throughout the war. Despite pressure from family, friends, and the American government, Sylvia Beach would not consider leaving her behind. A few days before the Germans entered Paris, she wrote to Bryher,

> . . . A certain number of persons have gone away to what
> they hope will be bomb-proof country. My friend in Jersey
> wants me to spend the rest of the war with her there. My
> father suggests returning to the U.S.A. . . . But as far as I can

ABOVE **Gisèle Freund's self-portrait, taken in Mexico after the war.**

see, I belong here and would only be gloomy elsewhere . . .
[Adrienne] is now wrestling with the new No. of the Gazette
which is to appear any minute . . . and I'm sure readers will
be joyful to have it to read war or no war, and I think they will
be quite reassured by the continuation of such things in the
midst of trouble.

The continuation of such things did not include Sylvia's bookshop which she had suddenly closed down after being threatened by a German officer. She managed to endure daily life in occupied Paris until August 1942, when a German truck showed up to collect her and carry her off to an internment camp in eastern France. There she remained for over six months with other American and British women who defied their governments' requests to leave the country.

Although they shared a loyalty to Paris and a deep sadness about its condition, the female Modernists were divided in their response to the war. Some were committed anti-fascists and worked in the Resistance; some saw fascism and communism as equally patriarchal and authoritarian; and a few even sympathized with the fascist cause. Colette claimed that she took her 'humble place among those who did nothing except wait.'[4] Actually she appealed to anyone who would listen, including numerous Nazis and their French collaborators, as she sought to find, and then secure the release of, her Jewish husband, Maurice Goudeker, who was arrested in 1941. Gertrude Stein, who had served as an ambulance driver in France during the First World War, wrote to Janet Flanner, 'neither we nor Noel [Murphy] are going to go to war. England and France could do as they wished.'

As the Germans invaded France, Janet Flanner and Solita Solano left Noel Murphy on her farm in Orgeval and set sail for New York. Noel survived from her garden vegetables and a false identity card which gave her an Irish name but French nationality. It is possible she was a Nazi collaborator, as some people accused her of being, although Janet herself refused to believe it. Noel also spent five months in the same detention centre as Sylvia Beach.

Hemingway showed up with a BBC crew to 'liberate' his favourite street, rue de l'Odéon, right after Germany surrendered Paris. He had the nerve to ask Adrienne Monnier, who loved good food, how she managed to survive without some sort of collaboration with the Nazis. By way of reply, she hinted that there are many ways of carrying out sabotage.

Janet Flanner, Bryher, and Nancy Cunard were also anti-fascist and, not being French, could afford to be more vocal about it than Adrienne Monnier. Nancy Cunard had initially retreated to Santiago and Mexico City at the outbreak of war, but when France fell to the Germans, she headed

ABOVE **The war took its physical toll on Noel Murphy (left), and Janet Flanner was shocked when she first saw her again after the liberation.**

RIGHT **War correspondents Janet Flanner and Ernest Hemingway, at their regular table in the Café des Deux Magots.**

back to Europe (something easier said than done at that time) to do what she could. She considered it 'my war too – insofar as it is (if only partly) against Fascism.'[5] From London she worked with Free French organizations, translated a book on the French Resistance, and compiled an anthology of poetry, *Poems for France*, which was published in 1944.

Bryher, as already noted, contributed not only her family wealth but also her own efforts to the Resistance by helping German Jews and radicals escape through Switzerland.

She felt she did no more than any human being who believed in morality would do, by saving over a hundred lives before having to flee herself. Of all the people she helped, only two did not make it to safety; one of these was the writer and philosopher Walter Benjamin, who was stopped at the Spanish border and took his own life. In 1940, Bryher escaped at zero hour across the Swiss border and back to London, in the midst of the Blitz. There she lived out the rest of the war with H.D. and their daughter Perdita.

Janet Flanner knew it was time to leave when her 'Letter from Paris' was censored in October 1939. Shari Benstock describes her departure from Paris as marking the end of the era:

> Janet Flanner was one of the last to leave, and when she fled
> Paris on the afternoon of 4 October 1939, she ran from
> encroaching darkness augured by the sounds of military air-
> craft and marching armies. The door of the culture she helped
> to create on the Paris Left Bank closed behind her.[6]

New York, London, Territet in Switzerland; Fiesole in Italy; Bilignin in France; Santiago, Buenos Aires, Mexico City – from these as well as other settings, their friendships persisted across the distances. Rarely could correspondence get through, and when it did, as with Natalie Barney's letters to Gertrude and Alice, the censorship prevented much from being said or read. More often friends relied on word of mouth, and in the absence of any news, blind faith. Bryher afterwards wrote

> of the joy H.D. and I had felt when a letter from [Sylvia
> Beach] had reached us in London after five years of silence, it
> seemed impossible that it could fall on the floor with a news-
> paper, a bill and some unimportant trifles, with your own
> handwriting on the envelope.[7]

It seems equally impossible that Janet Flanner, as a war correspondent, found time to read Gertrude Stein's *Paris France*, yet it was important enough to her that she managed to write some encouraging words to Gertrude about it, and review it in the *New Yorker*.

Sylvia celebrated the liberation of Paris by flying an American flag outside her window, and by writing a letter to Bryher 'after five years of silence'.

Dear Gertrude,

It's a *fine* book, full of just that sort of sense you have for things other people make nonsense out of – I enjoyed reading it very much . . . and have found it very fertilizing, it gives me new notions about many things . . .

Gertrude and Alice escaped to their summer house in Bilignin, American Jews defying the Nazi occupiers despite pleas from the American embassy to flee from France altogether. They received a letter there from Janet Flanner, instructing them that both of you must stay there with rocks and fresh eggs and air and Basket as long as possible – Love to you both, indeed all three [though I know Basket only slightly –] And my very sincere thanks – Yours Faithfully Janet

If Janet felt that Gertrude and Alice and their new poodle (named Basket as the first had been) were in idyllic retreat from the war, Gertrude and Alice themselves felt they were living through the war's darkest days, and that it was Janet who was in retreat. Upon receiving Janet's book review, Gertrude wrote to her in New York:

ABOVE *Life* magazine reported on the reunion of Americans Sylvia Beach, Janet Flanner and Ernest Hemingway upon the liberation of Paris.

Some one just sent me your review of Paris France and it is a beautiful review and has pleased me enormously, and thanks and thanks again, you know Janet even in the darkest days we talked about you, I used to say and it was only three days ago that I was saying it again, I am so sorry Janet was not in France for it all, she would have liked being here and Alice always answered, perhaps she would not have liked it at all and then we argued, well Janet, what is the answer. Oh Janet, someday well not too far away, you and Noel will come and spend that promised week and we could tell you so much. When are you coming back, well until you do come back Alice and I will continue to argue whether you would have liked being here or whether you would not have liked being here, bless you, come back to us soon and thanks and thanks again for the perfect review, lots of love from us both, always Gtde.

'Come back to us soon' is the refrain of the many letters written between friends divided by war. Returning from Italy, where she and Romaine Brooks sympathized with Mussolini, held anti-semitic views, and sun-bathed in trenches to avoid being spotted by aircraft, Natalie Barney wrote to Gertrude and Alice in Bilignin:

> Dear Gertrude and Alice dear, . . . I have dreamed of getting
> back to our old quarter so long, that, like a somnambulist, I
> shall find my way to your door, and see the doves of your
> bedroom flutter, and the easy chairs contain us as before, and
> your portrait seating you above us, looks down; uniting past
> and present to whatever future we have yet to live through –
> may it be in Paris . . .
>
> Love, Natalie and my friend Romaine

Gertrude did not have much future left, although she did live it through in Paris. She died of cancer in 1946, a year after the war ended. Devastated, Alice wrote, 'I wish to God we had gone together as I always so fatuously thought we would – a bomb – a shipwreck – just anything but this.'[8]

Natalie's condolences acknowledged the importance of Alice's work to Gertrude's career:

> Ah Alice what can I send you now? No words can match such
> a loss . . . Perhaps her works, which you will continue later
> on, may bring a feeling of accomplishing those duties which
> you have always filled to the utmost . . . I can never separate
> you from Gertrude nor Gertrude from you. So let her remain
> there ever between us uniting us more closely than ever . . .

The close network of friends kept each other informed of Alice's daily trials and tribulations in 'staying on alone'. Sylvia reported to Bryher about such mundane difficulties as what to do about the animals:

> [July 9th, 1947] Alice Toklas came to see me one day. She
> said she was so glad to hear Bryher was coming to Paris . . .
> Basket pulls too hard when she takes him for walks. He had a
> fit of jealousy when she took in a cat, and got eczema, the vet

said entirely on account of the cat. He refused to come into
the salon any more until Alice got rid of the cat . . . With
much love dear Bryher . . . Please give my love to H.D.

On many days, however, Alice had more substantial causes for despair. When Picasso's painting of Gertrude was collected for the Metropolitan Museum in New York, and Picasso came by to say farewell to it, 'It was another parting and completely undid me.'[9]

What became of the rest of Gertrude and Alice's art collection is a sad, often repeated story. Since Gertrude and Alice had of course no legal connection, Gertrude's nephew's children contested Alice's right to the collection, bought for virtually nothing but by now valued at over six million dollars. Without the paintings, one or two of which she could decide to part with *in extremis*, Alice did not have enough cash for her daily expenses. Janet called upon mutual old friends and created and administered a fund for Alice's support. She wrote to a friend, 'It drives me mad that Alice is driven to the generous charity of her friends when she is in reality an HEIRESS – ' Publicly she wrote about the fate of these famous paintings, perhaps in the hope that other contributors would come forward. But when Margaret Anderson mentioned to Janet that 'you gave so many interesting details about Gertrude's will that I suppose you were swamped with appreciative letters,' Janet replied, 'Not at all, not one. No one seemed to care.'

Readers of the *New Yorker* may not have cared, but Alice's friends certainly did. Thorton Wilder, Bryher, and Janet Flanner herself were among those who supported Alice in her old age, after she could no longer afford to write such proud letters as she had in 1956: 'So, dear Bryher, I am returning your cheque but keeping as a lovely gift your thought in sending it.'

Gertrude's was the first in a long string of deaths, stretched across four decades, which interrupted these extraordinary friendships. Adrienne Monnier was the next to go; plagued by maddening, unrelenting sounds in

LEFT **Natalie Barney longed to get back to Paris and see the doves
of Gertrude's bedroom flutter, but they were actually pigeons on
the grass, alas.**

ABOVE **Janet wrote on the back of this photo: 'The most widowed woman I know. I said this to Alice the first time I saw her after Gertrude's death.'**

her ears, she took her own life in 1955. Although Sylvia was glad that Adrienne had finally found peace and quiet, she wrote to Bryher, 'it is very hard for me who have lost Adrienne who was everything in my life . . .' Like Alice's hopes for a bomb or a shipwreck that would have taken them both, Sylvia too 'would have liked so much to have left at the same time as Adrienne,' which Adrienne had proposed, knowing how hard it would be for Sylvia without her. The rue de l'Odéon which had been her home for so many decades 'might be anywhere else with Adrienne gone – everything gone. Surgical instruments in Shakespeare & Company now and preferably at the Amis des Livres as well.'

Bryher responded with messages of comfort and love, but found herself next on the receiving end of the condolences. H.D. had a stroke and passed away three months later. Alice wrote to Bryher soon after:

> The other evening I hobbled to a lecture . . . and there spoke
> for a moment to Sylvia. When I asked her for news of you and
> H.D. she told me [of] H.D.'s death. It was inexpressibly sad
> for me . . . Nothing will replace for you the wonderful person
> she was . . . My deep sympathy, dear Bryher, and affectionate
> appreciation. Alice.

The one person who outlived all the rest was the isolated and embittered Djuna Barnes, who marked each death as 'one more nail in our own coffins'.[10] Back in New York, she saw no one, not even her beloved Thelma

BELOW Thelma and Djuna: still tortured forty years later.

THELMA WOOD
FAN HILL ROAD
MONROE, CONNECTICUT

April 14th 1969

darling, should have sent the photographs
earlier, but anything to do with us bothers
me, the pain is so unequal that i just natually
avoid it when possible, its been so long a time
too its too much. i have kept the pictures i
love and that belong to me alone.

i have a trembly right hand so the typing,
no hangover havent had a drink about ten years —
spring is here but as rachel carson said it is
silent, the people have taken everything.

i love you as always.

Thelma

Wood, although they spoke occasionally on the phone. In 1964, Djuna wrote of Thelma, '"Still beautiful?" I hear not, how can one be at 62. I think she has gained weight, wears glasses, and has white in her hair; poor child, she never knew such things could happen to her.'[11] Thelma developed cancer of the spine and spent her final years bedridden. Berenice Abbott had stayed in touch with Thelma throughout the decades and visited her just before her death which, Berenice reported, she met bravely and philosophically.

Djuna Barnes admitted that they were in 'the winter of our world' but she was not one to fall back on nostalgia. If she expressed any regrets, they were not sentimental ones. She wrote to Solita Solano in 1951, 'Sometimes I think I have made a mistake in this matter of "all for art" and nothing whatsoever for money.' When *The Little Review* was reprinted as a book in the late sixties, Djuna was not concerned with drawing public attention to the 'lost masterpieces' of the era or even with seeing something of hers back in print long after she had been forgotten. She wrote to Solita about potential royalties:

> . . . I see that the *Little Review* has been reprinted by some
> crook (that's what they are) in toto, and gather that no author
> has seen so much as the thin side of a dime for their part in it?
> Will you ask Margaret about this?
> . . . This is one of these upstart publishers tricks.

Djuna Barnes was not the only one to remain true to form as she grew older. At the age of 90, Natalie Barney still persisted with her lifelong cause, that of bringing recognition to the work of the many women artists and writers who were her friends. She wrote to Janet Flanner in 1967 as though it were still 1927, asking if she would write something in the *New Yorker* about the paintings of Romaine Brooks.

But if Natalie's role hadn't changed, Janet's certainly had: just as she had reported on and publicized the activities of her dear friends in the pre-war years, now with the passing decades she became the chronicler of their deaths. One by one, she paid posthumous respects to each in the pages of the *New Yorker*, rarely revealing how much her own life must have been diminished by each loss.

ABOVE **Old friends Sylvia Beach (right) and Bryher in 1959, at an
exhibit on Paris in the twenties, based on Sylvia's personal possessions.**

Her public letters are staggering evidence of the contributions this
extraordinary group of women, singly and together, made to western culture. But it is the private letters, both sent and received, that document the
vital, tenacious web of friendships, spun long ago in Paris. These friendships, sparked by something so intangible as the promise of Paris at a particular moment in history, made it possible for them to create the cultural
legacy they have left for us. Fifteen years after Gertrude's death, Alice sent
Janet Flanner and Solita Solano a postcard: 'My dearest dears . . . Paris and
the French still seduce me . . . Love love love Alice.'

N O T E S :

INTRODUCTION : PARIS WAS A WOMAN

1. Frederic Lefèvre, quoted in the *Paris Tribune* (8 June 1924), reprinted in Hugh Ford, ed., *The Left Bank Revisited: Selections from the Paris Tribune 1917–1934* (University Park: Penn State University Press, 1972), p. 96.

2. Bryher, *The Heart to Artemis* (London: Collins, 1963), p. 226.

3. Andrew Field, *Djuna: The Life and Times of Djuna Barnes* (New York: Putnam, 1983), pp. 133–134.

4. Gertrude Stein, *Everybody's Autobiography* (New York: Vintage Press 1973), pp. 102-103.

5. Katherine Anne Porter, 'Gertrude Stein: A Self-Portrait,' *Harper's Magazine* 195 (December 1947): 522.

6. Jessie Fausset, *Paris Tribune* (1 February 1923), reprinted in Hugh Ford, ed., *The Left Bank Revisited*, op. cit., pp. 47–48.

7. From a letter written by Gertrude Stein in 1939 to Gotham Book Mart's owner Miss Steloff in New York, who published it in her bookstore catalogue.

CHAPTER 1: ODÉONIA: THE COUNTRY OF BOOKS

1. Adrienne Monnier, 'Souvenirs de l'autre guerre,' *The Very Rich Hours of Adrienne Monnier: An Intimate Portrait of the Literary and Artistic Life in Paris Between the Wars*, translated, with an introduction and commentaries, by Richard McDougall (New York: Charles Scribners & Sons, 1976), p.11.

2. Janet Flanner, 'The Infinite Pleasure: Sylvia Beach,' *Janet Flanner's World: Uncollected Writings 1932–1975* (New York and London: Harcourt Brace Jovanovich, 1979), p. 310.

3. Noel Riley Fitch, *Sylvia Beach and the Lost Generation: A History of Literary Paris in the Twenties and Thirties* (New York and London: W.W. Norton and Co., 1983), p. 11.

4. Sylvia Beach, *Shakespeare and Company* (New York: Harcourt, Brace and Co., 1956), p. 16.

5. Adrienne Monnier, 'Memorial de la rue de l'Odéon,' quoted in *The Very Rich Hours of Adrienne Monnier*, op. cit., p. 40.

6. Katherine Anne Porter to Sylvia Beach, 6 February 1956, published in *Sylvia Beach: 1887–1962* (Paris: Mercure de France, 1963), p. 154.

7. Sylvia Beach, *Shakespeare and Company*, op. cit., p. 47.

8. Sergei M. Eisenstein to Sylvia Beach, December 11, 1933, published in *Sylvia Beach: 1887–1962*, op. cit., p. 125.

9. Sylvia Beach to Bryher, 13 January 1936, in the Bryher collection of the Beinecke Rare Book and Manuscript Library, Yale University.

10. Quoted in Noel Riley Fitch, *Sylvia Beach and the Lost Generation*, op. cit., p. 25.

11. Janet Flanner, 'The Great Amateur Publisher,' *Sylvia Beach: 1887–1962* op. cit., p. 48.

12. Sylvia Beach, *Shakespeare and Company*, op. cit., p. 27.

13. Bryher, 'For Sylvia,' *Sylvia Beach: 1887–1962*, op. cit., p. 18.

14. Bryher, *The Heart to Artemis* (London: Collins, 1963), p. 211.

15. Sylvia Beach, 'A Letter to Bryher' written for Bryher's birthday in 1950. Bryher collection, Beinecke Rare Book and Manuscript Library, Yale University.

16. Jules Romains, quoted in Adrienne Monnier, *The Very Rich Hours of Adrienne Monnier*, op. cit., p. 14.

17. Interview with Gisèle Freund, June 1992, for the *Paris Was a Woman* film project.

18. Adrienne Monnier, 'In the Country of Faces,' *The Very Rich Hours of Adrienne Monnier*, op. cit., pp. 231–232.

19. Simone de Beauvoir, preface to Gisèle Freund, *James Joyce in Paris*, quoted in Adrienne Monnier, *The Very Rich Hours of Adrienne Monnier*, ibid., p. 491.

20. Sylvia Beach to Bryher, September 21, 1935, in the Bryher collection, Beinecke Rare Book and Manuscript Library, Yale University.

21. Sylvia Beach, *Shakespeare and Company*, op. cit., p. 29.

22. Bryher, *The Heart to Artemis*, op. cit., p. 211.

23. Sylvia Beach, quoted in Jackson Matthews, 'My Sylvia Beach,' *Sylvia Beach 1887–1962*, op. cit., p. 25.

24. Janet Flanner, 'The Infinite Pleasure: Sylvia Beach,' *Janet Flanner's World: Uncollected Writings 1932–1975*, op. cit., p. 309.

25. Jackson Matthews, 'My Sylvia Beach,' *Sylvia Beach: 1887–1962*, op. cit., p. 26.

26. Sylvia Beach, *Shakespeare and Company*, op. cit., pp. 58 and 88.

27. Janet Flanner, 'The Great Amateur Publisher,' *Sylvia Beach: 1887–1962*, op. cit., 46–51.

28. James Joyce, quoted in Noel Riley Fitch, *Sylvia Beach and the Lost Generation*, op. cit., p. 328.

29. Sylvia Beach, *Shakespeare and Company*, op. cit., pp. 58–60.

30. Interview with Sam Steward, July 1992, for the *Paris Was a Woman* film project.

31. Interview with Gisèle Freund, June 1992, for the *Paris Was a Woman* film project.

32. Sylvia Beach to Holly Beach, quoted in Noel Riley Fitch, *Sylvia Beach and the Lost Generation*, op. cit., p. 318.

33. Robert McAlmon to Gertrude Stein, in the Stein collection, Beinecke Rare Book and Manuscript Library, Yale University.

34. T. S. Eliot, 'Miss Sylvia Beach,' *Sylvia Beach: 1887–1962*, op. cit., p. 9.

35. Interview with Gisèle Freund, June 1992, for the *Paris Was a Woman* film project.

36. Jean Amrouche, quoted in Adrienne Monnier, *The Very Rich Hours of Adrienne Monnier*, op. cit., pp. 60–61.

37. Shari Benstock, *Women of the Left Bank* (Austin: University of Texas Press, 1986 and London: Virago Press, 1987), p. 228.

38. Bryher, *The Heart to Artemis*, op. cit., p. 213.

39. Janet Flanner, 'The Infinite Pleasure,' *Janet Flanner's World*, op. cit., p. 314.

40. Sylvia Beach, *Shakespeare and Company*, op. cit., p. 215.

CHAPTER 2: THE WRITER AND HER MUSE

All quotes from letters not listed below are to be found in the Gertrude Stein collection, Beinecke Rare Book and Manuscript Library of Yale University.

1. Alice B. Toklas, *What is Remembered* (New York: Holt, Rinehart and Winston, 1963), p. 23. Also, Alice B. Toklas, interviewed by Roland E. Duncan, Paris, November 1952. Audiotape in the Bancroft Library, University of California at Berkeley.

2. Katherine Anne Porter, 'Gertrude Stein: A Self-Portrait,' *Harper's Magazine* 195 (December 1947): 519.

3. Janet Flanner, 'Introduction: Frame For Some Portraits,' *Two: Gertrude Stein and Her*

Brother and Other Early Portraits [1908–1912]: Volume One of the Yale Edition of the Unpublished Writings of Gertrude Stein (New Haven: Yale University Press, 1951), p. x.

4. Catharine R. Stimpson, 'Gertrice/Altrude: Stein, Toklas, and the Paradox of the Happy Marriage,' *Mothering the Mind: Twelve Studies of Writers and Their Silent Partners,* eds. Ruth Perry and Martine Watson Brownley (New York and London: Holmes and Meir, 1984), p. 126.

5. Natalie Clifford Barney, 'Foreword', *As Fine as Melanctha: Volume Four of the Yale Edition of the Unpublished Writings of Gertrude Stein* (New Haven: Yale University Press, 1954).

6. Gertrude Stein, *Everybody's Autobiography* (New York: Vintage Press, 1973), p.87.

7. Catharine R. Stimpson, 'Gertrice/Altrude: Stein, Toklas, and the Paradox of the Happy Marriage,' op. cit., p. 133.

8. Judy Grahn, *Really Reading Gertrude Stein* (Freedom: The Crossing Press, 1989), pp. 6–7.

9. Natalie Clifford Barney, 'Foreword', *As Fine As Melanctha,* op. cit.

10. Bryher, *The Heart to Artemis* (London: Collins, 1963), p. 215.

11. William Carlos Williams, 'MANIFESTO: in the form of a criticism of the works of Gertrude Stein,' manuscript in the Stein collection, Beinecke Rare Book and Manuscript Library, Yale University.

12. Bryher, *The Heart to Artemis,* op. cit., p. 208.

13. Pavel Tchelitchew, Martin A. Ryerson Lecture on Gertrude Stein, 20 February 1961 at the Yale Gallery of Fine Arts. This quote is from the transcript of the audiotape, Stein collection, Beinecke Rare Book and Manuscript Library, Yale University.

14. Janet Flanner, 'Foreword: Frame For Some Portraits,' op. cit., p. xvi.

15. Alice B. Toklas, *What is Remembered,* op. cit., p. 136.

16. Janet Flanner, *An American in Paris: Profile of an Interlude between Two Wars* (London: Hamish Hamilton, 1940), pp. 83-84.

17. Pavel Tchelitchew, Martin A. Ryerson Lecture, op. cit.

18. Undated letter from Gertrude Stein to a Miss Clair who had asked for biographical information in preparation for the publication of *Tender Buttons.*

19. Janet Flanner, 'Introduction: Frame For Some Portraits,' op. cit., p. xi.

20. Janet Flanner, 'Paris in the Twenties,' CBS Television, broadcast date 17 April 1960.

21. Sylvia Beach, *Shakespeare and Company* (New York: Harcourt, Brace and Co., 1956), p. 31.

22. Natalie Clifford Barney, 'Foreword', *As Fine as Melanctha.* Reprinted in Linda Simon, ed., *Gertrude Stein Remembered* (Lincoln: University of Nebraska Press, 1994), p. 30.

23. Pavel Tchelitchew, Martin A. Ryerson Lecture, op. cit.

24. Interview with Samuel Steward, July 1992, for the *Paris Was a Woman* film project.

25. Samuel Putnam, *Paris Was Our Mistress* (New York: Viking Press, 1947), p. 136.

26. John Richardson, 'Picasso and Gertrude Stein: Mano a Mano, Tête-à-Tête,' *The New York Times* (10 February 1991): 36.

27. Pavel Tchelitchew, Martin A. Ryerson Lecture, op. cit.

28. Gertrude Stein, interviewed at Colombia University on NBC Radio, November 12, 1934.

29. Alice B. Toklas, interviewed by Roland E. Duncan, Paris, November 1952.

30. Richard Wright, 'Gertrude Stein's story is drenched in Hitler's horrors,' *PM Magazine* (11 March 1945).

31. Jacqueline Morreau, 'Introduction' to Gertrude Stein, *Wars I Have Seen* (London: Brilliance Books, 1984), p. xiv.

32. Alice B. Toklas, interviewed by Roland E. Duncan, Paris, November 1952.

33. Virgil Thomson, 'A Portrait of Gertrude Stein,' *A Virgil Thomson Reader* (Boston: Houghton Mifflin Co., 1981), p. 75.

34. Katherine Anne Porter, 'Gertrude Stein: A Self-Portrait,' op. cit., p. 527.

35. Janet Flanner, 'Paris in the Twenties,' CBS Television, broadcast 17 April 1960.

36. Gertrude Stein, *Everybody's Autobiography*, op. cit., p.47.

37. Janet Flanner, 'Introduction: Frame For Some Portraits,' op. cit., p. xii.

38. Gertrude Stein, in Peter Neagoe, ed., *Americans Abroad* (The Hague: The Servire Press, 1932), p. 418.

39. Alice B. Toklas, interviewed by Roland E. Duncan, Paris, November 1952.

CHAPTER 3: *AMAZONES ET SIRÈNES*

All quotes by Natalie Barney not identified below are from her unpublished autobiography, *Memoirs of a European American*, in the Fonds Littéraire Jacques Doucet. All letters to her not identified below are housed in the Doucet collection; all other unidentified letters in this chapter can be found in the Stein collection, Beinecke Rare Book and Manuscript Library, Yale University.

1. George Wickes, *The Amazon of Letters* (New York: G.P. Putnam's Sons, 1976), p. 7.

2. André Germain, *Les Clés de Proust* (Paris: Sun [1953]), cited in Wickes, ibid., p. 93.

3. Natalie Barney, quoted in Wickes, ibid., p. 44.

4. Natalie Barney, quoted in Wickes, ibid., p. 48.

5. Marguerite Yourcenar, quoted in Jean Chalon, *Portrait of a Seductress: The World of Natalie Barney*, trans. Carol Barko (New York: Crown Publishers, 1979), p. 221.

6. Solita Solano, 'The Hotel Napoleon Bonaparte,' in John C. Broderick, 'Paris between the Wars: An Unpublished Memoir by Solita Solano,' *Quarterly Journal of the Library of Congress*, 34 (October 1977): 309–310.

7. Truman Capote, quoted in Wickes, op. cit., p. 255.

8. Natalie Clifford Barney, in a dedication to Berthe Cleyrergue dated 1929, quoted in Chalon, p. 147.

9. Interview with Berthe Cleyrergue, July 1992, for the *Paris Was a Woman* film project.

10. Janet Flanner, interviewed in Wickes, op. cit., p. 261.

11. Janet Flanner, introduction to Colette, *The Pure and the Impure*, transl. Herma Brifault (London: Penguin Books, 1971), p. 6.

12. Janet Flanner, introduction to Colette, *The Pure and the Impure*, ibid., p. 8.

13. Herbert Lottman, *Colette : A Life* (London: Secker and Warburg, 1991), p. 27.

14. Colette, preface to *Claudine at School*, transl. Antonia White (London: Penguin, 1963), pp. 5–6.

15. Colette, *Earthly Paradise: An Autobiography Drawn from her Lifetime Writings* by Robert Phelps (New York: Farrar, Straus & Giroux, 1966).

16. Janet Flanner, introduction to Colette, *The Pure and the Impure*, op. cit., p. 9.

17. Janet Flanner, in a draft of a speech in tribute to Colette, July 1966, in the Flanner/Solano papers, Library of Congress.

18. Letter from Colette to Janet Flanner, n.d., Flanner/Solano papers, Library of Congress.

19. Truman Capote, quoted in Wickes, op. cit., p. 256.

20. Interview with Berthe Cleyrergue, July 1992, for the *Paris Was a Woman* film project.

21. Natalie Clifford Barney, 'Foreword', *As Fine as Melanctha*. Reprinted in Linda Simon, ed., *Gertrude Stein Remembered* (Lincoln: University of Nebraska Press, 1994), pp. 31–32.

22. Natalie Clifford Barney, 'Foreword', *As Fine as Melanctha*, ibid., pp. 31–32.

23. Virgil Thomson, quoted in Wickes, op. cit., p. 248.

24. Elizabeth Eyre de Lanux, quoted in Wickes, ibid., p. 242.

25. Gabriel-Louis Pringue, *Trente Ans de Diners en Ville*, quoted in Chalon, op. cit., p. 160.

26. Janet Flanner, quoted in Wickes, op. cit., p. 261.

27. Letter from Dolly Wide to Janet Flanner, n.d., Flanner/Solano papers, Library of Congress.

28. Janet Flanner, quoted in Wickes, op. cit., p. 260.

29. Interview with Gisèle Freund, July 1992, for the *Paris Was a Woman* film project.

30. Sylvia Beach to Bryher, 15 January 1953, Bryher collection of the Beinecke Rare Book and Manuscript Library, Yale University.

31. Sylvia Beach, *Shakespeare and Company* (New York: Harcourt, Brace and Co., 1956), p. 115.

32. *Colette: Catalogue de l'exposition* (Paris: Bibliotheque Nationale: 1973), pp. 163–164, quoted in Lotman, op. cit., p. 207.

33. Janet Flanner, *Paris Was Yesterday: 1925–1939* (New York: Harcourt Brace Jovanovich, 1988), p. 48.

34. Natalie Clifford Barney, 'Foreword', *As Fine as Melanctha*. Reprinted in Linda Simon, ed., *Gertrude Stein Remembered*, op. cit., pp. 33–34.

35. Gertrude Stein, *Picasso* (Boston: Beacon Press, 1959), p. 8.

36. Germaine Beaumont to Solita Solano, 1964, in the Flanner/Solano papers, Library of Congress.

CHAPTER 4: CITY OF DARK NIGHTS

All letters to Djuna Barnes are to be found in the McKeldin Library, University of Maryland at College Park. All letters from Djuna Barnes to Emily Holmes Coleman are from the Emily Holmes Coleman papers at the University of Delaware Library. All letters to Natalie Barney are from the Fonds Littéraire Jacques Doucet. All other letters where no source is indicated are from the Beinecke Rare Book Room, Yale University.

1. Natalie Barney, quoted in George Wickes, *The Amazon of Letters* (New York: G.P. Putnam's & Sons, 1976), p. 180.

2. Kathryn Hulme, *Undiscovered Country* (Boston: Atlantic-Little, Brown, 1966), pp. 37–39.

3. Eugene Jolas, *Paris Tribune* (20 July 1924), reprinted in Hugh Ford, ed., *The Left Bank Revisited* (University Park: Penn State University Press, 1972), p. 97.

4. Virgil Thomson, 'A Portrait of Gertrude Stein,' *A Virgil Thomson Reader* (Boston: Houghton Mifflin Co., 1981), p. 69.

5. Janet Flanner, 'Introduction', *Paris Was Yesterday: 1925–1939* (New York: Harcourt Brace Jovanovich, 1988), p. xvii-xviii.

6. Janet Flanner, 'The Infinite Pleasure: Sylvia Beach,' *Janet Flanner's World: Uncollected Writings 1932–1975* (New York and London: Harcourt Brace Jovanovich, 1979), p. 309.

7. Djuna Barnes, *I Could Never Be Lonely Without a Husband: Interviews by Djuna Barnes*, ed. Alyce Barry (London: Virago Press, 1987), p. 288.

8. Sylvia Beach, *Shakespeare and Company* (New York: Harcourt, Brace and Co., 1956), p. 112.

9. Andrew Field, *Djuna: The Life and Times of Djuna Barnes* (New York: Putnam's, 1983), p. 84.

10. Allan Ross MacDougall, ed., *Letters of Edna St Vincent Millay* (New York: Harper and Brothers, 1952), p. 116.

11. Interview with Berthe Cleyrergue, June 1992, for the *Paris Was a Woman* film project.

12. See Cheryl Plumb, 'Revising Nightwood: "a kind of glee of despair,"' *The Review of Contemporary Fiction* 13, no.3 (Fall 1993): 158.

13. Andrew Field, *Djuna: The Life and Times of Djuna Barnes*, op. cit., p. 147.

14. Djuna Barnes, *The Paris Tribune* (2 September 1931), reprinted in Hugh Ford, ed., *The Left Bank Revisited*, op. cit., p. 142.

15. Sylvia Beach, *Shakespeare and Company*, op. cit., p. 112.

16. Shari Benstock, *Women of the Left Bank* (Austin: University of Texas Press, 1986 and London: Virago Press, 1987), p. 245.

17. Djuna Barnes to Solita Solano, 22 May 1964, Flanner/Solano papers, Library of Congress.

CHAPTER 5: LETTERS FROM PARIS

All letters to Janet Flanner or Solita Solano and all unpublished writings by Janet Flanner not identified below can be found in the Flanner/Solano papers of the Library of Congress. All other unidentified writings by Janet Flanner are from her 'Letter from Paris' column in the *New Yorker*.

1, Quoted in Brenda Wineapple, *Genêt: A Biography of Janet Flanner* (New York: Ticknor & Fields, 1989), p. 55.

2. G.Y. Dryanski, 'Genêt Recalls Paris in the 20's,' *Washington Post* (1967). Newspaper clipping from the Flanner/Solano papers in the Library of Congress.

3. Quoted in Brenda Wineapple, op. cit., p. 21.

4. Solita Solano, 'The Hotel Napoleon Bonaparte,' in John C. Broderick, 'Paris between the Wars: An Unpublished Memoir by Solita Solano,' *Quarterly Journal of the Library of Congress* 34 (October 1977): 313. According to John C. Broderick's footnotes, Janet interpolated the phrase 'of an intense blue' into Solita's manuscript.

5. Solita Solano, 'The Hotel Napoleon Bonaparte,' ibid., in John C. Broderick, pp. 308–309.

6. Solita Solano, 'The Hotel Napoleon Bonaparte,' ibid., in John C. Broderick, pp. 312–313.

7. Jane Cole Grant, *Ross the New Yorker and Me* (New York: Reynal & Co, 1968), p. 223.

8. Eugene Jolas, *Paris Tribune* (28 December 1924), reprinted in Hugh Ford, ed., *The Left Bank Revisited: Selections from the Paris Tribune 1917–1934* (University Park: Penn State University Press, 1972), p. 261.

9. Solita Solano, quoted in John C. Broderick, op. cit., p. 306.

10. Janet Flanner, draft of speech to The American Institute of Arts and Letters, in the Flanner/Solano papers, Library of Congress, n.d.

11. Patrick O'Higgins, 'In Her Own Words: Janet (Genêt) Flanner on her "Pets" from 50 Years in Paris (De Gaulle Wasn't One of Them),' *People* 3, no.7(24 February 1975) : 62.

12. Patrick O'Higgins, 'In Her Own Words,' *People*, ibid., pp. 60–61.

13. Janet Flanner, 'Introduction', *Paris Was Yesterday: 1925–1939* (New York: Harcourt Brace Jovanovich, 1988), p. xix.

14. Jane Cole Grant, *Ross the New Yorker and Me*, op. cit., pp. 223–4.

15. Janet Flanner, draft of speech on Colette, July 1966, Flanner/Solano papers of the Library of Congress.

16. Janet Flanner, Introduction, *City of Love*, ed. Daniel Talbot (New York: Dell, 1955).

17. Berenice Abbott, quoted in Morrill Cody, *The Women of Montparnasse* (Cranbury, NJ: Cornwall Books, 1984), p. 163.

18. *Paris Tribune* (20 May 1927), reprinted in Hugh Ford, ed., *The Left Bank Revisited*, op. cit., pp. 83-84.

19. Bryher, *The Heart to Artemis* (London: Collins, 1963), p. 208.

20. Janet Flanner, 'A Life on a Cloud: Margaret Anderson,' *Janet Flanner's World: Uncollected Writings 1932-1975* (New York and London: Harcourt Brace Jovanovich, 1979), p. 320.

21. Margaret Anderson, quoted in Morrill Cody, *The Women of Montparnasse*, op. cit., p. 151.

22. Margaret Anderson, 'Introduction', *The Little Review Anthology* (New York: Hermitage House, 1953).

23. Ezra Pound to Margaret Anderson, n.d. [January 1917] quoted in Gillian Hanscombe and Virginia L. Smyers, *Writing for their Lives: The Modernist Women 1910–1914* (Boston: Northeastern University Press, 1988 and London: The Women's Press, 1987), p. 181.

24. Robert Sage, *Paris Tribune* (18 January 1931), reprinted in Hugh Ford, ed. *The Left Bank Revisited*, op. cit., p. 71.

25. H.D. to Amy Lowell (19 September 1917), quoted in Gillian Hanscombe and Virginia L. Smyers, *Writing for their Lives*, op. cit., p. 183.

26. Margaret Anderson, *My Thirty Years' War* (New York: Covici Friede, 1930), quoted in Janet Flanner, 'A Life on a Cloud: Margaret Anderson,' op. cit., pp. 323–324.

27. Janet Flanner, 'A Life On a Cloud: Margaret Anderson,' ibid., p. 326.

28. Margaret Anderson, quoted in Janet.Flanner, 'A Life On a Cloud: Margaret Anderson,' ibid., p. 326.

29. Janet Flanner, 'A Life On a Cloud: Margaret Anderson,' ibid., p. 326.

30. Margaret Anderson, *My Thirty Years' War*, op. cit., p. 102; Shari Benstock, *Women of the Left Bank* (Austin: University of Texas Press, 1986 and London: Virago Press, 1987), p. 379.

31. T.S. Eliot to Gertrude Stein, 21 April 1925, Stein collection, Beinecke Rare Book and Manuscript Library, Yale University.

32. Janet Flanner, 'A Life On a Cloud: Margaret Anderson,' op. cit., p. 325.

33. Eugene Jolas, *Paris Tribune* (28 December 1924), reprinted in Hugh Ford, ed. *The Left Bank Revisited*, op. cit., p. 261.

34. Bryher, *The Heart to Artemis*, op. cit., p. 208.

35. H.D. to Ezra Pound, n.d. [1929], quoted in Janice S. Robinson, *H.D.: The Life and Work of an American Poet* (Boston: Houghton Mifflin Co., 1982), p. 266.

36. *Paris Tribune* (26 January 1930) reprinted in Hugh Ford, ed., *The Left Bank Revisited*, op. cit., p. 252–3.

37. Solita Solano, 'Nancy Cunard: Brave Poet, Indomitable Rebel,' in Hugh Ford, ed., *Nancy Cunard: Brave Poet, Indomitable Rebel* (Philadelphia: Chilton Book Co., 1968). p. 76.

38. Andrew Field, *Djuna: The Life and Times of Djuna Barnes* (New York: Putnam's, 1983), p. 104.

39. Brenda Wineapple, *Genêt: A Biography of Janet Flanner*, op. cit., p. 93.

40. Solita Solano, 'Both Banks of the Seine,' *D.A.C. News* (20 February 1932): 50.

41. Jane Cole Grant, *The New York Ross and Me,* op. cit., p. 224.

42. Shari Benstock, *Women of the Left Bank,* op. cit., p. 108.

43. Janet Flanner, speech to American Institute of Arts and Letters, in the Flanner/Solano papers of the Library of Congress, n.d.

EPILOGUE

1. Janet Flanner, 'Paris, Germany,' *New Yorker* (7 December 1940), reprinted in Janet Flanner, *Janet Flanner's World: Uncollected Writings 1932–1975* (New York and London: Harcourt Brace Jovanovich, 1979), p. 51.

2. Adrienne Monnier, 'Occupation Journal: May 8 to July 10, 1940,' *The Very Rich Hours of Adrienne Monnier* (New York: Charles Scribner's Sons, 1976), p. 394.

3. Colette, quoted in Herbert Lottman, *Colette: A Life* (London: Secker and Warburg, 1991), p. 240.

4. Colette, 'Fifteen hundred days: liberation, August 1944,' *Earthly Paradise: An Autobiography, Drawn from her lifetime writings* by Robert Phelps (New York: Farrar, Straus and Giroux, 1966), p. 458.

5. Nancy Cunard, quoted in Anne Chisholm, *Nancy Cunard* (London: Sidgwick & Jackson, 1979), p. 263.

6. Shari Benstock, *Women of the Left Bank* (Austin: University of Texas Press, 1986 and London: Virago Press, 1987), p. 140.

7. Bryher, 'For Sylvia,' *Sylvia Beach: 1887–1962* (Paris: Mercure de France, 1963), p. 18.

8. Alice B. Toklas to W.G. Rogers, 28 October 1947, published in Edward Burns, ed., *Staying on Alone: Letters of Alice B. Toklas* (New York: Vintage Books, 1975), p. 88.

9. Alice B. Toklas to Henry Rago, 16 March 1947, published in Edward Burns, ed., *Staying on Alone: Letters of Alice B. Toklas,* ibid., p. 57.

10. Djuna Barnes to Solita Solano, 7 September 1960, Flanner/Solano papers, Library of Congress.

11. Djuna Barnes to Solita Solano, 22 May 1964, Flanner/Solano papers, Library of Congress.

SELECTED BIBLIOGRAPHY

Adams, Bronte and Trudi Tate, eds. *That Kind of Woman: Stories from the Left Bank and Beyond.* London: Virago, 1991.

Barnes, Djuna. *Nightwood.* London and Boston: Faber and Faber, 1985.

Beach, Sylvia. *Shakespeare and Company.* New York: Harcourt Brace and Company, 1959.

Benstock, Shari. *Women of the Left Bank.* Austin: University of Texas Press, 1986.

Broe, Mary Lynn, ed. *Silence and Power: A Reevaluation of Djuna Barnes.* Carbondale: Southern Illinois University Press, 1991.

Bryher, *The Heart to Artemis.* London: Collins, 1963.

Colette, *The Pure and the Impure.* Translation by Herma Briffault, introduction by Janet Flanner. London: Penguin Books, 1971.

Flanner, Janet, *Paris Was Yesterday,* 1925–1939. New York and London: Harcourt Brace Jovanovich, 1988.

Fitch, Noel Riley, *Sylvia Beach and the Lost Generation.* New York and London: W.W. Norton & Co., 1983.

Grahn, Judy, *Really Reading Gertrude Stein.* Freedom, California: The Crossing Press, 1989.

Jay, Karla, *The Amazon and the Page: Natalie Clifford Barney and Renée Vivien.* Bloomington: Indiana University Press, 1988.

Monnier, Adrienne, *The Very Rich Hours of Adrienne Monnier.* Translation and introduction by Richard McDougall. New York: Charles Scribners & Sons, 1976.

Stendhal, Renata, *Gertrude Stein in Words and Pictures.* London: Thames and Hudson, 1995.

Stimpson, Catharine R. , 'Gertrice/Altrude: Stein, Toklas, and the Paradox of the Happy Marriage.' In Perry, Ruth, and Martine Watson Brownley, eds. *Mothering the Mind: Twelve Studies of Writers and Their Silent Partners.* New York and London: Holmes and Meier, 1984.

Wickes, George, *The Amazons of Letters.* New York: G.P Putnam's & Sons, 1976.

Wineapple, Brenda, *Genêt: A Biography of Janet Flanner.* New York: Ticknor and Fields, 1989, and London: Pandora, 1993.

PHOTO AND TEXT CREDITS

Permission to publish photographic and other visual work in this book has kindly been granted by the following sources:

Archives and Manuscripts, McKeldin Library, University of Maryland at College Park: pages 22, 142, 144, 145, 147, 149, 151, 154, 155, 158, 160, 161, 163, 165, 166, 169, 172.

The Baltimore Museum of Art: The Cone Collection, formed by Dr. Claribel Cone and Miss Etta Cone of Baltimore, Maryland: page 80.

Bancroft Library, University of California at Berkeley: pages 65, 85, 86.

The Beinecke Rare Book and Manuscript Library, Yale University: pages 37, 60, 69, 70, 72, 75, 91, 92-3, 159, 187 (© Man Ray), 204, 207.

Berlinische Galerie, Photographic Collection: page 16.

Department of Rare Books and Special Collections, Princeton University Libraries: pages 26, 28, 30, 33, 43, 45, 53, 54, 56, 59, 205, 224-5, 227, 233, 241.

The Estate of Carl Van Vechten, courtesy of Joseph Solomon, Executor: pages 24, 63, 89, 146, 236.

The Estate of Janet Flanner, courtesy of William B. Murray: page 95.

Fonds Littéraire Jacques Doucet: pages 35, 81, 101, 102, 103, 106, 108, 112, 115, 118, 124, 131, 139, 140.

Gisèle Freund: pages 14-15, 40-41, 51, 228.

National Museum of American Art, Washington D.C.: pages 104 (courtesy of Art Resources, NY), 109, 122, 135 (courtesy of Art Resources, NY).

Poetry-Rare Books Collection, State University of New York at Buffalo: page 46.

Prints and Photographs Division, Library of Congress: pages 113, 132, 174, 176, 177, 178, 179, 182, 189 (© Berenice Abbott), 191, 194 (courtesy of Wide World Photos), 196, 197, 199, 209, 210, 212, 215, 217, 218, 221, 223, 230, 231, 234, 238.

Books and articles quoted or cited in the text under the usual fair use allowances are acknowledged in the endnotes. For more extensive quotations and to quote from unpublished material, I wish to thank the following sources:

The Estate of Gertrude Stein for permission to quote extracts from the published and unpublished writings by Gertrude Stein, and Random House for permission to reprint selections from *Four Saints in Three Acts*, *The Autobiography of Alice B. Toklas*, *Everybody's Autobiography,* and *Wars I Have Seen*. The Estate of Sylvia Beach, courtesy of Frederic B. Dennis, for permission to quote from her unpublished letters. The Estate of Mina Loy, courtesy of Roger L. Conover, for permission to reprint Mina Loy's poem 'Gertrude Stein'. The Estate of Natalie Clifford Barney, courtesy of Francois Chapon, for permission to publish extracts from Natalie Barney's autobiography and letters. The Authors League Fund, New York, and the Historic Churches Preservation Trust, London, for permission to quote from *Ladies Almanack, Nightwood* and from the letters of Djuna Barnes. Liveright Publishing Corporation for permission to quote from *Staying On Alone: Letters of Alice B. Toklas*. The Estates of H.D. and Bryher, courtesy of Perdita Schaffner,for permission to publish extracts from their letters, and the Estate of Janet Flanner, courtesy of William B. Murray, for permission to quote from *Paris Was Yesterday* and from unpublished writings by Janet Flanner.

INDEX

Toddler's First Steps

A Best Chance Guide to Parenting Your 6- to 36-Month-Old Child

second revision second edition 2011
printed December 2011

Second edition first published in 2008. Also available on the Internet.

Library and Archives Canada Cataloguing in Publication

Toddler's first steps : a best chance guide to parenting your 6- to 36-month-old child. – 2nd Rev. 2nd ed.

Includes index.
Issued by British Columbia Ministry of Health
ISBN 978-0-7726-6097-8

1. Toddlers. 2. Child rearing. 3. Child development. 4. Child care—British Columbia. I. British Columbia. Ministry of Health II. Open School BC

HQ774.5.T62 2009   649'.122   C2009-900004-0

You may purchase this book through Crown Publications at 1-800-663-6105 or online at www.crownpub.bc.ca. Special discounts for bulk purchases are available.

Published by Open School BC, Victoria, British Columbia, Canada.
Printed by The Queen's Printer of British Columbia, Canada.

Contents

Acknowledgements

Many people in British Columbia helped review the information in Toddler's First Steps (2nd ed.). Thanks are given to them all. Thanks are also given to the people who worked on the first edition of the handbook. Their work has made this edition possible.

The Design Team included:

Lisa Rogers, Janice Lidstone	Ministry of Health Consultants
Michelle Nicholson	Project Manager/Readability Editor
Dini Steyn	Project Coordinator
Cindy Lundy	Senior Subject Matter Expert/Researcher
Carol Orom	Instructional Designer/Writer
Susan Doyle	Writer
Janet Bartz	Art Director/Book Designer
Ken Faulks	Illustrator
Keith Learmonth, Shannon Mitchell	Copy Editors
Laurie Lozoway, Dennis Evans	Layout Technicians
Ilona Ugro	Copyright Officer
Glen Brownlow	Print Coordinator
Sherry Brown, Eluned Davies	Distribution Coordinators
Frances Litman Photography Inc.	Cover Photographer
Madea Solberg	Cover Model

Individuals who attended a Provincial Advisory Committee Meeting include:

Radhika Bhagat	Vancouver Coastal Health
Margaret Chesterman	BC Speech and Language Pathology Council for Early Childhood Development
Laurie Ford	Department of Educational and Counselling Psychology and Special Education; and the Human Early Learning Partnership, University of British Columbia
Dr. Virginia Hayes	University of Victoria School of Nursing and Children's and Women's Health Centre of British Columbia
Dr. Jill Houbé	Division of Developmental Pediatrics, BC Children's Hospital
Mary Lou Matthews	BC Healthy Child Development Alliance
Dr. Carol Matusicky	BC Council for Families
Becky Milne	BC NurseLine

Plus several representatives from the Ministry of Health, Ministry of Children and Family Development, and the Ministry of Education

Subject Matter Experts who participated in the instructional design workshop and/or conducted extensive review of the content include:

Dr. Shelina Babul-Wellar	BC Injury Research & Prevention Unit, Department of Pediatrics, University of British Columbia
Radhika Bhagat	Vancouver Coastal Health
Dr. Jill Houbé	Developmental Pediatrics, BC Children's Hospital
Dr. Carol Matusicky	BC Council for Families
Becky Milne	BC Nurseline
Jane Wark	Registered Dietitian
Joanne Wooldridge	Vancouver Coastal Health

Other Content Advisors include:

0-6 Years Subcommittee	Community Nutritionists Council of BC
Marilyn Barr	Prevent Shaken Baby Syndrome (SBS) British Columbia, BC Children's Hospital
Diana Elliott, Mary Clifford	Aboriginal Infant Development Program
Marina Green	BC Baby Friendly Network
Dr. Pam Glassby	Vancouver Coastal Health
Dr. Clyde Hertzman	Human Early Learning Partnership of British Columbia
Linda Kirste	Dial-A-Dietitian
Ann Marie Newroth	BC Early Hearing Program, Provincial Health Services Authority
Dr. R.G. Peterson	Child Health BC
Irene Rathbone	West Shore Health Unit, Vancouver Island Health Authority
Barbara Selwood	BC Perinatal Health Program, Provincial Health Services Authority
Anita Vallee	Vancouver Island Health Authority

BC Government personnel who participated in the project include:

Ministry of Health

Healthy Children, Women, Seniors and Injury Prevention:
Joan Geber, Tessa Graham, Matt Herman, Janice Lidstone, Erin O'Sullivan, Lisa Rogers, Carla Springinotic, Anita Vallee, Lori Wagar, Kristen Yarker-Edgar

Other: Lisa Forster-Coull, Leah Davidson, Tristan Davis, Toby Green, Andrew Hazelwood, Debbie Leach, Linda Poirier, Pete Rose, Craig Thompson, Dr. Malcolm Williamson, Lori Zehr

Ministry of Education — Catherine Jensen, Susan Kennedy

Ministry of Community Services — Debbie Anderson

Ministry of Children and Family Development — Melanie Gordon, Jana Harley, Lynne Hol, Susan Perkin, Sandy Wiens, Lara Woodman

Public Affairs Bureau — Laura Stovel

We also appreciate the feedback provided by our parent focus groups from:

Pacific Spirit Community Health Centre, organized by Radhika Bhagat
Northern Interior Health Unit, organized by Michelle Fitt
Knee-Waas House, Port Alberni Friendship Centre's Urban Aboriginal Early Childhood Development Program, organized by Lori Gardiner and Jackie Wells

A special thanks to all those who provided reference photos for the illustrations.

Second Revision (2011)
Thank you to all those involved in the second revision (2011), including:
Ministry of Health – Joan Geber, Meghan Day, Adrienne Treloar, Carla Springinotic, Carolyn Solomon, Margaret Yandel and Melissa Raposo; Government Communications and Public Engagement – Laura Stovel; and External Reviewers – Barbara Selwood.

Preface

Welcome to the second edition of *Toddler's First Steps: A Best Chance Guide to Parenting Your 6- to 36-Month-Old Child* published by the Government of British Columbia. The first edition was published in 2002. This edition has been revised based on best practices and evidence and has practical information on child development, nutrition, health and wellness, parenting, and safety. This information will help you provide the environment and support that contribute to your toddler's optimal growth and development.

Baby Friendly Initiative

The second edition of *Toddler's First Steps* has been revised to meet the Baby-Friendly Initiative criteria. The Baby-Friendly Initiative (BFI) is a global program of the World Health Organization (WHO) and UNICEF to increase hospital and community support for promoting, supporting, and protecting breastfeeding. Accepted criteria have been established for designation of Baby-Friendly hospitals, maternity facilities, and communities.

More information on the Baby-Friendly Initiative can be found at:
- www.unicef.org/programme/breastfeeding/baby.htm
- www.bcbabyfriendly.ca/

How to Use this Handbook

How do you read a book? From cover-to-cover, or do you dip in and out seeking specific information? This book is designed for both types of reading. The following components will help you find the information you need, quickly and efficiently.

Contents

The table of contents will help you find a specific topic. Note that the book is divided into five main chapters:

- Child Development in the Toddler Years
- Healthy Eating for Your Toddler
- The Health and Well-Being of Your Toddler
- Parenting Your Toddler
- Toddler Safety

At the back of the book you'll find:

Resources

Need a phone number or contact information? See the Resources on page 191.

Index

Need to find a topic quickly? See the Index on page 201.

Websites

Throughout this book, there are many references to Internet websites. If you do not have Internet access at home, go to your local public library for free use of a computer with access.

Page Arrangement

The layout will help you sort information quickly.

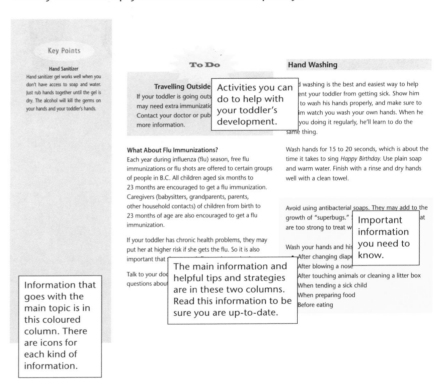

Key Points

Hand Sanitizer
Hand sanitizer gel works well when you don't have access to soap and water. Just rub hands together until the gel is dry. The alcohol will kill the germs on your hands and your toddler's hands.

To Do

Travelling Outside
If your toddler is going outs may need extra immunizatio Contact your doctor or pub more information.

Activities you can do to help with your toddler's development.

Hand Washing

d washing is the best and easiest way to help ent your toddler from getting sick. Show him to wash his hands properly, and make sure to im watch you wash your own hands. When he you doing it regularly, he'll learn to do the same thing.

What About Flu Immunizations?
Each year during influenza (flu) season, free flu immunizations or flu shots are offered to certain groups of people in B.C. All children aged six months to 23 months are encouraged to get a flu immunization. Caregivers (babysitters, grandparents, parents, other household contacts) of children from birth to 23 months of age are also encouraged to get a flu immunization.

If your toddler has chronic health problems, they may put her at higher risk if she gets the flu. So it is also important that

Talk to your do questions abou

Wash hands for 15 to 20 seconds, which is about the time it takes to sing *Happy Birthday*. Use plain soap and warm water. Finish with a rinse and dry hands well with a clean towel.

Avoid using antibacterial soaps. They may add to the growth of "superbugs." at are too strong to treat w

Important information you need to know.

Wash your hands and his
After changing diape
After blowing a nose
After touching animals or cleaning a litter box
When tending a sick child
When preparing food
Before eating

Information that goes with the main topic is in this coloured column. There are icons for each kind of information.

The main information and helpful tips and strategies are in these two columns. Read this information to be sure you are up-to-date.

Information Icons

Key Points   Important information you need to know.

FACTS & STATS   Interesting tibits of information that can help you.

Family Stories   Stories from parents relating their experiences.

Introduction from Dr. Clyde Hertzman

"The first years last forever." Our health, well-being, and coping skills throughout our lives are strongly affected by whether or not we get a good start. The period from conception to school age is especially important. During this time the brain develops rapidly. It organizes and reorganizes based on the stimulation, support, and nurturing that a child receives. By the time of school entry, a child's brain will have been shaped by these experiences, just like a house is shaped by the work of a homebuilder. One-quarter of Canadian children who enter school need extra support to help them develop. The sad fact is that for the most part this can be prevented.

A full range of early experiences affects the newborn:
- visual
- verbal
- emotional
- physical
- touch
- smell
- taste

Children who grow up in a stimulating environment have the best chance for a good start in life. We now know a lot about the kinds of early settings that work best. We know the value of reading to children. Taking the time to snuggle up with your child and read bedtime stories is one of the best things you can do. Children need chances to talk, to listen, and to explore their world through play. They need warmth and acceptance, and protection from teasing and punishment.

Effective parenting means making environments for children that have these characteristics. Children feel protected when they have a stable family and relationships that are close and supporting. They also need a sense of personal safety. But parents cannot do it all alone. Parents must have economic security and a workplace that supports them. They need neighbourhoods that are safe and caring of children. High-quality, affordable child care and family support programs make a big difference, too.

It is with these thoughts in mind that this book has been developed. Its aim is to provide parents of children ages six to 36 months with practical information on how to best support, encourage, and help their toddlers to grow and develop to their full potential.

Dr. Clyde Hertzman
Director, Human Early Learning Partnership of British Columbia

Introduction from Dr. R.G. Peterson

Toddlers are citizens in their own right. They are key to the future success of British Columbia. Our children trust us with a huge responsibility as their parents, grandparents, and caregivers. They rely on us to provide a safe, nurturing, and stimulating environment for them. We all take this responsibility very seriously. In return, and to our great fortune, we get a loving response for our efforts.

Infants and toddlers go through astonishing development in a short period. This development covers physical, intellectual, cognitive (including hearing, speech, and language), emotional, and behavioural growth. In each of these areas of development there are milestones. These milestones act like building blocks that must be in place before children can move to the next higher level. The final goal is that children reach the point where they can make their own lifelong contributions to their families and communities.

Toddler's First Steps is a wonderful companion for this adventure. Health-care providers, early childhood educators, and child development specialists worked together to create this reference for the early years of life. I encourage all parents, grandparents, and caregivers to enjoy its content. Please discuss it with those who partner with you in providing care to your toddler. Use it to generate your own questions regarding your experiences with your toddler.

You will find that most toddlers thrive in our environment. They'll continue to surprise and enrich you as they move through this unique period of development. However, we need to be aware of when to expect toddlers to move through the stages of development. We must recognize when to ask questions about their behaviour, language development, and the other aspects of normal childhood development. If we don't, we might not identify issues early. This can have important consequences for a child.

You will find many answers to your questions in this book. It can be a great help in understanding the amazing journey of your toddler's growth and development.

Use this opportunity to its fullest!

R. G. Peterson MD, PhD, MPH
Clinical Professor
Department of Pediatrics
University of British Columbia Faculty of Medicine
Director, Child Health BC

A network of health authorities and health-care providers dedicated to excellence in the provision of health services to infants, children, and youth in British Columbia.

Getting Started

Welcome to the world of parenting a toddler. As you travel on this joyful journey of growth and development with your toddler, you will see amazing changes in her. You will teach her and she will teach you. This is an exciting partnership for all. Welcome to this wonderful world!

It is important that you respond to your toddler in a loving and accepting manner time after time when she is sick, hurt, or upset. This will make her feel confident and secure.

Learning About Your Toddler

Attachment

Attachment is one of the key factors in raising a happy and confident child. Attachment is the coming together of a child and a parent (or caregiver) in a close and connected relationship. When a child is attached to a parent in a healthy way, she feels safe, secure, and protected on physical, emotional, and mental levels. The parent senses and responds to her cues (or what she needs and wants). Attachment occurs gradually over time, through day-to-day actions and routines.

When you respond to your toddler in a loving and accepting way time after time, she learns that someone is there to support and protect her. This is especially important when she is sick, hurt, or upset. She then feels free to explore the physical and social world with confidence. She knows she can return to the safety of a parent if something frightens or overwhelms her. Knowing this, she can take full advantage of opportunities to learn new skills. The basis of a secure attachment is that the parent always offers a safe place from which to explore the larger world.

Definition of a Toddler
In this book, a toddler is defined as a child between the ages of six months and 36 months (three years).

There are many things you can do to make sure your toddler develops a secure attachment.

Provide Comfort

As you grow with your toddler, you will learn to read her signals and determine when she is in need of comfort. She may become upset if she is sick, hurt, or lonely. She will want you to reassure, rock, or hold her. If you can respond this way regularly and predictably, your child will learn that she is safe when you are around. Be responsive, sensitive, and available, as much as you can.

Respond and Notice

Your toddler needs to know that he is important and that you will respond to him. He needs not only to be comforted when upset, but also to be given attention. He wants you to spend time with him and to help him with problems. Find activities that you both enjoy. Spend time talking with and listening to him, asking him how he feels about things, and taking him places. Read stories, go for walks, and play games together. Show interest in his activities and spend lots of one-on-one time with him. Tune in to your toddler, and let him take the lead. Keep these activities warm and intimate, even if they are sometimes brief.

Provide a Sense of Trust

Strike a balance between being sure your toddler is safe and encouraging her to explore the world in a trusting manner. Instil a sense of trust in your child by letting her know you believe that she can do things. Keep your home and environment as safe as possible, to allow your toddler to explore. Protect her independence without abandoning her. For example,

when she learns to crawl or walk, you can let her go off a short distance, but make sure you remain nearby so she can return to you.

Do not expose your toddler to scary accounts of tragic events or acts of violence on television. If she does have a frightening experience, give her lots of support and talk about what happened.

Review and Re-enact Experiences

Talk with your toddler about things that have happened in his life. As he gets older, tell him stories about when he was small. Show him photos of when he was younger, and answer any questions he may have. These memories can give him a sense of his past and create a feeling of security.

If your toddler goes through a difficult event, talk to him about it. Review it, play it out, and discuss it when he is willing and able to do so. This can help avoid nightmares and trauma. Events, such as the birth of a sibling or a friend leaving town, are important, and it helps to talk to him about these events. If you are going through the same trauma as your toddler, you may not be able to talk about it. If this is the case, it is important to find professional help for both you and your toddler.

Create Warm Memories

Keep good memories alive. Make a photo album and look at it with your toddler. Maintain a collection of her crafts and artwork. Keep a diary of her achievements. Make videos and keep a record of special events. Establish family traditions; they help her feel secure and able to look forward to things.

Provide a Sense of Security

Being away from your toddler once in a while will help his sense of attachment, but these separations need to be handled well. When leaving him with someone else, set up a goodbye ritual and leave with confidence. Provide him with some things to do while you are away. Give him a photo of yourself, a security blanket, or familiar toys to keep him calm. Let him know when you will return, and make sure to come back on time.

If your toddler is very upset about being away from you, try to do it gradually. Remain present during part of the first few days.

Be Predictable and Positive

Be as predictable as you can, to provide your toddler with an additional sense of security. Keep to a routine for meals, bedtime, and so on. Establish clear rules and follow through on them. Always comfort and soothe your toddler if she is sick, hurt, or upset.

Excerpted from the AboutKidsHealth website. AboutKidsHealth provides trusted answers from The Hospital for Sick Children for families' health questions. www.aboutkidshealth.ca

Temperament

Every person has a temperament, including your toddler. Temperament is his distinct nature or character; it is "who he is." Some children's temperaments are obvious right from birth, while others will show over time. Your toddler's temperament may be seen in a number of ways, such as activity level, how predictable he is, how he reacts to new situations, and how he adapts to things. Does he react strongly or mildly to events? Is he easily distracted or can he focus well? What's his attention span like? How is his general mood?

Your temperament may not be the same as your toddler's. If you're active and out-going, it may be harder for you to understand his if he is quiet and shy. If you love to spend time alone, it may be hard for you if he always wants to play with you or other children. Learning to accept and work with his temperament rather than trying to change it will make both your lives easier and more pleasant.

Your home environment and who your toddler spends time with will have some effect on his temperament, but it is mostly just an inborn part of the kind of person he is. Your job is to find ways to support him.

Supporting Your Toddler's Temperament

Try this exercise: If you are right-handed, take a pen in your left hand, and if you are left-handed, take the pen in your right. Now write your name and address. How did that feel? Difficult, uncomfortable, slow, unnatural, that you are not doing as good a job as you know you could? Now imagine trying to live your life that way. Forcing your toddler to be someone she's not is just as difficult for her as this writing exercise was for you. She may, with practice, be able to act in a certain way, but this won't be easy or feel natural to her. Understand that your toddler's temperament is not her choice, but rather how she naturally feels about things.

Here are some ways you can try to understand and work with your toddler's temperament:

- Try not to label her temperament. A child who grows up with the belief that she is shy or not good in sports will tend to live up to those expectations.

- Be prepared to change your ideas of what you may have thought she would be like. Boys are not always rough and tumble and not all girls like to play with dolls. Let her lead you to discover her talents and preferences.

Ways to Help Your Toddler Work With His Temperament

Try to find ways to help your toddler direct his tendencies into positive activities. This will make him more comfortable and will help him to learn ways of working with his temperament.

- A toddler who tends to be shy or slow to warm up may take longer to get used to a new playgroup. You can help by letting him sit with you and watch until he's ready to join in. Supporting his temperament does not mean that he can do whatever he wants. Not joining the playgroup is not an option, and neither is ignoring family and friends. But allowing him to join in at a slower rate or to play in a different way helps him to develop those skills he will need.

- If your toddler has lots of energy, provide ways for him to move around as much as possible and safely explore the world using his body. He may excel in sports or dance, or just simply enjoy running around the backyard for an hour. If he must be still for a period of time, give him something to do with his hands, such as playdough, or have him turn pages in a book or push a toy on his lap. Play games that give your toddler the chance to move. Let him help you around the house with chores and other tasks.

- If your toddler tends to be easily frightened, talk to him about his fears. Even if his fears seem silly to you, they are very real to him. Together think of ways to overcome fears, such as checking the closet together for monsters or holding him on your lap when near a dog. Let him know that you believe he can learn to cope with his fears. "Someday I bet you could be friends with that dog if we visit him often and get to know him."

- If your toddler is sensitive, bright lights and loud noises may bother him. Try to dim the lights and reduce noise from the radio or television. If tags in his clothing or wrinkles in his socks bother him, try to adjust his clothing so he feels better. Ignoring requests for clothing to be adjusted or noise to be decreased won't cure him of his sensitivities. He will only continue to be distracted by the discomfort and be unable to focus well on other tasks.

- If he has a strong reaction to new situations, try breaking new things down into simple, small steps, such as "This is how you sit on your bike, this is where your feet go, and this is where your hands go" instead of "Jump on and let's ride." Simplify your life—don't take him to places where he must stay quiet or sit for a long time. Restaurants and shopping malls may be too difficult for a spirited child at this age. Also, give plenty of warning before any change, such as leaving the park or bedtime. Be sure to praise him when he does well in difficult situations.

For a toddler of any temperament, it is important to provide routines and rituals so he will know what to expect. Being able to predict daily routines may keep stress lower in times of change. Meaningful rituals may provide a sense of belonging and foster a sense of who he is.

Temperament is your toddler's way of being in the world, both socially and emotionally. How you and others respond to his temperament can impact how he feels about himself as he grows.

Family Stories

Routines Are Important to Toddlers
I tried to make sure that my toddler went to bed at about the same time every night. We also got ready the same way every night—had a bath, read a book, and had a special way of saying goodnight. This helped my daughter wind down from a busy day of play and activities to bedtime.

Key Points

Definition of Parents
In this book, the words "parent" and "parenting" refer to both mothers and fathers or primary caregivers.

Growing as a Dad
Many men want to be active dads. They want to be involved in the care of their children right from the start. They want strong emotional bonds with their children. They want to have broader roles in the raising of their children.

For guidance on fathering, including information for teenage fathers, see "Fathering" in the Resources chapter.

Growing as a Parent

Your toddler is not the only one who will be growing and learning during the first 36 months of her life. You, too, will experience change and growth in your role as a parent. Remember to take time to celebrate your successes as you learn new parenting skills.

Your family, friends, and other experienced people can support you and help you understand and meet the changing needs of your growing child. Remember, "It takes a whole village to raise a child."

Here are some general tips that can help support you to parent a toddler:

- Keep learning. With each new stage of her growth, you will be learning new parenting skills. To keep learning, you could try parenting classes, talk with other parents, read books on parenting, and find out more about child development. (See the Child Development chapter on p. 9 for more information.)

- Find out how to get the help your family needs. Talk to your health-care providers or other professionals you connect with to learn how to get what you need for your child and your family. These could include additional income, extra child care, or help if your toddler has special needs. Your community offers many resources, from toddler playgroups to swimming lessons. Check the Resources chapter to find out what resources are available. (See p. 191.)

- Stay healthy and active. Check the state of your own health regularly, and try to get 30 to 60 minutes of moderate physical activity every day. Eat a healthy diet. Eat a balance of food from the four food groups, as outlined in *Eating Well with Canada's Food Guide*. (See p. 183.) Pay attention to your emotional well-being, and seek help if you are depressed or overwhelmed. (See p. 136 for more information on perinatal depression.)

For more information about parenting your toddler, see page 125.

Child Development in the Toddler Years

You may have heard the saying "the first years last forever." This means that the experiences that your toddler has in the early months and years of life affect her health, well-being, and coping skills for the rest of her life.

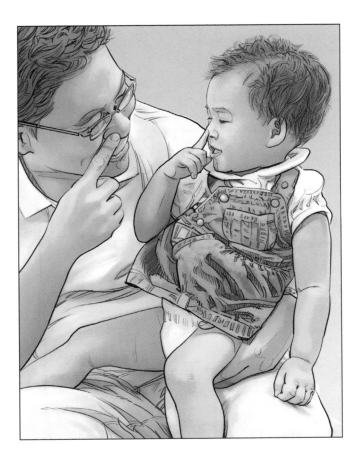

The Five Areas of Child Development

During the toddler years, your child will go through a time of rapid change in all areas of development. Many experts divide child development into five areas: physical, social, emotional, cognitive, and language.

The different areas of development are closely linked. The progress your toddler makes in one area affects—and is affected by—the progress she makes in another area. No one area of child development is more important than any other.

Many things affect your toddler's growth and development, including:
- The genes she inherited.
- The kind of nurturing and support she receives from you and her other caregivers.
- Her experiences in your home and community.

Learning about child development can help guide your parenting. The following table describes each area of child development. It also gives you some parenting suggestions for each area.

Portions of content provided by *Invest in Kids*. (For more information on *Invest in Kids*, see Child Development in the Resources chapter.)

Physical Development

Usually divided into gross and fine motor skills.

Gross motor skill is the control of the large muscles that he needs for physical activities such as sitting, crawling, walking, running, climbing, and jumping.

Fine motor skill is the control of the muscles in the hands and fingers. It also covers hand-eye co-ordination, needed for actions such as reaching for and picking something up.

Parenting Suggestions

Help him develop gross and fine motor skills through physical activity.

He'll do well when you:

- Create safe, interesting places and activities for him to explore and be active in.

- Respond to him with physical affection (hugs and cuddles). Physical touch helps his brain release hormones that he needs to grow.

Social Development

Learning to make friends and get along with others.

Parenting Suggestions

Help her learn to co-operate, trust, and become confident with others.

She'll do well when you:

- Respond as often as you can when she shows that she wants help and attention.

Emotional Development	Cognitive Development	Language Development

Emotional Development

Learning to know and show a full range of feelings.

Parenting Suggestions

Help her learn to see emotions in herself and others, and how to show feelings.

She'll do well when you:

- Help her know and show her feelings.

- Comfort her often.

- Set reasonable limits and consequences.

Cognitive Development

Learning to think, remember, imagine, gather and organize information, solve problems, and develop judgment.

Parenting Suggestions

Help him become a lifelong learner.

He'll do well when you:

- Give him safe and stimulating chances to play.

- Play with him.

- Praise and encourage him.

Language Development

Learning to communicate through talking and listening.

Parenting Suggestions

Help her develop language skills.

She'll do well when you:

- Tell her stories and talk to her.

- Listen to her and encourage her to talk.

- Read to her as much as you can.

- Sing, talk, and play with her.

- Respond to her signals, such as cries, sounds, movements, and eye contact.

Child Development by Age

The overall pattern of child development is the same for most toddlers. Most reach the milestones of development at about the same pace. However, sometimes a toddler will develop more quickly or more slowly than expected.

To Do

Keeping Track of Your Toddler's Development

As a parent, you are the best source of information about your toddler's development. To add to your knowledge, there are tools that you or your health-care provider can use to review your toddler's development. One tool is called the *Ages and Stages Questionnaires.* Another is the *Nipissing District Developmental Screen.* To learn more, contact your public health office or the infant development program in your community.

The charts on the following pages show the skills you are most likely to see at each stage. They will also give you ideas about how you can support your toddler's healthy development.

Physical Development

What Your Toddler is Likely to Do

- Sit steadily without help for longer periods.
- Sit and bounce on his bottom.
- Push up from his tummy onto his hands and knees, and rock back and forth.
- Sit up by pushing from a crawling position with his arms at his sides.
- Crawl with an object in one or both hands.
- Help when you pull him up to a standing position.
- Stand firmly on his legs when held in a standing position.
- Progress from holding things in his palm to using his thumb and first and second fingers.
- Rake at tiny objects with his hands.
- Pick up larger objects with his fingers.
- Chew or gum finely minced foods (six to seven months).
- Feed himself small pieces of food (by nine months).
- Pick up a cup and put it up to his mouth.
- Pick up, hold, and control an object using both hands.
- Bang objects together.
- Explore objects by grabbing, shaking, sliding, and banging them.

Other Things Your Toddler May Do

- Pull himself up using furniture.
- Move by shuffling on his bottom or turning in circles on his stomach.
- Stand by himself while holding on to your hands. He may then put one foot in front of the other.
- Extend his arms to keep from falling backwards.

- Lower himself to sitting from a hanging-on position.
- Crawl up stairs.
- Step sideways while holding on to furniture.
- Throw objects.
- Build a tower of two blocks.
- Point with his index finger.
- Poke his fingers into holes or anything that looks interesting.
- Take objects out of containers.
- Release objects with no fuss.

How You Can Help Physical Development

- Continue to breastfeed.
- Get down on the floor at his level.
- Provide safe places for him to crawl and explore.
- Encourage movement. For example, put some distance between you and him when playing on the floor, put toys just a bit out of reach, or hold his hands and go for a walk.
- Give lots of opportunities for "tummy time" and crawling. (See p. 16 for more information on tummy time.)
- Provide soft pieces of food for snacks and meals to develop finger control and chewing skills.
- Offer him a spoon (but he won't be able to use it correctly).
- Roll a ball back and forth on the floor with him while he's sitting.
- Make noisemakers with plastic bottles for him to grasp and shake.

6–9 months

Social Development

What Your Toddler is Likely to Do

- Play social games, such as peekaboo or patty cake.
- Want to take part in activities with people.
- Point to things for a reason.
- Seek attention.

Other Things Your Toddler May Do

- Show fear of people he doesn't know.
- Begin copying what he sees, such as sticking out his tongue or opening his mouth.
- Show he feels some control over his life. For example, he may show you a toy but won't give it to you.
- Learn to protect himself and his things.
- Won't do something he doesn't want to do. For example, he may push a spoon away when you try to feed him.
- Focus when doing something, ignoring other things that are going on.

How You Can Help Social Development

- Continue to respond when he shows that he wants help or attention.
- Keep to regular routines.
- Model good manners: use "please" and "thank you."
- Play "seeking" games to help him understand he is not part of you: "Where's Liam?"
- Play with him and invite others to play too.
- Join a playgroup for parents and toddlers.
- Follow his lead; let him decide what to do.
- Go slowly. Help him approach new people by following his pace.
- Have him eat at the table with you and others.

Emotional Development

What Your Toddler is Likely to Do

- Show strong feelings about likes and dislikes.
- Laugh.
- Not want to be away from you or other caregivers.
- Show fear (possibly by crying) if he is scared.

Other Things Your Toddler May Do

- Look worried about loud noises, such as vacuum cleaners, loud stern voices, or banging.
- Show clear likes or dislikes for certain people, objects, or places.
- Be sensitive to other children and perhaps cry if they cry.
- React to other people's moods. If you are sad, he may cry. If you are happy, he may laugh along with you.

How You Can Help Emotional Development

- Continue to breastfeed.
- Smile at him.
- Hold and comfort him, especially when he is upset, sick, or hurt.
- Create and stick to routines.

6–9 months

Crawling and "Tummy Time"

Putting your child on her tummy for some supervised play time helps her get ready for crawling. Tummy time is when you lay your child on her stomach or side when she is awake. Your child can be on the floor, on a safe firm surface, on your lap, or on your chest. It is a time when you can show her toys or pictures, sing or talk, or massage her back. When on her tummy, your child pushes up with her arms and raises her head in order to see around. Tummy time will help your child develop the upper body strength needed for crawling. Crawling usually develops between six and eight months.

Until she can roll over on her own, put her to sleep on her back to decrease the chance of Sudden Infant Death Syndrome (SIDS). (See p. 100 for more information on safe sleeping.)

Cognitive Development

What Your Toddler is Likely to Do

- Notice the size of objects, reaching for smaller objects with her finger and thumb and larger objects with both hands.
- Know whether objects are near or far.
- Understand how objects can be used. For example, she may bang blocks on the floor, shake a noisemaker harder, or push buttons on a toy.
- Search briefly for an object when it is taken away from her.

Other Things Your Toddler May Do

- Drop objects and then look for them.
- Understand the concepts of "in" and "out." For example, she may drop several large beads in a cup, dump them out, and repeat.
- Use problem-solving skills. For example, she may pull the string of a pull toy to get it closer.
- Start to combine known behaviours in new ways. For example, she may reach and crawl at the same time.
- May think of herself when she sees a child in photos or a mirror.

How You Can Help Cognitive Development

- Continue to breastfeed.
- Give lots of praise for her new skills.
- Give him a range of objects or toys (fill-and-dump toys; toys for stacking, nesting, and sorting; toys with a variety of textures, shapes, sounds, colours, and weights; childproof books). (See p. 48 for more information on toys.)
- Read toddler books with her.
- Play copy games, such as sticking out your tongue or banging a pan.
- Play hide-and-seek games.
- Play in-and-out games, such as putting blocks in a container and taking them out.
- Dance, play music, and sing with her.

Language Development

What Your Toddler is Likely to Do

- Say several sounds (ma, mu, da, di, ba) all in one breath.
- Repeat sounds (da-da-da, ga-ga-ga).
- Respond to some words, such as "Mommy," "Daddy," or "ball."
- Babble.
- Turn to listen to familiar sounds, such as the telephone.
- Look at you when you say his name.

Other Things Your Toddler May Do

- Recognize familiar words like "no-no."
- Do simple things, such as showing you a ball or waving goodbye, when asked.

How You Can Help Language Development

- Talk to him whenever you can. This is how he'll learn language: "Let's change your diaper," "Let's find your doll."
- Respond to his babbling sounds with the words he is trying to say. Say "mama" or "dada" when he gets close to the words.
- Give names and labels to things that catch his attention.
- Use simple sentences to talk about what each of you is doing: "We are looking at the cat," or "Daddy is throwing the ball."

Key Points

Sign Language

Many community centres offer sign language classes for toddlers and parents, even when both child and parent are hearing. This may be a fun way to communicate with your toddler before he learns to talk. Remember that he has learned to understand many more words than he can show with movement or sounds.

Family Stories

Just Out of Reach

When our daughter, Maya, was just starting to crawl and move around, I would get on the floor and sit or lie just out of her reach with a toy. She would work hard to reach the toy and me. I would then talk about the toy: "What a great teddy. Yes, it's teddy bear." Then I would pick up another toy and move a few feet away. Again, she would work away to get to me. It kept her occupied and active, and helped her learn words. If I were tired at the end of the day, I would lie there reading a book until she got to me. We both were happy.

9–12 months

Physical Development

What Your Toddler is Likely to Do

- Turn in a circle when sitting.
- Twist to pick up objects.
- Stand by flexing her knees and pushing off from a squat.
- Walk while holding on to furniture.
- Walk when supported by both hands.
- Crawl up stairs.
- Crawl very well.
- Use the tip of her index finger and thumb to pick up small items.
- Put objects in and take them out of containers.
- Point, poke, touch, and pry with her index finger.
- Place one block on top of another.
- Give objects to another person, if asked.
- Hold a spoon, although she will need help to use it.
- Chew small pieces of food.

Other Things Your Toddler May Do

- Walk, with one hand held.
- Squat down, stoop, bend over, then get up.
- Crawl up and down stairs.
- Climb two or three steps without help.
- Drop down from a standing to a sitting position.
- Use both hands freely.
- Pull off socks and hats.
- Hold large felt markers and make marks with them.
- Build a tower using two blocks.
- Feed herself with a spoon and drink from a cup.

How You Can Help Physical Development

- Continue to breastfeed.
- Provide lots of encouragement.
- Go for walks outside and give her practice walking with your support.
- While playing on the floor, place favourite toys just far enough away so that she has to reach for them.
- Let her practise climbing a few stairs, making sure you support her from behind or by holding her hand.
- Increase the variety of foods and textures. Place small pieces of food on her plate or tray.
- Offer water to drink from a cup.
- Show her how to place soft building blocks one on top of another.
- Create a safe play space in the kitchen with lots of different-sized plastic containers, bowls, wooden spoons, and other objects.
- Play finger games with her, such as *Round and Round the Garden*.
- Introduce her to toys that require handling, such as activity tables or toys that make a noise when a button is pressed.

Social Development

What Your Toddler is Likely to Do

- Know when a parent likes or dislikes her behaviour.
- Hold out her arms and legs while being dressed.
- Mimic simple actions.
- Imitate other children.
- Repeat sounds or movements that made you laugh.

Other Things Your Toddler May Do

- Show fear of strangers.
- Dance to music.
- Know routines.
- Try different ways of getting attention, such as copying sounds.
- Enjoy being the centre of attention.

How You Can Help Social Development

- Respond to her calls or signals for help and attention (whenever you can) to build her trust.
- Create and follow regular routines.
- Offer choices you are comfortable with. For example, "Do you want this cup or that cup?"
- Model good manners: use "please" and "thank you."
- Play face-to-face games, such as peekaboo, or make faces together.
- Talk about what happens next in routines or upcoming events.
- Provide safe places for her to explore.

9–12 months

Key Points

Introducing Books

It is never too soon to start sharing books together. Toddlers will flip the pages and stare at the pictures. It won't be long before your toddler is quietly listening to children's stories while you read. Visit your local library. There are many children's books that your toddler will enjoy. Make books a part of your toddler's world.

Emotional Development

What Your Toddler is Likely to Do

- Seek comfort when upset.
- Show many emotions, such as being sad, happy, mad, scared, hurt, or uncomfortable.
- Show distress when she does something wrong.
- Show that she always needs to be within sight and hearing of the caregiver.
- Display affection in hugs, kisses, pats, and smiles.

Other Things Your Toddler May Do

- Cry when you leave her with other caregivers.
- Show empathy, such as starting to cry when another toddler cries.
- Express a desire to do things herself.
- Show like or dislike of certain people and toys.
- Show discomfort when fearful or stressed.
- Express new fears and insecurity with situations that were fine before.

How You Can Help Emotional Development

- Continue to breastfeed.
- Smile at her.
- Cuddle her.
- Comfort her, especially when she is upset, sick, or hurt.
- Create routines and structure in her day.
- Turn everyday routines into playful moments.
- Talk about her emotions: "I see you are feeling sad/happy/frustrated."
- Ask her for hugs and kisses.
- Provide her with chances to play with other children and to be around people.

Cognitive Development

What Your Toddler is Likely to Do

- Try to find objects that you have hidden.
- Try out new actions to reach the same goal, or change old actions through trial and error.
- Connect animals with actions and sounds, such as meows, barks, or chirps.
- Copy the actions of others.
- Develop stronger memory skills.
- Become aware of parents as separate people from herself. She may point when asked, "Who's Mommy? Who's Daddy?"
- Recognize her own name, when spoken.
- Start to see cause and effect, such as the fact that things fall when dropped.
- Match shapes. For example, she may place a cube in a matching square hole.

Other Things Your Toddler May Do

- Enjoy looking at pictures.
- Point to the correct parts of the body when asked where they are.
- Know that smaller objects fit into larger ones.
- Search more for hidden objects.
- Repeat an action that gets a reaction, such as knocking over blocks.
- Put two ideas together, such as going to another room to get a toy and bringing it back.
- Leave an activity and return to it later.

How You Can Help Cognitive Development

- Continue to breastfeed.
- Praise her new accomplishments.
- Keep adding to the range of objects/toys you are providing for her.
- Play action games in which you and she take turns. Try blowing kisses, clapping, or peeking.
- Ask her to help you find lost objects.
- Talk about cause and effect: "You dropped Teddy, so now Teddy is on the floor."
- Read toddler books with her.
- Play music for her and encourage dancing and movement.

Family Stories

Copy and Learn

Whenever my friend, who was a teacher, would come to visit us, she would take the time to talk with our 10-month-old. She would also pull out keys, toys, or whatever and say the names of them carefully. Often our son would copy her and say the word (or something like the word). It was a good example of what I needed to be doing every day. I would just get busy and forget how kids copy and learn so much from us. She didn't need to tell me to do it. I just watched and copied her, just like our son did.

9–12 months

Play Dates

When our daughter was little we used to have play dates with other kids the same age. We moms would all laugh about it being a "play" day—the kids didn't really play with each other. It was the moms who loved it the most. We would visit, talk, and share stories and tips. Gradually, the kids got old enough to actually play with each other. It was the moms who formed the strongest bonds. We still get together now.

Key Points

Early Literacy

Early literacy does not mean trying to teach your toddler how to read or write. Reading, talking, chanting, singing, and having conversations with your toddler are the best ways to build early language and literacy skills.

Language Development

What Your Toddler is Likely to Do

- Babble in long, repetitive strings.
- Understand simple sentences, questions, and requests, such as "Please give the book to Daddy."
- Take turns making sounds with you.
- Copy speech sounds.
- Respond to her own name.
- Point and talk to specific objects.

Other Things Your Toddler May Do

- Copy sounds, such as "bow-wow" or "woof."
- Use a few words: "no," "baby," "bye-bye," "Mommy," or "Daddy."
- Use simple words with matching gestures. For example, she may say "no" and shake her head or say "bye-bye" and wave.
- Use a single word to express a whole thought, such as "more" for "I want more."
- Talk less while learning how to walk.

How You Can Help Language Development

- Talk to her whenever you can.
- Respond to her babbling sounds with the words she is trying to say.
- Continue to introduce new words to her.
- Talk to her while doing regular activities and tell her what you are doing.
- Describe her actions. For example, "You stacked the blocks into a tower."
- Read to her every day.

Physical Development

What Your Toddler is Likely to Do

- Walk alone.
- Crawl or walk upstairs one step at a time, holding on to a railing or your hand.
- Push and pull toys while walking.
- Squat to pick up a toy without falling.
- Climb by himself on things (for example, chairs, sofas, and tables) or climb by himself out of things (for example, cribs, high chairs, and strollers).
- Give an object to another person if asked.
- Pick up and eat small pieces of food.
- Drink from a cup.
- Turn a container upside down to get something out.
- Turn pages of a book.
- Stack three or more blocks.
- Scribble with a big crayon.

Other Things Your Toddler May Do

- Walk down stairs holding a railing, placing both feet on the same step.
- Try to kick a ball.
- Ride toys.
- Run, but fall and run into things.
- Walk backwards.
- Feed himself with a spoon.
- Throw a ball forward.
- Begin to unlatch, unscrew, open, and take apart things.
- Squeeze, poke, and pat playdough.
- Copy simple lines drawn on paper.

How You Can Help Physical Development

- Continue to breastfeed.
- Spend lots of time playing outdoors in safe places. Try running and kicking balls.
- Play favourite music or songs and encourage dancing.
- Build an obstacle course for him to crawl through using boxes, chairs, big pillows, and other objects.
- Provide different-sized balls to kick and play with.
- Let him feed himself with small pieces of food at mealtimes.
- Offer him plastic bowls for stacking and nesting.
- Provide big crayons and lots of paper.
- Provide pots with lids to encourage matching.
- Help him solve simple, large-piece jigsaw puzzles.

12–18
months

Social Development

What Your Toddler Is Likely to Do

- Love being the centre of attention.
- Begin to show a sense of humour.
- Play best by himself.
- Be unlikely to share toys.
- Copy adult activities, such as driving a car, reading, or cooking.
- Separate himself from you for brief periods of time.
- Change his food likes and dislikes often.

Other Things Your Toddler May Do

- Strongly resist the limits you set.
- Co-operate, or not.
- Want to do things on his own.
- Fight with other children as he is learning to share.

How You Can Help Social Development

- Create and stick to regular routines.
- Offer choices you are comfortable with: "Do you want to put your coat or your shoes on first?"
- Have happy goodbye routines when you and family members leave each other.
- Give him chances to help with chores. He could put clothes in the laundry basket, pick up toys, or put away clean clothes.
- Provide regular chances for him to play beside children the same age.
- Don't force him to play with other children.
- Play with him and teach sharing.
- Use "yes" and "no" to clearly set reasonable limits. Briefly explain your reasons and be consistent.
- Model good manners: use "please" and "thank you."

Emotional Development

What Your Toddler Is Likely to Do

- Enjoy familiar places.
- Boldly explore and try new things.
- Take risks, if a trusted adult is present.
- Identify himself in a mirror or photo.
- Hug and kiss parents and other very familiar people and pets.
- Enjoy being the centre of attention.

Other Things Your Toddler May Do

- Show jealousy when attention is given to other family members.
- Get frustrated easily.
- Display a sense of owning toys and people.
- Enjoy older children but not play with them.
- Have a security toy or blanket.

How You Can Help Emotional Development

- Continue to breastfeed.
- Comfort him, especially when he is upset, sick, or hurt.
- Set reasonable limits and consequences.
- Provide many chances for happy moments, such as family meals and bedtime routines.
- Give him many chances to feel successful.
- Provide chances for him to play on his own.
- Talk about emotions: "You seem to be really happy!"
- Read stories and look at pictures that focus on emotions.
- Talk about changes in routines.

12–18
months

Cognitive Development

What Your Toddler Is Likely to Do

- Realize things still exist even when he cannot see them.
- Find things in pictures when asked.
- Learn about the world by touching and moving things. He may fit things into holes, mix and dump sand, or stack items and knock them down.
- Expect events to follow in routines and be predictable.
- Follow simple directions, such as "Come and show me the ball."

Other Things Your Toddler May Do

- Group similar things, such as socks, shoes, or blocks.
- Use imagination in play. For example, he may move toy trucks around on the floor.
- Handle playdough, crayons, and paints.
- Show understanding of some colours and shapes.
- Show increased memory skills by asking for something you took away earlier.

How You Can Help Cognitive Development

- Keep adding to the range of things that you give him to play with.
- Talk about events and people that he remembers.
- Count things together in books and find the same things in your home.
- Point out colours and shapes when you talk to your toddler.
- Give him simple directions: "Put your truck and doll in the toy box, please."
- Make special books with him and read or enjoy them together.
- Read toddler books with him and encourage him to talk about and point to the pictures.
- Encourage him to make music and dance with shakers, pots, and pans.

Language Development

What Your Toddler Is Likely to Do

- Point to show you something.
- Understand far more words than he can speak. For example, he can point when asked, "Where's your belly button?"
- Use a vocabulary of five or more words to make short expressions such as "all gone."
- Use "no" correctly, often with a shake of his head.
- Form questions by making his voice rise at the end of a sentence: "Daddy go?"
- Try to sing songs.

Other Things Your Toddler May Do

- Begin to understand basic sentences.
- Name pictures in a book.
- Use one word to name things he sees or say what he wants. For example, he may say "More" for "I want more."
- Copy animal sounds.
- Use his own name to refer to himself.
- Follow simple directions.
- Look at what you are talking about.
- Start combining words to form two-word sentences. For example, "Mommy ball!" for "Mommy, I want the ball."

How You Can Help Language Development

- Expand on his language: If he says "Doggie," you say "Yes, that is a dog."
- Read to him as often as you can.
- Complete his sentences. For example, if your toddler says, "Daddy going . . .," say, "Daddy is going to the car."
- Read and sing nursery rhymes.
- Give him books to look at.
- Encourage him to point out things in picture books.
- Use different voices and lots of expression when reading to him.
- Monitor your use of "no," and use it only when needed for safety.
- Keep a diary of the words he says. It may surprise you how quickly he learns language.

Family Stories

Hugs and Kisses

We used to have a goodbye routine whenever one of us left for the day. We called it our "group hug," or as our toddler Taylor called it, our "dup ugh." We would all hug and say, "Let's kiss Daddy," "Let's kiss Mommy," and then, "Let's kiss Taylor." It was fun, took a minute, and made leaving easier for everyone.

18–24 months

Physical Development

What Your Toddler is Likely to Do

- Ride on a small-wheeled toy.
- Carry a large toy while walking.
- Kick a ball.
- Squat while playing.
- Walk backwards or sideways while pulling a toy.
- Back into a chair to sit down.
- Remove lids from containers.
- Nest cups and boxes inside each other.
- Take off her shoes, hat, and socks.
- String large beads with two hands.
- Raise and drink from a cup, then put it back on the table.

Other Things Your Toddler May Do

- Walk on tiptoes.
- Throw and go get objects.
- Jump in place with both feet.
- Catch a large ball.
- Open doors by turning knobs.
- Copy straight or circular strokes with a crayon.
- Snip with child-sized scissors.
- Fold paper in half.

How You Can Help Physical Development

- Continue to breastfeed.
- Spend lots of time playing outdoors in safe places, like a toddler playground. Try running and kicking balls.
- Look for child-sized versions of adult things, such as furniture, a soccer ball, a plastic baseball and bat, or garden tools.
- Try toys that allow pushing and pedalling with feet.
- Play with her by pretending to be an animal: "hop like a frog, fly like a bird, jump like a rabbit."
- Say her movements and actions as she does them. If she climbs the stairs, say, "You're climbing the stairs."
- Play different kinds of music for her to dance to, such as marches, rock 'n' roll, and waltzes.
- Encourage her to dress and undress on her own. Only help when needed.
- Provide lots of containers during bath time.
- Offer activities that require the sorting of shapes.
- Offer things like finger paints, paints and easels, ride-on toys, and push-pull toys.

Social Development

What Your Toddler Is Likely to Do

- Enjoy playing alone for short periods of time.
- Act like she owns certain objects.
- Like to do things without help.
- Help with simple household chores.
- Have trouble sharing. Say "no" and "mine." May hit, push, and grab to keep toys.

Other Things Your Toddler May Do

- See herself as a separate person. She may say, "No me do it."
- Put on simple clothing without help.

How You Can Help Social Development

- Use everyday routines such as walks and mealtimes to talk about family and friends.
- Talk to her ahead of time about new routines and events: "At playgroup, we will sing songs and listen to stories."
- Introduce her to a playmate.
- Watch her while she is playing with other children. At this age she will be better at playing beside rather than with another child.
- Talk about the play of other children: "Look, Kim is building a block tower."
- Let her help with chores, such as cleaning up spills, putting clothes in drawers, or putting away toys.
- Model good manners: use "please" and "thank you."

18–24
months

Emotional Development

What Your Toddler is Likely to Do

- Show concern for others.
- Show fear, but she can be settled down.
- Change between doing things on her own and wanting help or comfort.
- Be watchful around adults she doesn't know.

Other Things Your Toddler May Do

- Have mood swings and tantrums.
- Show aggressive behaviours such as biting and hitting.
- Say "no" a lot, especially if she hears "no" a lot.
- Sometimes share food, toys, and other items.
- Become familiar with routines.
- Be unhappy about any changes in routines.
- Develop new fears.
- Have a security toy or blanket.

How You Can Help Emotional Development

- Continue to breastfeed.
- Have fun with her. Laughing together builds good feelings.
- Talk about her emotions: "Your tears tell me you are feeling sad."
- Suggest ways to deal with feelings: "When you feel angry, come and get a grown-up for help."
- Sing simple songs about emotions, such as *If You're Happy and You Know It.*
- Read stories that explore emotions, and talk about them.
- Offer her choices to help her cope with her feelings: "You're feeling sad, do you want to cuddle or be alone?"
- Talk about how others feel: "John is sad because you took his truck."
- If she hurts another child, explain: "You cannot hurt others." Redirect her activity.

Cognitive Development

What Your Toddler is Likely to Do

- Use things the way they are supposed to be used. She may put a telephone to her ear or use a comb for her hair.
- Understand the passing of time and the meaning of phrases like "not now" or "when we go home."
- Recognize and name familiar people in photos.
- Show increased memory for details and routines.

Other Things Your Toddler May Do

- Explore the concept of counting.
- Understand the idea of "more than one."
- Show great interest in checking any new person, thing, or sound.
- Understand two-part requests, such as, "Please go to the shelf and bring back the blocks."

How You Can Help Cognitive Development

- Continue to breastfeed.
- Praise her successes.
- Watch her to learn what toys she needs. She will outgrow toys that are too simple. She might also ignore toys that are too hard for her to use. Notice what toys she used to like but is no longer interested in.
- Keep adding to the range of things that you are providing for her.
- Offer art supplies, such as crayons and markers for use on paper.
- Offer simple puzzles with two to four pieces.
- Point out familiar sounds, such as car horns, dogs barking, or fire truck sirens when walking or playing outside.
- Help challenge her skill levels, when she's ready. If she can stack three blocks almost every time, give her a fourth to try.
- Talk about numbers: "There are two blocks in the pail."
- Talk about time: "We are going over to Grandma's tomorrow."
- Talk about colours: "Here is your red ball."
- Read toddler books with her and encourage interaction with pictures.

18–24 months

Talk, Talk, Talk

I always talked to my daughter, Chloe, about anything and everything we were doing. Even when she was just under a year, we'd be crossing the street and I would say, "Is it safe to cross? Let's look for cars. Look, there are no cars, it's safe. Let's go." Or when we were getting groceries, I'd talk about the fruit: "This one is not ripe enough," or "This apple is nice and red. Let's buy this one." I wasn't surprised when Chloe talked at an early age. I think all the talking really helped her learn words.

Language Development

What Your Toddler is Likely to Do

- Use two- to three-word sentences: "More milk please."
- Use about 200 words.
- Ask for help using words or actions.
- Talk in a run-on flow of words while talking to stuffed animals or herself. The words may not make sense.
- Name some pictures in a book.
- Copy new words and phrases you say: "Go bye-bye." "Grandpa's car."

Other Things Your Toddler May Do

- Sing simple songs with words and actions.
- Begin to be understood by others outside the family.
- Start to use plurals.
- Use the past tense.
- Copy or request new words.

How You Can Help Language Development

- Ask simple questions starting with "what" or "where."
- Read to her as often as you can.
- Build upon what she says. For instance, if she says, "cat," respond with "Yes! That's a black cat."
- Listen carefully to her and try to find the meaning in what she says by asking her questions.
- Point out the names of things around your home and outside.
- Take her to the library to get books and stories on tapes or CDs.

To Do

Read, Sing, Rhyme, and Tell Stories
Nursery rhymes help toddlers learn language patterns. Tell stories to spark your toddler's imagination. Try *Itsy Bitsy Spider*.

Physical Development

What Your Toddler is Likely to Do

- Walk backwards and sideways.
- Walk upstairs and downstairs alone, placing both feet on one step.
- Run without falling.
- Jump in place, lifting both feet off the floor.
- Climb on a riding toy and make it move using both feet at the same time.
- Scribble, holding a crayon in his whole hand.
- Copy drawing up-and-down and side-to-side and horizontal lines.
- Build a tower of five or more blocks.
- String beads, picking them up with his thumb and index finger.
- Remove lids by turning his wrist.

Other Things Your Toddler May Do

- Walk on a narrow balance beam.
- Walk upstairs and downstairs using one foot and then the other, holding the handrail.
- Run without bumping into things.
- Jump forward.
- Pedal a simple tricycle.
- Begin to use thumb and fingertips when holding a crayon.
- Copy drawing a cross or a circle.
- Fold paper.
- Use small safety scissors to snip paper.
- Remove unbuttoned clothes and zip up zippers.
- Begin to show an interest in using the toilet.

How You Can Help Physical Development

- Continue to breastfeed.
- Play different music and dance with him.
- Spend lots of time playing outdoors in safe places, like toddler playgrounds. Try running and kicking balls.
- Encourage him to try new movements, such as jumping, rolling, stretching, marching, and walking.
- Set up some plastic bottles for bowling pins so he can knock them down with a ball.
- Play simple movement games where he can stop and go, change directions, and move quickly or slowly.
- Sing songs like *If You're Happy and You Know It*, name body parts, and do different actions.
- Praise his drawing efforts and describe the markings you see.
- Provide him with chances to practise dressing skills, helping him with buttons and zippers only when he needs help.
- Make playdough with him and create different shapes together.
- Supply him with costumes for pretend-play, including hats, shoes, coats, and pants.
- Offer art materials, such as markers, crayons, finger paints, paints and an easel.
- Offer ride-on toys and push-pull toys.
- Provide puzzles of different sizes, colours, and number of pieces.
- Invite him to help with simple cooking jobs, such as adding vegetables to a salad or stirring with a spoon.

24–30 months

Social Development

What Your Toddler is Likely to Do

- Try to do more independently. For example, he may say, "No! Me do it!"
- Enjoy playing near other children (parallel play). However, he is probably not yet able to play with other children (co-operative play). (See p. 45 for more information on types of play.)
- Have trouble sharing. Say "no" and "mine." May hit, push, and grab to keep toys.
- Become aware of the difference between boys and girls.

Other Things Your Toddler May Do

- Act shy around strangers.
- Pull hair, hit, or bite other children when upset.
- Willingly help put things away.
- Accept new people, if you have talked to them.
- Begin to start playing with others.
- Show patience.

How You Can Help Social Development

- Provide chances to play with other children, but keep it on a one-to-one basis.
- Teach him to practise sharing by using toys as examples: "Dolly's sharing her blocks with Teddy."
- Explain how conflicts make other people feel sad, angry, or frustrated.
- Share quiet times together by reading, telling stories, or cuddling.
- Give lots of praise for positive behaviours: "I think you're doing a great job putting your toys in the toy box."
- Provide chances for him to do things without help.

Emotional Development

What Your Toddler is Likely to Do

- Move back and forth between doing things by himself and wanting help.
- Demand his own way much of the time.
- Want routines.
- Connect feelings to language and pretend-play. For example, he may roar like an angry lion.
- Have many strong feelings that he has trouble expressing.

Other Things Your Toddler May Do

- Show clear likes or dislikes for certain people, objects, or places.
- Be more sensitive to other children and cry if they cry.
- React to other people's emotions.
- Have a security toy or blanket.
- Have tantrums.

How You Can Help Emotional Development

- Continue to breastfeed.
- Encourage him to show his emotions and talk about them: "It's OK to cry. Can you tell me what's making you sad?"
- Move him to a quieter place when he is having difficulty coping with his emotions.
- Provide chances for pretend-play with dolls and stuffed animals to help practise emotional responses.
- Give him chances to do things by himself, such as getting dressed and helping with chores.
- Read books that show how children or animals experience a range of emotions, such as jealousy, anger, and affection.
- Talk about how his behaviour may affect others: "You took away Tommy's toy, and now he has no toy to play with. I think this has made Tommy feel sad."
- Let him know ahead of time when you will be interrupting his play: "In five minutes it will be time to be put on our coats and pick up your sister from school."

24–30 months

Cognitive Development

What Your Toddler is Likely to Do

- Pretend-play with others.
- Begin to match and sort shapes, pictures, and some colours.
- Understand that things are different shapes and sizes.
- Become aware of the sequence of numbers, when spoken.
- Show an increased attention span.
- Begin to solve problems by trial and error.

Other Things Your Toddler May Do

- Sort groups of objects into sets.
- Complete simple puzzles.
- Combine toys and games in more complex ways, such as using playdough in dramatic play.
- Understand the concept of future time (soon, tomorrow) but not past time (yesterday).
- Begin to understand one-to-one actions, such as setting one plate per person.
- Recall past experiences.

How You Can Help Cognitive Development

- Continue to breastfeed.
- Praise his successes.
- Keep adding to the range of objects and toys that you are providing.
- Give him a broader range of art supplies and ask him to talk about the drawings and colours.
- Allow time for him to solve a problem; don't rush to help.
- Include shapes and colours in daily routines.
- Keep counting: "Let's count the blocks you used in your tower."
- Let him fill in the blanks while singing a song or reading a book.
- Play matching games. For example, match jars and lids together, or sort a mix of puzzle pieces and crayons back into their separate boxes.
- Read toddler books with him and encourage interaction with the pictures.
- Play singing and actions games with music.

Language Development

What Your Toddler is Likely to Do

- Use personal pronouns such as "I," "me," and "you."
- Put together simple two-word sentences.
- Say his first and last names.
- Answer simple questions, such as, "What's your name?"
- Enjoy looking at books and talking about the pictures.
- Sing parts of songs.
- Ask many questions.

Other Things Your Toddler May Do

- Use words that describe, such as "big," "dirty," "wet," or "hot."
- Talk more in interactions and during stories.
- Know and say details about himself, such as his name and age.
- Understand two-step directions: "Please go into the kitchen and bring me the big spoon."
- Recite a few simple nursery rhymes.
- Use plurals in a general way. He will likely say "foots" instead of "feet."

How You Can Help Language Development

- Talk and read to him whenever you can.
- Listen to audiotapes and CDs of nursery rhymes together.
- Use correct pronouns in sentences. For example, instead of saying, "Mommy is going out," say, "I am going out."
- Show him that you are interested in what he says by repeating what he says.
- Look at family pictures with him and use simple sentences to describe what is happening: "This was Sarah's birthday party."
- Play language games, such as "Where Is Your Ear?"
- Be prepared to answer a lot of questions.

Key Points

Encouraging Different Languages

If your family members speak more than one language, consider passing on this gift to your toddler. Here are some strategies:

- Use two languages from the start. For example, one parent or caregiver can use one language while the other parent or caregiver uses another language.
- Or, use only one language at home, and your toddler can learn the second language in the community, at daycare, or at playschool.

30–36 months

Physical Development

What Your Toddler is Likely to Do

- Take part in group activities that include running, galloping, crawling, rolling over, and twirling around.
- Walk on a narrow beam, putting one foot in front of the other for a few steps.
- Run without bumping into things.
- Climb the ladder of a slide or other play equipment.
- Pedal a tricycle.
- Hold a pencil as if to print.
- Copy drawing a cross, circles, dots, small lines, and swirls.
- Cut paper with small safety scissors. However, she may not be able to cut along a line.
- Turn pages of a book one at a time.
- Turn handles and doorknobs.

Other Things Your Toddler May Do

- Walk forward and backward on a narrow beam.
- Ride a tricycle, steering well and using the pedals.
- Kick a ball so it sometimes goes where she wants.
- Throw a ball overhand with fairly good aim.
- Take part in circle games with many players, such as musical chairs, hokey-pokey, or *The Farmer in the Dell*.
- Scribble with pencils, crayons, and markers.
- Draw squiggles and say that's her name.
- Join in songs and finger plays.
- Play with different manipulative toys (toys that she can hold and move), such as connecting straws, snap blocks, or folding paper.
- Put on and take off clothes.

How You Can Help Physical Development

- Continue to breastfeed.
- Cheer her on when she tries new physical challenges, making sure of safety.
- Set up a big target for her to aim at when throwing or kicking a ball.
- Be physically active with her by playing tag or rolling down a hill.
- Play music and provide colourful scarves to move and dance with.
- Show her movements like galloping and twirling by playing "follow the leader."
- Show her pictures of different animals and ask her to move like them: "Show me how you move like a fish!"
- Create a simple obstacle course with blocks and hoops.
- Praise her skill at drawing, dancing, climbing, and other activities.
- Let her turn the pages of the book while you are reading to her.
- Provide writing and art supplies, such as pencils, markers, crayons, or chalk. Supervise the activity and only give a few supplies at a time.
- Help her cut out small pieces of paper to use as tickets for a puppet show.
- Provide different kinds of dress-up clothes with snaps, buttons, and zippers.
- Talk about safety rules and explain how to use playground equipment carefully.

Social Development

What Your Toddler Is Likely to Do

- Show affection openly, for example, by hugging and kissing.
- Use social language, such as "please," "thank you," and "bye-bye."
- Play with others and take turns more easily.
- Play make-believe games and create imaginary characters.

Other Things Your Toddler May Do

- Copy adult behaviours, such as shopping, banking, parenting, breastfeeding, or cooking.
- Create an imaginary friend to talk to.
- Be more comfortable around new adults.
- Help other children to do things.
- Develop skills such as taking turns, sharing, and using words instead of fighting.

How You Can Help Social Development

- Introduce her to familiar neighbours and community workers.
- Show affection with hugs and loving words.
- Praise good behaviour. Instead of saying "good girl," say, "Sharing your teddy with Kim was very kind."
- Provide chances to play with other children.
- Encourage her to wash, dress, and feed plastic dolls to teach caring for others.
- Encourage imaginary play. Join in with questions: "Is the tea ready?"
- Make sure you are nearby to help her solve problems when playing with other children.
- Make sure a trusted adult is close by when children are playing.

30–36
months

Emotional Development

What Your Toddler Is Likely to Do

- Be upset with major changes in routines.
- Know and respond to other people's feelings.
- Become more comfortable with new people.
- Want to do things by herself, but she may fear new experiences.
- Want approval and need praise.

Other Things Your Toddler May Do

- Explain her feelings when asked about them.
- Understand the feelings of other children and talk about them.
- Stamp her feet when frustrated.
- Ask you to tell certain stories to help deal with her fears.

How You Can Help Emotional Development

- Continue to breastfeed.
- Praise her new skills and when she does something without help.
- Accept her feelings and talk about them.
- Give and use words for feelings: "disappointed," "hurt," "thrilled," "excited."
- Talk very simply about your own feelings as examples.
- Listen to and understand her fears.
- Sing songs and read stories about emotions. Talk about the feelings of a story's characters and why the characters might feel that way.

Cognitive Development

What Your Toddler Is Likely to Do

- Compare sizes of things and use words like "bigger," "smaller," and "really little."
- Try to play-act her thoughts and ideas. For example, she may pretend to be a dinosaur.
- Count three objects.
- Match and sort similar pictures and objects.
- Enjoy creative movement.

Other Things Your Toddler May Do

- Make a plan before taking action. For example, she may search for needed felt-board pieces before playing.
- Notice changes in nature, such as a seed that she planted growing a sprout.
- Use words related to time, such as "sleep time."

How You Can Help Cognitive Development

- Continue to breastfeed.
- Praise her successes.
- Keep adding to the range of things that you give her.
- Provide dress-up clothes and props.
- Give her a broader range of art supplies. Try sticks, cotton balls, paper, and cones.
- Use laundry time as a chance to talk and sort clothing.
- Introduce the concept of first, second, third in simple games. Ask: "Who is first? Who comes second?"
- Provide more complex puzzles with three to six pieces.
- Cook with her and explore different foods. Always remember to be safe in the kitchen!
- Continue to talk about time, shape, and colour concepts.
- Encourage her to tell stories.
- Encourage creative moves to music.
- Teach and play singing games like *Ring-Around-the-Rosie* and *London Bridge*.

30–36 months

Family Stories

The "Why" Game

Some days I would get tired of hearing my toddler ask "why" for what seemed like the hundredth time. I started answering, "Well, why do you think the sky is blue?" or "What do you think?" It seemed to make him stop and think for himself for a minute. He still asks why, but I can get him to participate more with different answers that make him think, too.

Language Development

What Your Toddler Is Likely to Do

- Ask a lot of questions.
- Tell stories, sing nursery rhymes, and do finger plays.
- Repeat five-word sentences.
- Talk to adults and other toddlers and be understood.
- Talk to herself about recent events and make-believe characters.
- Use social words: "please," "thank you," "hello."
- Name most body parts.

Other Things Your Toddler May Do

- Use and understand direction and position words, such as "around," "backwards," "forward," "inside," and "underneath."
- Comment on pictures in books.
- Show an understanding of story plots and act them out using puppets or dolls.
- Answer complex questions, such as "What is this?" or "How did you do that?"
- Respond to requests: "Go find your coat, please," or "Please get a paper towel."

How You Can Help Language Development

- Take time to talk to her and ask about the things that interest her.
- Sing number songs and rhymes like *Five Little Monkeys*.
- Ask open-ended questions: "What did you see on your walk?"
- Be prepared to answer lots of questions.
- Instead of always answering her questions, occasionally ask: "What do you think?"
- Make up silly rhymes.
- Invent songs.
- Read to her often.

Independence

Developing a sense of independence is an important step for toddlers. Independence is when your child does something by herself. This usually starts to happen between 12 and 36 months of age. Your toddler is starting to learn that she can control herself, her body, and sometimes those around her. She will love learning new skills and enjoy doing things by herself, including making choices.

When your toddler is learning to be independent, you will notice an increase in her willpower and self-control. You may feel frustrated when she wants to do things "her way" and not yours. However, you can also see it as a sign of her healthy development.

To help your toddler learn to be independent:

- Encourage her to do things by herself even if she fails or it takes extra time.

- Let her do whatever she can on her own, from dressing to washing, and praise her for it.

- Give her simple choices, such as choosing which cup to drink from.

- Encourage new activities that she has a good chance of doing well at.

- Let her be successful and build her confidence. Give her time to repeat each skill she learns so that she feels successful. For example, give her two blocks and let her stack them successfully before you give her a third block to add to the stack.

- Avoid shame and ridicule.

Empathy

Empathy is understanding and caring about how others feel. Teaching your toddler how to feel and show empathy is an important part of helping him develop into a responsible and caring person.

You can help your toddler develop empathy for others by:

- Responding to his needs and those of others in a caring, kind, and fair way. You are the most important role model of empathy.

- Using positive discipline with the goal to teach. (See p. 126 for more on disciplining your toddler.)

- Reasoning with him to help him understand how his actions can affect others. If he has hurt or upset someone, teach him why this is hurtful and what he can do to make it better: "When you hit your sister, it hurt her and made her sad. Please say you're sorry, give her a hug, and don't hit her again."

- Teaching him to share and be kind to others. "Look how happy Jessica is because you gave her a toy. That is so nice of you."

- Encouraging him to talk with you about his feelings.

Play

Play is the work of toddlers. It is one of the most important ways your toddler learns and develops. She discovers and learns to understand the world around her through play. It also helps her see how everything and everybody relates to each other. As a parent, you can provide the safe environment for play.

Experts recommend that parents support toddlers to:

- Play actively. Toddlers need at least 60 minutes of physical activity every day to help build strong bones, muscles, heart, and lungs. (See p. 91 for more on physical activity.) Try dancing, jumping, running, rolling, and skipping.

- Play with other children, when possible, to help them learn social skills like co-operating and sharing.

- Play in ways that help them to learn about the world around them.

- Play in ways that foster creativity and self-expression.

Types of Play

Children can learn through different kinds of play. You'll probably see your toddler play in the following ways:

- Solitary Play: This is when she plays by herself. All children like solitary play at times.

- Parallel Play: This is when she plays beside another child without interacting. She will, however, observe the other child and often imitate what they do. Toddlers enjoy parallel play.

- Imitative Play: This is when she copies another child and they copy her. One toddler starts to jump and soon they are all jumping. Or you are folding clothes and she tries to do the same.

- Social Bids: This is the first step toward having fun with others. Well before the age of 24 months, she will offer toys, looks, or words to other children. It's her way of communicating.

- Co-operative Play: As she gets older, she will start to play with other children. She might help to build a block village or take their stuffed animals to the doctor. Many children are not ready for this kind of play until they are 36 months of age or older.

Skills Learned Through Play

By encouraging your toddler to play, you are helping her physical, emotional, social, cognitive, and language skills to develop.

Area of Development	Examples
Physical skills	how to crawl, climb, walk, run
	how to make small fingers work
	how to see
	how to hear
Social skills	how to co-operate
	how to share
	how to be a leader
	how to say please and thank you
Emotional skills	how to identify her feelings
	how to tell others about feelings
	how to deal with feelings
Cognitive skills	how to solve problems
	how to make things work
	how things feel and look
	how things affect each other
	how shapes, colours, and numbers differ
	how close or far things are
	how to imagine
	how to explore
	how to paint and draw
Language skills	the names for things
	the words for some big ideas like love and share
	how to say a sentence
	how to tell a story
	how to listen
	how things sound

Play by Age

Each toddler is unique and will develop at his own pace. However, the following are general guidelines of what you will notice at different ages.

6 to 12 Months:
Explorers

During this time, your toddler will use his body to make discoveries. He will begin to sit up, crawl, pull up, and grab for everything within reach. He will start to understand cause and effect. He will also search for things that have become hidden—that may include you, as you go into another room. You will find yourself talking to him more and more as you begin to hear his first words. He will be busy dumping, stacking, and pouring. This is a good time to give him balls, sturdy toys on wheels, blocks, nesting toys, rattles, and bowls of different sizes.

12 to 24 Months:
Movers and Shakers

Between 12 and 24 months, your toddler will go through big changes. Once she can walk and talk, her play will become more complex. She will be able to handle smaller toys as her co-ordination improves. You will see her imagination develop, as she copies the things she hears and sees. You will also see her personality by the type of play she chooses. Does she prefer quiet play or active play? Does she tend to focus for quite a while on a single task, or does she do many tasks at the same time?

At this age, she will still not be able to play with other children (co-operative play). However, she will be able to play beside other children (parallel play). This is a good time to give her balls to chase and later to kick and throw. It's also a good time for toys to push, such as pop-up toys, or sit-and-ride toys.

24 to 36 Months:
Social Butterflies

Between 24 to 36 months, your toddler will become sociable and want playmates. Gradually, he will develop the skills to play with another child. Make sure you are nearby to help him solve possible problems when playing with other children.

Your toddler will also show much more imagination. Encourage imaginary play; join in and expand the play with questions. This is also a good time to supply dress-up clothes and props.

Blocks

If I were to advise parents on the one best toy to buy that will last for years, I would say to buy blocks. Old-fashioned wooden blocks are great. My school-aged kids still use their blocks.

Encouraging Your Toddler to Play

You toddler will learn best when she can choose what she wants to do from a couple of options. Here are some ways you can encourage her to play:

- Let play be directed by her.

- Be playful. If you like to sing or dance or do puzzles, do these things with her.

- Use your imaginations in play. For example, pretend to be animals. Move and make noises like the animals.

- Follow the cues she gives you, such as "Roll ball, Mommy."

- Provide a variety of toys appropriate for her age.

- Set aside time to play with her each day. If you are rushed, play singing, word, and guessing games while you are doing other things.

- When you put toys out, put others away, instead of having them all out at once. She may find it too much to handle if there are too many toys to choose from.

- Encourage a mix of both active and quiet play.

- Read to her every day.

- Take her outside and watch her crawl over logs, inspect insects, pick grass or stones, and explore nature.

- Let her help wash dishes, tear lettuce, dig in the garden, make beds, or whatever else interests her. What looks like work to you may seem like play to her.

- Encourage her to do artwork, using her own ideas. This may be gluing clippings of colourful paper onto a board or smearing paint with her hands. She may need your help to get started and to understand what she can do with the materials. Then, let her be creative.

- Show her that you value her play by giving her lots of praise. Tell others how good she is at climbing, painting, or building with blocks, and proudly show her work.

- Gently stop playing if she looks away or cries. She is probably tired, hungry, or overstimulated.

Toys

Many household items are perfect toys for children. Your toddler does not need fancy and expensive toys. He can use things like plastic bowls for filling and dumping, pillows for climbing or making a cave, and old clothing to play dress-up. Provide the old classics, like blocks, dump trucks, stuffed animals, toy hammers, play kitchens, garages, and farms. These toys great are for developing imagination. (See the following page for information on toy safety.)

"Natural" toys are free, fun, and easy to find, too. Children love getting down and dirty with earth and clay, water, sand, and stones. Playdough can substitute for clay. The bath is great for water play. (See pp. 173 and 174 for more information on bathing and water safety.)

(See pp. 173 and 174 for more information on bathing and water safety.)

To Do

Play at Child Care

If your toddler is in child care, she will be involved in lots of play. Spend some time observing this play when you have a spare moment. You might be able to pick up ideas for play at home. You can also see whether or not you think she is getting enough variety of play experiences. If you have concerns, talk with your child-care provider.

Toy Safety

Check the size of toys. Any toy that fits completely into your toddler's mouth is too small and can cause choking. Check that he cannot squash a larger toy, such as a sponge, into a smaller size and put it into his mouth. A good rule of thumb is that anything that can pass down the middle of a toilet paper roll is too small for a toddler. Toys should be at least 3.5 cm (1.4 in.) wide and 6 cm (2.4 in.) long.

- Make sure any paint on toys is non-toxic and cannot peel.

- To prevent choking, don't offer your toddler toys with strings, cords, or ribbons that are longer than 15 cm (6 in.). Longer ties can get wrapped around his neck and cut off breathing. Cut these cords off before giving the toy to him. Be careful about other things that can act like cords, such as audiotapes, pull toys, or skipping ropes.

- Avoid using polystyrene or Styrofoam material (egg cartons, packing materials, food containers) as toys. They can break into pieces and cause choking if your toddler puts them in his mouth.

- Check toys often for broken, sharp, or loose pieces. Fix or throw out broken toys right away.

- Watch when your toddler plays with battery-operated toys. Make sure he does not put batteries into his mouth. When the toy is not in use, store it and the batteries out of reach.

(See pp. 173 and 174 for more information on bathing and water safety.)

Family Stories

Keeping Toys for Older Kids Away From Your Toddler

When our daughter, Julia, was a toddler, we were worried about how we could keep her away from the small toys that our seven-year-old, Lucas, played with. We asked Lucas to take on the job of being the big boy in the house by helping keep his little sister safe. He said he would play with the smallest toys in his own room. This worked until we found Julia always crying outside the door. Lucas came up with the suggestion of putting a gate on the door so that she didn't feel so shut out.

We helped out during the play times, too—while our son was playing, we spent time with her. We also did a daily sweep of the house to make sure no small parts of toys were lying around.

- Be very careful with balloons. They can cause choking for children of all ages. Always blow up balloons for children. Never allow your toddler to chew on any unused balloons or those that have popped. Throw away balloons that have gone flat, and do not let your toddler suck or chew on inflated balloons.

- Put toys not being used into a toy box to prevent falls. Also, storing unused toys helps ensure that your toddler will not use toys unsupervised. The toy box should have a lid that will not trap him inside or slam down on fingers or head.

- Make sure that any toy (or toy box) that is large enough for your toddler to climb into and has a lid or door also has a source of air such as air holes or cut-outs.

- Buy washable toys and wash them often to prevent the spread of germs. Most stuffed toys can be put in a pillowcase with a knotted top and washed and dried with good results.

- When possible, give your toddler well-made toys. These last longer and are generally safer.

- Always read the safety information on a toy's warning label. Choose toys that are recommended for your toddler's age.

- To prevent suffocation, immediately throw away or recycle the packaging from new toys.

- Do not let noise from toys damage your toddler's hearing. If you have to raise your voice to be heard above the noise level of a toy, the toy is too noisy.

TV and Computer Games

It may be helpful to ask yourself if TV or computer games help your toddler grow and develop. Research and child development experts suggest that toddlers do not gain much from watching TV because only two senses are used: sight and hearing. Even TV shows created for young children often move too fast and are too much for your toddler to follow. Too much colour, movement, and sound all at once does not support your toddler's health and development. We know that childhood obesity is linked to watching TV. Researchers are also looking at how the large-screen TVs and "surround sound" affect children.

Choosing not to watch TV or play computer games gives you and your toddler quality time to do things that can help her be more creative, improve problem-solving skills, and get more physical activity. Limiting or cutting out TV watching also lowers how much she will see advertising for unhealthy food choices, violent images, and male and female roles that are stereotyped. Research shows that children who watch a lot of TV are more aggressive—in both words and actions.

The Canadian Paediatric Society recommends that preschoolers be limited to one hour or less of TV watching per day. The American Academy of Pediatrics recommends no TV for children under the age of 24 months (two years) and no more than one to two hours of quality TV and videos a day for older children.

If you choose to let your toddler watch TV, here are some tips:

- Limit her viewing to programs on children's channels or channels without commercials.

- Rent, borrow (from the library or friends), or buy children's videos. Ask other parents or caregivers to give you names of suitable videos for toddlers.

- If you allow her to watch or play with other media, set a limit on total screen time (that is, the time she watches TV or videos, plays video and computer games, and watches or uses a computer). Use a timer: when the timer goes off, her screen time is over—do not allow your mind to be changed.

- Discuss your decisions about TV watching with those who care for her, like grandparents or child-care providers.

- Monitor violence on TV or video games that others may be watching or playing while she is nearby. This includes television and radio news reports, which can be very violent and frightening. Television shows can be recorded and watched when she is not nearby.

Reading to Your Toddler

Reading aloud to your toddler can help his learning in many ways. Research shows that reading helps him learn new words as well as develop skills in listening, language, and math. Reading also helps him develop imagination and creativity.

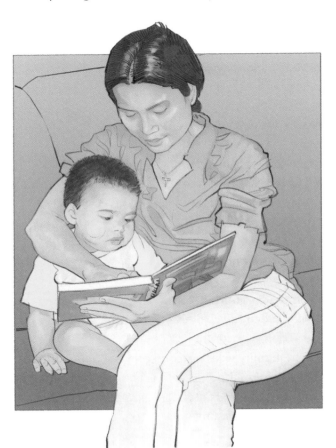

Influences on Children's Sexuality
Parents and caregivers have wide-ranging beliefs regarding sexuality. Normally, children will absorb these beliefs. You may want to examine your own beliefs and ask yourself whether or not you want your toddler to copy them.

Your toddler is likely to be exposed to sexual images on TV. Monitor the amount and type of TV she watches. (See p. 50 for more information on TV and toddlers.)

Sexual Development

The way you touch and talk about your toddler's body sends him important messages, even at an early age. When you give him a bath and clean his private parts in a matter-of-fact way, you are telling him that genitals are simply another part of the body.

Your toddler is curious about his own body, including his genitals. Here are some examples of typical behaviours you may see:

Sexual Development by Age

Birth to 24 Months
- May enjoy being naked.
- May like to touch and explore his own body, including genitals.
- May have an erection if a boy (or lubrication if a girl) for no reason.

24 Months to 36 Months
- May touch his genitals or masturbate for relaxation or soothing.
- Can identify whether someone is a girl or a boy.
- May explore bodies with a same-age playmate in a playful, curious manner (e.g., playing doctor).
- May want to watch you go to the bathroom.

Masturbation

Although children as young as seven months will explore their genitals, it is more common in toddlers 24 to 36 months old. This kind of investigation is just natural curiosity. It is as normal for your toddler to touch his genitals as to explore his toes and fingers. Once they make this discovery, most children realize quickly that this touching feels good. The way you react to your toddler's masturbation may affect his attitude toward sexuality. He may feel confused or guilty if he feels punished or ashamed about masturbation. The best approach is to ignore the activity. Teach him that sexuality isn't a secret.

Some parents feel uncomfortable if their toddler touches his genitals in public. If he is touching his genitals in public and is old enough to understand, provide him with limits. Tell him what he can do in public and what he can do at home: "Some things are private. You can do that at home in your room—how about playing with this toy for now?"

Exploring Body Parts With Other Children

You may find your toddler exploring his genitals with another child of similar age (usually 36 months and older). If this happens, try to be calm. Simply comment on what the children are doing: "I see you two are looking at each other's penises." You can let both children know that their genitals are private and should not be touched by other people. Then distract the children by directing them to other activities.

An older child should not be exploring genitals with a younger child. The younger child usually sees the older child as more powerful. Calmly talk with him about what happened in order to get the facts. Explain that no one should touch or look at his genitals without his permission. Talk to your doctor or public health nurse if you have concerns about your child being touched inappropriately by another child.

If You Have Concerns About Your Toddler's Development

There may be times when you worry that your toddler's development is not following the usual path. You may find that the milestones set out in the previous pages are very different from what is happening with your toddler.

Your toddler also may have already been diagnosed as having a special health, developmental, or behavioural need. As a result, it may be difficult to see how the usual developmental milestones relate to her. Children with special health-care needs do follow pathways of development in the same five areas of development. However, your toddler may reach milestones at a different pace.

Your toddler may also have been born early (preterm birth) or faced special health problems early in life; you may find that her health and development seem different from those of other children born at the same time. It is important to remember that a child born early or with health problems may develop differently during infancy and early childhood than other children the same age. These differences will become smaller as a child gets older.

Parents of children who had a serious illness at birth or were born very preterm are encouraged to follow

their growth and development closely. Try to understand the developmental milestones to support and guide your toddler. Find members of the community who can provide you with help and support. Look to these resources, such as public health nurses, family physicians, parent and child groups, neighbourhood resource centres, infant development programs, HealthLink BC , or child-care programs.

If you are concerned about your toddler's development, talk to a doctor, public health nurse or child development professional in your community. It is important for health-care professionals to hear your concerns about your toddler's development. They should follow up on your concerns. Follow-up might include watching your toddler playing, filling out a child development screening questionnaire with you, or referring you to another child development or health professional in your community.

To Do

Do you need more Information?

For more information on government support for children with special needs, visit the Ministry of Children and Family Development's Special Needs Supports and Services web page. (See "Special Needs" in the Resources chapter for the web address.)

Healthy Eating for Your Toddler

You can help your toddler be healthy and eat well. Eating habits and attitudes will have an influence on his health and development throughout his life. Here are some ways to help him have healthy eating habits.

Key Ideas for Healthy Eating

Feeding "jobs." A healthy feeding relationship is one where both you and your toddler have feeding "jobs." Your "job" is to offer a choice of healthy foods at regular times each day. His "job" is to decide what to eat and how much to eat from the foods that you have offered.

Let your toddler's hunger and fullness cues guide you. He knows when he is hungry or full. Watching for and responding to his cues will help you understand how much food to offer.

Continue breastfeeding to 24 months or longer. The World Health Organization, Health Canada, Dietitians of Canada, and the Canadian Paediatric Society recommend that you continue breastfeeding until your toddler is 24 months of age or older.

Introduce your toddler to a variety of healthy foods. By starting to introduce solid foods at six months, you can introduce him to a full range of foods that provide all the nutrients he needs to grow and develop into a healthy, active child.

Help your toddler develop healthy eating habits and attitudes. Family life is busy at the best of times. It can be hard to find the time to support your toddler in eating well and learning healthy eating habits. Here are some ways to help:

- Create a calm, relaxed eating environment. A calm and relaxed environment helps him eat better. Good food and good feelings will create the setting where he can learn healthy eating habits and attitudes.

- Eat together. Taking the time to sit down and eat with him shows him the importance of eating together. It also helps him develop important language and social skills. Right from the start, you can include him in the family meal by having him join you at the table.

- Be a healthy-eating role model. Modelling healthy eating habits yourself is a powerful way that you can show your toddler the importance of healthy eating. Healthy eating habits that you can model include:
  - preparing and eating a variety of healthy foods
  - eating at regular times
  - sitting down to enjoy your meal

- Offer meals and snacks at the same times each day. When children "graze," or eat on and off all day, they may not eat a healthy, balanced diet. Grazing raises the chance that your toddler will become overweight. It also increases the risk of tooth decay.

The Eating Relationship

Your toddler has a lot to learn about healthy eating. By choosing an eating relationship with feeding "jobs" and following her hunger and fullness cues, you can help her develop healthy eating habits. Children who experience healthy eating from an early age have the best chances to become lifelong healthy eaters.

Feeding Jobs

Thinking of yourself and your toddler as having feeding "jobs" can start you off on the right path toward healthy eating. Following the feeding "jobs" can also help to avoid fighting about food.

Your "job" is to:
- Offer a choice of healthy foods.
- Offer enough food.
- Offer meals and snacks at the same times each day.
- Watch and respond to your toddler's hunger and fullness cues during meals and snacks.

Your toddler's "job" is to:
- Choose whether to eat.
- Choose what to eat from what is offered.
- Choose how much to eat.

Hunger and Fullness Cues

Your toddler knows when he is hungry or full. He will usually give you signs, or "hunger and fullness cues," to show that he does or doesn't want to eat. By reading and responding to these cues, you can help him be healthy, eat well, and enjoy food.

You can tell if he is hungry when he:
- Opens his mouth when offered food.
- Leans forward excitedly, kicks his feet, or waves his hands when offered food.

You can tell when he has had enough food when he:
- Closes his mouth when food is offered.
- Turns his head away when food is offered.
- Pushes food away.

Your toddler's appetite will vary from day to day. Sometimes he will eat a lot and at other times he will have no interest in eating. By never forcing him to eat, you will support him in following his body's own feelings of hunger and fullness.

When the Feeding Cue Is "NO!"

Sometimes you may get a strong "No!" from your toddler at a meal or snack time. If this happens, end the meal naturally and remind him when the next meal or snack will be offered. By doing this, you are supporting his feeding "job" of choosing whether to eat.

Here are some other helpful tips when the feeding cue is "No!":

- Allow him to leave the table.

- Wait until the next regular meal or snack time to offer food or drinks.

- Avoid using dessert or other foods and drinks as a bribe for finishing food.

- Avoid using food for comfort. Try offering playtime, attention, and affection instead.

Here are some questions that you can ask yourself if you are not sure whether your toddler's feeding cue is "No":

- Is he overtired, excited, or sick? Schedule some quiet time or check out your suspicions.

- Is he full? Check the amount of cow's milk or juice being consumed. More than 500 ml (2 cups) of cow's milk per day leaves little room for food. Offer water instead. Juice is not necessary. If you choose to offer juice, toddlers six to 12 months old should have no more than 60–125 ml (1/4–1/2 cup) of juice a day. Children one to six years old should have no more than 125–175 ml (1/2–3/4 cup) of juice a day.

Breastfeeding Your Toddler

The World Health Organization, Health Canada, Dietitians of Canada, and the Canadian Paediatric Society recommend that at the age of six months, you start to offer your toddler other food in addition to breast milk. Breast milk is still the healthiest food you can offer your toddler. Breast milk has many benefits and is not just for babies.

Benefits of Breast Milk for Your Toddler	Benefits of Breastfeeding for Mom
Breast milk:	Breastfeeding:
• Is an excellent source of nutrition.	• Decreases the risk of certain cancers.
• Is the best type of milk for young children.	• May decrease the risk of osteoporosis.
• Helps prevent colds, ear infections, and other infections.	• Costs less than formula.
• Helps your toddler develop healthy teeth.	• Is convenient and time saving (no bottles).
• May help prevent diabetes, heart disease, and obesity later in life.	• Is environmentally friendly (no waste).
• May improve brain development (higher IQ).	

Breastfeeding also helps you give comfort and cuddling, and be close to your toddler.

Breastfed children and many formula-fed children need a vitamin D supplement. (See p. 60 for more information.)

If you do not breastfeed, choose an iron-fortified infant formula. (For more information on infant formula, see "BC HealthFiles" in the Resources chapter.)

Frequently Asked Questions About Breastfeeding Your Toddler

You may have questions about how to enjoy and be successful at breastfeeding your toddler. Talking with other moms who are breastfeeding toddlers can be a great way to find answers to questions you may have.

Here are some frequently asked questions and answers about breastfeeding a toddler:

Can I continue breastfeeding . . .

If I return to work outside the home?
Yes. You will be able to breastfeed your toddler before you leave and when you see her after work.

Also, many workplaces support a breastfeeding mother's need to change break times and the need for a private place where breast milk can be expressed. With a little planning you can store this milk and have it given to your toddler the next day. For more information, see the resource *Baby's Best Chance: Parent's Handbook of Pregnancy and Baby Care* (third revision, sixth edition), or visit the Best Chance website, at www.BestChance.gov.bc.ca. Check out the chapters on breastfeeding and working, and expressing and storing breast milk.

You can get help and advice on returning to work and breastfeeding. Contact your public health nurse, lactation consultant, La Leche League, or breast-feeding support group. (See "Breastfeeding" in the Resources chapter.)

If I want my toddler to learn to become independent?
Yes. In fact, some studies show that toddlers who are breastfed longer than 12 months achieve independence at their own pace and become more secure than children weaned at a younger age.

If I have to take prescribed medication?
Most medications are safe to take while breastfeeding, although there are a few medications that must not be taken while breastfeeding. In this case, your doctor may be able to prescribe something else. If your doctor wants you to take a medication, be sure to say that you are breastfeeding. If you are unsure about a medication, your doctor, pharmacist, and public health nurse are all good resources for information on medications and breastfeeding.

In public?
Yes. If you feel reluctant to breastfeed in public because of the comments or reactions of others, know that breastfeeding is a normal and healthy activity.

If I get pregnant again?
Yes. You'll need to be extra careful to get enough nutrition for your unborn child, your breastfeeding toddler, and yourself. Talk to your health-care provider or a public health nurse about taking a vitamin supplement to meet your need for extra vitamins.

Family Stories

The Breast Is Best for Toddlers
I didn't plan to breastfeed my daughter, Madison, for very long. I thought breastfeeding was just for babies. But then I saw the pictures of toddlers breastfeeding in the books and read about how good breast milk is for toddlers too. That changed my mind. I ended up breastfeeding her until she was two and a half years old.

Pizza and Breastmilk?
A Great Combination!
One night, when I asked my older son, Jason, what we should have for dinner, Madison (who was breastfeeding at the time) came off the breast and said, "Pizza Mommy!" It seemed hysterical that she would breastfeed and ask for pizza at the same time. It's amazing how we can change our ideas about what's normal and healthy.

A Time to Love

The thing I love the most about breast-feeding my toddler, Noah, is seeing the "baby" in him still. When he is pulled in close to my body, skin on skin, I forget about the rough-and-tumble kid. I don't see the boy who frustrates me when he colours on the wall or upsets his brother when he takes his toys. When I breast-feed, he is my baby once again, even if only for a moment. I know I am giving him the best gift ever.

Best Times

The best times of my day are when I get to breastfeed my 15-month-old, Kelsey before and after a busy day at work. It is a chance for us to connect, reinforce our bond, and snuggle.

If I drink alcohol or use street drugs?

It's best not to drink alcohol at all while breastfeeding. Alcohol may affect your toddler's sleep or decrease the amount of milk she takes at feeding time. However, if you choose to have a drink, feed your toddler first. Since breast milk is so good for her, you do not need to stop breastfeeding if you have a drink. Alcohol is not trapped in breast milk. It is continually circulated into and out of breast milk.

If you are taking street drugs or drinking alcohol in large amounts, do not breastfeed. These substances pass through your breast milk and can affect your toddler. Talk with your doctor, pharmacist, health-care provider, public health nurse, or HealthLink BC about getting help. Or call the Motherisk Alcohol and Substance Use Helpline. The Alcohol and Drug Information and Referral Service also has information about drug and alcohol programs. (See "Alcohol and Drug Use" in the Resources chapter.)

If I smoke cigarettes?

Cigarette smoking is not recommended if you are breastfeeding. Nicotine and other harmful ingredients in cigarettes pass through your breast milk. They can affect your toddler. Smoking can also reduce the amount of breast milk you produce. It may lead to earlier weaning. However, because breastfeeding is so good for a toddler, it is better to breastfeed than not. This is true even if you do not stop smoking.

If my toddler bites me?

Toddlers bite while breastfeeding for many reasons. If your toddler bites, it does not mean that she should be weaned or you should stop breastfeeding. Try to determine why she is biting you. Is she teething? Does she have a cold or ear infection?

If your toddler bites you, remove her from the breast and firmly say, "No biting. Biting hurts mommy," then try breastfeeding again. You may have to repeat this message a few times before the biting stops. She cannot bite while breastfeeding if she is properly latched onto the breast and sucking. If she tends to bite at the end of the feeding, remove her from the breast as soon as active sucking stops. You can also offer a teething ring for biting if her teeth are coming in. (See "Breastfeeding" in the Resources chapter.)

Vitamin and Mineral Supplements

If your toddler is eating a variety of foods from all the food groups, is growing well, and looks healthy, he probably does not need extra vitamins or minerals, except for the following:

Vitamin D

Breastfed toddlers up to 12 months need 400 IU of vitamin D each day from vitamin drops. Formula-fed toddlers need vitamin D drops if they drink less than 1000 ml (4 cups) of formula each day. If your toddler drinks both breast milk and formula, he needs vitamin D drops. For more information about vitamin D supplements, call HealthLink BC at 8-1-1 to talk to a dietitian.

Vitamin D helps to build healthy bones and teeth. Vitamin D may also help prevent some chronic diseases later in life, such as diabetes.

In the past, when the dangers of too much sun were still unknown, toddlers made enough vitamin D from being in the sun. We now know they should be protected from the sun. Also, from October to March, the Canadian sunlight is too weak for toddlers to make vitamin D. So they need the vitamin D in their food to meet their bodies' needs.

Other Vitamins and Minerals

Iron deficiency is a concern for growth and brain development. If your toddler is not eating iron-rich foods or is a vegetarian or vegan, talk with your doctor. (See p. 63 for a list of iron-rich foods.)

Do not give cod-liver oil to your toddler. Cod-liver oil is too high in vitamin A for toddlers. Overdoses of vitamin A can be poisonous.

If you give your toddler a vitamin and mineral supplement, choose one approved for his age. Speak to your pharmacist who can help you find the right one. Help keep your toddler safe from overdoses by not calling supplements "candy" or "sweets" and keeping them out of his reach.

When Your Toddler Stops Breastfeeding

As your toddler grows, she will learn to feed herself solid foods more and more independently. This begins the natural process of weaning. When she is ready, she will begin to wean herself from breast-feeding. You do not have to wean her, it occurs naturally—she will gradually stop breastfeeding at her own pace.

Allowing your toddler to decide when to stop breastfeeding lets:

- You and her adjust more easily to the end of your breastfeeding relationship.

- Your body reduce the amount of milk it produces in a natural way, which will prevent your breasts becoming overfull and uncomfortable.

If You Decide to Wean Your Toddler

If you need or want to stop breastfeeding before your toddler completes the process herself, here are some tips on how to do it. The time it takes to stop breastfeeding will vary, depending on you and her. If possible, try not to rush the process. Mothers can find that breasts become sore and full of milk if they wean too quickly. Weaning gradually helps to give your body time to adjust to the reduced demand on breast milk production.

Taking Time with Weaning
Weaning can come with emotional feelings. Taking time with weaning allows your toddler to get used to new ways to eat and feel close. It also allows your body's hormones to change more slowly, so you feel comfortable emotionally.

Here are some tips to help the weaning process be comfortable for both you and your toddler:

- **Plan:** Choose a non-stressful time to start. Starting to wean her on your first day of work or child care, or during a move, can add to the stress of these situations.

- **Start slowly:** Choose to replace one feeding every day for the first week. You may wish to pick the feeding that provides the least comfort for her. This is often the late-afternoon feeding. To provide enough nutrition, replace the skipped feeding with expressed breast milk and food.

- **Skip one more:** After one week, or when you feel comfortable, replace one more feeding.

- **Continue to skip:** Keep replacing one feeding per week with food and other fluids.

- **Last to go:** Last of all, replace the feeding that provides the most comfort. Often these are the morning and bedtime feedings. When you are ready to stop the morning or bedtime feeding, it may work best to have your partner or another family member take over the routines at this time.

- **Be ready to give more comfort and cuddles:** You may be looking forward to fewer demands on your time and energy when you stop breastfeeding. However, this most likely will not be the case. Your toddler may need more attention and love during and after weaning. You may find that you are spending more time holding, comforting, and settling her.

Changing From a Bottle to a Cup

To make the change from a bottle to a cup easier, you can use a cup with your toddler's meals and snacks. Start this when he is six months old. Using a bottle is not necessary. Breastfed toddlers can begin using a cup while continuing to breastfeed.

You may wish to slowly cut down the amount of milk you give in a bottle for each feed. This way your toddler may not notice the change. If he requests more to drink, offer a small amount of water in a separate bottle.

To prevent choking and spills, ask your toddler to sit down with you when he drinks from a cup. This is safer than walking around with it.

Your toddler's teeth may decay if he is still drinking from a bottle filled with anything other than water. This is especially true during rest and sleep periods. Tooth decay can occur if he walks around with a bottle during the day and always sips from it. (See p. 107 for more information on how to prevent tooth decay.)

Introducing Solid Foods

The World Health Organization, Health Canada, Dietitians of Canada, and the Canadian Paediatric Society recommend that when your toddler is six months old, you keep breastfeeding but also offer solid foods.

You will know she is ready for solid food when she:

- Sits and holds her head up.

- Watches and opens her mouth for a spoon and closes her lips around the spoon.

- Does not push food out of her mouth with her tongue.

Getting Started With Solid Food

To get started, pick a time when your toddler is alert and has an appetite but is not too hungry. Seat him on your lap or facing you while secured in a comfortable high chair. (For more information on choosing a safe high chair, see p. 167.) It is a good idea to give him a second child-sized spoon. That way he is less likely to grab your spoon.

Place a spoonful of meat or single-grain iron-fortified infant cereal close to his lips. Give him time to look at it, smell it, and taste it. Once he opens his mouth, put the spoon in. If he takes the food, offer another spoonful. If he spits out the food, wait a few minutes and try again.

You can expect that most of the first solid food you offer will end up on his bib, face, and high-chair tray. This is normal—you are getting him used to eating solid foods.

Gagging

When toddlers try foods with more texture, they sometimes gag. This is a normal part of learning to eat. A toddler's gag reflex is very sensitive—and very effective in preventing choking. Gagging is normal and healthy; your toddler is learning how to eat without choking. If he gags, don't panic because it could startle him and make him afraid to try new foods. Stay calm and reassure him.

Choosing a First Food

The best "first foods" are meat or an infant cereal that is single-grain and iron-fortified. Rice cereal is an example of a single-grain cereal. (For more information on how to prepare meat, see "Getting Started With Meat" on p. 64.)

Wait a few days before adding each new food. To make sure your toddler is getting enough iron, offer iron-rich foods at least twice a day.

Iron-rich Foods

Iron-rich foods include:

- Meats: beef, pork, lamb, veal
- Cereals: iron-fortified infant cereals
- Poultry: chicken, turkey
- Fish
- Tofu
- Beans and other legumes
- Egg yolks

For more information about iron, see "BC HealthFiles", p. 191 in the Resources chapter.

Getting Started With Meat

Mix water, mashed vegetables, or gravy with meat to make sure that it is moist enough for your toddler to chew. Shredding or grinding the meat into very small pieces also helps make it easy to chew.

Ground meat is easier to chew. You can use it in casseroles, meatloaf, or patties. If you are serving chicken, you can mince some of the dark meat, which is moister than the white meat. Fish is another good choice because it is tender and easy to chew.

To reduce the risk for food poisoning, cook meat well. When you cut into well-cooked meat or poultry, the juices should be clear, with no traces of pink.

Meat, fish, and poultry are well cooked when they reach the following safe temperatures. Use a thermometer to check the temperature.
- Beef (roast, steaks): 63°C (145°F)
- Ground beef: 71°C (160°F)
- Poultry (chicken, turkey): 74°C (165°F)
- Pork: 71°C (160°F)
- Or, safe and easy to remember: cook all meats to 74°C (165°F)

Homemade Baby Food

Both homemade baby food and store-bought baby food are options for feeding a toddler. To make homemade baby food, mash the foods your family eats. It is not necessary to purée your food. Even without teeth, your toddler can enjoy food that is well mashed.

Following these steps can help make sure that homemade baby food is safe:

- Wash counters and equipment with soap and water immediately after use. Clean with 5 ml (1 tsp.) of liquid household bleach added to 750 ml (3 cups) of water. It is especially important that you clean up after contact with raw meats.

- Discard worn cutting boards where germs can hide.

- Store leftovers for no longer than two to three days in the refrigerator. If you freeze leftovers, use frozen portions within two months.

Safe Microwave Cooking and Reheating

Following these steps for microwave safety will help protect your toddler from food or drinks that are unevenly heated.

- Cover, stir, or turn foods at least once midway through cooking or reheating.

- Check the temperature of food by tasting it before giving it to her.

- When cooking foods in a microwave, heat them to a temperature at least 14°C (25°F) higher than what is recommended for other types of cooking.

- When reheating food in a microwave, heat to 88°C (190°F). Then allow it to stand covered for two minutes after heating.

- It's safer to heat bottles in hot water because liquids heated in a microwave can heat unevenly.

Learning to Drink

At six months of age, a toddler can learn to drink from a regular cup. Sip cups don't help your toddler learn to drink from a cup because most sip cups are just bottles in disguise. The valve to stop spills makes him suck rather than sip.

Instead of using a sip cup, encourage your toddler to sit down with you when he has a drink from a cup, rather than walking around with it. This will help prevent choking and spills.

Feeding by Age

The charts on the following pages are based on the four food groups from *Eating Well with Canada's Food Guide* (see Appendix p. 183). The charts give guidelines and suggestions on foods that match your toddler's development age. The amounts given are guidelines only. Don't worry if your toddler does not eat the same amounts. Remember, her appetite will depend on age, body size, activity level, and growth rate.

Right from the start you can include your toddler at the family meal table. Sharing good food and good feelings can help create a setting where she will learn healthy eating habits.

Key Points

Use Safe Containers for the Microwave

It can be unsafe to microwave food or liquids in containers that look damaged, are stained, or smell bad. If you use plastic containers or plastic wrap in the microwave, be sure they are labelled "microwave safe".

6–9
months

6–9 Months

Typical Eating Skills of Toddlers From 6–9 Months

- Picks up food with fingers or palms and puts in mouth.
- Bites off food.
- Closes lips around a cup held by an adult.
- Chews by:
  - moving food to sides of mouth
  - moving food from front to back of mouth
  - munching up and down
  - grinding food with jaws

Feeding Tips for 6–9 Months

Here are some ideas to help you promote healthy eating habits:

- Offer solid foods after breastfeeding.

- Offer small amounts of water from a cup. At six to nine months your toddler is learning to drink from a cup. However, keep in mind that she needs the nutrition from breast milk.

- To reduce the chance of allergies, offer one new food at a time and wait a few days before offering a new food.

- Feed solids with a spoon; do not put solid foods in a bottle.

- You can use a fork to mash soft, cooked foods and use that instead of store-bought puréed baby food.

- Give your toddler lots of chances to feed herself—she can use the practice.

Daily Food Suggestions for Toddlers Aged 6–9 Months

At six months, offer a variety of solid foods two to three times per day, plus breast milk. By nine months, offer a variety of solid foods three to four times per day from each of the food groups, plus breast milk.

Milk and Alternatives	Grain Products	Vegetables and Fruit	Meat and Alternatives
	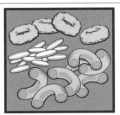		

Milk and Alternatives

- Breast milk (breastfeed according to your toddler's hunger and fullness cues).

Grain Products

- Single-grain iron-fortified infant cereal. Start with about 5 ml (1 tsp.) and increase to 60–125 ml (4–8 tbsp.).
- Progress to rice, pasta, "oat ring" cereals, noodles, crackers by eight to nine months.

Vegetables and Fruit

- Cooked, well-mashed vegetables (potatoes, yams, squash, carrots). Progress to small pieces by nine months.
- Soft fruit (banana, kiwi) and cooked hard fruit (apples, pears).
- Start with small amounts and progress to 60–125 ml (4–8 tbsp.) of fruit and vegetables.
- Juice is not necessary for your toddler. If you decide to give juice, choose 100% unsweetened juice and offer it in a cup as part of a meal or snack. Limit to no more than 60–125 ml (1/4–1/2 cup) of juice a day.

Meat and Alternatives

- Fully cooked, well minced meat, poultry, fish, shellfish, mashed cooked egg, mashed tofu, legumes.
- 15 g (1 tbsp.) peanut or nut butter.
- By 9 months, aim for 100–125 ml (6–8 tbsp.).

9–12 months

Typical Eating Skills of Toddlers From 9–12 Months

- Chews up and down.
- Uses thumb and finger to pick up small pieces of food.
- Holds a cup in two hands.
- Twists and turns hand when using a spoon.
- Drops things from a high chair.
- Wants to sit at the family table and feed herself.
- Feeds herself with fingers or spoon but usually needs some help.

Feeding Tips for 9–12 Months

Here are some ideas to promote healthy eating habits:

- Sit and eat with your toddler to show that you value healthy eating.

- Offer solid foods *before* breastfeeding to best meet her nutrition needs.

- This is a great age to increase the variety of flavours offered.

- Offer water in a cup to quench thirst and help her learn to drink from a cup.

- To keep her safe, be aware of choking hazards. (See p. 82– 83.)

- Wait until after 12 months to offer egg white or honey.

Daily Food Suggestions for Toddlers Aged 9–12 Months

Offer a variety of solid foods three to four times per day from each of the food groups, plus breast milk.

Milk and Alternatives	Grain Products	Vegetables and Fruit	Meat and Alternatives
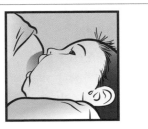	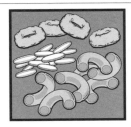		

Milk and Alternatives

- Breast milk.
- Small amounts of whole milk may be offered once your toddler is 9 to 12 months old and is taking a variety of solid foods.
- Introduce milk products (such as yogurt, cottage cheese, pasteurized cheese).

Grain Products

- Iron-fortified infant cereal: about 125 ml (1/2 cup) or more.
- Whole-grain toast, pasta, rice.
- Small pieces of bannock, tortillas, roti.

Vegetables and Fruit

- Soft fruits and vegetables: about 125–250 ml (1/2–1 cup), mashed or cut in small pieces.
- Small pieces of cooked vegetables (potato, yam, squash, carrots).
- Soft fruit (banana, kiwi) and cooked or small pieces of hard fruit (apples, pears).
- Juice is not necessary for your toddler. If you decide to give juice, choose 100% unsweetened juice and offer it in a cup as part of a meal or snack. Limit to no more than 60–125 ml (1/4–1/2 cup) of juice a day.

Meat and Alternatives

- Fully cooked, soft and diced meat, poultry, fish, shellfish, egg, tofu, legumes: about 100–125 ml (6–8 tbsp.).
- 15 g (1 tbsp.) peanut or nut butter.

Family Stories

Eating Together

I was amazed at how much better Nathan would eat when we sat together and ate the same foods. So I made meals that both of us could eat. For example, if I was making chicken with rice and vegetables, I would cut the chicken and vegetables into small pieces that he could pick up. It was so cute watching him study how I ate. Then, he'd try to copy how I used the fork to get the food from my plate into my mouth!

12–24 Months

Feeding Tips for 12–24 Months
Here are some ideas to promote healthy
eating habits:

- Include your toddler in regular family meals and snacks. This helps support healthy eating, language, and social skills.

- Be aware of choking hazards. (See p. 82 – 83.)

- Water is the healthiest drink to offer between meals and snacks.

- Limit foods high in salt, sugar, and caffeine (chips, chocolate, candy, pop).

Typical Eating Skills of Toddlers From 12–24 Months
- Feeds himself with fingers or spoon, but is messy.
- Sometimes eats very little, other times eats a lot.
- Puts food in mouth and takes it out again.
- Is easily distracted.
- May throw food.

Daily Food Suggestions for Toddlers Aged 12–24 Months

Offer a variety of food three to four times per day from each of the food groups, plus one to two snacks. Continue to breastfeed.

Milk and Alternatives	Grain Products	Vegetables and Fruit	Meat and Alternatives
	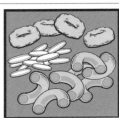		

Milk and Alternatives

- Breast milk.
- Give about 500 ml (2 cups) whole milk if your toddler is no longer breastfeeding.
- Offer milk products (yogurt, cottage cheese, pasteurized cheese, etc.).

Suggested portions:
- 25–50 g (1–2 oz.) of pasteurized cheese.
- 60 ml (1/4 cup) of cottage cheese.
- 75–175 g (1/3–3/4 cup) of yogurt.

Grain Products

Choose 100% whole-grain products.
- Offer five to six times each day.

Suggested portions:
- 1/2 to 1 slice bread, bannock, tortilla, roti.
- 125–250 ml (1/2–1 cup) whole-grain cereal.
- 75–125 ml (1/3–1/2 cup) of hot cereal, cooked pasta, rice, congee.

Vegetables and Fruit

Choose at least 1 dark green and 1 orange vegetable.
- Offer five or more times each day.

Suggested portions:
- 1/2 to 1 medium-sized vegetable or fresh fruit.
- 30–60 ml (2–4 tbsp.) fresh, cooked or mashed fruit.
- 60–125 ml (1/4–1/2 cup) of cooked vegetables.
- 60–125 ml (1/4–1/2 cup) of raw vegetables.
- Juice is not necessary for your toddler. If you decide to give juice, choose 100% unsweetened juice and offer it in a cup as part of a meal or snack. Limit to no more than 125–175 ml (1/2–3/4 cup) per day.

Meat and Alternatives

- Offer two to three times each day.

Suggested portions:
- 30–60 ml (2–4 tbsp.) of well-cooked, ground, chopped, or cubed lean meat, fish, shellfish, or poultry.
- 30–60 ml (2–4 tbsp.) of mashed legumes.
- 1 whole egg.
- 50–100 g (3–6 tbsp.) tofu or tempeh.
- 15 g (1 tbsp.) peanut or nut butter.

24–36 Months

Typical Eating Skills of Toddlers From 24–36 Months

- Holds cup in hand.
- Spills a lot.
- Feeds herself if food is cut up.
- Eats family foods.
- May eat a lot or very little.
- Can take a long time to eat.
- May show strong food likes and dislikes.

Health Canada recommends following *Eating Well with Canada's Food Guide* once your toddler is 24 months old. (See Appendix p. 183.)

Your toddler has now outgrown the need for whole (homogenized) milk and you can choose to switch from whole milk to 2% or 1% milk. Breast milk is also a healthy choice.

Feeding Tips for 24–36 Months

Here are some ideas to promote healthy eating habits:

- It is normal for your toddler's appetite to vary from day to day. Follow her hunger and fullness cues. This will support her in listening to her body's signals and eating in a healthy way.

- Include her in regular family meals and snacks. This will show her that you value healthy eating.

- Be aware of choking hazards. (See p. 82–83.)

- Water is the healthiest drink to offer between meals and snacks.

- Limit foods high in salt, sugar, and caffeine (chips, chocolate, candy, pop).

Number of Recommended Daily Food Guide Servings for Toddlers 24–36 Months:

- Vegetables and Fruit   4 servings
- Grain Products   3 servings
- Milk and Alternatives   2 servings
- Meat and Alternatives   1 serving

Sample One-Day Menu for Toddlers 24–36 Months

Foods	Number of Food Guide Servings				
	Vegetables and Fruit	Grain Products	Milk and Alternatives	Meat and Alternatives	Added Oils and Fats
Breakfast					
• 1/2 bowl of whole-grain cereal (15 g)		1/2			
• 125 ml (1/2 cup) of 2% milk			1/2		
Snack					
• 60 ml (1/4 cup) carrot sticks and broccoli florets with salad dressing	1/2				✔
• water					
Lunch					
• 1/2 salmon sandwich on whole wheat bread (made with 30 g or 1 oz. of canned salmon and mayonnaise)		1		1/2	✔
• 60 ml (1/4 cup) red pepper strips and cucumber slices	1/2				
• 125 ml (1/2 cup) milk			1/2		
• 1 peach	1				
Snack					
• oat rings cereal (15 g)		1/2			
• 125 ml (1/2 cup) milk			1/2		
Dinner					
• 125 ml (1/2 cup) spaghetti with tomato and meat sauce (about 40 g or 1 1/2 oz. of meat)	1/2	1		1/2	✔
• 125 ml (1/2 cup) milk			1/2		
• 125 ml (1/2 cup) applesauce	1				
Snack					
• 1/2 banana	1/2				
Total Food Guide Servings for the Day	**4**	**3**	**2**	**1**	

Source: *Eating Well with Canada's Food Guide, A Resource for Educators and Communicators,* Health Canada, 2007: Adapted and reproduced with the permission of the Ministry of Public Works and Government Services Canada, 2007.

Eating Well with
Canada's Food Guide

Health Canada recommends following *Eating Well with Canada's Food Guide* once your toddler is 24 months old. The entire *Eating Well with Canada's Food Guide* is in the Appendix.

Canada's Food Guide
First Nations, Inuit and Métis

Eating Well with Canada's Food Guide - First Nations, Inuit and Métis is a new guide that reflects the values, traditions, and food choices of Aboriginal populations. (See "Aboriginal Resources" in the Resources chapter for information on how to get a copy.)

Vitamin and Mineral Supplements

If your toddler is eating a variety of foods from all the food groups, is growing well, and looks healthy, she probably does not need extra vitamins or minerals, except for the following:

Vitamin D

Breastfed toddlers up to 12 months need 400 IU of vitamin D each day from vitamin drops. Formula-fed toddlers need vitamin D drops if they drink less than 1000 ml (4 cups) of formula each day. If your toddler drinks both breast milk and formula, she needs vitamin D drops. For more information about vitamin D supplements, call HealthLink BC at 8-1-1 to talk to a dietitian.

Children over 12 months of age need 600 IU of vitamin D each day. You can stop giving your toddler vitamin D drops once she is eating enough solid food to get 600 IU of vitamin D from food most days.

Food sources of vitamin D include:
- 1 egg yolk   25 IU
- 5 ml (1 tsp.) margarine   25 IU
- 30 g (1 oz.) salmon   100 IU
- 250 ml (1 cup) cow's milk   *100 IU
- 250 ml (1 cup) formula   100 IU

* Cow's milk is NOT recommended for children under 9 to 12 months.

Vitamin D helps to build healthy bones and teeth. Vitamin D may also help prevent some chronic diseases later in life, such as diabetes.

In the past, when the dangers of too much sun were still unknown, toddlers made enough vitamin D from being in the sun. We now know that they should be protected from the sun. Also, from October to March, the Canadian sunlight is too weak for them to make vitamin D. So they need vitamin D in their food to meet their bodies' needs.

Other Vitamins and Minerals

Iron deficiency is a concern for growth and brain development. If your toddler is not eating iron-rich foods or is a vegetarian or vegan, talk with your doctor. (See p. 63 for a list of iron-rich foods.)

Do not give cod-liver oil to your toddler. Cod-liver oil is too high in vitamin A. Overdoses of vitamin A can be poisonous.

If you give your toddler a vitamin and mineral supplement, choose one approved for her age. Speak to your pharmacist to help you find the right one. Help keep her safe from overdoses by not calling supplements "candy" or "sweets" and keeping them out of her reach.

Ideas for Healthy Meals and Snacks

Here are handy ideas for you when you are planning meals for your toddler. They are based on *Eating Well with Canada's Food Guide*.

- For each meal, aim to offer food from all four food groups.
- For each snack, offer food from at least two food groups. You can use the following suggestions to help plan combinations of food that will make sure your toddler is eating from the four food groups.

Meal and Snack Builders

- baked beans and toast
- buttered toast spread with fruit purée
- carrot or pumpkin bread spread with cream cheese
- chili, dahl, or lentils, and rice with vegetables
- congee or rice porridge with small pieces of meat
- dessert tofu with fresh fruit
- fish served in a whole wheat bun or bannock
- fresh fruit cut into wedges, with seeds and tough peels removed
- fresh fruit pieces and yogurt for dipping
- grated carrots, beets, or cabbage in salad
- grated or small cubes of cheese with whole-grain crackers
- macaroni and cheese
- meatballs with pasta
- milk or yogurt shakes blended with fruit
- oatmeal or cream of wheat with whole milk
- pancakes or waffles topped with applesauce
- raw or cooked vegetables with dip or hummus/dahl
- rice or pasta and meat with vegetables

- rice and raisin pudding with whole milk
- scrambled eggs and toast
- small muffins and orange wedges
- soft tortillas filled with beans or ground meat
- soups made with milk, and a whole-grain bun
- spaghetti with tomato or meat sauce
- tomato or mixed vegetable juice
- vegetable, split pea, or bean soup with whole wheat crackers, bannock, or roti
- whole-grain cold cereal with whole milk and fruit pieces or berries
- whole-grain crackers or rice cakes spread with cottage cheese or mashed avocado
- whole wheat pita/roti and hummus/dahl
- whole-grain toast spread with butter, fruit purée, or non-hydrogenated margarine
- yogurt mixed with pieces of fruit or applesauce
- yogurt with crackers or roti

List your ideas for meal and snack builders:

- _____
- _____
- _____
- _____
- _____
- _____
- _____
- _____
- _____
- _____
- _____
- _____
- _____
- _____

Offering Safe, Healthy Food and Drinks

Drink Choices

Water

By offering your toddler small amounts of water starting at six months, you will be helping him get used to the taste of water. If you think he is thirsty, try offering small amounts of water in a cup. Breast milk is still an important source of nutrition, so water should not replace it altogether. A healthy habit to aim for is to drink milk with meals and drink water to quench thirst.

Generally, tap water is safe and bottled water is not needed for safety. If you have your own private water supply, you should have your water tested. (See "BC HealthFiles" in the Resources chapter.) It is important to follow all public system "boil water" advisories or notices in your area. If you have concerns about your water supply, check with your public health office about using this water.

Milk

Your toddler does not need any milk other than breast milk if he continues to breastfeed. If he's no longer breastfeeding, you can safely offer him whole (homogenized) cow's milk or goat's milk occasionally when he is eating a variety of solid foods. It is safest to wait until he is between 9 to 12 months old to start offering whole (homogenized) milk.

Toddlers who are younger than 24 months need a lot of energy for growth and development. Choose whole (homogenized) cow's milk until your toddler is at least 24 months. You can switch him to 1% or 2% milk after 24 months.

Since milk is not a good source of iron, offer high-iron foods twice a day to make sure your toddler gets enough iron. For a list of iron-rich foods, see "Choosing a First Food" (p. 63).

Sometimes toddlers would rather drink cow's milk or goat's milk than eat solid foods. But too much cow's or goat's milk fills up a toddler's small tummy and leaves little room for other healthy foods. Toddlers who drink too much cow's or goat's milk are at higher risk for not getting enough iron (iron deficiency). Limit to 500 ml (2 cups) of cow's or goat's milk a day.

All milk sold in stores is pasteurized. Some farmers may have access to raw milk. Raw milk may contain harmful bacteria that can cause your toddler to become very sick or even die.

If you choose goat's milk, make sure it is pasteurized and full-fat. Most goat's milk does not contain vitamin D. Be sure to give your toddler a vitamin D supplement if you give him goat's milk. For more information about vitamin D supplements, call HealthLink BC at 8-1-1 to talk to a dietitian.

Soy or rice beverages are safe choices after your toddler is 24 months old. For healthy growth and development, choose a soy or rice beverage that is fortified with calcium and vitamin D. A beverage's label will say if it has added calcium and vitamin D.

Juice

Toddlers do not need juice. After 6 months, if you decide to give juice, choose 100% unsweetened juice. Offer it in a cup as part of a meal or snack. Give no more than 60 to 125 ml (1/4–1/2 cup) of juice a day to toddlers 6 to 12 months old. Offer no more than 125 to 175 ml (1/2–3/4 cup) of juice a day to children one to six years old. Giving your toddler juice in a bottle can lead to tooth decay. Instead of juice, offer her whole fruit or whole vegetables. They are more nutritious than juice.

Only drinks that say "100% juice" are juice. If the label says "made with real juice," the drink is mostly water and sugar with a little bit of juice. You can find sugar in the ingredient list by looking for words ending in "ose" (e.g., sucrose and high fructose corn syrup). These drinks are not recommended for toddlers.

Unpasteurized juices may contain harmful bacteria. These bacteria can cause young children to become very sick or even die. Most juice is pasteurized. Unpasteurized juice will say "unpasteurized" on the label.

Sweet Drinks

There is a lot of sugar in fruit-flavoured drinks, fruit beverages, drinks made from powders or crystals, pop, and slush drinks. They are not recommended for toddlers because they have little nutrition. Offer healthier choices such as water or milk.

Drinks With Caffeine

Toddlers can easily get more caffeine than the safe levels recommended by Health Canada. Caffeine can cause a rapid heart rate and can make your toddler excited and anxious. Caffeine is found in many soft drinks, sports drinks, coffee and coffee-slush drinks, tea, and chocolate. To be safe, choose not to offer drinks that have caffeine in them.

Toddler Nutritional Supplement Drinks

Toddlers do not need toddler nutritional supplement drinks.

Food Choices

Vegetables and Fruit

Local food is fresher and may be more nutritious than imported food that must be trucked a long way to get to a store near you. The freshest vegetables and fruit will be the ones you grow or pick yourself.

Foods labelled "certified organic" may have lower levels of pesticides and herbicides.

Frozen vegetables and fruit can be just as high in nutrients (and sometimes higher) than fresh vegetables and fruit.

Whether you choose "certified organic," local, fresh, or frozen vegetables and fruit, know that you are making a good choice. Healthy eating includes lots of vegetables and fruit.

Honey

Because honey may contain botulism spores that can make your toddler sick, wait until she is 12 months old before offering honey. Don't add honey to baby food, use honey on a soother, or offer foods that contain honey, such as graham wafers. The botulism spores are not a risk for adults or children older than 12 months.

Undercooked Meat and Eggs

Undercooked meat, poultry, fish, seafood, and eggs can cause food poisoning. To reduce the risk of food poisoning, cook all meats until they are brown—NOT PINK—and the liquids run clear. Braising, stewing, and sautéing are good ways to cook meats thoroughly while keeping them soft to chew. Cooking fish until it flakes with a fork reduces the risk of food poisoning. Cooking eggs until hard, with no soft or runny yolk, reduces the risk for food poisoning.

Sprouts

Do not offer raw or lightly cooked sprouts (for example, alfalfa or mung bean sprouts). These sprouts may contain harmful bacteria. Check for sprouts in salads or sandwiches from restaurants and vending machines. Only sprouts that are thoroughly cooked in stir-fries or soups are safe for your toddler to eat.

Fast Foods

Offer your toddler healthy choices such as vegetables, fruit, whole-grain foods, and milk products instead of fast foods. Fast foods are high in fat and salt. Also, they are usually poor sources of nutrition. Offering fast foods prevents your toddler from getting high-quality nutrition from other foods.

Unpasteurized Cheeses

Choose cheeses made from pasteurized milk. This will lessen the risk of food poisoning. Cheeses made from unpasteurized milk may contain harmful bacteria. These bacteria can cause toddlers to become very sick or even die. Cheese made from unpasteurized milk will say "unpasteurized" on the label.

Seafood

Fish is part of healthy eating. Fish provides many nutrients, such as protein and omega-3 fats. Omega-3 fats are important for brain and eye development.

When you choose fish, it is important to know that some fish are high in mercury and have recommended serving limits. Mercury is a metal found naturally in the environment. Even small amounts of mercury can damage a growing brain. Mercury cannot be removed or reduced by cleaning, preparing, or cooking fish. So it is important to choose fish low in mercury more often and to limit the number of servings of higher mercury fish.

The BC Ministry of Health and BC Centre for Disease Control have developed the recommendations in the following tables for choosing and eating fish specifically for British Columbians. These recommendations can help you provide the healthy benefits of fish while keeping mercury levels low.

Note: Information about the mercury levels of other types of fish is not yet available. If you eat fish that are not included on the lists, do not eat large amounts of the same fish very often. Instead, eat a wide variety of fish.

Recommendations for Choosing and Eating Fish

Mercury Level of Fish	Children 6 – 24 Months	Children 2 – 12 Years
Low in Mercury • Salmon, wild or farmed, fresh, frozen or canned • Albacore Tuna, fresh, frozen or canned, from B.C. or Canada • Shrimp • Prawn • Rainbow Trout • Mackerel, Atlantic • Sole or Dover Sole	**No Limit**	**No Limit**
Moderate in Mercury • Canned Tuna, all varieties • Albacore Tuna, fresh or frozen (often used in sushi) • Cod, Atlantic • Bass or White Bass • Halibut, Pacific • Lake Trout • Sablefish, Black Cod or Alaskan Black Cod • Sea Bass	**2 servings a month**	**3 servings a month**
High in Mercury • Bigeye Tuna, fresh or frozen (often called Ahi Tuna) • Shark • Marlin • Swordfish	**Do not eat**	**1 serving a month**

Left margin labels: Eat Freely · Moderate · Limit

One serving is equal to 75 g (2.5 oz.) or 125 ml (1/2 cup).

For more information, or for healthy eating advice for people of all ages, call HealthLink BC at 8-1-1 to speak to a dietitian. (See "Nutrition" in the Resources chapter.)

Preventing Choking

WARNING: Do not give whole nuts, whole peanuts, whole grapes, popcorn, gum, cough drops, or hard candy to children under four years of age. These foods are very likely to cause choking.

The greatest risk for choking is in children under four years old. Their mouth muscles are not developed enough to control hard or slippery foods. The airway of a small child is about the same diameter as a pencil.

You can help prevent choking by staying with your toddler while she eats. Also, to help prevent choking, do not let her eat while she is walking, in a stroller, or riding in a vehicle.

Be careful that you do not give children younger than four years of age foods that they could choke on. These foods are very likely to cause choking. By following the directions in the chart on the next page, you can make the food you give safer to eat.

Identify and Reduce Choking Hazards

Think about food that is:	Examples:	Steps to make food safer:
Round	Whole grapes, small tomatoes or large berries, hot dogs, sausages	Slice lengthwise into quarters
Hard	Fruit with pits or seeds	Remove pits and seeds
	Raw vegetables that can break into chunks, such as carrots	Grate or chop finely, cook and slice into thin sticks
	Whole nuts or peanuts	Chop finely
	Seeds	Chop finely
Sticky	Globs of peanut butter	Spread thinly on toast or crackers
	Raisins and other dried fruit, marshmallow	Cut into small pieces
Stringy	Celery and citrus fruit, such as oranges and grapefruit	Remove large, stringy sections
	Leafy vegetables	Cut into small pieces
Chunky	Chunky peanut butter or nut and seed butter	Choose smooth nut butters or seed butters; spread thinly on toast or cracker
	Large chunks of meat or cheese	Cut into small cubes
Easy to eat by handfuls without chewing	Pretzels, chips	Serve small amounts onto plate or bowl rather than out of bag
Bones	Chicken and whole fish	Remove bones from chicken and fish; flake fish before serving. Rub between fingers to feel for bones

Eating Together

Offer Meals and Snacks at the Same Times Each Day

Toddlers often do well with regular routines. By sitting down for meals and snacks at the same times each day, your toddler can focus on learning to eat a variety of foods and learning the skills to feed himself.

"Grazing" between meals and snacks is not a healthy eating habit and is especially harmful to teeth.

Offering water between meals and snacks is a healthy way to quench thirst.

Making Meals Enjoyable

Sitting down or having a family member sit with your toddler while he is eating can be a habit to choose as soon as he begins to eat solid foods. Studies show that children who eat meals with family members eat healthier and do better in school.

Mealtimes can be good times to learn and teach. Your toddler can use mealtimes to develop fine motor skills (such as picking up small pieces of food with his fingers). It is a good time to learn language skills (like talking and listening), and social skills (for example, using "please" and "thank you").

Your toddler will probably have a hard time staying in one place for any length of time. However, when he is hungry and eating, you can expect him to stay at the table. Let him leave the table when he loses interest in eating.

A great start is to securely seat your toddler in a high chair or booster seat, or on your lap. Reduce distractions to make the most of this special time. For example, keep toys away from the table, and let phone-callers leave a message. Remove any other distractions.

Promote language skills by choosing to turn off the TV. Watching TV disrupts family conversations. It also makes it harder to follow your toddler's signs of fullness. (See p. 50 for more information on TV.)

Eating together is a great opportunity to have pleasant conversation. It also gives you the chance to teach your toddler to say "no, thank you" instead of "yuck" or "gross."

Don't Stress About the Mess

Your toddler needs to explore food the same way she explores the rest of the world—with her eyes, hands, and mouth. This is an important part of learning. This also means a mess: food in the hair, food in the ears, and food all over the floor. She will make a mess because she doesn't have complete control of her hands and fingers. She may drop food on the floor by mistake—or on purpose, to see how you react. Be patient and remember that "being neat" is not important to her. Serve small portions and let her set the pace. Have a wet cloth nearby for cleanup after the meal or snack is over. Enjoy watching her learn to eat and develop fine motor skills. Before you know it, she will have learned and adopted all of your good manners. (See Child Development chapter on p. 9 for more information.)

Eating on the Go

There will be times when you are away from home at meal and snack times. You can still take the time to stop and sit down together to enjoy food and conversation with your toddler.

There are nutritious snacks that are easy to take on the go. Try packing dry cereal, cheese and crackers, or cut-up fruit or vegetables. Also, a small plastic drink container with a folding spout is handy for water.

Keeping a plastic bag handy with plastic knives and spoons and some wet wipes can make eating on the go easier. Carrying snacks in small containers with tight-fitting lids can help reduce mess and spills.

Talk to other parents to get more helpful tips on eating meals and snacks away from home.

Preventing Picky Eating—Offering a Variety of Healthy Foods

Many toddlers and their caregivers struggle with periods of picky eating. Providing many opportunities for your toddler to smell, touch, and taste new foods

gives her time to accept the foods. Let her eat at her own pace. Offer a new food along with something that she already likes.

Providing foods with a variety of textures from an early age can help your toddler accept new foods. Children who have eaten only puréed, store-bought baby food often won't eat foods with lumpier textures.

Role modelling healthy eating can be powerful. It sends the message that healthy eating is important. You can be a role model for healthy eating by eating a balanced, healthy diet. Do this by following *Eating Well with Canada's Food Guide*. (See Appendix p. 183.) Your toddler is more likely to eat foods that she sees you and other caregivers enjoying. If you remove or limit junk food and soft drinks in your home, she will not see them and won't ask for them. If you have these foods around the home and she sees you eating them, she will want them too.

Involve your toddler as much as you can in planning and preparing meals and snacks to increase her interest in trying new foods. Many have found that children will happily eat foods that they have chosen in the store, grown, or "helped cook."

Being a Vegetarian Toddler

The term "vegetarian" can mean different things to different people. Some vegetarians choose not to eat red meat. Others choose not to eat red meat, fish, or poultry. People who call themselves "vegan" choose not to eat any food that comes from animals.

It Could Take Up to 30 Times!
Did you know that toddlers often need to see a new food 12 to 30 times before it is accepted? Give your toddler many chances to look at, touch, smell, and taste new foods. This will help her accept new foods more easily.

You may be a vegan and want your toddler to eat this way too. If so, consult a registered dietitian to make sure your toddler gets the nutrients she needs. Contact Dial-a-Dietitian or talk to the community nutritionist (registered dietitian) at your local public health office. (See "Key Resources for Parents" on p. 191 in the Resources chapter.)

By choosing foods carefully from all four food groups, you can make sure that your toddler is meeting his nutrition needs. You can find the food groups listed in *Eating Well with Canada's Food Guide.* (See Appendix p. 183.) If you choose not to offer meat, choose meat alternatives, including:

- Eggs
- Beans and legumes
- Tofu
- "Veggie" meats
- Nut and seed butters

If food choices are too limited, he may not get all the nutrients he needs. Your toddler will get the right foods if the meals you offer contain foods from all four groups. Offer snacks that contain food from two or more food groups.

If you are raising your toddler on a vegan diet that does not include any meat or milk products, following these steps can make sure that he is meeting his nutrition needs:

- Breastfeed for 24 months or longer. Note for breastfeeding vegan mothers: Make sure that you are getting enough vitamin B12 from fortified foods or from a daily supplement. This will make sure your toddler has good brain development.

- If you choose not to breastfeed, give your toddler soy protein–based formula that is fortified with iron. These should be used until he is 24 months old.

- Give him a vitamin D supplement. (See p. 74.)

- Introduce iron-fortified infant cereals at six months.

- For energy and protein, use meat alternatives: tofu, soy, or veggie "meats," beans, peas, lentils, nut and seed butters. For younger toddlers, mix nut or seed butters with breast milk, water, or other liquids. This will make it thinner and will prevent choking.

- Soy beverages (except formula) and rice beverages do not contain enough nutrients. They are not recommended until 24 months of age.

- Remember—your toddler needs sources of:
  - Energy: offer food from all four food groups.
  - Omega-3 fats: offer canola, flaxseed oil, breast milk, and/or infant formula with added DHA and ARA.
  - Protein: offer breast milk and/or infant formula, tofu, lentils, dry beans, nut butters.
  - Vitamin B12: is found only in animal foods and veggie "meats" with added vitamin B12. Offer foods with extra vitamin B12 added to them or give vitamin B12 supplements. This will prevent anemia and damage to your toddler's brain, spinal cord, and nerves.
  - Iron: offer iron-fortified infant cereal, enriched cereals, legumes, quinoa, peas, lentils, tofu, and blackstrap molasses.

- Calcium: better sources include breast milk, calcium-fortified orange juice, canned baked beans, and blackstrap molasses. Other sources include almond and sesame butter and oranges. Since it is difficult to get enough calcium without milk products, it is important to breastfeed your toddler until 24 months or older.

- Contact a registered dietitian by calling HealthLink BC at 8-1-1, or contact the community nutritionist at your local public health office.

Understanding Food Allergies

A food allergy occurs when the body mistakes a particular food as harmful. An allergic reaction is the body's immune system fighting back. It is not known why some children develop food allergies. Allergies tend to run in families.

Talk about your family history with your doctor to find out if your toddler is at risk.

For more nutrition information and advice on food allergies, call HealthLink BC at 8-1-1 and talk to a registered dietitian. Or, talk to the community nutritionist (registered dietitian) at your local public health office. (See "Key Resources for Parents" on p. 191 in the Resources chapter.)

Possible Signs of Food Allergy

Food allergy can vary and range from mild to severe. Signs can appear within minutes and often within two hours after exposure to the food. Signs can also occur hours later, but this is less common. **The most common signs include hives, redness, and rash.** Hives are red blotchy raised bumps that appear on the skin.

Other possible signs of food allergy include:
- Stuffy or runny nose with itchy, watery eyes
- Vomiting, stomach cramps, and diarrhea
- Moderate to severe eczema

Stop giving the food and get medical advice if you are concerned that a food is a causing an allergic reaction in your toddler.

Some signs of food allergy require immediate attention.

Signs of a severe allergic reaction include:
- Swelling of the mouth, tongue, and throat
- Trouble breathing
- Trouble swallowing, hoarse (rough) voice, trouble speaking
- Pale or blue colour of the face or lips
- Feeling faint, weak, or passing out
- Hives that are spreading

Call 911 or other emergency service immediately if you see signs of a severe allergic reaction.

Healthy Eating

The Health and Well-Being of Your Toddler

Your Toddler's Growth

Your toddler will grow very fast up until her first birthday. Between the ages of 12 and 24 months, her growth will slow, although she will continue to gain weight and grow taller.

Once your toddler is walking, she develops more muscle in her legs and arms. She will usually lose fat around the face and tummy. This makes her look less like a baby and more like a young child.

Here are general guidelines for growth from six months to 36 months of age:

Age	Weight	Length/Height
6 months	Birth weight has usually doubled by 6 months	Average length: 55–57 cm (21.5–22.5 in.)
12 months	Birth weight has usually increased by 2.5–3 times by 12 months	By 12 months, average growth is 25.5 cm (10 in.) in length since birth
12 – 24 months	Between 12–24 months of age toddlers gain an average of 1.4–2.3 kg (3–5 lb.)	Average growth is 7–12 cm (3–5 in.) between 12–24 months
24 – 36 months	Between 24–60 months (2–5 years) of age children gain an average of 1.5–2.5 kg (3.3–5.5 lb.)	Average growth is about 8 cm (3 in.) between 24–60 months (2–5 years)

If you are concerned about your toddler's growth, talk to your doctor or public health nurse.

Your Toddler's Weight

You can help your toddler stay at a healthy weight by combining enough physical activity with healthy food.

A growing concern among parents is the problem of children being overweight or obese. You can help your toddler stay at a healthy weight by combining enough physical activity with healthy food.

Here are some additional ways that you can help your toddler maintain a healthy weight:

- Breastfeed until she is 24 months and older.

- Encourage her to be physically active every day.

- Always offer wholesome meals with lots of fresh vegetables, fruits, and grains. *Eating Well with Canada's Food Guide* can help you plan meals. (See p. 183 for information on *Eating Well with Canada's Food Guide* and p. 55 for the chapter on Healthy Eating.)

- Let her eat the amount of healthy food that she wants. Avoid forcing her to eat. A healthy eating relationship is one where you provide healthy food choices at meal and snack times and she decides how much she wants to eat.

- Never take food away from her if she is still hungry.

- Avoid using food as a bribe or reward.

- Avoid giving her soft drinks and high-sugar or high-fat drinks or snacks.

- Have regular mealtimes as a family. Avoid grazing or snacking all day long.

- Set a good example for her. Eat healthy foods, eat meals at a table, eat slowly, and get enough physical activity.

- Limit the amount of time she spends in front of the TV or other media to a maximum of one hour a day or, better yet, none at all. (See p. 50 for more information on TV.)

Ask your physician, dietitian, or pubic health nurse if your toddler is at a healthy weight. Your health-care provider will look at her age, sex, height, and weight. If she is over 24 months of age, it might be possible to calculate her Body Mass Index (BMI). The BMI is useful for children 24 months of age or older because it allows you to see if they are at, over, or under the normal weight for their age and height.

Physical Activity

Regular physical activity is the best way to help your toddler stay at a healthy weight. Physical activity is also a way for him to play, have fun, and develop physically, socially, and emotionally. (See p. 44–48 for more on play and child development.)

Some of the other benefits of physical activity are:
- Better overall health
- More energy
- Improved fitness
- Stronger muscles and bones
- Better posture
- Improved self-esteem
- Less stress

Your toddler needs at least 60 minutes of physical activity every day to help build strong bones, muscles, heart, and lungs. Physically active children are much less likely to become overweight or obese. Being overweight or obese is a serious health concern for both adults and children in Canada, but it is especially serious in children.

Toddlers and Physical Activity—Key Ideas

- Physical activity includes any activity where most of your toddler's body is moving.

- Physical activity is a natural part of every day. It can easily fit into daily routines.

- Your toddler needs opportunities every day to use the large muscle groups of the body. (See "Physical Development" in the Child Development chapter starting on p.10 for more information.)

- Your toddler needs to develop confidence with basic movement skills like walking, climbing, and balancing.

- Your toddler needs active role models.

- Your toddler will learn new skills and try new physical activities when he is encouraged and praised for his efforts.

Helping Your Toddler Be Physically Active

You can get your toddler off to a good start by being active yourself for at least 30 minutes every day. Try a variety of activities and make them fun. Joining with other families is one of the best ways to have fun while being active.

A good way to keep your toddler active is to turn off the TV and computer and get outside. Limit his TV watching to no more than one hour a day—better yet, none at all. (See p. 50 for more information on TV watching.)

Unless he's sleeping, your toddler should not be sitting still for more than 60 minutes at a time. Notice how much time he spends sitting or lying and look for ways to help him be active. Encourage his natural need to move, play, run, jump, climb, and explore.

When our son, Caleb, was little I wanted to get fit again but found I didn't have much time. So I started using him as my "little weight" and would lift him instead of a dumbbell. It started small but gradually became a full weight-lifting and stretching workout to music. I would do sit-ups with him on my feet and use my arms to lift him over my head for a number of upper-body work-outs. He loved it and would roll around me on the floor whenever I wasn't lifting him.

Making It Safe for a Toddler to Move

When our son, Matthew, really started moving, I had to childproof our home all over again. So I crawled around with him and looked at everything that could be grabbed from that height. I was surprised at how many things were dangerous to a toddler who was crawling or walking. The stairs, coffee table corners, anything on tables, standing lamps—the list was very long. It took a few hours of looking, but we made the house safer just by being aware of what he could do now. (See p. 156 for more information on childproofing your home.)

Here are some other ways to help your toddler enjoy being active:

At 6–12 Months

- Put some toys just out of reach so he has to work to move toward them.

- Hold and rock him.

- Play physical games ("peekaboo"and "Patty Cake").

- Encourage him to crawl, roll, and explore in safe spaces, either indoors or outdoors.

- Choose toys that promote physical activity.

At 12–36 Months

- Do activities with him. Go outside and explore. Throw a ball, chase bubbles, or play at the park.

- Turn off the TV and other interactive media and get him moving. Limit the time he spends in front of the TV and other media to one hour or less per day—or better yet, none at all.

- Go to a park and teach him to use the slides, swings, and climbing equipment.

- Teach him basic sports skills (throwing and catching a ball and jumping).

- Include him in daily activities that are physically active (walking to the store, cleaning the house, washing the car, or gardening).

- Whenever possible, get him out of the stroller and have him walk with you. Your toddler is not active while in the stroller.

- Check with your local recreation centre or public health office about activities that he might be able to join (swimming, gymnastics, dance, and others).

Outdoor Protection for Your Toddler

When you are outside playing and being active with your toddler, it's important to protect her from the heat and cold.

Heat and Sun

Your toddler has sensitive skin that is easily damaged by the sun, even on cloudy or overcast days.

Protect your toddler from sunburns to reduce the chance of skin cancer in the following ways:

Stay out of the sun and heat

- Keep children less than 12 months of age out of direct sunlight.

- Try to keep her out of the sun between 10 a.m. and 4 p.m., when the sun's rays are the strongest.

- Never leave her alone in a car.

- Do not let her get overheated.

- Make sure she has plenty of water to drink in hot weather. Offer her a drink of water every hour or so.

- Dress her in loose clothing that offers protection from the sun.

- Make sure she takes regular breaks from activity.

Dress for protection

- Dress her in loose clothes that have a tight weave.

- Give her a large-brimmed hat with neck cover and no ties.

Use sunscreen

- Choose water-resistant sunscreens rated SPF 30 or higher and approved by the Canadian Dermatology Association. (Look for their logo or name on the label.)

- Teach her why using sunscreen is a good idea.

- Do not wait for signs of sunburn to get her out of the sun. Sunburns do not usually show up for six to 24 hours.

Put sunglasses on your toddler

- See p. 111 for more information on sunglasses.

Heat Exhaustion

Signs of heat exhaustion include fatigue, weakness, confusion, nausea, headache, muscle cramps, and pale skin that is cool and damp. If your toddler has these signs, bring him indoors or into the shade. Loosen or remove his clothing, and give him a cool bath and a drink of water. If your toddler still shows signs of heat exhaustion or starts to vomit, call or see your doctor.

Tips for Applying Sunscreen

- Use water-resistant sunscreen that works immediately.

- Apply about 15 ml (1 tbsp.) of sunscreen to all areas of skin that the sun will touch.

- Apply lip balm with sunscreen to the mouth area.

- Put on more sunscreen about every two hours if your toddler is out on sunny, cloudy, or overcast days without breaks spent indoors.

The 4-S Protection System

Seek shade.

Slip on a shirt.

Slap on a hat.

Slop on the sunscreen.

Cold

There are many fun activities to do with your toddler in the winter or during colder weather. Here are some tips on how to protect him from the cold while playing outside:

- Provide a warm, water-resistant coat. The sleeves should be snug at the wrist.

- Provide warm, slip-proof footwear that is water resistant.

- Give him mittens. Attach these to his coat sleeves.

- Choose a warm hat that fits well and does not have ties.

- Dress him in loose-fitting layers that will go under the coat.

- Make sure he is able to warm up every 30 minutes or so.

- Keep him indoors when temperatures are below −25°C (−13°F), or if the wind chill is −28°C (−18°F) or more.

Frostbite

If your toddler needs to be out in very cold weather for any length of time, watch for signs of frostbite or skin injury from cold. Do this by checking for whiteness and numbness on his cheeks, nose, ears, fingers, and toes.

If you think your toddler has frostbite:

- Bring him indoors immediately.

- Remove wet clothing. Wet clothes take heat away from his body.

- Put the frostbitten body part(s) in warm water until feeling has returned. Make sure you test the temperature of the water yourself, because he will not be able to feel heat or cold. He may cry from the stinging that will happen as the feeling returns.

Playground and Park Safety

The playground can be a lot of fun and give your toddler a place to develop and practise new physical skills. She can also learn social skills as she plays in the playground with other young children.

Always go with your toddler to the playground, and watch her closely. Playground falls are a major cause of serious injuries. She can also get caught in playground equipment. Never dress her in clothes that may become caught on equipment. Drawstrings, skipping ropes, scarves, bike helmet straps, and loose clothing can become tangled and strangle a toddler.

Use the following questions to check the safety of any playgrounds or parks you visit:

- Is the playground equipment in good condition, well anchored, and the right size and height for your toddler? If she can't reach it without help,

it's too big. Children younger than five should use playgrounds that are designed for preschool children. The playground equipment should be no more than 1.5 metres (5 feet) in height.

- Does the play equipment have guardrails and barriers to prevent injuries?

- Is the play equipment free of points, corners, hooks, joints, and other things that could catch clothing?

- Are the swing seats made of soft material to prevent injuries?

- Is there lots of space around the play equipment?

- Does the playground have proper surfaces? Sand, wood chips, and synthetic materials are best.

Sleep and Your Toddler

Just like adults, each toddler needs a different amount of sleep, but most children follow the pattern on the next page.

Sleep Patterns of Toddlers

At 6 months	• May sleep 11 to 12 hours at night and have two naps. • Usually naps once in the morning and once in the afternoon, with each nap lasting one to two hours. • May sleep at night for a stretch of several hours, or even through the night. Will start sleeping through the night at different ages; there is no correct age for children to start.
At 12 months	• May sleep about 14 hours per day. Part of this may be in morning and afternoon naps. Between 12 months and 18 months, the morning nap disappears and is replaced with one longer afternoon nap.
At 24 months	• May sleep 11 to 12 hours at night, with a nap in the afternoon lasting one to two hours.
At 36 months	• May sleep about 12 hours at night, and may or may not have a short nap.

Developing Good Sleep Habits

Here are some tips on how you can help your toddler develop good sleep habits:

Keep Regular Day Routines

• Try to set up daytime routines and habits. Your toddler thrives on routine.

• Keep a regular nap schedule, even on weekends (if you can). If your day is very busy and naps are missed, he may not sleep well at night.

• Offer him regular meals and snacks during the day.

Keep Regular Bedtime Routines

• Wind down the action at bedtime. Giving him a bath, followed by reading and quiet cuddle, helps teach him to slow down from the day. Ask other members of the family to share in this quiet time.

• Make bedtime a special time. Set aside time for talking about the day. This will help in later years as he comes to know that this is the time of day when he has your full attention.

• Give him some choices at bedtime—which story to read or which pajamas to wear.

• Avoid TV watching before bedtime. TV is stimulating, not relaxing.

Encourage Your Toddler to Settle

From time to time, your toddler may find it difficult to settle down to sleep. Stresses such as teething, being overtired, or being off a routine may all cause problems with settling.

Here are some tips on how you can help your toddler settle:

- Help him understand what to expect by giving a kiss and saying: "Now, it is time to sleep." He will gradually learn the meaning of this phrase.

- Teach him that it is bedtime by putting him into bed awake. This will help him learn to fall asleep and settle himself.

- He may have become used to being nursed and rocked to sleep as a baby. As he gets older, help him learn to fall asleep on his own so that when he wakes during the night he will know how to settle himself to sleep again. You can do this by gradually putting him down to sleep a little sooner—first before he's sound asleep, and then before his eyes are shutting.

- Don't try to sneak out. Instead, try patting him gently and quietly, singing a quiet song over and over, playing some relaxing quiet music and staying close by. When he is settling, say "Goodnight" and leave.

- If he is having a hard time settling, use this time as your relaxation time. Sit in a chair close by and read, listen to music, or just relax. Over a few days, move the chair farther and farther away until he is independent.

- If he seems afraid of the dark or is just more comfortable with some light, plug in a nightlight or leave the door open and turn on a light outside the room.

- Keep his sleeping area quiet.

- He may not easily let go of habits such as being rocked to sleep or held until asleep. Parents have different comfort levels when it comes to letting a toddler cry when settling to sleep. If you are comfortable with it and you know your toddler is not ill or hurt, you can try letting him cry for short periods of time. Make sure you check regularly until he falls asleep.

Night Waking

Night waking is very normal for small babies and even for toddlers. However, most parents want their toddler to sleep through the night once it is no longer necessary to have a night feeding. But it is not always easy. Children are quick to develop habits, and waking at night may have become a habit that stays even when your toddler no longer needs a night feeding. Sleep researchers have found that even adults never really sleep through the night. It's normal to wake up from time to time and go back to sleep without remembering the waking. Learning to resettle herself is a skill that your toddler will learn over time.

FACTS & STATS

Night Waking

About 30 per cent of children between one and four years of age wake during the night at least once a week. These night wakings tend to peak between 18 months and two years and then decline. Children may wake during the night because they are too hot or too cold. Or, they may be teething, or not feeling well. Attend to their needs. However, try to limit conversation and social interaction with them. These special times together should not become a habit.

Permission to reprint by UNH Cooperative Extension from fact sheet *Helping Young Children Sleep Better.*

Bedtime Reading

We have a bedtime routine that has lasted for over 12 years. We started reading to our daughter, Isabella, right before bed when she was just six months old. It helped her to slow down and realize it was time to sleep. This kept on every night even when it was a struggle to get her into bed sometimes. She always wanted a story, so that got her into bed. Now she's old enough to read herself, but she loves the close time with one of us. It also lets us have quiet time to chat about the day and unwind. I'm so glad we started this routine early on. Now I'm the one saying, "Let's get you into bed so I can find out what happens in the next chapter."

Here are some tips on how you can help your toddler end the habit of night waking:

- When you feed her in the middle of the night, keep the lights off. Don't make this a time to talk or play. Gradually shorten the feeding time. She may find it easier to resettle herself if she does not fully waken.

- Monitor daytime napping. You may need to gradually shorten or move naps to earlier in the day so that she sleeps better at night.

- Some parents choose to break the night waking habit by letting their toddler cry for a set period of time, perhaps two or three minutes, before going in. Do not pick her up or play with her, just calmly tuck her back into bed and say, "It's time to sleep now." Leave the room. You may have to do this more than once until she falls asleep. Over a few days, gradually increase the amount of time before going to her. It can be hard to listen to the crying, but it often works over time. (If at any time you have concerns for her safety or well-being, go and check immediately.)

- After making sure she is not ill or injured, you can also call out to reassure her but not go into her room.

- Some parents find it works to immediately get up, go into her room, and reassure her by saying: "This is sleep time."

- If your toddler is big enough and no longer sleeping in a crib, make a bed on the floor of your bedroom. She can come in and use it if she wakes.

To Do

Keep a Sleep Diary

If your toddler is not sleeping well, keeping a sleep diary might help. Write down when your toddler sleeps and for how long. Do this for about two weeks. This will help you see the patterns. You can then experiment with changes in nap times or routines.

Sleep Problems

Some of the most common reasons for sleep problems include:

- Inability to fall asleep by himself (for example, he is used to being rocked or fed to fall asleep and is unable to settle himself when he wakes in the night)
- Busy daytime schedules that are not regular
- Eating meals at different times from day to day
- Bedtimes or bedtime routines that change from one day to the next
- Lack of quiet and comforting bedtime routines
- Interrupted naps
- Not enough physical activity during the day
- Sickness
- Teething
- Having foods or drinks with caffeine (See p. 78 for more information on caffeine.)

Sleeping Arrangements

The Canadian Paediatric Society recommends that the safest place to sleep for infants under the age of 12 months is in their own crib. If your toddler is under the age of 12 months, he should be put to sleep on his back, in a crib meeting the Canadian government's safety standards. (See p. 101 for more information on crib safety.)

Bed sharing is when your toddler shares the same sleeping surface with you or another adult. Bed sharing is not recommended for infants under 12 months of age because it increases the chance of suffocation. This risk increases even more if your infant shares a bed with you (or with any other person) and you:

- Are a smoker, or he is exposed to second-hand smoke.

- Have been drinking alcohol or using drugs.

- Have taken any medicines that could make you extra sleepy.

- Are very tired, to the point where you would not be able to respond to him.

- Are ill or have a medical condition that might make it difficult to respond to him.

- Have long hair that is not tied back.

- Are obese.

When there is exposure to cigarette smoking, the risk of Sudden Infant Death Syndrome (SIDS) is further increased with bed sharing.

Room sharing is when your toddler is within arm's reach of you but is not on the same sleeping surface (for example, he is in a crib beside your bed). Room sharing can protect against SIDS.

"Back to Sleep"

If your toddler is under 12 months of age, put her to sleep on her back, called "back to sleep." It lowers the risk of suffocation. Once she is strong enough to turn over on her own (every time), there is no need to continue to place her in the back to sleep position.

Sudden Infant Death Syndrome

Sudden Infant Death Syndrome (SIDS), also known as "crib death," is the sudden and unexpected death of an apparently healthy child under 12 months of age. No one can explain why a child dies of SIDS, but there are steps you can take to lessen the risk:

- A smoke-free home will reduce the risk of SIDS.

- Children under 12 months of age should be put to sleep on their backs on a firm surface. The Canadian Paediatric Society recommends that for the first 12 months of life the safest place for a child to sleep is in his own crib.

- When your baby can roll over on his own from his back to stomach, usually at 5 - 7 months of age, there is no need to continue to place him on his back if he turns over in his sleep.

- Room sharing may protect against SIDS and is safer than bed sharing. Bed sharing is not recommended.

- Breastfeeding may help prevent SIDS.

- Keep your toddler warm, not hot. To check if he is too hot, place your hand on the back of his neck. He should not be sweating.

- When awake, give younger toddlers (aged 6 - 9 months) some supervised tummy time to help develop arm and neck strength. (See p. 16 for more on tummy time.)

Sleep Safety

At some point, you will decide it's time to move your toddler out of a crib and into a bed. Some 36-month-olds still sleep happily in a crib, while some 18-month-olds are already climbing out. If your toddler is trying hard to climb out of the crib, then it's time to move her to a bed.

- Place beds and cribs away from windows, heat sources, lamps, curtains, blinds, and electrical plugs and cords. Check for these or anything else that could be dangerous.

- She only needs a thin blanket if she is dressed in a sleeper. In a warm room, a sleeper and a light blanket or a blanket-weight sleeper should be enough to keep her comfortable.

- Do not use sheepskins, pillows, pillow-like items, quilts, comforters, stuffed toys, or bumper pads.

- Do not let her sleep on pillows, air mattresses, waterbeds, sagging mattresses, feather beds, reclining chairs, down comforters (or other loose bedding), beanbag chairs, sofas, couches, daybeds, or other soft surfaces. Avoid these soft surfaces, even for temporary sleeping arrangements (for example, during travel).

- Use a firm, flat mattress in a crib or a bed.

- Never cover her face or head with blankets.

- She should be warm but not hot.

- Top sheets are not recommended until she is an older toddler. Young toddlers can get caught in a top sheet.

- Car seats, seat carriers, and playpens must not replace the crib as a sleeping surface.

Crib Safety Checklist

Choose a crib that meets the federal government regulations for cribs and cradles. Cribs built before 1986 do not meet these regulations and are not safe. For more information, visit the Canadian Health Network website and search for "cribs." (See "Safety" in the Resources chapter for the web address.)

- Follow the manufacturer's instructions when you put the crib together.

- Check that there is less than 6 cm (2 in.) of space between the vertical slats (bars) on the sides, head, and foot of the crib.

- Use a crib mattress that is 15 cm (6 in.) thick or less, and fits the frame tightly. Only two fingers or less should fit between crib and mattress to prevent your toddler from getting stuck between the mattress and the bars.

- Keep the mattress placed at the lowest position if your toddler is able to sit up.

- Once in a while, check the joints to make sure screws are tight.

- Do not use plastic sheets, as they can get in the way of breathing.

- Lock the sides into place after putting your toddler in the crib.

- Avoid items that your toddler could climb on and then fall out of the crib.

- Keep the crib free of mobiles, activity gyms and other hanging objects after your child is five months old. Once he is able to get on to his knees, these kinds of toys can be a strangulation risk.

- Make sure that your toddler does not have a soother with a cord or anything else around his neck while in the crib.

- Do not leave loose objects (including bottles) in the crib.

Safe Bedding
Your toddler only needs a thin blanket if he is dressed in a sleeper. Do not use sheepskins, pillows, pillow-like items, quilts, comforters, stuffed toys, or bumper pads.

Bed Safety Checklist

- Choose a bed with a simple design. There should be nothing sticking out, no cut-outs, and no fancy headboard and footboard.

- Check the joints every few months to make sure screws are tight.

- There should be no spaces between the mattress and the headboard, walls, or other surfaces that could trap your toddler.

- Place the headboard (rather than the side of the bed) against the wall. This position prevents your toddler from becoming trapped between the bed and a wall.

- Choose a bed that is low to the floor. Put protection on the floor (carpet, quilts, and pillows) in case your toddler falls out of bed.

- Use safety rails that you can attach on all sides.

- Your toddler is safest in the lower bunk of a bunk bed set.

Learning to Use the Toilet

Toddlers learn to use the toilet at different times. Toilet learning can be a positive experience. Your toddler will discover a new skill and feel a sense of accomplishment. Try not to be pressured into making her use the toilet before you think she is ready. Rushing the process may make it more difficult and frustrating for both of you.

Most children learn to use the toilet between the ages of 24 and 48 months. Staying dry all night often takes longer, sometimes up to the age of six or older. Toilet learning is easy for some children, but most toddlers take between two weeks and six months to learn.

The Keys to Toileting Success

- Start only when your toddler shows you she's ready.

- Let your toddler be in charge of her toileting, but do your part, too. Have a potty chair close by, have a general routine with potty chair reminders, and praise her accomplishments.

- Do not pressure your toddler to use the toilet. Keep the toilet a battle-free zone.

Is Your Toddler Ready?

If you answer "yes" to most of the questions below, your toddler is likely ready to get started.

- Does he stay dry for a few hours at a time or occasionally wake up dry from a nap?

- Does he show in some way that he is aware when he urinates or has a bowel movement? For example, does he go into a corner or squat to have a bowel movement? Does he comment on soiled diapers? Does he notice when he has an "accident" without diapers on?

- Can he follow simple directions, such as, "Let's go to the toilet"?

- Can he let you know when he needs to use the toilet?

- Is he able to pull down his pants and underwear by himself?

Family Stories

Wet or Dry

The best piece of advice about toileting I was given came from a friend who had five children. She told me to start talking to Alexander about "wet" and "dry" right from birth. So I started saying something like, "That wet diaper can't feel good," or "You're dry, doesn't that feel good?" When it came time to start toilet learning, Alex already understood the concepts of wet and dry.

If your toddler doesn't want to have her bowel movements in a potty chair or toilet, let her continue to use diapers. This will keep her from becoming constipated. Constipation can cause painful bowel movements that may delay toilet learning.

Using Training Pants

Training pants are pull-up pants that look like normal underwear but are made from the same material as diapers. Not everyone agrees on the use of disposable training pants while a toddler is trying to learn to use the toilet.

Some people think that using them slows down toilet learning. Training pants feel the same as diapers and a toddler could forget that the goal is to use the toilet. Some parents prefer to put their toddler in normal underwear.

However, because a toddler's nighttime bladder and bowel control often is slower than daytime control, it is sensible to use training pants at night or when you're out and about with your toddler.

Helping Your Toddler Start Using the Toilet

- **Wait for a stable time** in your toddler's life to get started. The best time is when there are no other stresses going on, like going to a new daycare, a new sibling in the house, moving to a new home, illness, or other family changes.

- **Use reminders:** "I'm going to the bathroom—do you want to come too?" or "Your potty chair is waiting for you," or "It's potty time."

- **Give lots of praise for action.** When your toddler is successful, give lots of praise but direct it at her actions rather than at her "being good." Encourage her by saying something like, "It's great that you went pee in the potty chair!" instead of saying "Good girl!" That way you will help her see that using the toilet is the goal. You will show her that whether she succeeds or not doesn't make her good or bad in your eyes.

- **Let your toddler watch you go to the bathroom.** Explain what you are doing (if you are comfortable with it). Observing a same-sex parent or sibling is worth a thousand words.

- **Encourage your toddler to sit on and play with the potty chair.** Encourage her to help "dolls" toilet on the potty chair.

- **Explain how using the toilet is a good change:** "You won't have to wear diapers anymore." "You will be able to wear underwear like big kids."

- **Keep a potty chair next to the main toilet.**

- **Get a toilet seat that fits on top of the regular seat**, if your toddler is interested in the big toilet. Make sure this seat is stable, and provide a solid step stool for her to use to get up onto the toilet.

- **Let your toddler claim the potty chair as "my own."**

- **Use training pants** or clothes with elastic waists that can be pulled down quickly and easily.

- **Pants can be optional.** You may choose to let your toddler go without pants around the easily cleaned parts of the house or yard. If she feels the urge, she can sit on the potty chair quickly.

- **Place your toddler on the toilet immediately after she awakes.**

- **If your toddler gets bored** while sitting on the potty chair, give her something to do, like looking at a book. Check your library for books about toilet learning.

- **Do not use sweet treats as rewards** for success. If you do use a reward system, try stars on a chart, a coin in the piggy bank, or a song of success.

Helping Your Toddler Succeed

To help your toddler succeed at toileting, try to stay relaxed and be patient. Think of toilet learning in the same way as learning how to run. It's a new skill for him and it will take some time to learn. Praise his efforts and try not to be upset over accidents. Just clean up soiled pants and encourage him to use the potty chair next time.

Accidents will happen. Even older children forget to use the toilet, especially when they're sick, cold, or very involved in play.

Prepare to continue toilet learning away from home. If you can, find the locations of bathrooms before you go out. Bring along the potty chair if you're going to be away from home, and make any other preparations you'll need.

If your toddler is dealing with a major change or stress in his life, or just refuses the potty chair, be prepared to go back to diapers for a while. If this happens, remember that he is learning a new skill. It's normal to go two steps forward and one step back.

Looking After Your Toddler's Teeth

To prevent tooth decay, toddlers need to have their teeth brushed daily by an adult.

Your toddler's first teeth (called baby teeth) are important because they:

- Help him to stay healthy. Infections in the mouth and teeth can affect overall health and have lifelong health consequences.

- Help him eat and digest food properly.

- Play an important role in speaking.

- Help in jaw development and guide the permanent teeth into their proper position.

- Help him look good.

Your toddler's first tooth is likely to appear at about four to six months of age. By about 36 months of age, he should have 20 teeth (10 on the top and 10 on the bottom). These teeth will be replaced by permanent teeth starting when he is between five and seven years old. Some baby teeth do not fall out until age 11 or 12.

Once teething begins, it will continue for about two years. Many children have no problem with teething. Other children may have pain or trouble eating. A common sign that a new tooth is coming is increased drooling.

If your toddler has a fever or diarrhea while teething, it may not be related to the teething. If he has a fever, see p. 122 for more information. If your toddler has diarrhea, see "BC HealthGuide" in the Resources chapter.

Here are some ways you can help your toddler cope with teething:

- Use a bib to catch drool and wipe his face often to prevent chaffing.

- Give a clean, chilled wet face cloth or teething ring to chew on. Check the condition of teething rings frequently. Throw away any that are cracked or worn. Teething gels and ointments are not recommended.

- Avoid giving teething cookies or biscuits. These can lead to tooth decay.

- Give your toddler extra love and patience to help him through the teething process.

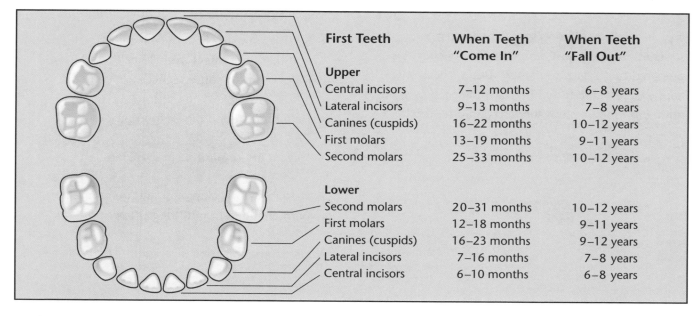

First Teeth	When Teeth "Come In"	When Teeth "Fall Out"
Upper		
Central incisors	7–12 months	6–8 years
Lateral incisors	9–13 months	7–8 years
Canines (cuspids)	16–22 months	10–12 years
First molars	13–19 months	9–11 years
Second molars	25–33 months	10–12 years
Lower		
Second molars	20–31 months	10–12 years
First molars	12–18 months	9–11 years
Canines (cuspids)	16–23 months	9–12 years
Lateral incisors	7–16 months	7–8 years
Central incisors	6–10 months	6–8 years

By about 36 months of age your toddler should have 20 teeth, 10 on the top and 10 on the bottom.

Preventing Tooth Decay

Tooth decay can start as soon as a tooth appears in your toddler's mouth. Bacteria that stick to the teeth mix with food and drink and make acid. This acid can break down tooth enamel and cause tooth decay.

Here are some tips on how to care for your toddler's teeth:

Brush Her Teeth

- Once baby teeth appear, gently brush her teeth (once in the morning and after the last evening feeding) with a child's toothbrush. She needs to have her teeth brushed daily by an adult.

- Have her lie comfortably in your lap, on a change table, or on the floor.

- Use a tiny (rice-sized) amount of toothpaste with fluoride. As more teeth appear, gradually increase the amount of toothpaste up to a pea-sized amount by the age of 36 months.

- Plan to brush her teeth at times when she is not too tired or hungry.

- Make time for frequent spitting.

- Make a game of teeth brushing. Sing a silly song, or tell a story about clean teeth.

- Keep toothpaste out of reach. Children should not swallow large amounts of toothpaste with fluoride.

- Replace toothbrushes frequently. Some children like to chew on the bristles, so these toothbrushes may need to be replaced more often.

Choose Her Food and Drink Carefully

- Do not offer her sugary drinks like pop, punch, or slush drinks.

- Avoid letting her drink milk or juice out of a bottle at naptime or bedtime.

- Offer regular meals and snacks. Avoid grazing (eating and drinking all the time, including from a bottle or a sip cup).

- If she is thirsty, offer only plain water unless it is a regular meal or snack time.

- When she is six to nine months old, serve drinks in a regular cup instead of a bottle or sip cup.

- Give hugs and attention for comfort, instead of food.

Check for Tooth Decay

Check her mouth often for any signs of tooth decay (chalky white crescent or spots along the gum line). See your dentist if you notice any tooth decay.

Visit the Dentist

The Canadian Dental Association recommends that toddlers see a dentist six months after the first baby tooth appears or no later than 12 months of age. During this first visit, the dentist will have a look in your toddler's mouth. This is also a good time to talk about daily dental care, fluoride, and eating habits.

If you have concerns about your toddler's teeth before she is 12 months old, see a dentist.

If you are on Premium Assistance through Medical Services Plan (MSP), your toddler may have dental benefits through the Healthy Kids Program. Contact the Ministry of Social Development for more information about Healthy Kids. (See "Dental Care" in the Resources chapter for contact information.)

Bottles and Tooth Decay

Your toddler's teeth may decay if she often drinks from a bottle filled with anything other than water, especially during rest and sleep periods. There is also a risk if your toddler walks around with a bottle, drinking box, or sip cup and sips from it all day long.

For information on how to stop your toddler's bottle habit, contact your dentist or local public health office. (See p. 62 for more information on how to help your toddler change from using a bottle to using a cup.)

Fluoride

Fluoride helps make tooth enamel stronger and better able to resist tooth decay. Some "baby" toothpastes do not contain fluoride. Check the toothpaste ingredients for fluoride.

Few cities add fluoride to the drinking water. To find out if your community water has added fluoride or about testing your well water for fluoride, call your local public health office.

Most children will get enough fluoride from using a small amount of fluoride toothpaste twice a day. However, some children may need more. Ask your dentist.

Floss Her Teeth

- Once her teeth touch each other, floss once a day.

- Use a floss pik or string floss. She could damage her gums if she uses floss on her own teeth, so it's best if an adult does the flossing.

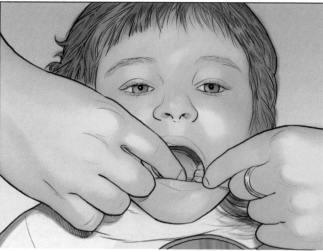

Start flossing your toddler's teeth once they touch each other.

Tooth Safety

Here are some ways to protect your toddler's teeth:

- Use size-appropriate car seats, booster seats, and seat belts to prevent injuries to his teeth if there is a car crash. (See p. 162 for more information on car seats.)

- Young toddlers may chew on almost anything. Keep him from chewing on hard things that could crack his teeth, are a choking risk, or could cause injuries.

- Children fall often when they are learning to walk. Do not allow him to walk around with a toy, sip cup, bottle, or anything else in his mouth.

Soothers

Soothers are also called pacifiers or dummies. Soothers are sometimes given to toddlers to help them satisfy their need to suck, beyond their need for nutrition. A soother should not be used in place of cuddling, comforting, or breastfeeding. Try finding out if your toddler wants something or is hungry, bored, or tired before giving her a soother.

Sucking on a soother is thought to be better than thumb-sucking because it's easier to break the soother habit later on. Try to use a soother only for sleep or when she wants extra sucking.

Soother Safety Checklist

- Make sure the soother is a one-piece design.

- Check regularly that the nipple is firmly attached to the handle by giving it a good tug.

- Replace the soother every two months. If the soother is sticky, cracked, or torn, throw it away. It can easily tear and become a choking hazard.

- Sterilize the soother before the first use by boiling it in water for five minutes and then letting it cool completely.

- Clean the soother in warm, soapy water. Avoid cleaning it in your own mouth, which can transfer bacteria from your mouth to your toddler's mouth.

- Never tie a cord to a soother and hang it around your toddler's neck or attach it to clothes. It can get tangled around her neck, causing her to strangle. You can use a clip with a short ribbon attached.

- Avoid letting your toddler chew a soother for teething. It can tear or break and become a choking hazard.

- Never dip a soother into honey, syrup, or any other sweetener. This can lead to tooth decay. Also, honey should not be given to children under 12 months of age. It may contain botulism spores that can make them sick. (See p. 79 for more information on honey.)

(See p. 79 for more information on honey.)

Key Points

Avoid Sharing Your Germs

The bacteria from your mouth may increase the chance of tooth decay in your toddler's mouth. Here are some tips to avoid sharing your germs:

- If he uses a soother, avoid putting it in your mouth.
- Use separate toothbrushes.
- Use one spoon to test baby food and another one to feed him.

Thumb-Sucking

Thumb-sucking in toddlers is usually not a problem. However, children who suck their thumbs a lot or intensely after their permanent teeth start to come in are at risk for dental or speech problems. If you are concerned about your toddler's thumb-sucking, talk to your dentist.

Helping Your Toddler Stop or Reduce the Use of a Soother

If your child sucks a soother or his thumb, it is best to help him stop at around four or five years of age — before his permanent teeth start to come in.

Children who use soothers have more ear infections than those who do not use a soother. Children who have frequent ear infections should have their use of a soother limited.

To help your toddler stop or reduce the use of a soother:

- Choose a time when no changes are happening.

- Start by limiting where and when he can have the soother, slowly getting it down to one place at one time. This often ends up being during naps or bedtime. Once he is asleep, gently remove the soother from his mouth.

- Use comforting and calming techniques like extra hugs, story times, and listening to music.

- Praise him for using the soother less (stars on a chart, a phone call to Grandpa to report on how long the soother has been put away).

- Avoid the use of punishment to make him give up a soother.

Looking After Your Toddler's Vision

To help your toddler develop healthy vision:

- Make sure her eyes are safe from injury.

- Protect her eyes from sun exposure. Use sunglasses:
  - with 99–100% UVA and UVB protection
  - with lenses that fully cover the eyes
  - that fit snugly and comfortably.

- Provide healthy food.

- Show things to her (mobiles, colourful images, patterns).

- Encourage her to climb, run on the playground with you, play with a ball and big puzzles, build with blocks and look at books.

- Have her eyes checked if you think there may be a problem with her vision.

When you are choosing sunglasses, make sure they offer 99–100 per cent UVA and UVB protection.

The following are typical vision skills of toddlers:

Typical Vision Skills of Toddlers

By 6 – 8 months	• Sees objects of interest and moves toward them. • Eyes appear "straight" and work together.
By 8 – 12 months	• Uses her eyes to help herself move around objects.
Over 12 months	• Shows interest in books/stacking toys. • Moves, climbs, and throws in a co-ordinated manner.

Keeping Your Eyes Open

It was my friend who noticed that my daughter, Hailey, had a problem with her vision. She noticed that Hailey would "root around" for her toys, and when things were handed to her, she would move her hand around until she hit the object. I hadn't noticed because I was so used to it.

The eye doctor was great. Even at Hailey's young age, he tested her vision. Since she started wearing glasses, she is so much happier and more active. She can actually see where she's going and all of the things around her that she couldn't see before.

Eye Safety

Here are some ways you can protect your toddler's eyes from injury:

- Do not allow her to play with sharp items (darts, scissors, or any pointed object).

- Keep her away from older children who are playing with sharp objects.

- Teach her not to walk or run while carrying sharp objects (pencils, Popsicle™ sticks, or other sharp or pointed objects).

- Keep your home and yard childproofed for safety. (See p. 156 for more information on childproofing.)

- Limit the amount of TV she watches to no more than one hour per day, if any. (See p. 50 for more on TV.)

- Keep her at least three metres (eight to 10 feet) away from a TV screen.

- Place your TV so there is no glare coming from the screen.

- Put a hat and sunglasses (if possible) on her when you go outside. (See more in the sun safety section on p. 93.)

Vision Warning Signs

Here are some other signs that could mean your toddler has problems with her vision:

- Difficulty following objects or people with her eyes.

- Constantly rubbing eyes, squinting, or frowning.

- Blinking more than usual.

- Complaining that her head hurts.

- Closing one eye or tilting or holding her head in a strained or unusual position when trying to look at an object.

- Difficulty finding or picking up small objects dropped on the floor (after 12 months of age).

- Difficulty focusing or making eye contact.

- Bringing objects very close to eyes to see.

- Eyes are red or watery or have a discharge.

- Eyes appear to be crossed or turned after six months of age. (You may notice this in a photograph of your toddler.)

If you think your toddler has a vision problem, talk to your eye doctor (optometrist or ophthalmologist), doctor, or public health nurse.

Looking After Your Toddler's Hearing

Your toddler starts to learn speech and language from the moment he is born. Hearing plays a key role in how he learns language and speech skills. It is also important for his social and emotional growth.

Every toddler develops at his own pace, but the following are their typical hearing skills at various ages.

Typical Hearing Skills of Toddlers

By 6 months	• Turns head toward sound. • Tries to imitate changes in voice pitch. • Babbles ("baba," "mama," "gaga").
By 9 months	• Imitates speech sound of others. • Understands "no-no" or "bye-bye." • Will locate sound source at eye level or below.
By 12 months	• Understands simple requests like "Look here," "Open your mouth." • Tries to say a few words. • Imitates different speech sounds. • Likes to repeat sounds. • Recognizes words for everyday people and items. • Can hear you call from another room. • Understands short sentences.
By 24 months	• Points to pictures when they are named. • Listens to stories, songs, and rhymes. • Uses several different words, "Mama," "Dada," "cat," "ball." • Points to body part when asked (for example, "Where's your nose?"). • Follows simple directions like "Get the ball." • Puts two words together: "My teddy."

Key Points

The Earlier the Better: Newborn Hearing Screening

The BC Early Hearing Program (BCEHP) provides hearing screening to all babies born in B.C. Newborn hearing screening is done shortly after birth in hospital or at a public health office. Newborn hearing tests are important for families because a lot can be done if hearing loss is caught early in a child's life.

Genes and Hearing Loss

Children can inherit hearing loss. If any of your toddler's relatives have had hearing loss early in their lives, tell your health-care provider. Also, be sure to have your toddler's hearing tested.

Protecting Your Toddler's Hearing

Here are some ways you can protect your toddler's hearing:

- Breastfeed. Breastfed toddlers have fewer ear infections. (See p. 58 for more on breastfeeding your toddler.)

- Avoid putting him to bed with a bottle. This can lead to ear infections, which can reduce hearing.

- Keep him away from second-hand smoke. Second-hand smoke increases the risk of ear infections.

- Use only a light towel when cleaning his ears. Avoid using cotton swabs or putting anything in the ear canal.

- Check the volume of the TV or music. If you have to raise your voice to be heard above the noise of other sounds, the noise level is too high.

- Provide ear protection like earmuffs if he must be around loud sounds, such as loud music or fireworks. Do not use earplugs, as they can be a choking hazard.

- Have him immunized on time. (See p. 115 for more on immunizations.)

Hearing Warning Signs

The earlier hearing problems are found and treated, the better. It is best if this can be done by six months of age.

Looking in a toddler's ear will only help find an ear infection. Testing a toddler's hearing takes special equipment and skills. Hearing testing for young children is available in British Columbia through public health hearing (audiology) clinics.

See your doctor or public health nurse, or call HealthLink BC at 8-1-1 if your toddler has any of the following conditions, which may lead to hearing problems:
- Ear discharge (runny ear)
- Earache (pain in the ear)
- Bad smell from the ear canal
- Reddened skin around the ear
- Wax totally blocking the ear canal
- An object in the ear canal

The following signs may indicate that your toddler already has a hearing problem. If he shows any of the following signs, speak to your doctor:
- Talks in a very loud or very soft voice.
- Seems to have difficulty responding when called from across the room, even when it is for something interesting.
- Turns his body so that the same ear is always turned toward the sound.
- Has difficulty understanding what has been said (after 36 months of age)
- Is rarely startled by loud noises.

Preventing Illness

You can help prevent your toddler from getting sick by doing three simple things: getting her immunized, washing her hands, and keeping surfaces clean.

Immunizations

Immunizations are also called vaccinations, boosters, or shots. They protect your toddler from serious childhood illnesses and diseases before they have a chance to make her sick. Immunizations are a safe and effective way to prepare her body to fight certain diseases and help her stay healthy.

Why Immunize Your Toddler

Immunizations have reduced several serious diseases in Canada (e.g., polio, diphtheria, tetanus, whooping cough, and measles). However, the germs that cause these diseases still exist. Immunizations are the best way to protect your toddler from serious diseases. By having her immunized, you help protect other children and unprotected adults from these diseases as well. In the long run, this helps to reduce the spread of disease and the chance of outbreaks.

Immunizations are often required for enrolment in childcare centres and schools because of the protection they offer to everyone.

How Immunizations Work

Immunizations help your toddler's immune system make antibodies. Antibodies fight diseases and protect her from getting sick. Because she gets an immunization, she doesn't have to get sick first to get protection.

Vaccines are given by injection, using a sterile needle or syringe. Children are given free immunizations as part of their basic health care in British Columbia.

Immunizations Are Very Effective

Most routine childhood vaccines are effective for 85 to 95 per cent of the children who receive the complete series. Some children can still get sick, even if they have the immunization. To protect these children, it is important for all children to be immunized, so the disease won't spread.

Diseases Immunizations Protect Against

British Columbia provides publicly funded immunizations to protect your child against these diseases: measles, mumps, rubella, hepatitis B, diphtheria, tetanus, pertussis (whooping cough), polio, rotavirus, Haemophilus influenzae type b disease (Hib), varicella (chicken pox), pneumococcal and meningococcal diseases, and human papilloma virus (for girls).

When to Immunize Your Toddler

Immunizations work best when they are given at certain ages. Some vaccines are only given once or twice. Some need to be given over a period of time in a series of properly spaced immunizations.

Children are usually immunized at: 2 months of age, 4 months of age, 6 months of age, 12 months of age, 18 months of age, 4–6 years of age, 11 years of age (Grade 6 level), and 14 years of age (Grade 9 level).

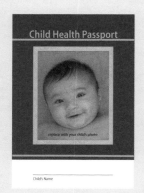

Child Health Passport

The *Child Health Passport* tells you the basic schedule for immunizations, and is a record of your child's immunizations. It gives you some suggestions about things you can do before, during and after an immunization visit to care for your child. It also provides information about monitoring your child's growth, and having their hearing, teeth and vision checked.

For more information, ask your health care provider, a public health nurse, or visit www.BestChance.gov.bc.ca/tools-and-resources/key-resources/index.html

If you have been following the recommended schedule for immunizations, your toddler will have already had visit #1 (at 2 months) and visit #2 (at 4 months). Visit #3 will be needed when your toddler is 6 months old.

The immunization schedule can change. To find out more about the current immunization schedule, visit www.immunizebc.ca.

Immunizations are Safe

Immunizations are very safe for your toddler. Sometimes immunizations may cause minor side effects, but these are temporary. These side effects might be soreness where the needle went into the arm or leg, or a slight fever. These do not usually last long. Serious side effects from immunizations are very rare. If your child gets one of these diseases, the risks of the disease are far greater than the risk of a serious reaction to the immunization.

For more information about the immunization schedule, or if you have questions about side effects or how to make your toddler more comfortable if he gets a fever or a sore arm or leg, ask your health care provider, public health nurse, or call HealthLink BC at 8-1-1.

Protection from the "Flu"

The influenza vaccine protects against the 3 strains of influenza viruses that health experts think will likely cause influenza—often called the "flu"—during the flu season. It does not protect against other viruses or bacteria that may cause colds or stomach illnesses (the stomach "flu"). The virus changes (mutates) every year, which means a new seasonal flu immunization must be given every year.

Influenza (flu) vaccine is recommended for all children 6–23 months of age, as early as October of each Fall. Children 6–23 months of age can get free influenza immunizations. Caregivers (parents, grandparents, babysitters, other household contacts) of children from birth to 23 months of age are also encouraged to get a flu immunization. Older children with certain health conditions can also get free influenza immunizations.

If your toddler has chronic health problems, they may put her at higher risk if she gets the flu. So it is also important that she get an influenza immunization.

Talk to your doctor or a public health nurse if you have questions about immunization for influenza.

Preparing for an Immunization Visit

Here is a quick checklist of reminders to help you prepare for an immunization visit:

- Bring your toddler's *Child Health Passport* with you to the appointment. You may have been given one on your first public health visit. If you do not have one, tell your public health nurse at your visit.

- Dress your toddler in clothes that can be easily removed from her arms and legs.

- Bring your toddler's favourite toy or blanket for comfort.

- Tell your toddler what is happening: "You are going to get an immunization that will help you stay healthy. I will be with you the whole time."

During the Immunization Visit

- Distract your toddler during the immunization by using toys or get her to blow out or take deep breaths.

- Be prepared to stay for 15 minutes after the immunizations.

- Book your next visit when you take your toddler in for her immunizations.

Reactions to Immunizations

Immunizations cause very few serious reactions. Those that do occur are far less serious than the actual diseases that immunizations help prevent. Most reactions to vaccines are mild and do not last very long. The most common reactions include:

- Redness, mild swelling, or soreness where the vaccine was given

- Mild fever (about 38°C [100.4°F] or less taken under the arm)

- Drowsiness, irritability, and poor appetite

- A mild rash that may occur seven to 14 days after the chicken pox or measles, mumps, rubella (MMR) vaccines

Severe reactions to immunizations are rare. These could be a very high fever (over 39°C [102°F] under the arm) or difficulty breathing. If your toddler has either of these signs, tell your public health nurse or doctor and seek medical care right away.

If you are worried about your toddler's reaction to immunizations, talk to your public health nurse or doctor, or call HealthLink BC. (See "Key Resources for Parents" in the Resources chapter.)

Key Points

Immunizing a Sick Toddler

There is no need to delay immunization if your toddler is sick with a cold, cough, or mild fever. If your toddler has a more serious illness on the day of the immunization, talk to your public health nurse or doctor.

To Do

Travelling Outside of Canada?

If your toddler is going outside of Canada, he may need extra immunizations for protection. Contact your doctor or public health office for more information.

What About Flu Immunizations?

Each year during influenza (flu) season, free flu immunizations or flu shots are offered to certain groups of people in B.C. All children aged six months to 23 months are encouraged to get a flu immunization. Caregivers (babysitters, grandparents, parents, other household contacts) of children from birth to 23 months of age are also encouraged to get a flu immunization.

If your toddler has chronic health problems, they may put her at higher risk if she gets the flu. So it is also important that she get an influenza immunization.

Talk to your doctor or public health nurse if you have questions about the influenza immunization.

Hand Washing

Hand washing is the best and easiest way to help prevent your toddler from getting sick. Show him how to wash his hands properly, and make sure to let him watch you wash your own hands. When he sees you doing it regularly, he'll learn to do the same thing.

Wash hands for 15 to 20 seconds, which is about the time it takes to sing *Happy Birthday*. Use plain soap and warm water. Finish with a rinse and dry hands well with a clean towel.

Avoid using antibacterial soaps. They may add to the growth of "superbugs." Superbugs are bacteria that are too strong to treat with antibiotics.

Wash your hands and his hands often, especially:
- After changing diapers or toileting
- After blowing a nose
- After touching animals or cleaning a litter box
- When tending a sick child
- When preparing food
- Before eating

Keeping Surfaces Clean

Cleaning surfaces and the other things that your toddler or her food touches is another good way to prevent her from getting sick.

Some of the most important things to keep clean are:
- Food preparation areas and kitchen utensils
- High chairs, bibs, her dishes and cups
- Strollers, toys
- Cribs, changing tables, other furniture that she touches
- Garbage containers
- Pet litter boxes, pet toys, pet beds

Tips to help make cleaning quicker and easier:

- Keep cleaning supplies in one area where they are handy but locked away from your toddler.

- Clean the most important areas first. You may have time to get to other things later.

- Normally, plain soap and water are all you need for cleaning. Antibacterial household products may reduce the spread of germs. However, their use in the home is not yet proven. Using them may add to the growth of superbugs.

- When cleaning up vomit, diarrhea, blood, or pet droppings, use a mixture of one part bleach to nine parts water, and wear rubber gloves.

- Wash cleaning cloths frequently.

- Avoid using a dishcloth to wipe her face. You could spread germs. Use a clean face cloth.

- You may find it easier to have paper towels and disposable wipes on hand.

- If possible, divide up cleaning tasks between people in the house.

When Your Toddler Is Sick

Your toddler can get sick very quickly. She may be playing happily one minute and then, unexpectedly, start feeling sick. You may have already learned her early signs of getting sick. You might notice glassy eyes, more crying or clinging, or pale skin. Be alert to these behaviours and watch her more closely when you see them.

British Columbia has a number of health resources that can help you when your toddler gets sick.

B.C. Health-Care Resources

BC HealthGuide

The BC HealthGuide provides helpful information you can trust on many medical concerns. To use the guide, look in the index to find your toddler's symptoms. Follow the instructions about home treatment and when to seek help from a health professional. You can get this guide at no charge from your pharmacy or at www.healthlinkbc.ca

HealthLink BC

When you need information right away, you can call HealthLink BC. The registered nurses will give you 24-hour confidential information and advice. You can also speak to a pharmacist about medication concerns. The pharmacist is available from 5 p.m. to 9 a.m. every day.

When you call the service, have your Personal Health Number from your B.C. Care Card ready to give. Also, have a clear idea of the symptoms or concerns you want to discuss. Note: If you do not have your B.C. Care Card number available, you still will be able to get service.

Anywhere in B.C.   8-1-1

TTY (Deaf and hearing impaired)   7-1-1

Translation services are offered in over 130 languages.

Public Health Offices

You have a local public health office near you. It provides many supports for you and your toddler. Typical programs and resources include:

- Child immunization programs

- Programs and services for parents of infants and preschoolers

- Assessment and screening of child development and progress

- Education and support for families of children with asthma, allergies, and eczema

- Resources on pregnancy and parenting (pamphlets, brochures, books, videos, and more)

- Telephone contact with all new mothers and follow-up home visits

- Breastfeeding support

- Postpartum depression screening

- Support for women during postpartum adjustment or those who are experiencing postpartum depression

- Education and support for parenting concerns (safety, healthy lifestyle choices, parent support services, and more)

For more information, see "Key Resources for Parents" and "Health Authorities" in the Resources chapter.

Other Health-Care Professionals

If you have any doubts about your toddler's health or development, talk to any of the following health professionals:
  - Family doctor
  - Dentist

- Optometrist
- Pharmacist
- Members of your local public health office.

Helping Your Toddler With Health-Care Visits

Visits to health-care professionals can be a stressful experience for your toddler. He may be at the developmental stage when he is afraid of strangers. And it is likely that this "stranger" may need to touch and look closely at him.

Here are some tips to help prepare your toddler for health-care visits:

- Talk about what is happening. Explain where you are going and why. Use simple language: "The nurse is going to give you an immunization in the arm. It will sting for a minute, but I'll hold you on my lap the whole time."

- Answer his questions simply and directly.

- Book health-care appointments during times when he is well rested and not hungry.

- Model what a health caregiver might do, such as listening to his chest or looking in his ears.

- Encourage him to play "doctor" or "dentist" with a toy.

Key Points

For a fever:

- Let your toddler breastfeed more, or offer more to drink
- Take off extra clothes that your toddler is wearing
- Give your toddler medicine to help bring down the fever and make her more comfortable
- Give your toddler a lukewarm bath

If you are concerned about a fever, call HealthLink BC (at 8-1-1), your public health office, or your family doctor.

- Bring along items that will make him more comfortable (a favourite blanket, toy).

- Read children's books about visits to a doctor, dentist, optometrist, or nurse.

- Praise his behaviour and efforts to co-operate (even if he cried the whole time). "You held so still when the doctor looked in your ears!"

Fever

A toddler has a fever if her temperature is 37.4°C (99.4°F) or higher measured in the armpit. (A temperature taken in the armpit is also called an axiliary temperature.) A fever itself is usually not harmful. However, it can cause discomfort and dehydration. A fever in a healthy toddler is usually not dangerous. This is especially true if the toddler does not have other symptoms and the fever goes away in three to four days.

It is important to look for other symptoms of sickness besides fever. The degree of fever may or may not tell how serious your toddler's illness is. For example, a cold may cause a high fever of 39°C (102°F). Then again, a very serious infection may cause only a mild fever or none at all.

How Do You Know If Your Toddler Has a Fever

Simply touching your toddler's forehead or neck may or may not tell you if she has a fever. Taking her temperature will tell you how high your toddler's fever is. It will also allow you to keep track of how long she has her fever.

Taking a rectal (in the buttocks) temperature is the most exact way to measure fever. However, taking a rectal temperature is not recommended for toddlers. This method might cause injury.

The best way to take your toddler's temperature is in the armpit with an easy-to-read thermometer (such as a digital thermometer). Place it high up in the centre

of her armpit. Make sure it is touching bare skin on all sides. Tuck the arm snugly against her body. Hold her arm close to her body, and wait at least three minutes. Comfort and distract her while taking her temperature.

If the reading is high or you are not sure if it is accurate, wait a few minutes and take her temperature a second time.

Here are some other tips for taking your toddler's temperature:

- Mercury (glass) thermometers are not recommended. If the thermometer breaks, she might be exposed to the mercury, which is poisonous.

- Forehead strips or pacifier thermometers are not accurate.

- Do not use a thermometer in the mouth of a child under five years. Young children cannot keep the thermometer under their tongue long enough. Never use a glass thermometer in a toddler's mouth.

- An ear (tympanic) thermometer is quick, but it may not be accurate. Talk with your public health nurse about how to use your ear thermometer correctly.

If you are concerned about a fever, call HealthLink BC (at 8-1-1), your public health office, or your family doctor.

Coughs and Colds

Most children get several mild colds and coughs every year. These usually improve within a week and go away within 14 days. A toddler under the age of three who has a cold or cough needs to be watched closely. He can become more ill than older children.

When your toddler has a cough or cold, you might notice he has a runny nose, cough (which may or may not produce mucus), fever, or sore throat. He may also be irritable.

How Do You Treat Coughs and Colds?

- Let your toddler rest.

- Keep the room temperature comfortable but not too hot.

- Give your toddler plenty of fluids (breast milk, water, other fluids).

- Use a cool air humidifier.

- Use saline drops in your toddler's nostrils to help clear a stuffy nose.

- Raise the head of your toddler's bed by 2.5–5 cm (1–2 in.) by placing blocks under the legs of the bed.

- Give extra attention.

- Practise good hand washing. (See p. 118 for more information on hand washing.)

(See p. 118 for more information on hand washing.)

Antibiotics and Colds

Antibiotics cannot cure colds. Colds are caused by viruses, which cannot be treated with antibiotics. There is a risk of side effects from antibiotics, including allergic reaction. More common side effects include: nausea, vomiting, diarrhea, rashes, and yeast infections. Antibiotics also kill good bacteria. The unnecessary use of antibiotics adds to the growth of dangerous superbugs that antibiotics can't treat.

- Do not use decongestant or antihistamine medications unless recommended by your doctor.

- Use acetaminophen to reduce pain or fever. Always check the label carefully so that you give the right amount. Phone HealthLink BC at 8-1-1 for guidelines if needed.

If you are concerned about your toddler's cough or cold, phone HealthLink BC, or contact your public health office or family doctor.

Parenting Your Toddler

Being a parent can be one of the most important and rewarding things you do. It is also hard work. There is no instruction manual for the challenges you will face as a parent. You will learn to parent as you go, based mostly on the way you were brought up. You may also base your parenting on what you see others do or what you read in books and magazines.

Toddlers grow and learn so quickly that you may need to change the way you parent every day. It can help if you try to keep learning what resources your family needs and stay healthy and active.

Why Toddlers Behave the Way They Do

What is happening when you and your toddler disagree or she is doing something you don't like?

Are you expecting too much? Do your expectations match your toddler's needs and temperament? (See p. 5 for more on temperament.)

Is it part of your toddler's stage of development? She sees herself as the centre of the world. She also has little or no control over her impulses. When a feeling arises, she simply goes with the first idea that comes, whether it is hugging or biting. She can easily become upset by her lack of control over her world. She may not be able to say how she feels because she doesn't know the words to do that. (See p. 9 for more on child development.)

Is she stressed? A tired or hungry toddler will often act out if there are too many activities that are too close together.

Has something changed in her life? Changes in your home or routine can be unsettling for her.

Sometimes she'll act out more until the change becomes routine.

Is she getting enough attention? She may be misbehaving in order to get your attention.

Is the setting suitable for her? Some settings are just not meant for toddlers. Try to avoid settings that require more control than she has.

Thinking About Discipline

Take a few minutes to reflect on your beliefs about discipline. For example, think about your own experience as a small child. What worked and what didn't? Think about your goals for guiding your toddler's behaviour. Consider ways you can develop your skills. For example, you might want to watch videos or read some books about discipline. You may also want to join a parenting group or have friends over for coffee to share ideas.

Positive Discipline

The goals of positive discipline are to teach and guide your toddler as he grows. The aim is to keep him safe and to help him to become a responsible person and to act in acceptable ways.

There is a fine line between punishment and positive discipline. Punishment is an unpleasant consequence that follows an action. Punishment can be physical, verbal, or emotional. Hitting or slapping is physical punishment. Shouting is verbal punishment. Shaming or disgracing is emotional punishment.

Positive discipline should not be used to punish or to make your toddler obey. Rather, it should help him understand how to fit into the world in a thoughtful, healthy, and productive way.

Your toddler will benefit most from positive discipline that is:

- Based on respect for him and his feelings. Name calling, blaming, or talking in a hurtful way is not positive discipline.

- Seen as fair by your toddler (although he may not feel this at the time).

- Right for his age and what he can do.

- Consistent.

- Given at the time when the problem behaviour occurs.

- Explained in a way he can understand. This helps the discipline become a learning experience.

- Built on the trust and love between you and him.

The following section gives you information on how to promote positive behaviour and how to deal with problem behaviour. It also provides information on how to guide your toddler's behaviour as he gets older.

How to Promote Positive Behaviour

You can help promote positive behaviour in your toddler. This can prevent problems from developing in the first place. Here are some tips on how to promote positive behaviour.

Communicate With Your Toddler

Much of your communication with your toddler is a form of teaching. Your words should be simple. Some days it can feel like you each are speaking a different language. You will sometimes have to listen hard to learn what she wants to tell you.

Here are some tips for communicating with your toddler:

- Get her attention before you speak.

- Get down to her level. You may have to sit on a chair, stoop, or sit on the floor.

- Make eye contact.

- Use a gentle touch.

- Keep your words clear, simple, and direct. Saying "Please put that down" is more direct than "Cut it out."

- Make only one request at a time. She cannot react to two or three requests at the same time.

- Use positive communication. Try to tell her what to do instead of what not to do. Saying, "Please ride on the sidewalk" is more positive than, "Don't ride on the street."

- Listen carefully to her. If you are too busy to listen, say, "I can't listen right now, but I will be able to in five minutes."

- Focus on her behaviour. Saying, "How wonderful that you went pee in the potty" instead of, "Good girl" helps her understand what behaviour you want from her.

- For every "No," try to offer two reasonable choices. "No, that paper is for Daddy. But you can play with this book or this toy."

- Use "please" and "thank you" whenever you can.

Provide a Safe and Stimulating Environment

- Supervise your toddler.

- Childproof your home for safety. (See the Safety chapter on p. 155 for more information.)

- Provide a range of interesting toys and activities.

- Set up play areas in the kitchen, living room, garage, and yard, so you can be close to your toddler.

- Provide tools and toys for play cooking, office work, and gardening. You don't need to buy fancy toys. Just use items that you have around the house.

Keep Routines

- Organize your day so there are regular naps and mealtimes.

- Keep to bedtime routines.

- Balance active and quiet times.

- Tell your toddler about any changes in routine that will be happening.

- Give your toddler regular attention, even if you are busy.

Set Good Examples

- Be calm and patient.

- Model the behaviour you want to see in your toddler (such as sharing or taking turns).

- Gently remind your toddler about limits—she has a short attention span and can quickly forget what you've said.

- Avoid reacting in angry or defensive ways.

Family Stories

More Is Caught Than Taught

My aunt, who was a teacher, once told me, "More is caught than taught." Children watch us and learn from what we do in our daily life. As our daughter, Sophia, gets older, I hear her saying things I have said or doing things I have done. So I don't smoke or swear (usually), and I try to be fair and reasonable with her. I see myself every day through her eyes, and I try to make sure I like what I see.

Dinnertime Solution

Dinner was the worst time of the day for us. Both my toddler, Breanne, and I were tired and hungry, and I was trying to clean up and make dinner. When my husband, Wayne, came home, I would be yelling and Breanne would be in tears—not a pretty picture for him every night. So I decided to stop the pattern. At five o'clock Breanne sits on the couch with her blanket and has quiet time with soft music, a toy, and a small snack of fruit. I put my feet up and relax as well. When Wayne comes home, he plays with Breanne in the other room for half an hour while I have time to make dinner. We eat a little later but we are all calm and much happier. I had to rethink how I was doing things that no longer worked for us.

Praise Good Behaviour

- "Catch" your toddler behaving well and tell her right away: "I really like the way you are playing gently with your sister."

- Tell your toddler what you like about her behaviour: "Thank you for using your quiet voice at Grandma's house," or "I really like that you are holding my hand while we cross the street."

Focus on Co-operation, Not Control

- Offer appropriate choices, usually no more than two.

- Show your toddler how to negotiate: "I will read you a story after you've picked up the blocks."

- Talk about conflicts: "I can see that you are angry at Tim for taking the ball."

- Offer solutions to conflict: "Maybe you can let Tim have a turn and then he will give you a turn."

- Let your toddler know that other children have needs too: "Tim wants to have a turn with the ball too."

- Help your toddler express feelings and desires: "Does that song make you feel happy?"

How to Deal With Problem Behaviour

When your toddler wants to do something that you don't want him to do, he is not testing you. He is testing his ideas, boundaries, and power. Learning to be independent is an important part of his development. (See p. 43 for more on independence.)

Here are some positive ways to guide behaviour:

Offer Choices

"Would you like to wear your yellow T-shirt or your red T-shirt?" Your toddler will respond to being able to make simple choices. This helps give him a sense of control. Try to limit choices to two options. More than two options may confuse him. Making choices helps him develop independence and cognitive skills.

Redirect

"Let's throw your ball out on the deck. No one will get hurt out there." Use this strategy when your toddler is doing something that is all right, but the way in which he is doing it is not. If he is throwing blocks in the kitchen, take him to find a ball and a place where it is safe to throw. You can say: "This is where it is safe to practise throwing, and a ball is safer to throw than a block."

Set Limits

"Remember to hold my hand when we cross the street." Let your toddler know what the limits are and what is expected or what you want. If possible, state limits in a positive way. The most important limits you set are around safety. A simple "no" is an effective way to make the limits clear: "No. We don't hit." Be consistent in sticking to the limits you set. Remind him of limits when you need to: "You need to be buckled in your car seat before we drive to the park," or "Be gentle with your little brother."

Make your directions clear and simple enough for your toddler to follow. Be fair and consistent. Don't let him bite you one day and laugh it off, then get angry when he does the same thing the next day. Biting is always wrong. (See p. 132 for more on biting.)

Distract

"Look at this book." Distraction can work very well with even very young children. If he is doing something you don't want him to do, switch to something else. Show him a toy, ask him to read a book with you, or do a quick finger play. Distraction works because young children have very short attention spans.

Use Consequences

"That's too bad—the bubbles are all gone now." Older toddlers can learn from experience. Make sure you tell your toddler ahead of time what is likely to happen. Then he has a choice. If he is going to pour bubble-making soap on the grass, tell him, "There won't be any bubble soap left if you pour that out." And, if he decides to pour it out anyways: "That's too bad—the bubbles are all gone now." He may cry and may need a hug for comfort. But he'll learn quickly that some actions have consequences. Use consequences that teach.

Remove Your Toddler From the Situation

"It's time to take a break. Come and have some quiet time with me." If your toddler is nearing 36 months of age, removing him from a difficult situation can work well. This gives him a chance to calm down. Give him something quiet to do, like looking at a book or doing a puzzle. Once you feel he has calmed down, praise him. If he is going to go back to the same situation, remind him of what you expect: "You seem ready to play with your sister again. Remember to play gently with her."

Use a Short Time Out

"You need a time out." Time out is when you take your toddler away from a situation where she is doing something unacceptable. You then move her to a spot by herself, such as a quiet corner. This allows her time to calm down. It also teaches her that her behaviour is not acceptable.

Learning Control

I was sick of always fighting with my son, Jasper. It seemed like he was the one in control most of the time. Then my mother gave me a tip. She suggested that I let him be in control of some things, that it was something he needed to be learning at this stage in his development. So I started with, "Jasper, do you want to wear your blue shoes or your black shoes today?" instead of, "Put your shoes on now!" It worked. So I tried it with lots of different things: "Do you want to eat your carrots first or your tomatoes first?" "Do you want to play with your blocks or ball?" Suddenly, I wasn't fighting with him anymore to get things done. Once he was able to make decisions regularly, he was happier, and I knew I was helping him learn to be independent.

Time out is a teaching tool that works only if a toddler is old enough to understand why it is being used. Some experts say time out works for children between two and 12 years of age. Other experts say it doesn't work until the age of 36 months. Ask yourself if you think your toddler understands why a time out would be used.

If you choose to use time out, keep it short. Time outs should last no more than one minute for each year of your toddler's age. For example, if she is two years old, her time out should only be two minutes. She may become frightened of being alone or separated from her caregiver. So if you are going to use time out, stay near to supervise her. (For more information on time out, see "BC HealthGuide" in the Resources chapter.)

Learn to Compromise

A compromise is a middle way that is safe and will work for both of you. Your toddler may be at the stage when she needs to try things out for herself. Sometimes she may want to do something that you don't want her to do. In these situations, a compromise might work. Compromising is a skill that she will use to get along well with others.

For safety reasons, some things are not open for compromise. She should learn that safety comes first. For example, tell her, "No, you can't play with matches, you could burn yourself." She will soon learn that there is no compromise for some things.

Positive Discipline by Age

The way you guide your toddler's behaviour is going to change as he gets older. No single strategy will work for all stages. Try to change what you do as he gets older.

6 Months to 12 Months	12 Months to 24 Months	24 Months to 36 Months
A regular schedule of rest, feeding, and play is the best way to support and guide your toddler at this age. If your 10-month-old spills his milk, he is not being bad, but he may have been trying to move the glass. Consequences do not work as a form of discipline between 6 to 12 months of age.	At this age, your toddler will begin to try to exercise control over her world as she develops a stronger sense of self. She may be demanding and easily frustrated, and she may have a very short attention span. Remember, she is not misbehaving to upset you. She is simply testing and exploring.	Between 24 and 36 months of age, your toddler is struggling to master his world, going between independence and dependence. He is trying to figure out who he is. You may find he is very possessive and demanding at this stage. This can be difficult for both him and you. Outbursts and temper tantrums are likely. Stay patient, try to have empathy, keep your routines, give careful supervision, and set limits. (See p. 132–133 for more on tantrums.) Try to have realistic expectations of his skills and explain the reasons for limits in simple ways.
It is helpful for your toddler to experience some frustration so that he learns to comfort or soothe (or settle) himself. You don't always have to pick him up the moment he fusses, as long as you comfort him in other ways.	Her desire to explore, along with her short attention span, make safety a very important concern at this age. Try to be patient and keep a close eye on her. Children between 12 and 24 months of age should not be left alone.	
Some of the best ways to support your toddler at this age are to: • Spend quiet time together. • Give him a comfort toy. • Redirect. • Distract.	Time outs should not be used with this age group because they may increase separation anxiety or fear of being abandoned. Some of the best ways to support your toddler at this age are to: • Childproof your home. • Offer choices. • Redirect. • Distract.	Some of the best ways to support your toddler at this age are to: • Childproof your home. • Offer choices. • Redirect. • Set limits. • Use consequences. • Distract. • Use a short time out, if you choose.

Challenging Behaviours

Children do not come into this world knowing how to work well with others. It is during the toddler years that they begin to learn what they can and cannot do. This is the time for you to help your toddler learn the basic skills she needs to think, care, and act responsibly in the future. She will misbehave for a number of reasons. Very few (some would say none) of these reasons have to do with wanting to make you angry with her.

Some behaviours can be very challenging for parents, such as biting, tantrums, fighting, whining, and dawdling.

Biting

At one time or another, your toddler might try biting. It is unclear why he may bite, but it's best if he learns that it is something he must not do. If your older toddler bites:

- State the limit clearly and simply: "No, please don't bite. It hurts."

- If he bites while breastfeeding, loudly say, "Ouch, that hurts. Please don't bite!" and remove him immediately from the breast. Then try breastfeeding again. Just because he bites does not mean you need to stop breastfeeding.

- Avoid biting him back. It will frighten and confuse him and will not stop him from biting.

- Avoid laughing or taking biting lightly. A nibble on your leg may not seem serious, but a deep bite on a playmate is.

Tantrums

Tantrums can be normal events for toddlers. Your toddler is at a stage where he gets upset easily and reacts quickly. He wants to be in charge of his world, but he does not have the language or emotional skills to do it well. He can also easily become overtired, hungry, and anxious. Tantrums are usually more about how he is feeling overall than the event that seemed to start the tantrum.

How to Avoid or Cut Down on Tantrums

- Make sure your toddler has regular rest, physical activity, and meal and snack times. If you are out, take healthy snacks and water with you. (See p. 75 for more information on healthy snacks.)

- Let him know ahead of time what is going to happen and what you want him to do. When going into the store, tell him what you have planned, "We are going to the store for milk and fruit. You can help me choose the bananas."

- Find helpful ways for him to share strong feelings. This could be throwing a ball, running fast, or talking about his feelings ("mad," "sad").

- Try not to say "no" to every request.

- Give him control over little things. This will help lower his frustration level.

- If you see a tantrum coming on, try to redirect or distract him. Or try correcting whatever the problem is. Give him quiet time or some food if he's hungry or tired.

What to Do During a Tantrum

- If the tantrum has started, don't try to stop it or talk to your toddler. He is out of control, cannot stop, and will not hear what you say.

- Stay calm. Take 30 seconds to think about what to do. Do not scream at or spank him.

- Some children are better able to move back into control if they are held firmly but lovingly. Others find this closeness even more upsetting and their tantrum may become worse.

- If you are in a public space during a tantrum, keep in mind that most people will understand. Many people have been in the situation themselves.

- Make sure that he is somewhere safe, where the flailing, rolling, or pounding will not hurt him or others, or damage property. If he is in a shopping cart, make sure you hold on to him for safety.

- When the tantrum is over, cuddle and comfort him. Praise him for regaining control.

- Recognize his feelings: "I know you are upset about not being able to get that toy."

- Avoid giving in to whatever the tantrum may have been about. You do not want him to learn that a tantrum will make you change your mind.

Fighting

Have you watched your toddler around her playmates or siblings? You have probably seen that she doesn't always get along with them. She is beginning to understand ownership. She wants control over other people. She is likely to have at least a few fights in her toddler years. Think ahead about how you will handle a fight. Here are some tips that might help:

- Help her come up with solutions: "What do you think you should do?" She will need lots of coaching to arrive at solutions.

- Step in and offer solutions that are fair: "Let's take turns. Let Michael have the toy for a few minutes. Then he can give it to you."

Family Stories

Sometimes Nothing Works

When my daughter, Julia, was two, we were walking to the library to return a book on parenting. She had a meltdown right on the road. It was a classic, kicking, screaming down-in-the-dirt tantrum. I had no energy left or ideas on how to stop it. So after making sure that she was safe, I sat down on the curb and reread the chapter in the book about tantrums! None of the suggestions were helpful at that moment. But by the time I'd finished reading the chapter, Julia had stopped the tantrum on her own and was looking at me. Maybe she was wondering why her mother was relaxing on the side of the road while she was having a meltdown!

Key Points

Spanking

Never spank a toddler. Spanking is not recommended by the Canadian Paediatric Society or early childhood educators. This is because you can really hurt your toddler when you are angry. Spanking can also lead to anger and resentment. It can cause him to lose trust in you. Spanking also teaches that him that hitting others is all right.

What should you do if you feel you are beginning to lose control? Make sure he is safe, and take some time to cool down. If these feelings persist, talk with your health-care provider.

- If you feel the children are safe, step back for a few minutes to see if they can solve the problem themselves.

- If you are worried about their safety, step in right away and stop the fight.

Whining

Whining is that unpleasant tone between talking and crying. It bothers most parents much more quickly than other challenging behaviours. Whining often happens when your toddler is tired or hungry. You may hear it when he feels no one is listening to him, or he cannot find the words to tell you what's wrong.

Here are some tips to help prevent whining:
- Make sure he is not hungry, tired, or uncomfortable.
- Praise him when he is not whining: "I like your grown-up voice."
- Keep in mind that "more is caught than taught." Try to be a role model.
- Say, "I can't hear you when you whine."
- Do not give in to the demands of the whining.

Slowness or Dawdling

Time does not have the same meaning for your toddler as it does for you. She doesn't dawdle to make your life difficult. She is just more focused on an activity than she is on time. It is normal for her to take a long time when she is learning new skills, going somewhere, or getting something done.

Since it's almost impossible to get your toddler to stop dawdling, here are some tips to help:
- Give her plenty of notice that you are going to change from one activity to another.
- Build in extra time when you are organizing your day and week.
- Clearly and simply tell her what you want: "Put on your coat now, please."
- Get rid of distractions when you are in a hurry. Get yourself ready ahead of time, turn off the TV, and put toys away.

Staying Cool as a Parent

Parenting can be very rewarding, but once in a while almost all parents lose their tempers with their toddler. And most parents wish they had not. Here are some tips to help you stay calm:

- **Stick to routines.** Your toddler likes routines. It helps her to co-operate if she knows a certain thing will happen at the same time each day. Keeping routines for sleeping and eating will go a long way.

- **Adjust your expectations**. Sometimes parents have expectations of themselves and their toddlers that are much too high. Learn about child development to get a better idea of what to expect from your toddler at different stages. (See p. 9.)

- **Rest.** Sometimes taking a nap when your toddler does can help you feel less overwhelmed or angry.

- **Make time for yourself.** Build in some regular time for your own relaxation. Trade time with family members, friends, or another parent. Do something you enjoy.

- **Know that you don't always have to fix everything.** It can be difficult to hear your toddler cry. But if she hasn't learned to talk yet, crying may be her only way to express herself. You do not have to "fix it" every time she cries. If she's not hungry, hurt, or otherwise in need of your attention, and if she seems to be crying because she is upset or angry, it is fine to let her cry for a little while. Don't ignore her, but wait to see if she is able to calm herself down.

- **Keep a journal.** Try to figure out what triggers your temper. You may find that you tend to get angry at mealtimes when you are busy and your toddler is hungry. If this is true, plan a late snack, have a short rest together, or make some quiet time with a toy before making the meal.

- **Talk about the challenges.** Talk to someone close to you about the challenges you are having and how you are feeling. It is best not to do this in front of your toddler.

- **Get to know other parents.** Connecting with other parents of toddlers can help you build a support network.

- **Protect your toddler.** If you are feeling overwhelmed and afraid you might lose control and hurt your toddler, get help immediately. Put your toddler somewhere safe and call a family member, a friend, HealthLink BC, your public health office, or your doctor. (See the Resources chapter and Shaken Baby Syndrome below.)

Shaken Baby Syndrome

Shaken Baby Syndrome (or neurotrauma) is the name for the injuries that can happen when a baby or toddler is shaken. Shaking a toddler can cause serious injury or death. Shaking can cause brain damage, blindness, paralysis, and seizures.

Shaken Baby Syndrome often happens when a parent or caregiver loses control because a child won't stop crying. The parent or caregiver gets angry and ends up hurting the child.

To prevent Shaken Baby Syndrome:

- Learn how to calmly cope with your toddler's crying.

- Do not leave your toddler in the care of someone who has problems controlling their anger.

- Tell others who care for your toddler that crying is normal. Ask them to call you if they get frustrated, so you can return.

- Learn how to control your anger. If you are very angry, put your toddler in a safe place, such as the crib, and walk away until you are under control again. If you feel unable to cope or are afraid that you may hurt him, make sure he is safe. Then call someone for help. Never pick up a toddler when you are angry about the crying.

Every Parent Makes Mistakes

Nobody is perfect. Everyone makes parenting mistakes. When this happens, follow up with your toddler: "I'm sorry I yelled at you. I was afraid that you would drop the vase." This will model the kind of behaviour you expect from your toddler.

Perinatal Depression

As many as one in five women in B.C. will experience a major depression tied to her pregnancy and childbirth. Perinatal depression occurs among women of all ages, cultures, and levels of education.

Call a family member, a friend, HealthLink BC, your public health office, or your doctor.

See "Shaken Baby Syndrome" in the Resources chapter for more information.

Parenting Issues

As a parent, you will likely face situations that you were not expecting. This section gives you information about special situations including perinatal depression, nurturing your relationship with your partner and dealing with differences in parenting. It also includes information about cultural diversity, parenting on your own, and parenting a toddler with special needs.

Postpartum Depression

"Perinatal" means "around the time of birth". Perinatal depression is depression that happens any time from when you first become pregnant to one year after your baby is born. Postpartum depression is perinatal depression that happens after birth. It can also affect women who have had a miscarriage, stillbirth, or who have adopted a child. It is different from "baby blues" where mothers feel more irritable, restless, tired or tearful in the first two or three weeks after a baby is born. Most mothers experience "baby blues", but this gradually disappears.

Postpartum depression is a serious health concern and requires that mothers get help from health care providers. It can affect your body and mind, and upsets your thinking, emotions, behaviour, and habits.

Common symptoms of postpartum depression include:

- Difficulty sleeping, extreme fatigue or exhaustion
- Lack of self care, e.g., not eating or emotional overeating
- Uncontrollable crying
- Feeling upset or angry over things that usually wouldn't bother you
- Depressed feelings or extreme mood swings
- Unable to enjoy your child
- Feeling unfit or unable to care for your child
- Thoughts of harming yourself or your child
- Strong feelings of guilt, failure or worthlessness
- Panic attacks where you feel your heart is racing, you are out of breath or shaking and sweating
- Lack of interest in things that you usually enjoy

It is important to get help. Without treatment, postpartum depression affects both you and your toddler. A mother who is depressed for a long time can have difficulty bonding and caring for her toddler. He may not feel safe and loved, and may not be able to develop secure attachments. Over time, he might struggle with relationships.

If you think you, your partner or family member may be experiencing postpartum depression, ask your doctor or public health nurse for help. There are many effective supports and treatments that can help with recovery from this serious illness. The best help usually comes from a mix of support from health care providers, family, friends, self-help, and the community.

How to Help Yourself

Ask for help from your health-care providers.
Some women have a hard time asking for help, but it is important to talk to your doctor, midwife, or public health nurse about how you are feeling so that they can help you.

One treatment may include local support groups who know about the feelings you are having. Other treatments could be individual counselling, and sometimes, medication. You should be able to continue breastfeeding while using medication. Talk to your doctor.

Ask for help from your friends, family, and community. Mothers who have had postpartum depression report that having a strong circle of supportive people helped them recover. If possible, talk to your partner about how you are feeling. Talk with someone you trust and who you think will understand your feelings. Ask your partner, family members, or a babysitter to care for your toddler so that you can take regular breaks. It is also a good idea to find a support network, such as a mother-child group.

Self-help. Try to get enough sleep, eat well, and exercise regularly. Sleep while your toddler naps, take a daily walk with your toddler, have a friend over, and keep in contact with friends.

How Partners and Family Members Can Help

A mother who is trying to cope with postpartum depression needs support. You may feel helpless during this difficult time and may think there is little you can do, but you can make a difference.

Here are some suggestions that may help a mother with postpartum depression:

- Encourage the mother to talk about her feelings. Show that you are trying to understand.

- Help with or take over household chores and responsibilities.

- Let her know that she is loved and valued.

- Let friends know when she doesn't feel like having company.

- Say yes when friends or family offer to help with things like cleaning the house or helping care for the toddler. She needs some time away from her toddler.

- If you are a partner, be loving without asking for sex.

- Try not to act like you think she is making a fuss over nothing. Postpartum depression is a serious health issue.

- If you have concerns about how the mother is coping, show your support and concern. One way to do this is by going with her to visit her health-care provider and sharing your concerns.

- Find support for yourself. Talk with someone you trust and who you think will understand your feelings. Talking with others can provide you with hope and support.

Taking Care of Your Relationship

Parenting a toddler can be a very stressful time in a relationship. It is easy for parents to neglect each other because the toddler can take most of the focus and energy of the family. It is important that you find time to take care of your relationship.

Here are some ways in which you can nurture your relationship:

- Go on regular dates together. Write them on your calendar and have a babysitter or trusted family member take care of your toddler.

- Make mid-week dates, even if it is just for a coffee. Use this time to reconnect.

- Make time for a healthy sexual relationship.

- If possible, travel to and from work together.

- Allow your toddler to occupy himself sometimes. He can learn how to amuse himself and to be independent. You just need to be close enough to supervise him.

- Take an evening class together.

- Plan and cook meals together.

- Connect every day. This could be some quiet time before your toddler is up in the morning or after bed in the evening. Even 10 minutes to talk about the day may work.

Differences in Parenting

Consistent parenting offers your toddler a safe and nurturing environment. Sometimes, parents do not agree with each other about the best way to handle their toddler's behaviour. It seems to be healthy for toddlers to see their parents sometimes not agree. It helps toddlers learn that people may see things differently. It also teaches them how to be flexible.

Sometimes, however, parents find they never agree. This can be confusing for a toddler. It can give her unhealthy power within the family, where she takes sides and plays one parent against the other. This is especially likely if parents argue in front of her.

There are three main parenting styles:

- **Permissive Parenting Style**—Parent takes a relaxed attitude and usually lets children do want they want. Children know they are loved but don't learn consequences.

- **Authoritarian Parenting Style**—Parent takes control, is strict, and expects obedience. Children learn good behaviour, but often with the threat of punishment, and may rebel.

- **Authoritative Parenting Style**—Parent is gentle but firm, is consistent, explains the reasons, and models good behaviour. Children feel secure and have self-respect.

Research shows that the "authoritative" style of parenting is the most successful. It helps children grow into responsible, thoughtful, healthy, and productive adults. Discuss your parenting style with your partner.

Here are some other things you can do to help you and your partner work together on parenting:

- Respect and talk about your differences. Try to understand the reasons for your disagreement. Do this in private where your toddler cannot hear you.

- Be prepared to make compromises and negotiate with your partner. Remember, some differences in parenting styles are healthy for your toddler.

- If you seem stuck, get help. Take a parenting course, talk with friends and family, read books, or talk with a counsellor.

Cultural Diversity

If there are differing cultural beliefs and traditions within your family, you can use these to teach your toddler and enrich her life. She can gain a lot from being around cultural diversity. Parenting styles and what is expected of children differ from culture to culture. What is thought to be strict or respectful in one culture may not be the same in another culture. The value placed on children, the rules, and the role of relatives in raising a child can vary greatly. Who is allowed to discipline children also varies. In some cultures, extended family members as well as parents are responsible for the actions of young children. In other cultures, only parents are responsible for a child's behaviour.

It's a good idea for parents and families to discuss their childhood beliefs, practices, and traditions about parenting and the meaning of family.

Here are some tips for supporting cultural diversity:

- Acknowledge and respect the cultural differences. Listen to each other and try not to judge. Try to find out what your partner and family members believe and value.

- Think about your own culture and beliefs. Try to understand exactly why you parent the way you do. Do you consider your position more "normal" than your partner's? Do you believe something is important because it was traditional in your family? Have you questioned whether it really is important? Have you questioned the long-term consequences of your beliefs? Is your belief based on your own fears or your own experiences?

• Try combining your values and beliefs and using the best from all cultures involved. Combine and celebrate holiday traditions. Read stories to your toddler in all the languages used in your family. Cook and value traditional foods. Choose positive discipline strategies that are consistent and promote child development.

Parenting on Your Own

Being a single parent can be hard work. You may be struggling with increased financial pressures or with trying to juggle your time and energy between your many demands. You may be going to school or working while carrying the full load of parenting. You may find yourself having to work long hours, leaving little time for yourself and your toddler.

Families of any description build strong connections by:

• **Creating a stable, nurturing home.** Your toddler will thrive in a loving environment with routines that are predictable.

• **Developing support**. Build support for your toddler and yourself through family, friends, and community. Try to find people who can provide emotional support, companionship, emergency help, child care, and other help and support.

• **Giving positive discipline.** Set firm, clear limits for your toddler. These should match her development stage. Use the recommended disciplining practices described earlier in this section (See p. 131 for more on positive discipline.)

• **Giving your toddler quality time.** It's not just the amount of time that you spend with her that counts; it's what you do when you are together. Try to support, encourage, and listen to her.

• **Finding time.** If you are looking for more time with your toddler, be creative. Maybe your employer will be flexible with your hours. Arrange to trade babysitting with other single parents. Join activities with other parents and their kids.

• **Taking care of yourself.** Don't forget about yourself and your own health. Eat a healthy diet, get exercise, and try to get enough sleep. Find ways to take care of yourself—whether it is taking a nap, playing a sport, reading a book, or learning relaxation techniques.

- **Avoid treating your toddler as an adult**. Use your adult relationships to talk over issues and troubling events. Your toddler cannot take on adult roles.

- **Ask for help**. When you feel overwhelmed, depressed, or exhausted, get help. Look to friends, family members, and professionals.

Parenting a Toddler With Special Needs

Parenting a toddler with special needs brings both joys and challenges. Your health-care provider will be able to help you understand your toddler's development and individual needs. Your health-care provider can also tell you about the services available to assist you.

Here are some suggestions that may be helpful in parenting a toddler with special needs:

- Talk with other parents or join a support group for parents of children with special needs. Talking with parents who have had similar experiences can provide you with emotional and practical support.

- Expect to go through many changing emotions about your toddler's needs. Know that these emotions are normal.

- Have open discussions with members of your immediate family. Give yourself, family members, and friends time to adjust.

- Remember that you are not alone. Ask for help from professionals, extended family members, and friends. Contact organizations that focus on your toddler's special needs.

- Take care of yourself and make sure your needs are met. Exercise, eat well, get enough sleep, get regular medical care, and give yourself some time off from child care.

- Take time to enjoy your toddler and celebrate his strengths and abilities.

It is important to remember that, even if your toddler has a special need, he will still go through stages of development. He may not reach these stages at the same age or at the same rate as other children, but he will make progress.

Your toddler's needs are also very similar to those of other children. He needs chances to play, to try out new skills, and to be praised for his successes. Most of all, he needs your love and attention.

Teamwork

Parenting a toddler with special needs usually means working with a team of specialists and professionals. You are the key member of the team and the expert in your toddler's needs. You understand her better than anyone else. You know her history, her daily routine, her strengths, and her ongoing needs. This knowledge can help professionals develop the best plan for therapy, treatment, or support.

Here are some other tips for building a team that supports you and your toddler:

- Get support as soon as possible. Research shows that the sooner your toddler gets support for her needs, the better her chances are for healthy development.

- Make sure that all members of your team know what the other members are doing to help your toddler.

- When you meet with your team, ask a lot of questions. Remember, all questions are good questions.

- Take notes during visits with your team.

- Consider bringing a friend or family member to meetings for support. That person can also help take notes, keep track of information, and review the discussion with you later.

- Keep a journal about your toddler's condition, including any changes in behaviour, times of day they occur, and triggering events. You can use it to review and make decisions.

- Since you know your toddler best, be a champion for her. Think about the recommendations made to you by professionals. Then decide what would be best for her. This way you can join in the problem solving with the members of your team.

- If you have a concern about your toddler that you feel is being overlooked, trust your instincts. Let others know about your concern. You may be able to see something that everyone else is missing.

To Do

Who Are the Health Professionals on Your Team?

As your child grows from being an infant to a preschooler, you may wish to get other forms of support. Check the following professionals and services that may also help you and your toddler:

- Specialized doctors/pediatricians
- Public health nurses
- Mental health professionals
- Child development centres/infant development programs (you can contact them yourself, no referral needed)
- Social workers
- Speech-language pathologists
- Supported child development consultants
- Occupational therapists
- Public health audiologists
- Physiotherapists

Helping Your Toddler Adjust to Change

Toddlers are most comfortable with regular routines. Regular routines can make your toddler feel safe and protected. However, sometimes changes happen. Some children react very strongly to changes, while others don't seem to notice them.

Your toddler may not be able to tell you how he is feeling in words, so when there is a change in his life, he may show you how he feels by:

- A loss of appetite
- Crying
- Nightmares or sleep problems
- Outbursts of anger or temper tantrums
- Clinging
- Being very quiet or withdrawn
- Going back to old habits (thumb sucking, wearing diapers)
- Having trouble being apart from parents and caregiver

You can help your toddler adjust to change by showing him that he is loved and will always be taken care of. Keep in mind that he cannot be a support to you when things are difficult for you. He is too young. If you are upset and crying, tell him that you are upset right now, but you will feel better soon. If you need to, ask a safe, caring person to look after him while you talk with a friend, doctor, counsellor, or crisis centre.

It also helps to monitor how your toddler is adjusting. You know his temperament best and can predict the reactions he might have. Finally, it's important to tell him that the change is not his fault.

Expected Changes

This next section may be helpful if you are expecting big changes, such as welcoming a new baby to the family. It also provides information on how to help your toddler deal with death or a family breakup.

There are some changes that you know about, such as the birth of a new baby or a move to a new house. Here are some ways you can help prepare your toddler for a change:

- Talk to her about the expected change in a positive way.

- Listen to her concerns and reassure her.

- Read books to her about the expected change. If you are moving, read stories about families that move.

- Provide toys that allow her to act out the change. Use a baby doll to talk about a new baby. Use a toy moving truck to talk about moving to a new home.

- Try not to have more than one change at a time. Don't try moving her to a bed and start toilet training at the same time.

- Be warm and loving to make her feel safe and secure.

- Her concerns are real, even if they may seem small to you. If keeping a favourite teddy bear or pair of shoes out of the moving box helps, then make sure they do not get packed away.

Living together as a family, you can help your children to be close and loving to each other. Here's how you can help:

- Recognize and value their differences. Try not to compare them with each other.
- Encourage them to play together and give them time away from each other.
- Let each one know they are special.
- Try not to give them labels (such as "the baby," or "the big brother").
- Have clear rules for how they should treat each other.

- Try to make time every day for the usual things she enjoys, such as a favourite story, food she likes in her special bowl, or a cuddle before bed.

Welcoming a New Baby

How your toddler changes when a new baby is in the house will depend on a number of things, such as:

- His age
- How he usually responds to change
- How much he knows and understands

It does help to know that it is very common for toddlers to be upset by the arrival of a new baby. Toddlers don't like changes in their day or any change in the amount of time with their parents. A new baby in the house changes routines and can take time that may have been your toddler's.

Here are some ways to help with making the coming of a new baby easier for all of you:

Preparing for the Baby

- Tell your toddler about the new baby and answer his questions simply and honestly.

- Let your toddler feel the baby kicking and help him talk to the baby "in Mommy's body."

- Read books about babies and big brothers and sisters.

- Show your toddler his baby pictures and talk about what he was like as a baby.

- Find a baby doll for your toddler to "parent." He can change the diapers or cuddle the doll.

- Make any changes in your toddler's life, such as moving out of a crib to a bed, changing rooms, or toilet learning, long before the birth, if possible.

- Talk to your toddler about what a baby does and needs. He may expect someone to play with, not someone who cries or sleeps most of the time. If possible, visit friends who have babies so he can see for himself.

- Have a plan for your toddler's child care when the new baby arrives, and explain it to him.

- If you plan on having your toddler present at the birth, arrange for someone, other than your partner, to be his main support. This person must be able to leave the room with him if the labour or birth becomes upsetting or frightens him.

- Plan to have your toddler see and visit the baby soon after the birth. It is better to do this when no other visitors are there. Time his visit so you can focus on introducing him to the baby. Tell him ahead of time what he might see, such as any medical equipment in the room or on you.

On the Day of the Birth

- A daily plan is important. Make sure your toddler knows who will take care of him when you go into labour. Try to plan it so that his day is as normal as possible.

- Help your toddler safely hold and talk to the baby.

- Talk about how much your toddler looks like the baby or how the baby is looking right at him.

- Encourage your toddler to interact with the new baby as much as possible when you are all together.

At Home After the Birth

- Try to keep the routines you had before your new baby arrived. This will help your toddler feel safe and loved even as changes are made for the new baby.

- Try to make time to do the special things that you used to do with your toddler. You might want to give him a chance to suggest activities.

- Be patient with your toddler. He may want to return to old habits, such as sleeping in a crib or wetting his pants. (This can happen even if he knows how to use the toilet.) This is normal. Let him take these few steps back into babyhood for a short time. Praise him for the skills he shows you, like eating with a spoon or talking.

- Include your toddler when you can. This may be as simple as having him sit beside you or your partner during breastfeeding or throwing a soft toy back and forth with him while the baby rests beside you.

- Try not to use the baby as the reason for not doing something. Say, "When I've finished feeding the baby, let's read a story," instead of "I can't play with you now because I have to feed the baby."

Helping Your Toddler Deal With Loss and Grief

Your family may have to deal with the death of a loved one or a separation. Even if you don't tell your toddler, she will be able to sense that something is different. It is important to understand that she can sense these changes and to support her through her own fears and grief.

When you can, it helps to prepare your toddler for a loss. Try to find simple ways to tell her that something has changed. It is also important to keep her temperament in mind when you are trying to help her cope with loss and grief. (See "Temperament" on p. 5.)

Helping Your Toddler Deal With Death

Your toddler has little to no understanding of time and that some things are final. She may have little or no reaction to someone's death. Or, she may react with tears, anger, or fear that someone else may die. If a friend or family member dies, don't keep it a secret from her. She will know that something is wrong and may be more afraid if you don't talk to her about it.

When talking with your toddler, use simple terms that she can understand, such as "Grandma was very sick and died last night. She won't be with us anymore." Your toddler may want to know where Grandma is. You may choose to answer using your religious beliefs as a guide. Remember to keep your explanations simple and non-frightening. Allow her to express her feelings. Give details only if she asks for them.

Before There Is a Death

- Take any chance that comes up to talk to her about the cycle of life and death. Plants in the garden, the changing seasons, and the death of an insect—all provide a chance to show your toddler that death is a part of life.

- Be truthful and open about death. Your toddler might ask difficult questions, such as, "Will you die? Will I die?" Try to answer as honestly as you can without creating new fears: "Yes, we all die, but Mommy and Daddy won't die for a very long time and neither will you."

When a Loved One or a Pet Dies

- Include your toddler in your own grief. That will let her know that feeling sad and showing grief is normal when a loved one dies. Let her know that painful feelings are part of living and that, over time, the pain will decrease: "We are feeling sad. Sad things happen to us. But we'll feel better after a while."

- Use language that will not confuse your toddler. Use the words "die" and "dead." If you use protective terms like "asleep" or "gone away," she may develop fears of sleeping or travelling.

- Try to keep daily routines the same. This can help your toddler keep her sense of security in knowing what to expect each day.

- Keep thoughts of the person or animal alive by talking about them or by looking at pictures. If your toddler does not show an interest, it's all right. Some children avoid the feeling of loss by refusing to talk about the person or look at their picture.

- Think about how your toddler might feel. Pay attention to the way she acts. Is she afraid of being away from you after the death of Grandma? She may be thinking that you will not come back.

- Give extra love, attention, and support. This will help your toddler develop healthy emotional skills.

To Do

The Death of a Pet

The death of a pet can be very sad for you and your toddler. Be honest with him about the death of a pet. Listen to his questions and try to understand his concerns. It is an opportunity for you to talk with him about death and help him learn how to cope.

Helping Your Toddler Through a Family Breakup

A family breakup can a difficult time for everyone. The changes to daily routines may leave your toddler feeling upset and confused. During a family breakup, he needs to feel safe and secure. No matter how difficult your separation or divorce is, try to keep him out of the tension and discussions.

Here are some more tips for helping your toddler through the difficult time following a family breakup:

- Try to keep calm, even though you may feel upset, sad, and scared.

- Give him lots of love and attention, and tell him that you will not leave him.

- Keep the same routines and the same limits as you had before, and use the same type of discipline. This will help him feel safe.

- Give him chances to ask questions and talk about the changes in your family. Be direct and simple in your answers. You might be tempted to talk about adult problems such as responsibility or trust. It is much clearer to him if you say that you and the other parent are not happy together and will be happier if you live apart.

- Be patient with him. Be prepared to have the same discussions over and over to help him process and understand what is happening.

- Be sure he understands that he is not the reason for the breakup. He may think he is to blame.

- Let him talk happily about your ex-partner. When he can hear you, keep your comments about your ex-partner calm and neutral. He needs to know that his parents are still there for him even if you are not together anymore.

- Be prepared for angry reactions or difficult behaviours such as tantrums, thumb-sucking, or going back to diapers. Give extra love and support. These behaviours will stop in time. (See p. 132 for more information on challenging behaviours.)

- Your toddler may stay with a parent away from his main home. When this happens, make sure there are toys, clothes, and other things to make this new home feel comfortable and welcoming.

- Always make sure pickup and drop-off plans are clear with your ex-partner. You may have problems being calm with your ex-partner. If so, try to arrange for pickup and drop-off through a friend or relative. This way, you are not both present at the same time. If your toddler is in child care, one parent can drop off and another can pick up.

- Work out the best way to take toys and other favourite things back and forth between homes.

See "Family Resources" in the Resources chapter for more information.

Child Care

The majority of parents work outside the home. Both parenting and paid work are becoming more and more equally shared between moms and dads. Finding a way to balance the demands of work and parenting your toddler can be a challenge.

Here are some ideas to help balance the demands of combining paid work and parenting:

Develop a strong child-care partnership. Choose the best-quality child care you can. Think of your caregiver as a key support in raising your toddler. Keep your caregiver up to date about events in his life. Visit the child-care setting, and if possible make time to volunteer. This will help you form relationships with other children and parents. (See p. 149 for more information on choosing child care.)

Try to make the mornings run smoothly. Avoid letting the morning become a stressful time. Follow the same routines each morning so that your toddler learns what to expect. To help mornings go smoothly, it may help to get things ready in the evening. You may also find it helps to make time for yourself before your toddler wakes up.

Take a break before rejoining your toddler. Try to take a few minutes for yourself after work before rejoining your toddler. Walk home, read on the bus, or just take a few minutes for yourself. This will help ease the transition between work and parenting. Keep to routines so that everyone knows what to expect.

Simplify. Try to be reasonable with what you expect about work and parenting. You don't need to do everything and you don't have to be perfect. Choose to do those things that matter most and keep your life simple. A good rule of thumb when choosing what is most important is to always put your toddler's health and safety first.

Manage household chores. If you have someone else to share the work at home, try to agree about how the tasks will be shared. Negotiate with each other. Take care to keep things fair to prevent resentment from growing. If you are handling the household work on your own, don't expect too much of yourself. Spread the tasks out over the week so that you don't feel there is too much work and too little time.

Develop a sick plan with friends and family. Your toddler will likely become sick at some point and need to stay home. Plan ahead so that you can avoid a crisis. With your partner, friends, or family, discuss how to arrange keeping your toddler at home when he is sick. Talk to your employer to develop potential plans and to find out if you have benefits that cover family illness. Line up friends or family members who can stay with him on short notice.

Child-Care Choices

Choosing child care is an important and sometimes hard decision. There are many child-care choices available. Child-care options can be divided into two main types: outside your home and inside your home.

What Will Work for Your Family?

- How much care do you need? Full-time? Part-time? When do you need care? Regularly? Overnight? Only occasionally? A few days a month?

- Can you take your toddler to child care or does the caregiver need to come to you?

- How will you transport your toddler to the child-care setting? How much travelling time will it take?

- What kind of care approach do you want? Something that really helps your toddler develop? Lots of time with people? Free play time?

- How much can you pay?

What Will Work for Your Toddler?

Children can be happy in many different sorts of child-care settings. Here are some questions to think about:

- Does your toddler like large groups, small groups, or one-to-one attention? What kind of care suits her temperament?

- Do you think your toddler would like being at home? Near your home? Near your work?

- Does your toddler like going out and having lots of things to do, or does she like quiet times the best?

To Do

Finding Child Care

Start trying to find child care long before you need it. Child-care spaces fill up quickly. Once you have an idea of the kind of child care your family needs, in or out of home, you will need to search out the options in your community:

- Talk to other parents.
- Check your public health office for referrals.
- Check with neighbourhood groups.
- Check local newspapers, Yellow Pages, community bulletin boards.
- Contact the Child Care Resource and Referral (CCRR) program in your local area. (See "Child Care" in the Resources chapter for contact information.)

Key Questions for Child Care

You will want to interview possible child-care providers. Here are some key questions to consider whenever you place your toddler in the care of others:

- Will your toddler be safe?
- Are the caregivers qualified?
- Do you agree with their approach to child care?
- Will they help to encourage your child's development?
- What are their values and beliefs about children?
- What is the financial cost of the child care?
- Do you trust the caregivers with your toddler?

Child Care Outside Your Home

If you choose child care outside your home, your options are: centre care, family care, or a babysitter, relative, or nanny.

Licensed Child Care

Licensed child care can be in a public building like a community hall, a church, or a specific child-care centre. It can also be provided in the caregiver's home. It often has set hours. There are caregivers who step in for absent staff members. Often there are children of the same age group, and larger groups of children.

Regulations that licensed child-care facilities must meet include:

- Staff must have certain qualifications for schooling and practice.
- The centre must have the right number of staff for the number of children.
- Staff must undergo criminal record checks.
- The program must cover everything and be organized.
- Space and equipment must meet regulations.
- The food must meet standards.
- Emergency plans must be in place.
- No one is allowed to smoke.

License-Not-Required Child-Care Options

License-not-required (LNR) child care is given in an informal child-care setting. This is usually in the caregiver's home. LNR care is allowed for one or two children of any age in addition to the caregiver's own children. Family care may have more flexible hours. The children can be of different ages. If the caregiver becomes ill or has to be absent, care may not be available. Sometimes the care may be stopped with little warning.

To Do

Helping You Choose Between Family Care and Centre Care

Narrow down your options by using these questions:

- Do you prefer centre-based child care or family care?

- If you prefer centre-based care, does the facility take children of your child's age?

- Do the hours of operation suit your needs?

- Is the location good for you?

- Can you afford the child care? You may be able to get financial help. For information, contact your local Ministry of Children and Family Development office. (See the Resources chapter of this book for contact information.)

Child Care in Your Home

In-home care is where you get someone to look after your toddler in your own home. In-home child care can range from having the help of a grandparent to hiring a nanny who lives with you full time. An in-home caregiver may be called a nanny, an *au pair*, or a babysitter. Parents may hire an in-home caregiver directly or use a "nanny agency."

There are both advantages and disadvantages to in-home child care. Your toddler will be able to stay in the place he knows best. Travel time is not required. There are no special arrangements to be made if he becomes ill. On the other hand, you will have to bring a new person into your home. You will need backup plans for times when your caregiver is not available. Also, your toddler may be upset if your caregiver leaves.

Parents who use in-home care are considered employers. They must make both Employment Insurance and Canada Pension Plan payments. If you are interested in in-home care, please contact both the Canada Revenue Agency and WorkSafeBC. (See "Child Care" in the Resources chapter.) They will tell you more about your duties as an employer.

Some ways to find an in-home caregiver include:
- Ask family members and friends.
- Call a placement or nanny agency.
- Check newspapers and bulletin boards for advertisements.
- Call a child-care resource centre.

Key Points

Child Care and Culture

In-home child care can sometimes meet specific cultural needs of parents. This might mean that family holidays and traditions are honoured. Family languages can be taught if the caregiver is from the same cultural group.

Family Stories

Thank You Grandma!

I was very lucky to have my mother take care of our daughter, Grace, as I had to return to work when she was nine months old. My mother, who grew up in Iran, was great with keeping the daily routine that my daughter was used to. One thing that my mother and daughter attended regularly was a local family drop-in held in Farsi. My mother was able to meet with mothers and grandmothers, while my daughter was able to play with other children. It was win-win all the way.

Leaving Can Be Hard to Do
The first day I left my daughter, Brianne, on her own at the child-care centre, I started crying outside the door. It was very hard for me to leave her. But when I looked back inside, I saw her playing very happily. I reminded myself that I had checked out the child care and everything was safe. My toddler was prepared, but I had forgotten to prepare myself. I left for work with my makeup all smeared.

Babysitters

You may be looking for a casual or evening babysitter. A good guideline is, "The younger the child being watched, the older the babysitter should be." Generally, children under 12 years of age are not old enough to deal with problems that could come up when looking after your toddler. Choking, poisoning, or other emergencies may be too much for them to handle. Most babysitting courses require that children must be at least 12 years old to join. Before leaving your toddler with anyone, make sure you are comfortable with the person's maturity and ability to care for your toddler.

For more information about choosing a child-care option and checklists, see the Ministry of Children and Family Development *Parents' Guide to Selecting and Monitoring Child Care in BC*. (See "Child Care" in the Resources chapter for more information.)

Helping Your Toddler Adjust to Child Care

Once you have decided on the type of child care you want, talk to your toddler about it. You may want to read books together about child care. Let him meet the caregiver(s) and other children and spend time with them before you leave him on his own.

Here are some additional tips to help your toddler get used to child care:

- Plan to stay as long as you need to on the first day. When you do leave, arrange with the caregiver to give extra attention to him.

- Have him choose a blanket or toy to take with him (if the child care is outside of your home).

- Tell him that you will return.

- Tell him that you are leaving. Don't just disappear when he starts to play. Although it may seem hard to say goodbye, he will become sure that you will tell him about changes and will be less anxious.

- Develop a leaving ritual or routine. Say and do the same things each time you leave.

- Telephone your caregiver if your plans change. This will help to stop your toddler from worrying or being afraid that you won't come back.

- Develop a returning ritual or routine. Give your toddler special attention.

- Talk to him about what he did while you were away and tell him what you did.

- Ask the caregiver about his day.

- Be aware that there may be a "honeymoon phase." He may seem to be happy for several weeks and then unhappy.

If your toddler seems unhappy with the child care:

- Discuss his unhappiness with the caregiver. Ask if the caregiver has noticed anything unusual. Maybe he has not been napping or eating well.

- Call the caregiver to see how he is doing or drop in and see for yourself.

- Find out whether he stays upset after you have gone. Ask another parent to watch your toddler, or wait and listen outside the door.

- If he is old enough to talk, listen to what he says. Ask what he likes and doesn't like.

- If he continues to be unhappy, think about other child-care options.

Supported Child Development Program

If you have a toddler with special needs, you may be able to get extra financial help through the Supported Child Development (SCD) Program. The SCD Program is a family-centred child development program. Some children with developmental delay or disability need extra help to join child-care settings. The SCD Program helps place your toddler in a child-care setting that follows government regulations and includes all children.

You can find out more about the SCD Program by visiting the Ministry of Children and Family Development (MCFD) website. Or you can contact your local MCFD office. (See "Special Needs" in the Resources chapter.)

Child Care Subsidy

If you need help paying for child care, consider applying for a subsidy. British Columbia has a government program that helps families with low or middle incomes pay for child care.

If you wish to apply for a subsidy, contact your local Ministry of Children and Family Development office. You can also call the Child Care BC Help Line. Or, you can visit the Child Care Subsidy web page of the Ministry of Children and Family Development. (See "Child Care" in the Resources chapter for contact information.)

Toddler Safety

During her toddler years, your child will begin to crawl, walk, run, and jump. Toddlers are very curious about the world, and she will use her new skills to explore her world. She will climb on, touch, or taste just about anything. She will discover and test her new abilities. It is almost impossible to think of all of the ways to keep her safe, but using the information in this chapter will get you off to a good start. (For more information, see "Safety" in the Resources chapter.)

Key Safety Points

- Supervising your toddler is the best way to prevent injuries.

- Childproofing will help make your home safer. Childproofing is an ongoing process.

- Reading and following the manufacturer's instructions for toddler equipment is important.

- Securing your toddler in a child car seat is a must when you are travelling in a vehicle. Make sure the seat has been installed properly.

- Staying within arm's reach when your toddler is close to or playing in water is the best way to keep her safe around water.

Nothing Is Completely Childproof

There is no such thing as "completely childproof." Safety latches make it more difficult for children to open cupboards. But they don't make it impossible. The child-resistant caps on some products may keep some children from getting into them. But some children may be able to open the caps if they try long enough. Remember: keep harmful products locked up, out of sight, and out of reach.

Family Stories

Floor Scanning

One Sunday morning, I heard a noise in the living room, where my 15-month-old daughter, Rachel, was with her Dad. It turned out that she had found a peanut under the coffee table and stuffed it into her nose. By the time her Dad picked her up, she had pushed it way up. We rushed off to emergency. Now, I always scan the floor for small items.

Childproofing Your Home

You may be surprised at how quickly your toddler learns and shows you new skills in her first 36 months. It may amaze you how much you have to watch and know to keep up. Your toddler may not have been able to climb onto the couch yesterday. However, today you may find her up on the couch and starting to climb the bookcase beside it.

Childproofing your home will help to create a safer environment. To childproof your home, remove as many dangers to your toddler as possible.

To begin, get right down on the floor and crawl around on your hands and knees. At that level, you will be able to see exactly what your toddler may be interested in and what may be dangerous. Check for small objects that she could swallow or choke on. See if there are any cords that she could get caught in. Are there any large or heavy items that she could pull down? Check for any poisonous or harmful things she could reach or open.

General Home Safety Tips

- Keep emergency numbers by each phone in your house. Include 911 and the numbers for poison control and your doctor. You may know these numbers, but other caregivers may not.

- Know basic first aid. It is important to know what to do if someone is choking. If a child stops breathing, you need to know cardiopulmonary resuscitation (CPR). Contact your local St. John Ambulance, Red Cross, or community centre to sign up for classes.

- Drawstrings on children's outfits are very dangerous. Remove all hood and neck strings from children's outerwear, including jackets and sweatshirts. Drawstrings could get caught on the corner posts of a crib or on playground equipment. Many manufacturers have stopped making clothes with hood or neck strings. They have put on snaps to prevent this type of injury.

- Keep items such as toys, clothing, and household items with strings, cords, or ribbons that are longer than 15 cm (6 in.) out of your toddler's reach. Longer ties can get wrapped around her neck and cut off breathing.

- Cords on blinds and drapes must be removed or tied up where your toddler cannot reach them, even when she climbs on the furniture.

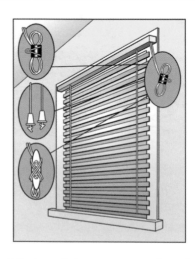

Tie cords on blinds and drapes up out of reach or clip them shorter, cut them off, or fasten them high and to the side.

Preventing Fires and Burns

- Check your home smoke detectors or alarms every month. Press the test button to make sure that the batteries are working. If the detector is wired into the electrical system, this will test if the alarm itself is working.

- Replace the batteries of your home smoke detector or alarm. The best time to do this is when you change your clocks in the spring and fall for daylight time. If you have extended-life batteries, check the manufacturer's instructions and follow them.

- Fireplace glass and other hot surfaces are really dangerous and can burn your toddler's hands very quickly. Fireplaces or inserts should be completely screened when a fire is blazing or at a low burn and even if the fire has gone out.

- Set the water temperature in your hot water tank at 49°C (120°F) to prevent burns. If you live in an apartment, it might not be easy to turn down the temperature on your hot water heater. If so, you can attach an anti-scald guard to the tap, tub, or showerhead faucet to slow the water if it gets too hot. You can restart the flow by turning up the cold water. Most hardware stores sell anti-scald guards.

- The best thing you can do for your toddler is to have a smoke-free home. Do not smoke or let anyone else smoke when she is around. Also, make sure that she cannot touch ashtrays, matches, lighters, or cigarettes.

Preventing Falls

- Keep gates at the bottom and the top of the stairs until your toddler shows you that he can use the stairs easily all the time. At about the age of 24 months, he will start going up and down stairs on his own. Teach him to go up and down facing the stairs. (See page 166 for more information on gates.)

- Keep toys off the stairs, and put away any loose carpets that are on them.

- Soften edges on furniture, countertops, and fireplaces. To do this, put homemade or store-bought corner guards or cushioned strips on the corners and edges.

- Your toddler may want to reach something up high or look out the window. He could use a laundry basket or box to prop himself up, so be sure you've put them out of reach.

- Make sure that you have window locks on all windows. Always lock the doors to rooms that contain things your toddler should not have.

- Your toddler is not steady on his feet and can fall easily. It is dangerous for him to carry breakable things such as glass when he is walking. It is wise to stop your toddler from walking with a sucker or Popsicle™ in his mouth.

- Put decals, cut-outs, or your toddler's artwork on your glass doors at his eye level to help him see that there is glass.

See page 166 for more information on gates.

Family Stories

Outlet Covers

After watching me plug in things that make noise, my 18-month-old, Justin, tried to poke a paper clip into an outlet. I put outlet covers on all the electrical outlets that same day!

- Your toddler probably loves to climb. Secure bookcases, TV cabinets, or other furniture to the wall with safety screws. This will prevent the furniture from falling on him.

- A chest freezer can be a danger for the older toddler, who can fall in when reaching for frozen treats. Be sure to keep your freezer locked and store the key where your toddler cannot get to it.

Preventing Choking

Purses can contain coins, small mints, and medications that can harm your toddler. Keep purses high up and out of reach.

Preventing Poisoning

The average home contains 250 poisons. Your toddler explores her world with her mouth. She does not know about or understand the same warning signs as adults do.

Poisonous	Flammable	Explosive	Corrosive

Poison warning symbols: You can start to teach your toddler that these warning symbols mean "Danger! Do not touch." However, do not expect your toddler to understand or remember. Keep all poisons locked up and out of reach.

Your toddler may not understand that a substance can hurt her. Many household items are poisonous for her if they are used in the wrong way or taken in the wrong dose. The most common of these are cough and cold medications, vitamins, fluoride, antibiotics, cleaning products, and plants.

Poison-Proofing

- Keep all poisons, including alcohol, drugs, medications, vitamins, home cleaning, and personal care products, in their original containers. Make sure they are well labelled. Place them on high shelves or locked up away from sleeping or play areas. Even hair shampoo can be dangerous.

- Do not tell your toddler that medicine is candy, and do not take medicine or vitamins in front of her.

- Never mix household chemicals together. Some mixtures can produce harmful gases.

- Remove poisonous houseplants from your home, and watch your toddler around plants in other people's homes.

- Be careful with your recycle bin: your toddler may want to chew on the newspapers, which contain ink that can hurt her if she eats large amounts. She may want to play with magazines or brochures and may suck on them. So keep those away from her, too. The bright colours in the magazines can contain lead and be harmful.

Tin cans may also be in your recycle bin. Their sharp edges can cut.

- Children of any age should not be exposed to mothballs or their odour.

- Never leave alcohol where your toddler can get to it. Lock liquor cabinets and use the back of the highest shelf in the refrigerator to store alcohol. Always clear away leftover drinks in the evening. Your toddler may get up early and drink what is left in the glasses. It does not take much alcohol to make her very sick.

- Secure your diaper pail with a tight-fitting lid. Deodorant disks are poisonous.

- If you are buying something that is poisonous, make sure it has child-resistant packaging. But remember that child-resistant does not mean childproof. Your toddler may be able to get into a package that is supposed to be childproof. Lock it up out of reach.

- Help visitors store their handbags and briefcases in a safe place out of your toddler's reach. Bags often contain medications.

- Protect your toddler from lead-based paints, trinkets, mini-blinds, or other products that have lead.

- Install carbon monoxide monitors in your home and work areas.

For more information on poisonous substances, visit the Drug and Poison Information Centre website. (See "Poison Control Centre" under "Safety" in the Resources chapter for the web address.)

If you think your toddler has been poisoned:
- Call the BC Poison Control Centre immediately: 1-800-567-8911.
- Have the following information ready:
  - the name of the substance you think may be poisonous
  - the amount your toddler took
  - the time your toddler took it
- Follow the first aid instructions on the label of any product taken.
- Get medical help by going to your hospital emergency. Take the container and label with you. Or call 911 if you don't have a way to get to the hospital quickly.

Safety In the Bathroom

Many things in the bathroom, such as soaps or shampoo, smell nice. They smell so nice that your toddler may want to taste or drink them. He may also watch you as you put on makeup or shave in this special room. These activities can be very interesting to him and he may try to do what you do. Most bathrooms have low cupboards under the sink. They may have dangerous things in them, so lock these cupboards.

Bathroom Safety Checklist

- Always supervise your toddler every moment that he is near water or in water (including the bathtub). If you must leave the bathroom, even for a minute, take him with you.

- Keep all medications, cosmetics, nail polish, mouthwash, hairspray, hair dye, and cleansers out of reach or locked up.

- Put away hair dryers, electric razors, and curling irons after you use them.

- Keep sharp objects like razors, scissors, and nail files out of reach or locked up.

- Use a non-skid bathmat on the bottom of the bathtub or shower.

- Close the lid on the toilet seat and install a toilet seat lock. Your toddler could lean over and fall in, and not be able to get out by himself.

- Keep baby powder, talc, cornstarch, diaper pins, and other baby-care objects well out of your toddler's reach.

Safety In the Kitchen

Your toddler loves to be where you are and to be part of what is happening in her home. In many homes the kitchen is where all the action is. She will likely be spending a lot of time in that room.

Kitchen Safety Checklist

- Turn pot handles toward the back or middle of the stove, and not over another element.

- Keep a fire extinguisher in the kitchen, away from the stove. Keep it near a door to the outside so you can use it and leave if necessary.

- Use the back burners of the stove for hot temperatures and the front burners for lower temperatures. It is even better if you try to cook using only the back burners.

- Keep hot oil out of reach and make sure it cannot splash or spill onto your toddler.

- Teach your toddler that the area in front of the stove is off limits as a play area.

- Unplug and keep small appliances out of reach.

- Keep small foods that could cause choking, such as beans or nuts, out of reach.

- Secure tablecloths so that they cannot be pulled down.

- Keep the dishwasher locked and the soap container empty until ready for use.

- If you have a chest freezer, keep it locked or in a locked room to prevent your toddler from falling in. Keep the key out of reach.

Car Safety

Child Car Seats

Finding a child car seat that is right for your toddler can be a challenge. Use the information on the next page to help you find the right seat for your toddler's age and weight.

Child Car Seat Guide

Rear-Facing Until 12 Months

It is the law in B.C. that every child must be placed in a child car seat. Your toddler must be in a child car seat that faces the rear until he is 12 months old. However, it is recommended that you keep him in a rear-facing car seat until he is at least 9 kg (20 lb.) or at the upper weight limit for rear-facing child car seats.

Type of Child Car Seat	Use
Stage 1: Rear-Facing Infant Car Seat	• Up to 9 kg (20 lb.). • Choose a rear-facing infant car seat with at least two sets of shoulder harness slots. The infant car seat should also have two crotch strap slots to allow for adjustment as your toddler grows. • It is the law in BC that every child who rides in a vehicle must be in a child car seat. The child car seat must face the rear until your toddler is 12 months old. It is recommended that you keep her in a rear-facing infant car seat until she is at least 9 kg (20 lb.).
Stage 1: Rear-Facing Convertible Car Seat	• Used after 9 kg (20 lb.) or 12 months old. • Convertible car seats have a five-point harness. • Switch to a rear-facing convertible car seat if your toddler has outgrown her infant car seat. • Look for an infant/child car seat that has a weight limit of 15 kg (33 lb.) when it is rear-facing. • It is the law in BC that children must stay facing the rear in a car seat until they are 12 months old. However, it is recommended that your toddler stay facing the rear until she reaches the upper weight limit for rear-facing car seats.
Stage 2: Front-Facing Car Seat	• Once your toddler is over 12 months and 9 kg (20 lb.), you can switch to a car seat that faces the front. However, it's best to keep her in a car seat that faces the rear until she's reached the upper weight limit for rear-facing car seats. • Your toddler should continue using this car seat until she is at least 18 kg (40 lb.).
Stage 3: Booster Seats	• Once your toddler has reached the maximum weight for the front-facing car seat, you can switch to her to a booster seat. • Booster seats lift your toddler so that the seat belt fits properly. • It is the law that all children must use booster seats while riding in vehicles until their ninth birthday unless they have reached 145 cm (4′9″) tall.

Be sure the child car seat has the Canadian Motor Vehicle Safety Standards (CMVSS) label.

Source: National Safety Mark, http://www.safety-council.org/news/sc/2007/children's_car_seats.html. Transport Canada. Reproduced with the permission of the Minister of Public Works and Government Services Canada, 2007.

Be sure the child car seat has the Canadian Motor Vehicle Safety Standards (CMVSS) label. Do not buy a child car seat in the United States or another country—it will not have this label.

Look for a child car seat that is easy to use and fits in your vehicle. Try it in your vehicle before buying it. Be sure it is easy to use so you will use it correctly every time.

Look for a child car seat with at least two sets of shoulder harness strap slots to allow room for growth. Make sure they are easy to adjust.

You can choose from two types of harnesses used in child car seats:

- Three-point harness: Restrains your toddler at the shoulders and buckles up between the legs.

- Five-point harness: Restrains your toddler at the shoulders and over the hips, and buckles up between the legs. **A five-point harness is recommended.**

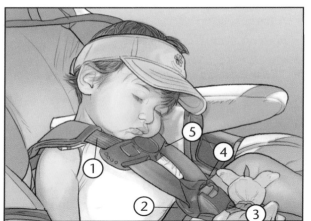

A five-point harness is recommended. It restrains your toddler at the shoulders (1, 5) and over the hips (2, 4), and buckles up between the legs (3).

Second-Hand Car Seats

Second-hand car seats are not recommended. However, if you are going to use a second-hand car seat, make sure it meets all Canadian Motor Vehicle Safety Standards (CMVSS). Check that it is not on a recall list and make sure it is the right type and size for your toddler.

A second-hand car seat should not be used if:

- The CMVSS label is not attached, or the manufacturer's instructions are missing.

- There are cracks in the plastic shell.

- The tubular frame is bent or rusted at the rivet points.

- It is older than 10 years or past the manufacturer's expiry date.

- A harness strap or padded liner is frayed, torn, or coming away from the seat.

- The tether strap or tether anchor is frayed, torn, or missing.

- You are unsure of the car seat's history. It could have been damaged in a crash.

General Child Car Seat Safety Tips

Here are the most important ways you can protect your toddler in a car:

Securing Your Toddler in a Child Car Seat

- Make sure she is always correctly buckled into an approved child car seat, even for very short trips.

- The safest place for children under 12 years is in the back seat, centre position. Avoid placing an infant car seat in the front seat.

- Keep track of her weight so you know when to move her to the next stage of car seat. Check the car seat directions for upper weight limits.

- There should be no more than a finger-width space between the harness and her collarbone.

- Make sure the harness straps are straight and not twisted.

- Make sure the harness fits her and is not covering bulky blankets or bunting bags. Dress her so that you can latch the buckle between her legs.

- Keep the chest clip (that holds the harness) at the level of her armpits.

- Make sure the harness straps pass through the slots in the back of the car seat so that they are level with her shoulders or slightly below. Almost all car seats can use the top set of harness slots only when in the forward-facing position. Check the manufacturer's directions.

- Never leave her sleeping alone by herself in the car seat, either in the car or in your home.

Installing Your Child Car Seat

- Never place a car seat in the front seat of a vehicle with an active passenger airbag. Serious injury or death may result if an airbag opens and hits a car seat.

- Make sure the child car seat is installed according to the manufacturer's directions. Secure the car seat with the car's seat belt or a system that uses anchors to keep the car seat in place.

- Check that the child car seat does not move from side to side or forward and back more than 2.5 cm (1 in.) each time you use the car seat.

- Make sure to check the expiry date given by the manufacturer.

- Anchor the forward-facing car seat to the frame of the car using the tether strap located on the back of the car seat. All cars built after 1989 (except convertibles) have an anchor slot that is already drilled and threaded for a bolt.

Safety In and Around Vehicles

- Never place your toddler in a car seat on a counter, on the car, or on any raised surface. He could move suddenly and flip over.

- Teach your toddler to be wary of cars and to hold a grown-up's hand in the street or parking lot.

- Always wear your own seat belt, and make sure all passengers wear theirs, too.

- Never drive while talking on your cellphone or text messaging. Pull over and stop first.

- If your toddler needs your attention or you need to do something while driving, pull over.

- Always put away loose objects in cars. These may include unused child car seats, anti-theft clubs, and other objects. In a crash, they could fly around and hit or injure you or your toddler.

- Keep your car free of small objects that can roll around and get stuck under the brake pedal.

- Never allow your toddler to play with power windows. Keep windows locked from the main control panel.

- When you raise or lower power windows, check that your toddler's fingers, head, and arms are inside.

- Keep pets behind screened partitions.

Equipment Safety

Choosing safe, approved equipment will go a long way to creating a safe environment for your entire family.

General Safety Tips for Equipment

- Use caution when using second-hand equipment unless it meets the latest safety requirements.

- Always inspect and check for recalls before using second-hand or older child equipment.

- Check all equipment regularly for sharp edges or tears or holes in the upholstery. Your toddler can bite off and choke on a piece of torn vinyl. Also check for loose wheels or brakes that don't work.

- Choose equipment that is right for your toddler's height, weight, and age.

- Make sure that all the sides are firmly fixed in the fully raised position and latches are in the fully locked position.

- Use safety straps and be sure that equipment is installed according to the manufacturer's instructions. Follow all manufacturer's instructions for assembly, care, and use.

- Never leave your toddler unsupervised in equipment.

Key Points

Airbags and Car Seats Don't Mix!
Never place a car seat in the front seat of a car with active airbags. If an airbag inflates, your toddler could be seriously injured or killed.

If you have to transport your toddler in the front seat, turn off the airbag, put the seat back as far as it will go, and secure him properly.

Be aware of side airbags, and keep your toddler away from them.

Toys

See p. 49 for information on safe toys.

Beds and Cribs

See p. 100 for information on safe sleeping.

Gates

Gates can be an important piece of equipment to keep your toddler safe and to give you peace of mind. It is wise to get a gate before you think your toddler will need it. You will then be ready for the day when a new skill appears.

Use the following tips to assess the safety of any gates in your home:

- Use gates manufactured after 1990.

- Accordion-style or expandable gates are not safe. The wide, V-shaped openings along the top or large diamond-shaped openings along the sides can trap your toddler.

- Check the gate for a safety-approved label.

- Ensure the gate has a smooth finish and is free of splinters, cracks, snags, and rough parts.

- Make sure the gate is the right size and style for the space being blocked.

- The best gate for stairs is a swing gate that attaches to one side of the wall and opens on the other side. Mount one of these gates at both the top and bottom of stairs, and do not remove them until your toddler can climb stairs on his own, without help.

- Pressure gates can be pushed over, so they are only useful for between rooms or in hallways, not for stairs.

- Avoid raising the height of the gate by lifting it off the floor; your toddler may try to crawl under it.

Chairs

Safe seating that is right for your toddler's age and size will make mealtimes easier and more fun for everyone. Use the following tips to check the safety of his chairs:

High Chairs

- Choose a high chair with a wide base, a safety strap, and strong tray locks. If it is a foldaway high chair, make sure it has proper locking devices.

- Always use the waist and leg straps.

- Check that your toddler's hands, arms, and legs cannot get caught in any moving parts when the chair or tray position is being changed.

- Make sure that older children do not use the chair. They could tip it.

- Place the chair away from hard surfaces that your toddler could push against (walls, doors, counters), causing the chair to tip.

- Place the chair away from appliances, windows, blind cords, mirrors, and sharp corners.

Booster Chairs/Seats (for eating)

- Booster chairs are useful when toddlers grow out of a high chair but are still too small for an adult chair.

- Booster chairs are placed on a regular chair and are held in place with a safety belt.

- The belt normally goes around the back of the chair. If possible, select a booster chair with a strap that keeps your child secure.

- Safety straps that cross over his chest should be placed low enough that they cannot reach his neck, even if he slips down in the chair.

Hook-On Chairs

Hook-on chairs are not recommended, as they can fall off under your toddler's weight or when he moves. However, you may find that you have to use a hook-on chair once in a while because nothing else is available, such as in a restaurant.

Here are some safety tips if you choose to use a hook-on chair:

- Make sure the hook-on chair is attached to a strong, sturdy table.

- Place the chair away from table legs. Your toddler could push against the table leg and push the chair off the table.

- Test the chair after it is hooked to the table but before you put him in it. You can test the chair by pulling it backwards.

- Use a different kind of chair if he is over 13.5 kg (30 lb.) or is very active.

Playpens

If you put your toddler in a playpen, (also called a play yard), check to make sure it meets these guidelines:

- Playpen walls should be mosquito-type netting. His little finger should not be able to pass through the mesh.

- It has only two wheels or casters. His actions in a playpen with four wheels can make it move.

- The walls are at least 48 cm (19 in.) high.

- Hinges should be designed not to pinch or collapse accidentally.

- All parts that are small enough to choke on are firmly attached.

- Vinyl rails and mattress pads are in good condition and not torn.

- The space is free of all cords, scarves, necklaces, and similar items.

- Toys strung across the top of the playpen have been removed.

Jumpers

Jumpers (also called Jolly Jumpers™) do not help your toddler walk sooner. They may even cause more injuries because he will tend to try to walk before he has good leg control. It is better to let him explore and be active on the floor.

Baby Walkers Are Dangerous!

Never use a baby walker, whether new or second-hand. Baby walkers with wheels were banned in Canada in April 2004. A toddler in a baby walker could tip over, roll down stairs, or fall into a swimming pool. A toddler in a baby walker could also reach dangerous items.

Choose a child activity centre that does not move (without wheels). Make sure you put it in a safe place where your toddler can't reach dangerous things while playing in it.

Strollers

It is a good idea to let your toddler walk whenever possible. However, sometimes a stroller can make it easier to be out in the community.

Stroller safety tips:

- Strollers are not safe for sleeping or playing.

- Make sure the stroller has a good security strap, and always use it.

- Check to see that there are no openings that your toddler could slip through when the stroller is in a fully reclined position.

- Watch out for fingers when you're folding or unfolding the stroller. Also, be careful when you're switching the handle from one side of the stroller to the other.

- Always set the brake when the stroller is not moving.

- Do not overload a stroller with heavy bags—it may overturn.

- Follow the manufacturer's instructions on assembly, care, and use.

Child Carriers

Child carriers help you to carry your toddler while keeping your hands free.

Back carriers are considered safe for children aged five months or older.

Front Carriers

If you are going to use a front carrier, be sure to follow the manufacturer's instructions. Some carriers have weight restrictions.

Back Carriers

Back carriers are considered safe for children aged five months or older. Look for a back carrier that:

- Has a proper safety strap.

- Has leg openings that are small enough to keep your toddler from slipping out but are large enough that they will not rub his legs.

- Is light but well made.

- Has a folding frame that will not pinch your toddler.

- Has a padded covering over the metal frame nearest your toddler's face.

Helmets, Tricycles, and Bicycles

When your toddler is playing on a riding toy or tricycle, provide a properly fitting helmet. Watch carefully, and make sure she is playing in a safe place.

Helmets

The illustration below details the four S's that can help you check your toddler's bike helmet for safety:

- Size
- Strap
- Sticker
- Straight

Other Helmet Safety Tips:

- Choose a bike helmet made especially for young children.

- Choose a bright colour so your toddler can be seen.

- Store helmets on handlebars, ready for the next ride. Store helmets out of the sun. Don't store them in the back window of cars.

- Replace old helmets. Their lifespan is only five years, because the foam lining breaks down.

- Do not use a helmet that has been in a crash, dropped, or damaged.

Straight: A helmet must be on your toddler's head in a straight position and not tilted.

Strap: Make sure the strap is adjustable and has a quick-release buckle.

Size: Make sure the helmet covers the upper part of the forehead and sits level on the head.

Sticker: A helmet must be approved. Look for the right stickers (CSA, Snell, ANSI, ASTM, BSI, or SAA).

Remember to use the four S's to help you check your toddler's bike helmet for safety.

- It is not recommended to buy a second-hand helmet. You won't know how old it is or whether it has been in a crash.

- Choose round helmets rather than "aero"-shaped ones. The tail of an aero-shaped helmet forces your toddler's head forward when it rests against the back of the seat. This is not good for her neck.

- It is not recommended to put stickers on helmets because this can affect the condition of the shell so that it does not protect properly.

Tricycles

Most children are well into their third year before they start to ride a tricycle.

Tricycle Safety Tips:

- Start early to get your toddler used to this rule: no helmet, no bike ride.

- Always supervise your toddler closely while she learns to ride.

- Don't offer a tricycle until your toddler can control it and ride it safely.

- Make sure the tricycle is solidly built.

- Make sure the tricycle is the right size for your toddler. She should be able to pedal while sitting squarely on the seat.

- Avoid all areas that are close to cars, swimming pools, or other dangers.

Bicycles

Children under the age of 12 months should not ride with you on a bicycle. They should not be put in a bicycle-mounted trailer, child seat, sidecar, or any other carrier. A very young child's back and neck muscles are not strong enough to withstand the jostling of bike riding. They also cannot support the extra weight of a helmet. Wait until your toddler can sit well without support and is able to wear a helmet. Both of you should always wear a certified bicycle helmet whether your toddler is in a trailer or a bike seat. You must also have the safety belt done up.

Only skilled cyclists should carry young children on bicycles or in trailers. These bike rides should be only in safe areas, such as parks, bike paths, or quiet streets. Practise turning, stopping, and hill climbing with some weight (such as a bag of flour) before putting your toddler in a carrier. This will help you learn how to manage the extra weight.

Bicycle Child Trailers

Trailers have a lower centre of gravity and are more stable than child seats mounted on a bike. They can be used for one or two children weighing up to 45 kg (100 lb.).

Here are some bicycle child trailer safety tips:
- Use a bike flag to increase visibility.

- Make sure the trailer has a tail light and reflector.

- Choose quiet, protected areas in which to ride.

- Do not ride with your toddler during bad weather or when road conditions are bad.

- Your toddler should not be able to reach the wheels while in motion.

- Make sure the trailer is stable. Make sure the hitching bar and connection that joins the trailer to the bike is strong.

- Your toddler should be well protected from sand and grit thrown up by the bike tires.

- Check that your toddler's harness is well designed and secure.

Bicycle-Mounted Child Seats

These seats can be used until your toddler reaches 18 kg (40 lb.) in weight.

Here are some bicycle-mounted child seat safety tips:

- Buckle the harness snugly around your toddler.

- Check that your toddler's feet, hands, and clothing are well away from the spokes or other moving parts of the bike.

- Be prepared to be thrown off-balance if your toddler moves suddenly.

- Never leave your toddler alone in a bicycle-mounted child seat.

Water Safety

Playing in and around water is fun and soothing for toddlers. It can also provide great learning experiences. Your toddler may play in the bath, at the beach, or in the backyard with a wading pool, a water table, or a bucket. Water is also a good source of fun, exercise, and family time.

Protect your toddler around any water by being close enough to reach her and watch her at all times. Parents should buy a child-sized life-jacket. Check the labels for the right size and weight. Even if your toddler is wearing a life-jacket, you still need to watch her carefully. Always hold on to her hand when on a dock or near a pool, since she might suddenly run toward the water.

Follow these water-safety tips to make water play safer—while keeping it fun:

- Always supervise your toddler every moment that she is near water or in water (including the bathtub). If you must leave, even for a minute, take her with you.

- Keep bathroom doors closed, put the toilet lid down, and use a toilet seat lock so your toddler cannot fall in the toilet.

- Do not leave water in a bucket or other container near your toddler.

Swimming lessons may help your toddler develop confidence, be physically active, and learn to enjoy the water.

But don't assume that swimming lessons will make your toddler safe in the water. There is no evidence to support this. You still need to supervise him in the water and stay within arm's reach.

Safe Bathing

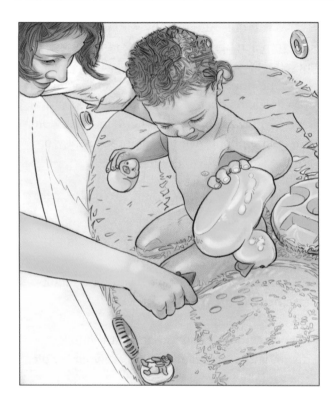

Never leave your toddler alone in the bathtub.

- Check the bath water temperature on your wrist or elbow, before placing your child in the water. The water should feel warm, not hot.
- Do not let your toddler play with the hot water tap.
- Teach your toddler to sit, not stand, in the bathtub.
- Bath rings and bath seats are not recommended. They have been linked to childhood injuries and drowning.

Swimming Pools and Garden Ponds

- Empty your toddler's yard pool when it's not in use and turn it upside down so rainwater won't collect in it.
- Remember that flotation devices, such as water wings or air mattresses, will not keep your toddler safe.
- Put a life-jacket on your toddler when around water or boats. Use only a government-approved life-jacket, and make sure it is the right size. Set a good example by always wearing a life-jacket when you are in a boat.
- Cover and lock your hot tub when it's not in use.
- Your toddler can very easily become overheated and should not be allowed in a hot tub.
- Make sure your swimming pool is properly fenced with a fence that is 120 cm (4 ft.) high on all four sides, and there is a self-latching, spring-locked gate that your toddler cannot open.
- A pool alarm is not enough to keep your toddler safe. By the time you hear the alarm, it could be too late. Your toddler must be supervised at all times when near water.
- Teach your toddler about safe play around the pool or pond (no running, pushing, diving, or unsupervised swimming).

- Remove all children's riding toys from near the pool or pond.

- Always clear away chairs, toys, tables, or other things that your toddler could use to climb into a fenced pool or pond area or an above-ground pool.

- Empty your pool at the end of the season, and cover it securely with an approved tarp. Keep pool or pond covers drained.

- Make sure all pool chemicals are safely stored and locked away.

Safety in the Community

Your toddler needs fresh air and space where she can run and play, have fun, get dirty, and make noise. You need to be with your toddler outdoors to share her fun and energy and to keep her safe.

Streetproofing Your Toddler

Keeping your toddler safe in the community is very important. You can help your toddler develop self-protection skills and learn to be cautious, but she is still too young to protect herself. She is still too young to be street smart. You must take responsibility for her safety.

Unfortunately, the majority of people who harm young children are known to them. Often the person who harms a child is a family member, someone quite close, or someone who your toddler knows. It does not help just to tell your toddler "never talk to strangers."

To help protect your toddler:

- Always know where she is.

- Never leave her with anyone unless you thoroughly trust the person.

- Stay well informed of the possible dangers in the community.

One of the ways to prepare your toddler for her increasing independence is called streetproofing.

A tip I used to teach my daughter our phone number was to sing it as a little song. Twenty years later and now living in another province, we both can still recall our old phone number by singing the song!

Streetproofing is helping her develop and use good sense if she is in traffic, around strangers, or lost. You can help streetproof your older toddler by teaching her how to react to situations that could be dangerous. Teach her to know what to do and practise doing it with her.

Some things you can teach your toddler to keep her safe are:

- Her first and last names.
- Your first and last names.
- The proper names for genitals (See p. 52 for more information on sexual development.)
- The name of the street you live on—repeat the street name often when you talk to her.

Check With Me First

Your toddler will probably find great pleasure in talking with people and in giving and getting small gifts and treats. With your support, being around people that he doesn't know can be a positive experience. Learning trust in his environment and community is a part of normal development. One way of keeping safety in mind and helping him to learn about his world is to teach the "Check with me first" approach. Teach him to check with you or a caregiver first before going anywhere with anyone or taking a gift or treat. Teach him that you need to know where he is all the time and what things are given to him. Let other caregivers know that you use this system so that they can do the same thing and teach him about safety the same way you do.

Toddlers Learn by Example

Your toddler learns by watching and copying you and other caregivers. So talk to him as you do things. It will help teach him safe behaviour. For example, say, "We're carefully looking both ways first—see the car?" "We won't run out here because there may be a car coming—let's look for a crosswalk or clear spot first." "What do we all do when we get in car? Buckle up." Be very clear in your communication. Say, "Look up the driveway when you ride," or "You must wear your helmet when you're on your bike," instead of "Be careful on the tricycle."

Keep Instructions Simple

Start off with what instructions must be followed and talk about the reasons in a simple way. It will help your toddler to learn more quickly if you use the same words and ideas over and over. Also, your actions should be the same as your instructions—you always walk in a crosswalk to cross the street when going to the store, even if it means walking half a block more.

Show Your Toddler

Show your toddler what you want him to do to help him develop a safety zone, or limits. For example, walk with him around the yard and show him how far he can go: "You can play anywhere in front of the big tree, but you can't go past it." Remember, he does not yet have the ability to make good decisions and may forget what was learned yesterday, so remind him often. Also, help him get to know his neighbourhood. Point out houses of neighbours and landmarks. Point out police officers, and explain that police help people.

Be Prepared

If you are in or have left a difficult relationship, keep a recent picture of your toddler and your ex-partner. Make sure to have a current list of the telephone numbers and addresses of your ex-partner's family and friends. As well, keep on record the make and year of your ex-partner's car and its license plate number. In the event of abduction, the police can work faster if they have this information. Some communities have child identification events where you can have a picture taken and fingerprints done for you to keep. Many communities also have block parent programs that you may want to know more about or be part of. (See "Safety" in the Resources chapter for more information.)

Violence

Toddlers are greatly affected by violence. Watching or experiencing violence can change your toddler's ability to learn about and reach out to adults and other children. Don't be fooled into thinking that your toddler is not upset by violence because she doesn't show you she is upset each time she experiences it. At first she may cry to get your attention. If this does not help, she may soon shut down and become silent. Although she does not continue to tell or show you that she's upset, she will be having the same physical and emotional reactions. Some research shows that a child who is around violence a lot may always feel upset or anxious. This may be true even though your toddler doesn't show or tell you how she is feeling.

Abuse in the Home

Violence and abuse happen in all kinds of homes and in many ways. Abuse is not always physical or violent. It can also be an ongoing pattern of threats, emotional or verbal abuse, neglect, isolation, sexual abuse, or financial control.

Abuse occurs in all cultures and is carried out by both men and women. It occurs in same-sex as well as opposite-sex relationships. It may be directed at a partner (male or female) or at a child.

Abuse does not affect the victim alone. A toddler in the home is also exposed to fear and stress. She may be directly injured by an abuser or may be exposed to abuse by hearing the conflict, seeing the injuries, being blamed for the abuse, or being used as part of the abuse.

Exposure to abuse can change how your toddler thinks and feels about you, herself, and the world in general. Even if she doesn't actually see the abuse, she can still feel the tension and fear in a house.

On the following page are some of the ways your toddler may be affected by abuse in the home.

Family Violence
In Canada, about 100,000 women and children seek shelter from violence every year.

She may:

- Have short- and long-term problems. These can include behaviour problems such as aggression and emotional problems such as depression and anxiety.

- Be more likely to accept violence as a "normal" response to stress. She may feel that she doesn't deserve happiness or respect.

- Be more likely to have learning difficulties.

- Lack the positive parenting role model she wants and needs. She may also miss out on learning positive ways of solving problems and treating people in her life.

- See the abused parent as unworthy of respect. She may not trust her parents to keep her safe and can come to view the world as an unsafe place.

- Develop negative beliefs about herself.

What to Do If There Is Abuse in Your Home

Sometimes parents feel quite helpless to do anything about the violence in the home. But there is help. **If you find yourself in violent situations, you must make a move to protect both you and your toddler right away.** Talk with your crisis line, local women's shelter, child protection social worker, doctor, or public health nurse.

Anyone who has a reason to believe that a child is in a violent or abusive situation must report this to the closest child protection social worker. You may have had violent experiences in your life. If so, it might help you to learn more about identifying violent situations early. You can get this information by talking with a community counsellor or a social worker. (See "Abuse or Neglect" in the Resources chapter for more information.)

How to Prepare for Your Safety During a Violent Incident

If you are living in an abusive relationship, here are some ways you can prepare to protect yourself and your toddler:

- Keep your wallet and keys where you can easily get to them.
- Teach your toddler to call 911.
- Decide where to go if you leave.
- Tell neighbours you trust to call 911 if they hear something suspicious.
- Practise getting out of your home safely and quickly.

If you feel you are in danger at any time, take your toddler, leave, and call 911.

Sexual Abuse

Sexual abuse is very different from normal sexual play between children of the same age. Sexual abuse is a criminal activity. It includes any sexual activity that the child is not able to understand or agree to. This includes obvious sexual acts, such as intercourse, fondling, or any form of sexual touching. It also includes acts such as a person exposing their genitals to a child, watching children when they are naked, and showing pornography to a child.

Most abusers are not strangers to their victims. Most sexual abuse of children is by someone they know. Toddlers are too young to be able to effectively protect themselves from a determined sexual abuser.

Be sure your toddler is safe by:

- Always knowing where he is.

- Making sure he is cared for by someone you fully trust.

- Being aware of who may be around him when he is in someone else's care.

- Encouraging him to tell you if he is not comfortable with anyone he is around or who cares for him. This means that as a parent you must listen carefully to him and encourage him to talk to you about his feelings, especially about friends and relatives. Pay attention when he shies away from someone.

You can also support your toddler to develop personal boundaries by not forcing him to kiss or hug others. Allow him to refuse unwanted kisses and hugs or tickling. It helps him learn that "no means no" when it comes to someone touching his body.

If you believe he has been sexually abused, contact the police.

Safety With Pets

Animals can be excellent friends for your toddler. She can learn valuable social and emotional skills by interacting with and helping to care for pets.

Safety With Your Pet

- Keep dry pet food out of your toddler's reach. It is a choking hazard.

- Thoroughly wash your hands and your toddler's hands after handling pets.

- Never leave your toddler alone with an animal, even if you trust the animal.

- Teach your toddler to recognize the signs of aggression in a pet.

- Model gentle caring for a pet. Remember, your toddler learns from what she sees.

- Explain in simple terms how to act with animals:
  - "The dog likes to be patted gently."
  - "The puppy's barking or growling is his way of telling you to stop."
  - "That's the puppy's special toy and he wants to chew on it now."

- If you are thinking about getting a pet, it is best to wait until your child is five or six. At an older age, she will be better able to understand how to be gentle with an animal.

Reptiles as Pets

Children younger than five years should not touch turtles or other reptiles, such as snakes or iguanas, or objects that touch these animals. Salmonella bacteria can make toddlers very sick, and they are often found on these animals.

Overcoming a Fear of Dogs

A big dog knocked down my son, Ryan, when he was only 11 months old. He became terrified of dogs. This became a real problem, as we love dogs. So we had to find a way to help him get over his fears. What we did was ask a friend who had a small, quiet dog to come over and let us handle the dog together. We found that by keeping Ryan on our lap so that he was a bit higher than the dog and taking as much time as our son needed, we solved the problem.

- Keep your pet healthy by taking it to the vet regularly, and keep your pet's immunizations current. Also, keep your pet away from wild animals.

- Do not keep wild animals, including ferrets, as pets.

Safety With Other People's Pets and Animals

- Always keep your toddler away from animals you do not know. Teach him not to go near an animal unless there is an adult around and the owner gives permission.

- Don't be shy about asking someone to put his dog on a leash. A toddler's safety comes before a dog's right to roam freely. Many parks have rules that dogs must be on a leash or well controlled.

- Always be with your toddler around animals, even ones you trust.

- When near a new mother cat or dog, do not go very close since they may feel threatened and bite or claw.

- If people bring their dog when they visit, ask them to put the dog on a leash for a while. This gives your toddler a chance to warm up to it, and the dog can become comfortable with everyone. It also gives you a chance to check whether it is safe for the dog to be off leash.

Animal Bites and Scratches

Certain diseases can spread from pets to people through biting, scratching, or direct contact. Cat bites are usually thin and deep, and they may not look very serious. However, they are often more serious than dog bites.

Prevent the spread of disease by training your dog or cat not to bite or scratch. If your toddler does get a bite or a scratch, thoroughly clean the area with soap and water. If the area does not seem to be healing normally, ask your doctor about the possibility of an infection.

If your toddler is bitten by an animal that is not yours, call your doctor, local public health office, or HealthLink BC if:

- There was no obvious reason for the animal to bite.

- The animal is not acting normally.

- The animal seems sick.

- The wound looks serious.

If you suspect that your child has had contact with a bat, even if there is no sign of a bite, call your doctor, local public health office, or HealthLink BC at 8-1-1 as soon as possible.

A Final Note on Toddler Safety

Over the next couple of years, your toddler will scrape his knees and bump his head. It is almost impossible to protect him from all threats of injury, but you can reduce the chance of injury by making his world safer. Creating a safe environment is an ongoing process. As your toddler begins to walk, run, jump, and climb, you will need to make more changes to protect him. The exciting news is that you've already started to make his world safer by reading this chapter. The next step is to use what you have learned. Revisit this chapter often as your toddler passes through these different stages.

Safety

Health Santé
Canada Canada
Your health and
safety... our priority.
Votre santé et votre
sécurité... notre priorité.

Eating
Well with
Canada's
Food Guide

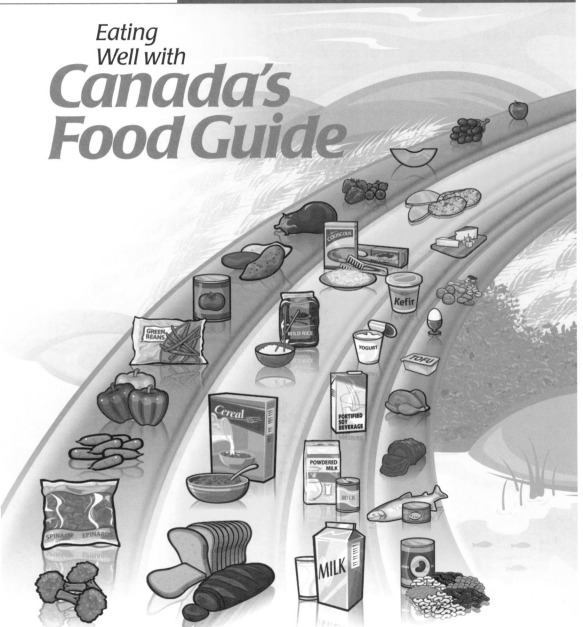

Recommended Number of Food Guide Servings per Day

The following chart shows how many Food Guide Servings you need from each of the four food groups every day.

	Children			Teens		Adults			
Age in Years	2-3	4-8	9-13	14-18		19-50		51+	
Sex	Girls and Boys			Females	Males	Females	Males	Females	Males
Vegetables and Fruit	4	5	6	7	8	7-8	8-10	7	7
Grain Products	3	4	6	6	7	6-7	8	6	7
Milk and Alternatives	2	2	3-4	3-4	3-4	2	2	3	3
Meat and Alternatives	1	1	1-2	2	3	2	3	2	3

What is One Food Guide Serving?
Look at the examples below.

Fresh, frozen or canned vegetables
125 mL (½ cup)

Leafy vegetables
Cooked: 125 mL (½ cup)
Raw: 250 mL (1 cup)

Fresh, frozen or canned fruits
1 fruit or 125 mL (½ cup)

100% Juice
125 mL (½ cup)

Bread
1 slice (35 g)

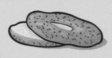
Bagel
½ bagel (45 g)

Flat breads
½ pita or ½ tortilla (35 g)

Cooked rice, bulgur or quinoa
125 mL (½ cup)

Cereal
Cold: 30 g
Hot: 175 mL (¾ cup)

Cooked pasta or couscous
125 mL (½ cup)

Milk or powdered milk (reconstituted)
250 mL (1 cup)

Canned milk (evaporated)
125 mL (½ cup)

Fortified soy beverage
250 mL (1 cup)

Yogurt
175 g (¾ cup)

Kefir
175 g (¾ cup)

Cheese
50 g (1 ½ oz)

Cooked fish, shellfish, poultry, lean meat
75 g (2 ½ oz)/125 mL (½ cup)

Cooked legumes
175 mL (¾ cup)

Tofu
150 g or 175 mL (¾ cup)

Eggs
2 eggs

Peanut or nut butters
30 mL (2 Tbsp)

Shelled nuts and seeds
60 mL (¼ cup)

Make each Food Guide Serving count...
wherever you are – at home, at school, at work or when eating out!

▸ **Eat at least one dark green and one orange vegetable each day.**
- Go for dark green vegetables such as broccoli, romaine lettuce and spinach.
- Go for orange vegetables such as carrots, sweet potatoes and winter squash.

▸ **Choose vegetables and fruit prepared with little or no added fat, sugar or salt.**
- Enjoy vegetables steamed, baked or stir-fried instead of deep-fried.

▸ **Have vegetables and fruit more often than juice.**

▸ **Make at least half of your grain products whole grain each day.**
- Eat a variety of whole grains such as barley, brown rice, oats, quinoa and wild rice.
- Enjoy whole grain breads, oatmeal or whole wheat pasta.

▸ **Choose grain products that are lower in fat, sugar or salt.**
- Compare the Nutrition Facts table on labels to make wise choices.
- Enjoy the true taste of grain products. When adding sauces or spreads, use small amounts.

▸ **Drink skim, 1%, or 2% milk each day.**
- Have 500 mL (2 cups) of milk every day for adequate vitamin D.
- Drink fortified soy beverages if you do not drink milk.

▸ **Select lower fat milk alternatives.**
- Compare the Nutrition Facts table on yogurts or cheeses to make wise choices.

▸ **Have meat alternatives such as beans, lentils and tofu often.**
▸ **Eat at least two Food Guide Servings of fish each week.***
- Choose fish such as char, herring, mackerel, salmon, sardines and trout.

▸ **Select lean meat and alternatives prepared with little or no added fat or salt.**
- Trim the visible fat from meats. Remove the skin on poultry.
- Use cooking methods such as roasting, baking or poaching that require little or no added fat.
- If you eat luncheon meats, sausages or prepackaged meats, choose those lower in salt (sodium) and fat.

* Health Canada provides advice for limiting exposure to mercury from certain types of fish. Refer to www.hc-sc.gc.ca for the latest information.

Having the amount and type of food recommended and following the tips in *Canada's Food Guide* will help:

- Meet your needs for vitamins, minerals and other nutrients.
- Reduce your risk of obesity, type 2 diabetes, heart disease, certain types of cancer and osteoporosis.
- Contribute to your overall health and vitality.

Oils and Fats

- Include a small amount – 30 to 45 mL (2 to 3 Tbsp) – of unsaturated fat each day. This includes oil used for cooking, salad dressings, margarine and mayonnaise.
- Use vegetable oils such as canola, olive and soybean.
- Choose soft margarines that are low in saturated and trans fats.
- Limit butter, hard margarine, lard and shortening.

Enjoy a variety of foods from the four food groups.

Satisfy your thirst with water!

Drink water regularly. It's a calorie-free way to quench your thirst. Drink more water in hot weather or when you are very active.

Advice for different ages and stages...

Children

Following *Canada's Food Guide* helps children grow and thrive.

Young children have small appetites and need calories for growth and development.

• Serve small nutritious meals and snacks each day.

• Do not restrict nutritious foods because of their fat content. Offer a variety of foods from the four food groups.

• Most of all... be a good role model.

Women of childbearing age

All women who could become pregnant and those who are pregnant or breastfeeding need a multivitamin containing **folic acid** every day. Pregnant women need to ensure that their multivitamin also contains **iron**. A health care professional can help you find the multivitamin that's right for you.

Pregnant and breastfeeding women need more calories. Include an extra 2 to 3 Food Guide Servings each day.

Here are two examples:

• Have fruit and yogurt for a snack, or

• Have an extra slice of toast at breakfast and an extra glass of milk at supper.

Men and women over 50

The need for **vitamin D** increases after the age of 50.

In addition to following *Canada's Food Guide*, everyone over the age of 50 should take a daily vitamin D supplement of 10 µg (400 IU).

How do I count Food Guide Servings in a meal?
Here is an example:

Vegetable and beef stir-fry with rice, a glass of milk and an apple for dessert		
250 mL (1 cup) mixed broccoli, carrot and sweet red pepper	=	2 **Vegetables and Fruit** Food Guide Servings
75 g (2 ½ oz.) lean beef	=	1 **Meat and Alternatives** Food Guide Serving
250 mL (1 cup) brown rice	=	2 **Grain Products** Food Guide Servings
5 mL (1 tsp) canola oil	=	part of your **Oils and Fats** intake for the day
250 mL (1 cup) 1% milk	=	1 **Milk and Alternatives** Food Guide Serving
1 apple	=	1 **Vegetables and Fruit** Food Guide Serving

Eat well and be active today and every day!

The benefits of eating well and being active include:

- Better overall health.
- Lower risk of disease.
- A healthy body weight.
- Feeling and looking better.
- More energy.
- Stronger muscles and bones.

Be active

To be active every day is a step towards better health and a healthy body weight.

Canada's Physical Activity Guide recommends building 30 to 60 minutes of moderate physical activity into daily life for adults and at least 90 minutes a day for children and youth. You don't have to do it all at once. Add it up in periods of at least 10 minutes at a time for adults and five minutes at a time for children and youth.

Start slowly and build up.

Eat well

Another important step towards better health and a healthy body weight is to follow *Canada's Food Guide* by:

- Eating the recommended amount and type of food each day.
- Limiting foods and beverages high in calories, fat, sugar or salt (sodium) such as cakes and pastries, chocolate and candies, cookies and granola bars, doughnuts and muffins, ice cream and frozen desserts, french fries, potato chips, nachos and other salty snacks, alcohol, fruit flavoured drinks, soft drinks, sports and energy drinks, and sweetened hot or cold drinks.

Limit trans fat

When a Nutrition Facts table is not available, ask for nutrition information to choose foods lower in trans and saturated fats.

Read the label

- Compare the Nutrition Facts table on food labels to choose products that contain less fat, saturated fat, trans fat, sugar and sodium.
- Keep in mind that the calories and nutrients listed are for the amount of food found at the top of the Nutrition Facts table.

Take a step today...

- ✓ Have breakfast every day. It may help control your hunger later in the day.
- ✓ Walk wherever you can – get off the bus early, use the stairs.
- ✓ Benefit from eating vegetables and fruit at all meals and as snacks.
- ✓ Spend less time being inactive such as watching TV or playing computer games.
- ✓ Request nutrition information about menu items when eating out to help you make healthier choices.
- ✓ Enjoy eating with family and friends!
- ✓ Take time to eat and savour every bite!

For more information, interactive tools, or additional copies visit Canada's Food Guide on-line at:

www.healthcanada.gc.ca/foodguide

or contact:

Publications
Health Canada
Ottawa, Ontario K1A 0K9
E-Mail: publications@hc-sc.gc.ca
Tel.: 1-866-225-0709
Fax: (613) 941-5366
TTY: 1-800-267-1245

Également disponible en français sous le titre :
Bien manger avec le Guide alimentaire canadien

This publication can be made available on request on diskette, large print, audio-cassette and braille.

Nutrition Facts
Per 0 mL (0 g)

Amount	% Daily Value
Calories 0	
Fat 0 g	0 %
Saturates 0 g	0 %
+ Trans 0 g	
Cholesterol 0 mg	
Sodium 0 mg	0 %
Carbohydrate 0 g	0 %
Fibre 0 g	0 %
Sugars 0 g	
Protein 0 g	

Vitamin A	0 %	Vitamin C	0 %
Calcium	0 %	Iron	0 %

Source: *Eating Well with Canada's Food Guide*, Health Canada, 2007: Adapted and reproduced with the permission of the Ministry of Public Works and Government Services Canada, 2007.

Resources

Key Resources for Parents

911 Emergency Contact

BC Poison Control Centre
Phone toll-free: 1-800-567-8911
Website: www.dpic.org

The Best Chance Website
An easy-to-use website for pregnant women and parents of babies and toddlers up to the age of 36 months. Filled with up-to-date and practical information on pregnancy, child health, parenting, safety, child development, healthy eating and much more.
Website: www.BestChance.gov.bc.ca

HealthLink BC
British Columbians have trusted health information at their fingertips with just a phone call or a click away with HealthLink BC. HealthLink BC gives you quick and easy access to non-Emergency health information and services.
You can:
- Speak with a nurse about your symptoms
- Talk to a pharmacist about your medication questions
- Get healthy eating and nutrition advice from a dietitian
- Find the health services and resources you need that are close to you.
Phone: 8-1-1. For deaf and hearing-impaired assistance (TTY), call 7-1-1.
Translation services are available in over 130 languages on request.
Website: www.HealthlinkBC.ca

HealthyFamilies BC
Website: www.healthyfamiliesbc.ca/healthy-start.php

Public Health Offices/Community Health Centres
Offer a wide range of services to promote the optimal physical development, communication and cognitive abilities, healthy emotional attachment, and positive social development for all infants and children. Services include: breastfeeding clinics, nutrition information and consultation, parent and infant drop-in, child health clinics, and family and infant follow-up. Contact your local health authority for more information. (See "Health Authorities" p. 196.)

Aboriginal Resources

Aboriginal Head Start is a Health Canada–funded, early-intervention strategy for First Nations, Inuit, and Métis children and their families living in urban centres and large northern communities.
Phone toll-free: 1-866-225-0709
Website: www.phac-aspc.gc.ca/hp-ps/dca-dea/prog-ini/ahsunc-papacun/

Aboriginal Health Services: See the blue pages of your phone book under Health Authorities, Key Word Listings. For other Aboriginal and Métis organizations, see the Yellow Pages of your phone book.

The **BC Aboriginal Child Care Society** is a non-profit provincial organization serving Aboriginal early childhood programs throughout British Columbia.
Website: www.acc-society.bc.ca

The **BC Aboriginal Infant Development Program** offers services for Aboriginal children. It is a parallel organization to the BC Infant Development Program. For information on local programs, contact your public health office.
Phone: 250-388-5593
Website: www.aidp.bc.ca/links.html

BC Association of Aboriginal Friendship Centres. Aboriginal friendship centres aim to improve the quality of life of Canada's Aboriginal people and to protect and preserve Aboriginal culture for the benefit of all Canadians.
Phone toll-free: 1-800-990-2432
Website: www.bcaafc.com

Eating Well With Canada's Food Guide: First Nations, Inuit and Métis is a new tailored food guide that includes both traditional foods and store-bought foods that are generally available, affordable, and accessible across Canada.
Phone toll-free: 1-866-225-0709
Website: www.hc-sc.gc.ca/fn-an/pubs/fnim-pnim/index-eng.php

Abuse or Neglect

Helpline for Children
A child is anyone under the age of 19. Abuse can be physical, emotional, or sexual. Abuse can be abandonment, desertion, neglect, ill treatment, or failure to meet the physical, emotional, or medical needs of a child. Anyone can call the Helpline for Children for help 24 hours a day, including parents who are afraid they might hurt their child or if you know a child is being abused. You can call anonymously.
Phone: 310-1234 (no area code needed)
Website: www.mcf.gov.bc.ca/getting_help/help.htm

Alcohol and Drug Use

To learn about programs for people with alcohol and other drug problems, ask your health-care professional or check in the Yellow Pages under "Alcohol" or "Drugs."

HealthLink BC provides 24-hour, confidential health information and advice, including referrals to other services.
Phone toll-free in B.C.: 8-1-1
TTY (Deaf and hearing impaired) phone toll-free: 7-1-1

The **Alcohol and Drug Information and Referral Line** offers a confidential, toll-free information line for alcohol and other drug programs in the province.
Phone toll-free: 1-800-663-1441

Motherisk offers information on the use of alcohol and other drugs while breastfeeding. Visit the Motherisk website or call its Alcohol and Substance Use Helpline.
Phone toll-free: 1-877-327-4636
Website: www.Motherisk.org

Breastfeeding

The **La Leche League Canada** encourages, promotes, and provides mother-to-mother breastfeeding support and information.
Website: www.lllc.ca

Dietitian Services, HealthLink BC
Dietitian Services at HealthLink BC is staffed by registered dietitians who can answer healthy eating and nutrition questions. Translation services are available in 130 languages.
Phone: 8-1-1. For deaf and hearing-impaired assistance (TTY), call 7-1-1.
Website: www.HealthlinkBC.ca

Public Health Office or Hospital
Public health offices or hospitals in your area may offer additional breastfeeding services such as lactation consultants, breastfeeding support groups, and phone consultation. Contact your local health authority for more information. (See "Health Authorities" on p. 196.)

Child Care

Your local Ministry for Children and Family Development office or public health office can give you information to help you select a child care facility. The BC HealthGuide (www.healthlinkbc.ca) and the Public Health Agency of Canada (www.publichealth.gc.ca) also offer tips and information on choosing child care providers.

The **BC Aboriginal Child Care Society** is a non-profit provincial organization serving Aboriginal early childhood programs throughout British Columbia.
Website: www.acc-society.bc.ca

The **Canada Revenue Agency** administers tax laws for the Government of Canada and for most provinces and territories; and various social and economic benefit and incentive programs delivered through the tax system.
Website: www.cra.gc.ca

The **Child Care BC Help Line** provides information for service providers and parents on child care funding and subsidies.
Phone toll-free: 1-888-338-6622
In Victoria: 250-356-6501
Website: www.mcf.gov.bc.ca/childcare/parents.htm

Child Care Licensing Regulations describe what is required of child care operators in British Columbia.
Website: www.health.gov.bc.ca/ccf/child_care.html

Child Care Resource and Referral Program (CCRR) is a source of information on child care in your local community.
Toll-free in B.C.: 1-888-338-6622
In Victoria: 250-356-6501
Website: www.mcf.gov.bc.ca/childcare/cc_resource.htm

Ministry of Children and Family Development: Information for Parents. Helpful information on how to select child care and local child care options.
Website: www.mcf.gov.bc.ca/childcare/parents.htm

Parents' Guide to Selecting and Monitoring Child Care in BC
This brochure from the B.C. government is full of information that will help you make decisions about child care.
Website: www.mcf.gov.bc.ca/childcare/parents.htm

WorkSafeBC is dedicated to promoting workplace health and safety for B.C. workers and employers.
Website: www.worksafebc.com

Child Development

A **Simple Gift** is a series of award-winning videos and guides for parents about the importance of the attachment relationship with parents in clear, easy-to-understand language. Videos include *Comforting Your Baby, Helping Young Children Cope with Emotions,* and *Ending the Cycle of Hurt.*
Website: www.sickkids.on.ca/imp/

The **BC Aboriginal Infant Development Program** offers services for Aboriginal children. It is a parallel organization to the BC Infant Development Program. For information on local programs, contact your public health office.
Phone: 250-388-5593
Website: www.aidp.bc.ca/links.html

The **Infant Development Program of BC** offers help to B.C. children and parents. The program has specialized practitioners who are trained to foster healthy child development. These practitioners work in your local health area. Contact your local Infant Development Program of BC office or public health office.
Email: info@idpofbc.ca
Website: www.idpofbc.ca

Invest In Kids is a national charitable organization dedicated to helping parents become the parents they want and need to be. For activities and tips based on the Comfort, Play & Teach™ approach, as well as information about child development and parenting, visit their website.
Website: http://fnih.investinkids.ca/

LEAP BC provides children from birth to age five with a strong foundation in literacy, physical activity, and healthy eating, through fun activities and play. This new program values the learning and bonding that happen when children and caregivers play together.
Website: www.2010legaciesnow.com/leap_bc/

Ready, Set, Learn is a BC government initiative that helps families connect with the school system and community agencies.
Website: www.bced.gov.bc.ca/early_learning/rsl/

Child Support

Family Justice Services InfoLine. Phone for information about government support for families.
In Vancouver/Lower Mainland: 604-775-0796
Elsewhere in BC: 250-356-5995
Phone toll-free: 1-800-668-3637

Ministry of Social Development: Family Maintenance Program.
See the website for information on government financial support for families.
Website: www.mhr.gov.bc.ca/PUBLICAT/bcea/fmp.htm#info

Dental Care

BC Dental Association
Phone: 604-736-7202
Toll-free: 1-888-396-9888
Website: www.bcdental.org

BC Dental Hygienists' Association
Phone: 604-415-4559
Website: www.bcdha.bc.ca

The **BC Healthy Kids Program** helps low-income families with the costs of basic dental care for their children. For more information, visit the website or talk to your public health office.
Phone toll-free: 1-866-866-0800. Press 4 and then 2.
Website: www.eia.gov.bc.ca/publicat/bcea/HealthyKids.htm

Kidsmiles.ca is a program created by the BC Dental Association, in collaboration with the B.C. government, to help parents, guardians, and other caregivers learn more about caring for the oral health of young children in B.C.
Website: www.kidsmiles.ca/index.htm

Family Resources

Support programs and family resource centres offer programs and services to support families and single parents. Contact your local public health office or public health nurse for more information.

For advice on financial support, including B.C.'s Family Bonus or family maintenance, contact the Ministry of Finance. For information about enforcement of maintenance orders, contact the Ministry of Attorney General. Check the blue pages of your phone book for the nearest office.

The **BC Association of Family Resource Programs** is a not-for-profit provincial organization dedicated to raising awareness of the importance of community-based family resource programs.
Website: www.frpbc.ca

The **BC Council for Families** is a province-wide community service that works on behalf of families and people who serve families.
Phone toll-free: 1-800-663-5638
Website: www.bccf.ca

B.C.'s **Representative for Children and Youth** supports children, youth and families who need help in dealing with the child-serving system and pushes for changes to the system itself. The Representative is responsible for advocating for children and youth and for protecting their rights. The Office works to help to improve the system of support for children and youth, mainly those who are most vulnerable. This includes those who are:

- in-care and live in foster or group homes
- in the home of a relative under a government program
- or in youth custody.

The Representative for Children and Youth is an Independent Officer of the Legislature and does not report through a provincial ministry.
Phone toll-free in B.C.: 1-800-476-3933
Website: www.rcybc.ca

The **Vanier Institute of the Family** is a national charitable organization dedicated to promoting the well-being of Canadian families. Its website offers resources on many family-related issues.
Website: www.vifamily.ca/library/resources/resources.html

Family Violence

When violence happens, get help.

In case of emergency, call 911 or the operator and ask for the police.

Crisis lines and transition houses in your community are listed under the Emergency tab in the first portion of the Telus (BC Tel) phone book. (Note: In Vancouver, this information appears inside the front cover page.)

BC Women's Hospital Woman Abuse Response Program
Phone: 604-875-3717
Website: www.bcwomens.ca/Services/HealthServices/WomanAbuseResponse/PlanForSafety.htm

BC / Yukon Society of Transition Houses
Website: www.bcsth.ca

Kids Help Phone is Canada's only toll-free, 24-hour, bilingual and anonymous phone counselling, referral and Internet service for children and youth.
Phone toll-free: 1-800-668-6868
Website: www.kidshelpphone.ca

National Clearinghouse on Family Violence is a resource centre for information on violence within relationships of kinship, intimacy, dependency, or trust.
Website: www.phac-aspc.gc.ca/ncfv-cnivf

VictimLINK is a province-wide telephone help line for victims of family and sexual violence and all other crimes. VictimLINK operates 24 hours a day, seven days a week, and provides service in 130 languages. It will help you find information on the victim services closest to you.
Phone toll-free: 1-800-563-0808
Access for hearing impaired: TTY 604-875-0885
Website: www.victimlinkbc.ca

Fathering

BC Council for Families provides educational resources on topics such as parenting, childhood development, parent-teen relationships, work-life balance, suicide awareness, and more. Information about involved fathering and parenting in general is available on the website. Print resources on fathering can be purchased as well.
Website: www.bccf.ca

HealthLink BC

British Columbians can get trusted health information by phone or online from HealthLink BC. HealthLink BC combines the BC HealthGuide, BC HealthFiles, BC NurseLine, and pharmacist and dietitian services, to help B.C. residents find the publicly funded health services they need, closest to where they live.

HealthLink BC provides a confidential telephone nursing service available 24 hours a day, seven days a week. It includes a pharmacist service for medication inquiries. The pharmacist service is available from 5 p.m. to 9 a.m. daily. It also includes dietitian services. Registered dietitians are available Monday to Thursday 8 a.m. to 8 p.m. and Friday 8 a.m. to 5 p.m. You can get answers to your health-care questions and concerns, including when to see a doctor or visit Emergency. Translation services are available in 130 languages.
Anywhere in B.C., phone toll-free: 8-1-1
TTY (Deaf and hearing impaired) phone toll-free: 7-1-1
Website: www.healthlinkbc.ca

The **BC HealthGuide** is a handbook that has information on how to recognize and cope with common health concerns. Pick up your free copy of the:
- English handbook – available at your local pharmacy or Government Agent's Office.
- Chinese or Punjabi handbook – available at many community or multicultural organizations, temples or English Language Services for Adults providers.
- French handbook – available through your local francophone organization.

Or, you can call to request a copy. Phone toll-free in B.C.: 8-1-1

BC HealthGuide OnLine is a reliable website that offers in-depth health information.
Website: www.healthlinkbc.ca

The **BC HealthFiles** is a series of easy-to-read fact sheets on a variety of environmental, public health, and safety topics. Several BC HealthFiles are available on topics related to parenting your toddler, including *Iron Content in Foods - #68d* and *Should I Get My Well Water Tested? - #45*. You can access the BC HealthFiles online or request a copy from your local provincial health unit/department and various other offices (e.g., employee health and wellness services, native health centres, and physicians' offices/clinics).
Website: www.healthlinkbc.ca

Health Authorities

Northern Health
Phone: 250-565-2649
Website: www.northernhealth.ca

Interior Health
Phone: 250-862-4200
Website: www.interiorhealth.ca

Vancouver Island Health Authority
Phone: 250-370-8699
Website: www.viha.ca

Vancouver Coastal Health
Phone: Toll-free 1-866-884-0888 or 604-736-2033
Website: www.vch.ca

Fraser Health
Phone: 604-587-4600
Website: www.fraserhealth.ca

Provincial Health Services Authority of BC
Phone: 604-675-7400
Website: www.phsa.ca

Hearing

The BC Early Hearing Program is the first province-wide screening program to check hearing in babies born in British Columbia.
Website: www.phsa.ca/AgenciesAndServices/Services/BCEarlyHearing

Immunizations

BC HealthFiles contain information on many immunization topics.
Website: www.healthlinkbc.ca

ImmunizeBC. This website has information about immunizations in B.C., including common questions.
Website: www.immunizebc.ca/

Vaccination and Your Child. This web page of the Canadian Paediatric Society answers many common questions about having your child immunized.
Website: www.caringforkids.cps.ca/handouts/vaccination_and_your_child

Medical Resources

BC College of Family Physicians
Phone: 604-736-1877
Website: www.bccfp.bc.ca

Canadian Health Network is a national, bilingual health promotion program found on the Web. Their goal is to help Canadians find the information they're looking for on how to stay healthy and prevent disease.
Website: www.ccohs.ca/chn/

Canadian Mental Health Association is a nationwide, voluntary organization that promotes the mental health of all and supports the resilience and recovery of people experiencing mental illness.
Website: www.cmha.ca/bins/index.asp

Canadian Paediatric Society promotes quality health care for Canadian children and establishes guidelines for pediatric care. The organization offers educational materials on a variety of topics, including information on immunizations, pregnancy, safety issues, and teen health.
Phone: 613-526-9397
Website: www.cps.ca

Caring for Kids is a website designed to provide parents with information about their child's health and well-being. Developed by the Canadian Paediatric Society.
Website: www.caringforkids.cps.ca

Nutrition

Eating Well with Canada's Food Guide is available through the Canada's Food Guide website or from your health office.
Website: www.hc-sc.gc.ca/fn-an/food-guide-aliment/index-eng.php

Dietitian Services, HealthLink BC
The HealthLink BC's help line is staffed by registered dietitians who can answer general and medical nutrition questions. Translation services are available in 130 languages.
Phone: 8-1-1. For deaf and hearing-impaired assistance (TTY), call 7-1-1.
Website: www.HealthlinkBC.ca

Parenting

Support groups, such as Parents without Partners, Mother Goose! and Nobody's Perfect, and the family resource program (Family Place) are available in many communities. Contact your local public health office, mental health agency, or family resource centre about programs. If you plan to return to school, the Ministry of Advanced Education may be able to help you look at options for your education and planning your career.

Nobody's Perfect Parenting Program is a parenting education and support program for parents of children from birth to age five. It helps parents develop knowledge, skills, and self-confidence in child-raising and encourages the development of support networks among parents, families,and friends.
BC Council for Families
Phone: 604-678-8884
Website: www.bccf.ca/professionals/programs/nobodys-perfect

Perinatal and Postpartum Depression

For information about postpartum depression support groups, contact your public health nurse.

BC Mental Health Information Line offers information and advice 24 hours a day.
Phone toll-free: 1-800-661-2121
Website: www.health.gov.bc.ca/mhd/infoline.html

BC Reproductive Mental Health Program provides counselling to women with depression in pregnancy and after birth. They have information and resources on their websites.
Websites:
www.bcwomens.ca/Services/HealthServices/ReproductiveMentalHealth/default.htm
www.bcwomens.ca

Pacific Post Partum Support Society is a non-profit society dedicated to supporting the needs of postpartum mothers and their families. They also publish *Postpartum Depression and Anxiety: A Self-Help Guide for Mothers*.
Phone: 604-255-7999
Website: www.postpartum.org

Physical Activity

Canada's Physical Activity Guide shows you how to make active living part of everyday life. Includes guides for children and youth.
Website: www.phac-aspc.gc.ca/hp-ps/hl-mvs/pa-ap/

Healthy Weights for Women
Website: www.healthypregnancybc.ca

Prescription Drugs

PharmaCare subsidizes eligible prescription drugs and designated medical supplies.
Phone toll-free outside Lower Mainland: 1-800-663-7100
Lower Mainland: 604-683-7151
Website: www.health.gov.bc.ca/pharmacare

Safety

BC Injury Research and Prevention Unit provides useful fact sheets by e-mail.
Website: www.injuryresearch.bc.ca

Canada Safety Council is a national, non-government, charitable organization dedicated to safety. The CSC provides resources for safety information, education, and awareness in all aspects of Canadian life—in traffic, at home, at work, and at leisure. The CSC website offers a wide variety of safety-related information and education materials for the general public.
Phone: 613-739-1535
Website: http://canadasafetycouncil.org/

Canadian Health Network offers information on many child safety topics on its website. Use the search function to find a specific topic.
Website: www.ccohs.ca/chn/

The Canadian Red Cross teaches emergency child care first aid, CPR, and basic skills for dealing with emergencies.
Phone toll-free: 1-888-307-7997
Website: www.redcross.ca

Child Seat Information Line
Phone: 1-877-247-5551
Website: www.bcaaroadsafety.com/

Health Canada: Consumer Product Safety
Phone: 1-866-662-0666
Website: www.hc-sc.gc.ca/cps-spc/index-eng.php

ICBC/BCAA Traffic Safety Foundation Child Passenger Safety Information Line. Call to find out more about child car seat clinic (how to install them correctly).
Phone toll-free: 1-877-247-5551
Website: www.icbc.com/road-safety/safer-drivers/child-seats

Lead in Your Home: Canada Mortgage and Housing Corporation. Call for a copy of this brochure.
Phone toll-free: 1-800-668-2642

National Highway Traffic Safety Administration. This U.S. traffic safety website provides information on child car seat recalls.
Website: www.nhtsa.gov

Poison Control Centre. The BC Drug and Poison Information Centre provides 24-hour poison information services.
Phone toll-free: 1-800-567-8911
Website: www.dpic.org

Provincial Emergency Program offers help with emergency planning or to create an emergency kit.
Website: www.pep.bc.ca

Safe Kids Canada is a national injury prevention program provided by the Hospital for Sick Children in Toronto. The website provides information on keeping children safe and preventing injuries.
Phone toll-free: 1-888-723-3847
Website: www.safekidscanada.ca

Safe Start is an injury prevention program of BC Children's Hospital. It provides information to parents and caregivers on how to make homes and cars safer.
Phone toll-free (outside Lower Mainland): 1-888-331-8100
Lower Mainland: 604-875-3273
Website: www.bcchildrens.ca/KidsTeensFam/ChildSafety/SafeStart/default.htm

Transport Canada provides information on child restraints.
Website: www.tc.gc.ca/eng/roadsafety/safedrivers-childsafety-index-53.htm

Shaken Baby Syndrome

Prevent Shaken Baby Syndrome British Columbia
Phone: 1-888-300-3088
Website: www.dontshake.ca

You Can Prevent Shaken Baby Injuries – HealthLink BC
An easy-to-read fact sheet on Shaken Baby Syndrome and what to do if a baby does not stop crying.
Website: www.healthlinkbc.ca

The Crisis Intervention and Suicide Prevention Centre of British Columbia. The Distress Line provides confidential, non-judgmental, free emotional support 24 hours a day, 7 days a week for people experiencing feelings of distress or despair.
Phone: 1-800-784-2433
Website: www.crisiscentre.bc.ca/

Special Needs

Your public health nurse can help if you think your toddler has a developmental problem or a disability. Most communities have an Infant Development Program for children. Staff in this program can help you with activities for your toddler that will encourage development. You will also have help finding other support services.

Ministry of Children and Family Development: Special Needs.
For information on government support for children with special needs. This resource will give you details on programs for young children with special needs residing in B.C.
Website: www.mcf.gov.bc.ca/spec_needs/

Ministry of Children and Family Development: Supported Child Development. Supported Child Development Consultants can help determine your family and child's needs and match these with the resources available in your community. Visit the website or contact your local MCFD office.
Website: www.mcf.gov.bc.ca/spec_needs/scd.htm

The Infant Development Program of BC offers help to B.C. children and parents. The program has specialized practitioners who are trained to foster healthy child development. These practitioners work in your local health area. Contact your local Infant Development Program of BC office or public health office.
Email: info@idpofbc.ca
Website: www.mcf.gov.bc.ca/spec_needs/idp.htm

Speech Therapy

British Columbia Association of Speech/Language Pathologists and Audiologists
Phone toll-free: 1-877-BCASLPA (222-7572)
Website: www.bcaslpa.ca

Vision

The **BC Healthy Kids Program** helps low-income families with the costs of prescription eyewear for their children. For more information, call, visit the website, or contact your public health office.
Phone toll-free: 1-866-866-0800. Press 4 and then 2.
Website: www.eia.gov.bc.ca/publicat/bcea/HealthyKids.htm

Index